SOCIAL IDENTITY IN IMPERIAL RUSSIA

SOCIAL IDENTITY IN IMPERIAL RUSSIA

ELISE KIMERLING WIRTSCHAFTER

NORTHERN ILLINOIS UNIVERSITY PRESS

DEKALB 1997

©1997 by Northern Illinois
University Press
Published by the Northern
Illinois University
Press, DeKalb, Illinois 60115
Manufactured in the United States
using acid-free paper
Design by Julia Fauci

Library of Congress Cataloging-in-
Publication Data
Wirtschafter, Elise Kimerling.
Social identity in imperial Russia /
Elise Kimerling Wirtschafter.
          p.   cm.
Includes bibliographical
references and index.
ISBN 0-87580-231-1
(alk. paper)
1. Social classes—Russia.
2. Russia—Social conditions.
I. Title.
HN530.Z9S646643 1997
305.5'0947—dc21   97-3293
          CIP

TO GARY,

WHO GIVES PEACE OF MIND,

AND TO OUR CHILDREN,

ERIC, CARLA, AND VALERIE,

FOR THEIR SPIRIT AND ENTHUSIASM—

WITH LOVE

CONTENTS

PREFACE

Inspired by the difficulty of conceptualizing imperial Russian society and by the rich results of the available archival research, this book addresses questions derived from my earlier studies of social categories—soldiers' children, common soldiers and noncommissioned officers, and the "people of various ranks" *(raznochintsy)*. These groups, while enjoying limited privileges, occupied ambiguous outsider statuses within a social framework constantly redefined by an activist state. Attention to formal social categories in turn has led me to emphasize long-term patterns of development that can account for the Russian empire's ability to integrate multiple societies and cultures in an enduring, flexible, though ultimately fragile, polity.

Having been trained at a time of widespread optimism about the "new social history," with its emphasis on measuring socioeconomic realities and writing "history from below," I first focused on the institutional and material parameters that defined the lives of common soldiers and their families. My effort to explore the connection between social structure and popular attitudes or mentalities quickly revealed that the historical record of the early nineteenth-century soldier, who rarely expressed himself in writing, is in large measure a governmental one. Official sources say a great deal about how administrative practices and economic conditions affected lesser servicemen, but little or nothing about their innermost struggles, thoughts, and feelings.

From the rewards and frustrations of the historian seeking to reconstruct the experiences of ordinary people, I moved into the history of social and political language *(Begriffsgeschichte)*, which, like cultural history, draws attention to the beliefs and values embedded in textual representations. My exercise in *Begriffsgeschichte* revealed additional shortcomings in the documentary record. Meanings and definitions of social categories and the relationships these categories described were multiple even in a single context, suggesting that the relationships themselves were fluid and indeterminate. After focusing on the ever-malleable designation *raznochintsy,* my research led me to a selective synthesis and interpretation of the highly diverse historiography of social categories in Russia. The result is a history of Orthodox Great Russian society in the period of the empire—or more precisely an extended essay, that explores the relationships between state building, large-scale social structures, and everyday life.

. . .

The work leading to this book was supported in part from funds provided by a Fellowship Grant from The National Council for Soviet and East European Research, under authority of a Title VIII Grant from the U.S. Department of State. Neither the Council nor the U.S. Government is responsible for its findings or contents. The writing of this book was also supported by the Research, Scholarship, and Creative Activity Program of the California State University; by a Faculty Development Award from California State Polytechnic University, Pomona; and by research funds from the History Department and College of Letters, Arts, and Social Sciences of California State Polytechnic University, Pomona. Previous research trips were supported in part by grants from the International Research and Exchanges Board (IREX), with funds provided by the National Endowment for the Humanities, the U.S. Information Agency, and the U.S. Department of State. None of these organizations is responsible for the views expressed. Lenia Veintraub and Katia Gerasimova provided crucial research assistance in Moscow, as did the officers and staff of the various libraries and archives where I have had the pleasure to work: in Moscow, the Russian State Archive of Ancient Acts (RGADA), the State Archive of the Russian Federation (GARF), the Central State Historical Archive of the City of Moscow (TsGIAgM), the Russian State Military Historical Archive (RGVIA), the Russian State Library (RGB); and in St. Petersburg, the Russian State Historical Archive (RGIA). Closer to home, Sue Benney and her staff in Document Delivery at the California State Polytechnic University library worked tirelessly to locate research materials through interlibrary loan. The New York Public Library and the libraries of Columbia University provided pleasant working environments and access to invaluable sources. The editors at Northern Illinois University Press took great care with the typescript; at all stages in the production process, they exemplified efficiency, professionalism, and modesty. Without the assistance of these individuals and institutions, this book could not have been completed.

I am grateful to Mary Lincoln and Bruce Lincoln for first urging me to write this book—to Mary for quietly determined editorial support and to Bruce for insisting that now was the time. Local colleagues have provided piecemeal readings and discussion. For their sustained collegiality, I thank Tony Brundage, Bob Edelman, Choi Chatterjee, Steve Englehart, Stephen Frank, Arch Getty, John Hatch, Lynn Mally, Georg Michels, and Hans Rogger. Other not so local colleagues—Ben Eklof, Dan Kaiser, Peter Pozefsky, and Christine

Worobec—commented on sections of the manuscript. I am particularly grateful to colleagues across the continent (some of whom I have never met) for sharing work in various stages of completion. Their generosity allowed me to incorporate recent research prior to formal publication: Lee Farrow, Stephen Frank, Greg Freeze, Bob Geraci, Steve Hoch, Dan Kaiser, Alan Kimball, Val Kivelson, Gail Lenhoff, Laurie Manchester, Georg Michels, David Ransel, Doug Smith, and Christine Worobec.

Most especially, I wish to express my gratitude to Marc Raeff for repeatedly helping to light the way (in multiple spheres over the long duration), to Greg Freeze for more than two decades of inspiration and laughter, to Bob Crummey for a careful reading and thoughtful critique of the completed manuscript, to Isser Woloch for his generosity and fruitful comments on draft chapters, and to Steve Hoch for his willingness to fight tooth and nail in making his point. My parents, Rita and Sol Kimerling, continue to facilitate my research by entertaining their grandchildren, and my mother once again provided expert proofreading. My husband, Gary, remains as ever a wondrous and enduring source of tolerance, balance, and creativity, and our children—Eric, Carla, and Valerie—of energy, exhilaration, enlightenment, and love. I dedicate this book to them.

SOCIAL IDENTITY IN IMPERIAL RUSSIA

European Russia
in the Nineteenth Century

SIBERIA

URALS

Perm

Ufa

Orenburg

Viatka

Kazan

Samara

Simbirsk

MIDDLE VOLGA

Nizhnii Novgorod

EASTERN STEPPE

Penza

Saratov

Astrakhan

Kostroma

NON-BLACK SOIL CENTER

Iaroslav

Vladimir

Moscow

Riazan

Tambov

BLACK SOIL CENTER

Tula

Voronezh

Don Cossack Region

Kaluga

Kursk

Tver

Novgorod

Orel

Chernigov

Khar'kov

SOUTHERN STEPPE

LEFT-BANK UKRAINE

Poltava

Ekaterinoslav

Smolensk

Mogilev

SOUTHWEST

Kiev

Kherson

Tauride

Pskov

BELARUS

Minsk

Volynia

Podolia

Bessarabia

Vitebsk

LITHUANIA

Vil'na

Grodno

Kovno

POLAND

Kurland

BALTIC

Livland

Estland

St. Petersburg

NORTH

Vologda

Arkhangel'sk

Olonets

FINLAND

White Sea

Baltic Sea

Black Sea

Caspian Sea

CAUCASUS

Miles

0   100   200   300

CHAPTER ONE

THE **INSTITUTIONAL SETTING**

When in October 1721, Peter I assumed the title "Father of the Country, Emperor, and Great,"[1] he also formally constituted the Russian empire *(Rossiiskaia imperiia)* as an entity distinct from the Muscovite tsardom, which preceded it and which continued to impart to it many basic historical patterns. In this act of symbolic self-fashioning Tsar Peter, the arbitrary and often erratic systematizer, proclaimed his bold and enduring legacy to Russia, Europe, and the world—a legacy embodied in countless prescriptive laws and decrees that fundamentally restructured the formal institutional framework of Russian imperial society. With restless energy and ruthless force, Peter imposed the capitation (poll tax) on all unprivileged males, personally directed the creation of a modern navy, and eliminated traditional militia forces in favor of a "standing" army. At the head of the Orthodox Church, he replaced the patriarchate with a collegial body, the Synod, composed of appointed bishops and supervised by a lay chief procurator. Finally, in order to assure administrative continuity and coordinate central government, he established the Table of Ranks, Senate, and colleges. In the cameralist tradition of the well-ordered police state *(Policeystaat)*,[2] Peter connected these innovations to a "society"—by no means fully conceptualized—that would provide the material and human resources needed to achieve the "common good." Agglomerated from the numerous Muscovite ranks *(chiny)* and based upon the Law Code *(Ulozhenie)* of 1649, Petrine "society" consisted of ascriptive legal-administrative categories, generally called *sostoianiia* (sing., *sostoianie)* or *sosloviia* (sing., *soslovie*), which until the collapse of the autocracy in February 1917 functioned as important sources of social identity and large-scale societal integration

STATE AND EMPIRE BUILDING

Theoretically the most absolutist of the European monarchies, the tsarist autocracy was the creation of the grand princes of Moscow, who in the mid-fifteenth century began to fashion a centralized state and succeeded in establishing themselves as the all-powerful, if not undisputed, rulers of the Russian lands. Possessing unlimited authority in principle and ordained to rule by the Judeo-Christian God, the Russian monarch was further sacralized by religious traditions that, beginning in the early eleventh century, encouraged the unofficial veneration and in some cases the formal canonization of deceased rulers. Pagan ancestor worship and religious syncretism set the stage for repeated glorifications of Kievan and Muscovite princes. This practice, which continues to the present day, underscored popular faith in the tsar as the earthly fountain of justice, legitimate authority, and redress for his or her subjects.[3] At all levels of Russian society, the image of the good and merciful tsar stood joined with that of the good tsarina, who in the seventeenth century received petitions and exercised patrimonial rulership on her personal estates. Although there is virtually no research devoted to the royal wives and grand duchesses of the eighteenth and nineteenth centuries—the educational and charitable activities of Paul's wife, the Empress Mariia Fedorovna, have received some attention—the religious and secular functions of the Muscovite tsarina help to explain the ease with which women assumed the imperial throne following Peter's death.[4] The idea of the tsar encompassed the imperial consort and, whether embodied in a male or female sovereign, suggested imagined relationships through which people interpreted social and political realities. This was so regardless of whether the tsar's subjects actually internalized the image or merely simulated belief in order to justify their own behavior and achieve their own ends. In either scenario, the idea of the tsar defined a moral standard that provided disfranchised groups with legal grounds for expressing grievances and demanding just amends. The concrete benefits to people were on the whole quite meager, yet the possibilities offered by the tsarist principle provided a firm foundation for the enduring legitimacy of the monarchy.

The concept of the tsar was real and meaningful in defining justice and delimiting administrative and social power, yet it also masked the vulnerability of autocratic authority and was to some extent the source of its fragility. The extent to which the Muscovite boyar aristocracy and the imperial landowning and service elites actually accepted the ruler's status as divinely sanctioned is questionable. Peter himself institutionalized instability when he decreed that the reigning sovereign was free to select his or her own successor. In seeking to concretize the absolutist authority of a secular emperor, Peter prevented the establishment of a predictable, regularized succession. The resultant ambiguity bolstered the informal influence of the court elite in crowning rulers and formulating policy. Throughout the eighteenth century, both "legitimate" and "illegitimate" monarchs were easily enthroned and just as easily toppled by political groupings at court, in the military, and at the highest levels of officialdom. Seven different individuals occupied the Russian throne between 1725 and 1762, and in 1730 Anna Ivanovna, Duchess of Courland, became empress after allegedly agreeing to specified conditions of power dictated by the eight powerful magnates who sat on the Supreme Privy Council. Equally revealing, Princess E. R. Dashkova, a friend and courtier of Catherine II (1762–1796), unabashedly applauded the assassinations of two emperors, Peter III (1762) and Paul (1796–1801), who in her view were ignorant, tyrannical, and simply unfit to rule. According to Dashkova, and most historians would agree, Catherine survived because of her political skills, concrete achievements, and ability to persuade rather than threaten.[5] Her estranged son, Paul, ended the dynastic uncertainty by enacting a precise order of succession, which did not, however, spare him a murderous overthrow. Following Paul's death, Russia's rulers became visibly more secure. Still, Nicholas I (1825–1855) faced two rebellions led by elite military officers, Alexander II (1855–1881) was assassinated by revolutionaries, and the last reigning Romanov, Nicholas II, readily gave up his throne when confronted by the opposition of courtiers, high-ranking army commanders, and Duma politicians. God's anointed rulers were dangerously vulnerable, and their divinely ordained power remarkably brittle.

Muscovite and imperial monarchs may have felt impelled to consult, cajole, and persuade in order to exercise and preserve their authority, but courtiers and elite servicemen remained dependent on the goodwill of the sovereign for position, power, and prestige. To be sure, great magnates as well as lesser nobles maintained their socioeconomic standing through inheritance, marriage, private land transactions, and the material rewards of service. Muscovite precedence placed vague formal limits on the tsar's powers of appointment, and in the local world of the landed estate, the mighty and the humble could achieve relative security for their families. Even so, in the larger arena of the Muscovite tsardom and Petrine empire, traditional boyars and imperial aristocrats promoted and sustained their influence through proximity to the ruler. In the reign of Catherine II (the Great), Dashkova was ever mindful of the slightest signs of monarchical favor, exhibited not only toward herself but also toward her husband, children, relations, friends, and enemies. Although in her memoirs she consistently professed indifference to the benefits of her closeness to the sovereign, the princess energetically sought advantageous appointments for family members and associates. She presented these efforts in the context of her own service and sacrifices on behalf of the empress— Dashkova served as director of the Academy of Sciences and president of the Russian Academy of Letters—however, she repeatedly relied on imperial largesse to acquire property, meet personal expenses, and pay off the debts of her spouse and children. Equally revealing, despite her enduring wealth and social stature, Dashkova was banished from court by Catherine's successor, Tsar Paul, and it was in the aftermath of this exile and humiliation that she wrote her self-justificatory reminiscences.[6] Whether one looks directly at the Russian monarch, the governing classes, or the relationship between the two, power and peril marched hand in hand.

Putting aside the presumption of obedience to the divine will, the image of the ruler encouraged political and social stability, as long as Russians believed that they could employ it effectively to mediate authority and hierarchy. The legal-administrative structures of Russia's abiding old regime, which combined custom with state prescriptions and kept institutional boundaries amorphous, allowed the principle of autocracy and the idea of the good tsar to transcend concrete conditions. As eighteenth- and nineteenth-century processes of state building and economic modernization gave clearer written definition to political and social relationships, significant numbers of people began to have concrete experience of imperial administration. Increasingly, the gap between the ideal and the reality of just monarchy was exposed. The ruler's personal authority (and that of his or her appointed officials) kept the system of governance malleable and dynamic, but once a reigning sovereign, due to individual failings, was no longer free from responsibility, all formally constituted power was threatened. Personalized authority meant that individuals answered for injustice, and if popular hopes of redress and expectations of fulfillment were disappointed, the monarch also appeared directly responsible. In this context, court elites justified the coups of the eighteenth century, and virtually all of society rejected tsarist legitimacy in the revolutions of 1905 and 1917.

The frailty of supreme political authority cannot be understood apart from larger patterns of state building that at once extended administrative control and desacralized the monarchy. Across time and space there were numerous customary, institutional, and technological limits to the exercise of autocracy. No legal-administrative act became law without first receiving the monarch's "So be it," an indication of the personal absolutism exercised by imperial rulers; yet from the Kievan era on, the monarch's divinely sanctioned power was mediated through law codes and Christian morality, and from the fifteenth century, through "bureaucratic" institutions as well. Seventeenth-century state building created new mechanisms of administrative control, unprecedented in their reach and effectiveness; but it was Peter I who consciously articulated the idea of a regularized government, distinct from the person of the monarch, that would operate on the basis of written laws, protocols, and procedures. In this arrangement, the sovereign was bound to obey the laws of the land, though he or she also could change legal norms at will. Petrine rulership combined personal absolutism with the rule of laws (not the rule of law), and the tension between the two was never resolved.[7] Because there was no functioning first minister or cabinet before 1905–1906, the ruler represented the sole point of systemwide integration in the state apparatus. He or she also controlled all high-level official appointments, and in the name of efficiency, necessity, or justice bypassed established administrative structures and at any moment could intervene in the normal operations of government.

Until the end of the old regime, limited revenues, insufficient manpower, primitive communications, and the enormous size of the empire meant that the Petrine autocracy of procedures depended heavily upon countless local decisions and individual discretions. A chronic discrepancy between resources and intentions perpetuated personalized authority, even as explicit rules of administration promoted uniformity and delimited arbitrariness. The very goals of regularized government—justice with order, the protection of all subjects living within imperial borders, the collection of taxes, and the mobilization of human and material resources—required improvisation and the frequent violation of legal prescriptions. In addition, the bureaucracy was fragmented into distinct yet frequently overlapping administrative and ministerial domains. All avenues of secular government led to the monarch, and all instrumentalities of rule radiated out from the monarch's person. If the sovereign's personal authority was strengthened by the dispersion of bureaucratic power, it also was weakened by the lack of a clear distinction between lawmaking and administration. Because the state apparatus could not function without ad hoc local interpretations of legal formulas, administrators became de facto lawmakers; however, they were lawmakers whose pronouncements could be overturned by superiors at multiple levels of review, reaching from provincial offices all the way to the throne. The state's limited administrative capabilities and atomized institutional structures thus made it difficult to establish secure linkages between society and government. This in turn undermined the effective impact of official regulations on actual conditions.

Throughout the imperial period, projects for political reform, including proposed "constitutions," addressed the twin problems of integrating administration and connecting governmental structures to society. Before the revolution of 1905 and the establishment of an elected legislative assembly in 1906, enlightened reformers did not think in terms of placing formal limits on monarchical power. The autocracy's authority already was contained by custom, specifically by the tsarist tradition of consulting representatives of society in times of national emergency and in preparation for major legislative initiatives, as well as by the popular practice of directly petitioning officials or even the ruler for redress of grievances. Of course, not all communities and social groups enjoyed equal access and representation, but all subjects, including serfs, enjoyed some "rights" to present complaints and submit lawsuits before higher authorities and courts. The tsarist tradition of informally conferring with representatives of society may explain why Russian elites did not seek to impose juridical limits on autocratic power, despite its vulnerability throughout the eighteenth century. Informal but customary consultations between rulers and ruled in effect made the legislative process interactive.[8] Although imperial society lacked codified constitutional powers, local courts and administrative offices for nobles, peasants, urban "citizens," and minorities were to some extent elective and brought the representatives of society into the state realm. Plans for political reform were essentially projects for administrative restructuring, designed to regularize and institutionalize communication between ruler and subjects.[9] In this spirit, loyal public opinion repeatedly indicated that society did not seek elected or even estate-based legislative authority but rather aspired to participate in meaningful and sincere consultations with lawmakers and the sovereign in order to meet the needs and protect the interests of particular social groups.[10]

Perhaps the greatest informal limitation on the monarchy in imperial Russia arose from institutional weakness and its concomitant, community autonomy. In Britain and France, early modern rulers temporarily asserted their abstract absolute power by encroaching upon the judicial and administrative prerogatives of formally constituted bodies. In Russia, there were no intermediary bodies to be appropriated.[11] Instead, there were self-administered and for the most part economically self-sufficient peasant and urban societies. The story of state and empire building in imperial Russia is the story of official efforts to construct bureaucratic mechanisms and societal organizations capable of integrating myriad local communities with governmental structures. The monarchy never fully succeeded in this endeavor. Not only did it lack the resources needed to maintain an effective bureaucracy in such a vast empire, individual communities jealously guarded their informal freedom of action. As long as modern communications and transportation were absent, large-scale administrative and social arrangements remained fluid. At the lowest levels of society, where imperial authority rarely penetrated, institutional fluidity translated into arbitrariness but also allowed ordinary people to evade and manipulate prescribed norms. Across time and space, the government's inability to achieve the intended control over social life gave wide latitude to the empire's diverse localities.

Looking at the Russian process of state and empire building from the mid-seventeenth to the twentieth century, there was an incremental, irregular, and often erratic extension of governmental authority into local society, culminating in a very rapid and dramatic collapse. Historians have long recognized that the autocracy remained feeble in its ability to influence social development, or at least the development it desired, and that the viability of the juridical society it sought to define depended upon the popular reception of its official definitions. Whenever and wherever the ascribed categories served as tools for coping with concrete realities, they acquired immediate meaning and extended state power. This was so even if the tsar's subjects misused the administrative prescriptions for designs that went against official goals and interests. Ironically, the monarchy's willingness to accommodate informal and, in some borderlands, formal local independence helped to maintain and expand central authority. In the Baltic provinces and Finland until the late nineteenth century and in the Kingdom of Poland between 1815 and 1830, the autonomy and privileges of indigenous elites far exceeded the norms prevailing in Russia proper. In territories, such as Ukraine, that were aggressively incorporated into tsarist administrative structures already in the eighteenth century, loyalty to the empire coexisted with regional and local identities. At no time in any of the imperial domains were language, political allegiance, and ethnic affiliation necessarily equivalent, and at no time did "central rule" mean "central control."[12]

For centuries, Russia's rulers measured their power over minorities and borderlands in terms of political loyalty, the payment of taxes, and the delivery of recruits.[13] By the second half of the nineteenth century, their sense of security and effective control had disappeared. As the idea of nationality penetrated Russian educated society and the intelligentsias of certain minority peoples, the eighteenth-century goal of full administrative incorporation began to imply linguistic and educational uniformity. Increasingly, the integrity of the tsarist empire seemed to require Christianization and Russification. State repression of native religions, languages, and schools varied widely. Although the toleration of Orthodox dissent and non-Orthodox (including non-Christian) confessions had long been a cornerstone of imperial policy, religious particularism never precluded bureaucratic regulation of minority faiths or meant that all viable churches received formal recognition. Despite growing nation-mindedness, local autonomy remained viable in legal-administrative relationships. In the cultural arena, by contrast, the effort to combine pluralism and imperial standardization broke down. Once political identity became associated with indigenous (local) culture, Russian officials ceased to believe that bureaucratic supervision was a sufficient basis for ensuring the empire's unity. With ever greater virulence, the idea of nationality affected policy in the borderlands, and subject peoples developed their own nationalistic cultural identities. As time passed, minority intellectuals and public figures began to think about local independence in abstract political terms, their understanding of the traditional rights and spheres of activity that defined autonomy broadened, and popular expectations of fair treatment from the Russian ruler faded away.[14] Nationalism also drove a wedge between ruler and ruled within Russian society. Although some Great Russians found in the idea of the nation a source of pride and positive identification, the monarchy itself never became fully Russified in its policies and ideology. Rather than employ the concept of Russian nationality to integrate society with the state, it subordinated all forms of nationalism to the categories of dynasty and empire.[15]

Family and the Imperial Framework

Imperial Russian society, like all societies, consisted not of men and women and children, but of men, women, and children together. This was true despite the realities of ethnic or religious difference, social hierarchy, patriarchal authority, and gender- or age-based subordination. Official social definitions hinged upon the idea of a patrilineal family unit, which assumed the presence of women and children whose legal status derived from that of their husbands or fathers. At the moment of birth, children acquired the legal standing of the father; consequently, a father whose formal station changed in his lifetime could have children who belonged to different social categories. For women, marriage might effect a change in juridical placement, with the important exception that noblewomen who married commoners retained their birth status but could not pass it on to their children. The gendered prescriptions that subordinated wives to husbands allowed men to achieve upward mobility through service, education, and economic success, whereas women relied upon marriage to attain social elevation. The law also required that wives obey their spouses, and children their parents, while insisting that husbands and parents bear responsibility for the well-being of the women and minors in their charge. However unequal the mutual obligations of husbands, wives, and children may appear from the perspective of the late twentieth century, in the official family, duty was a reciprocal concept that set a moral standard and implied interdependence rather than difference.

Because church law governed legal marriage and divorce and because the state rarely intruded into the immediate autonomy of the household and community, women and children seemed to be absent from legally defined society. Few women in imperial Russia held official titles, none were conscripted into the army, and virtually all lived under the formal authority of fathers and husbands. Female social roles appeared primarily in the arenas of family, local economy, official and unofficial religion, court politics, and the intellectual salon. When women and children belonged to social contexts outside the boundaries of autochthonous communities and the private familial sphere, the government assigned them to official categories that carried specific rights and obligations. Until the 1860s, peasants and townspeople drafted into the army were formally excluded from their communities of origin, so that any children born to them after they entered active service belonged to the military domain, attended special garrison schools, and were destined for careers in the armed forces or bureaucracy.[16] In addition, their wives became legally free women, who, in rural society, frequently faced accusations of depravity and as a result found it difficult to remain in their native villages.[17] Regardless of how individual households and communities treated a soldier's wife (soldatka)—and local conditions differed significantly—the law allowed that with her husband's permission, she could obtain a passport, move about unencumbered, live in towns, and engage in urban trades.[18] For such a woman, patriarchal values and patrilineal family arrangements did not necessarily translate into unambiguous gender inequality. In subordinating soldiers' wives to their husbands, the law also emancipated peasant women from the formal bonds of serfdom or the registered community, giving them access to economic activities that their male cohorts could only pursue illegally.

In the civilian population, orphaned, abandoned, and illegitimate children also acquired by their legal-administrative status a social position sometimes denied them by family and community relationships. During the seventeenth century, displaced children found occasional protection in almshouses, hospitals, and shelters maintained by church hierarchs and monasteries. Tsars, tsarinas, and wealthy individuals also gave generously to the poor. Bureaucratic social welfare joined personal and community almsgiving when Peter I decreed that hospitals for illegitimate children be established in every province. Serious and systematic care arrived only in the reign of Catherine II, who ordered the building of substantial foundling homes in Moscow and St. Petersburg. Despite horrendous living conditions and high rates of mortality and disease among their wards, these homes—like the military schools for soldiers' children—successfully provided basic subsistence, limited education and vocational training, and access to a social-occupational calling *(zvanie)* for people who might otherwise have become the victims of infanticide or lethal neglect. By the mid-nineteenth century, the Moscow home accepted seventeen thousand foundlings a year and supervised over forty thousand children living with wet nurses and foster parents in the countryside. The St. Petersburg home received nine thousand infants annually and managed over thirty thousand foster children.[19] Little is known about what happened to these abandoned children once they came of age. There is some evidence that those assigned to a common place of employment preserved a collective identity as well as ties to particular institutions and foster parents.[20] Whatever destiny awaited them, the examples of both soldiers' families and foundlings show that tsarist policies accommodated women and children without according them a clear-cut civic identity. Concentrated in socioeconomic contexts that generally were not subject to governmental control, these groups lacked visibility in official society; yet when familial and informal community structures excluded them, legal-administrative definitions offered rights, obligations, and a place in the imperial framework.

More important than the issue of whether official social categories incorporated women and children, which certainly they did, is the question of how understandings of gender and relations between the sexes affected the development of the groups within these categories. Recent scholarship highlights the central importance of control over female reproductive functions in the organization of society. Inheritance and property rights in Muscovy and imperial Russia indicate that gendered roles and relationships frequently derived from the need to preserve the patrilineal kinship group in a society where male offspring inherited equally, and where, at least until the end of the nineteenth century, security and status depended almost entirely on the possession of land. Marriage and successful procreation were crucial to the survival of both noble and peasant families, a convergence that explains why legal formulas regulating private testators were in their broad outlines so similar to the inheritance practices of villagers. In both contexts, women were vulnerable because of the ambiguous position they occupied either as family members destined to depart through marriage or as outsiders living among a spouse's kin. For nobles and ruling dynasties, marriage alliances played a crucial role in the pursuit of political and economic power.[21] For peasants, viable husband-wife work teams were the key to physical survival.[22]

Leaving aside the emotional and moral bonds of family life, a woman's authority in her own household, her husband's kinship group, and the village as a whole derived from her age, economic contribution, and role as the mother of healthy sons. From the standpoint of individual families and larger rural communities, peasant brides remained marginalized laborers until they fulfilled the expected and absolutely necessary reproductive function. In her natal family, a woman played no role in perpetuating blood relationships, unless the household lacked male heirs, and an adoptive son-in-law willing and able to leave his own domicile could be found. Except in households that owned private fields, a growing category in the late imperial period, peasant women lacked legal property rights enforced by tsarist courts. Instead, familial and community practices (and before emancipation, sometimes the intervention of a seignior) guaranteed their access to subsistence and usually also to land. Married women obtained communal allotments as members of husband-wife work teams. Some single women and virtually all widows received their own individual plots. Because marriage in rural Russia was nearly universal and occurred at a young age, there were significant numbers of widows who required assistance from local communities. Practices varied widely, and comprehensive research is lacking; but it seems likely that even within a single village, property rights and the resolution of inheritance disputes depended on particular circumstances and fluctuating norms. In general, a widow who had adult sons remained in her deceased husband's household or continued to live with his extended family and received a portion of his movable and immovable property. Widows also acted as trustees for land inherited by underage sons; as heads of nuclear families, they acquired allotments on the same basis as men. Daughters rarely inherited from their fathers, though one purpose of the widow's portion was to provide for girls until marriage. In addition, brothers were morally obligated to support their orphaned sisters, and spinster daughters who were beyond marriageable age might even be granted a land share equal to that of a male sibling. Some young widows remarried; others returned to their natal kin. In either situation, the widow's portion, if in fact awarded, stayed with a woman until death and only then reverted to the deceased husband's unmarried daughters or male heirs.

The diverse means for accommodating widows in peasant society depended upon economic conditions, family relationships, and values that accorded honor to parents and elders. Control over a widow's share of land gave women leverage in individual households and villages; but without the labor of adult children or the sanctuary of an extended family, an independent economic existence was difficult. Childless widows and those with very young children, or only female children, often became family and community outcasts. Some communities or households denied them a widow's portion outright. Other communities quickly deprived them of allotted plots when they failed to pay feudal rents, the capitation levied on minor sons, redemption dues, or various local taxes.[23] Rural society offered few options to dispossessed widows, who, like soldiers' wives, relied upon communal welfare and the goodwill of relatives, or simply left the village. Although similar misfortunes could befall any peasant family, including one with an able-bodied adult male, women were particularly vulnerable to administrative abuses and material deprivation. If, on the other hand, they enjoyed the protection of an extended family, women effectively exercised authority as wives, mothers, inheritors of property, and even household heads. Alongside and in collaboration with men, they used marriage and land rights to secure economic gain, prevent ruin, and care for their families. In the late imperial period, they also participated in collective acts of resistance—blocking surveyors, resisting property confiscations to offset tax arrears and debts, and even seizing food and fodder when necessary.[24] The malleability of property relations within a community suggests that patrilineal partible inheritance ensured relative status and security for women, based on customs that recognized their essential contribution to the survival and good fortune of children, men, kinship groups, and the community as a whole. Women may have been more easily victimized than men, and generally there were more widows than widowers; but within agrarian communities, widowers who lacked wives or brothers also found it difficult to maintain themselves and their children.

In elite society, where until the mid-nineteenth century the ownership of land was an essential source of social prestige and political power, women had enjoyed codified property rights since medieval times.[25] Before Peter the Great's inheritance law of 1714 eliminated the already blurred distinction between patrimonial estates *(votchiny)* and service lands *(pomest'ia),* both of which could be hereditary, patrilineal norms dominated the transmission of property.[26] Preservation of these norms required that sons inherit patrimonial lands. Seventeenth-century law preferred male heirs within any generation; only in their total absence did daughters succeed to the patrimony. As affines rather than direct kin, wives possessed especially limited property rights in their conjugal families. A noblewoman's importance, like that of her peasant counterpart, depended almost exclusively on her reproductive function. Widows who had borne children received land shares, which technically could not come from a husband's patrimonial estate.[27] Childless widows, by contrast, usually were returned to their natal families, dowries in hand. While Muscovite legal practice treated wives "as extensions of their husbands,"[28] it also protected the right of mothers to material sustenance, preserved dowries as the personal property of wives, and within their natal families, made women heirs to fathers who lacked direct male descendants.

Eighteenth- and nineteenth-century laws were more generous to women and to some extent explicitly elevated the nuclear family over the patrilineal clan by guaranteeing widows and daughters a minimum share of land and liquid assets.[29] By 1731, legal norms prescribed that widows receive one-seventh of immovable and one-quarter of movable patrimonial (inherited) property, while daughters were entitled to portions of one-fourteenth and one-eighth, respectively. A married daughter's right to one-fourteenth of her father's estate remained problematic until the end of the century, when the Senate ruled that the allotment of one-fourteenth included the value of her dowry. As before, a wife's dowry remained her individual property, which she bequeathed directly to her heirs; if she died without issue, it reverted to her natal kin. Both the dowry and statutory shares of patrimony established women as estate owners possessing potential economic independence. In addition, a law of 1715 allowed female landowners to execute deeds of purchase and mortgages in their own names. From the time of the Legislative Commission (1767), they participated indirectly in district elections to noble assemblies, voting through personal male representatives.[30] Although widows and daughters presumably received less property than sons, who were entitled to equal shares of a father's patrimony, their legal rights nonetheless promised more than a maintenance portion.

Litigation and wills revealed propertied women to be active and effective economic power brokers in their families and in local society during the eighteenth and nineteenth centuries. As so often happened in officially regulated social life, the laws defining property rights were vague, open to multiple interpretations, and easily abused. Even so, tsarist courts consistently upheld the legitimate claims of women against husbands, brothers, uncles, nephews, and other male relatives. While a testator could leave to his wife and female children or to any beneficiary as much acquired property as he liked, the rules governing patrimonial (inherited) estates ensured that men could not completely disinherit women.[31] Indeed, by the second half of the nineteenth century, the issue of individual testamentary freedom aroused concern among liberal jurists who objected to the traditional obligatory portions granted to the heirs of patrimonial property. Incremental judicial practice and eventually a reform act of 1912 expanded the testamentary power of property owners, without, however, fully eliminating the guaranteed shares. On the contrary, the new regulations raised a daughter's entitlement to one-seventh of immovable assets.[32] Clearly, imperial inheritance laws protected wives and children from arbitrary heads of households and potentially rapacious patrilineal kin by securing their right to a share of the patrimony and by treating the dowry and personal property of a woman as her separate domain.[33] This allowed women to gain power as estate owners who enjoyed economic autonomy and transmitted wealth to their heirs.[34]

Ongoing disputes over land boundaries plagued the Russian countryside both before and after emancipation. Because the use of violence and coercion to establish or refute property claims was reportedly common,[35] the dictates of tsarist justice may well have benefited women and children, who were vulnerable to abuses of patriarchal authority in a patrilineal system of inheritance that unflinchingly favored males over females. In practice, however, wives and daughters may not always have been in need of official intervention and may even have preferred to evade the legal guarantees when it suited them. Regardless of gender, nobles universally resisted the Petrine inheritance law, the first to assign a specified share (one-fourth) of movable and immovable patrimonial property to widows.[36] Scholars may very well discover that the law did not in fact give shape and definition to property relationships in Muscovy or imperial Russia, but simply imitated and codified the fluid customs of private life.[37] Evidence from the seventeenth century indicates that provincial service ranks in the Vladimir-Suzdal region systematically provided for the members of their immediate nuclear families, leaving sizable portions of purchased and service lands to wives and daughters.[38] Whether they would have done the same with patrimonial estates, which reportedly they rarely possessed, is unclear.

Equally important, in the eighteenth century, wives and husbands often failed to keep their individual properties separate, a situation that not only generated abuses but also led to litigation among rival heirs. Legally and morally obliged to obey their husbands, women were not always equal partners in the economic arena of conjugal life. Indeed, husbands sometimes used their authority illegally to control the property of their wives. Although historians know precious little about the fraudulent transactions between spouses that made these abuses possible,[39] violations of property laws are on the whole well documented and obviously resulted from both coercion and collusion. As plaintiffs and offenders in property disputes, women behaved no differently from men. Parents of both sexes looked after the needs of the nuclear family, without ignoring those of the larger clan, and to that end they used their public power and promoted the material interests of their children and spouses in similar ways.[40] Much depended on the type of property, inherited or acquired, that they owned and on whether competing claims could be adequately documented. Formal definitions and informal practices were exceedingly complex, and lawsuits dragged on for decades. While there was sufficient flexibility within the patrilineal system to permit women and men to exploit their resources successfully, confusion and uncertainty were widespread. Whatever guarantees the heirs to land holdings achieved as a result of legislative enactments, their status as landowners was not necessarily secure. Chronic litigation over estate boundaries and testamentary claims threatened the property rights of men and women. For every family able to piece together adequate dowries and inheritances for its members, there was likely to be another whose descendants became impoverished, landless, or dependent on alternative sources of income.

There is little concrete research on the fluctuating fortunes of individual families, though it is clear that as the size of the noble category grew in the eighteenth and nineteenth centuries, the proportion of its cohorts who depended upon inherited estates decreased, and the absence or loss of land ceased to be an inevitable marker of economic and social decline. Even in the seventeenth century, noninherited properties acquired through service, marriage, and individual purchases had been crucial to the survival strategies of nuclear families and larger kinship groups. Increasingly, and by the reign of Catherine II, in the provinces as well as the capitals, elite standing depended less upon ownership of land and more upon education and administrative power. When Peter I ordered that aristocratic women leave the traditional seclusion of their separate living quarters *(terem)* in order to attend mixed social gatherings at court, he made clear that in his conscious association of noble status with Western culture, women played a prominent role. Educated ladies quickly embraced this opportunity to participate in public sociability.

While such women rarely emerged as powerful political personages—the empresses of the eighteenth century, Princess E. R. Dashkova, and the salon hostesses of the late eighteenth and early nineteenth centuries represented important exceptions—poets such as V. K. Trediakovskii (1703–1769) and especially N. M. Karamzin (1766–1826) extolled their contributions to Russian language and literature.[41] Not surprisingly, as culture became a more valued attribute of nobility, as landed property became less essential to status honor, and as men and women from the ruling and service classes became better educated and more likely to pursue professional careers, controls on women eased.

Once the welfare of a family no longer depended upon patrilineal succession, elite women who were capable of articulating challenges to legal inequality and limited educational and employment opportunities began to imagine familial and social arrangements that elevated individual aspirations and personal desires over the female reproductive function. Although childbearing and beneficial marital unions remained paramount in family relations and continued to define the social roles assigned to and welcomed by women, as alternative occupations outside of service and independent of landed wealth became increasingly available to the educated classes, daughters and wives also could entertain the possibility of careers in medicine and teaching.[42] Even if the search for higher learning among women sometimes was born of personal rebellion or economic necessity, it was consistent with serious governmental efforts, dating back to the reign of Catherine II, to expand education for all groups in society and to provide formal schooling for young girls from the nobility and urban classes. Long before feminist and radical publicists of the mid-nineteenth century began to think in terms of gender equality or to demand the legal emancipation of women from fathers and husbands, official policy and public opinion assumed that education, though certainly not at the higher or professional levels, enhanced the ability of mothers to care for their children and fulfill their obligations to society. The cult of domesticity reached Russia by the early nineteenth century, and as a result, the notion of distinct public (male) and private (female) spheres, together with the relegation of women to the domestic milieu, entered elite social consciousness where it became attached to the separate identities of men and women.[43]

By the 1860s, an activist minority among educated women revolted against the dualistic notion of separate male and female realms. These women struggled to acquire higher education, escape the constraints of patriarchal family life, and achieve an independent economic existence and professional standing. Politically, they divided into liberal and revolutionary camps and as a result, pursued their shared goals in divergent ways. Liberals fought for legal equality with men, including eventually the right to vote, and worked to expand educational and occupational opportunities for women. Their radical socialist opponents rejected bourgeois political goals, frequently shunned marriage and motherhood, and explicitly subordinated narrow feminist issues to the broader cause of social justice for all. The reformist advocates of women's rights never attracted a mass following, and even among politicized and radicalized women, they represented an isolated minority. In their political impotence, they differed little from their constitutionalist male peers, a situation at least partly attributable to the relatively late appearance of national parliamentary politics in imperial Russia. More important, the context in which their feminist consciousness evolved was largely irrelevant to the vast majority of women, who neither thought in terms of public and private spheres nor sought alternative careers and professional recognition.[44]

In the countryside and among working-class families, the combined, constant labor of males and females was indispensable. Gender and age governed the assignment of particular tasks, yet when necessary for the well-being of family and community, peasant women and children readily performed the heavy field work of adult males. On noble lands as well, women effectively managed familial properties and resources, though they and their children were spared the drudgery of harsh physical labor. The modern industrial distinction between domestic and productive functions simply did not apply to the economies of peasant households or noble estates, even when these were tied to the capitalist market.[45] To be sure, domicile and place of employment could be separate among factory workers, but at Russia's early stage of industrialization, survival demanded that husbands, wives, and sometimes also children bring home a wage. Where survival depended upon direct farming or daily earnings, husbands and wives were so materially interdependent and the fruits of their labor so inextricably intertwined that notions of gender difference and equality held little meaning.

The same was true of social and political relations, where the nineteenth-century distinction between the public (male) and private (female) spheres scarcely applied. Like the vast majority of Russians, women generally were excluded but not completely isolated from the corridors of institutionalized power. In the eighteenth century, women at court acted as authoritative representatives of family and clan interests, soliciting and achieving preferential treatment and appointments for their relatives and associates.[46] In the early nineteenth century, founders of women's charitable societies and learned salon hostesses also emerged as influential public figures. In aristocratic society, admired ladies such as the Grand Duchess Elena Pavlovna, an early advocate of agrarian reform and emancipation, encouraged and on occasion influenced policy debates at the highest levels of government.[47] Among the revolutionary intelligentsia, trusted salon hostesses provided havens for illegal organizing and for the radical education of ordinary workers.[48] In the absence of parliamentary government, the salon in Russia remained what it had been in old regime France: a realm of independent communication located within the private sphere.[49] Women may have possessed still greater public authority in the countryside, where female landowners exercised indirect voting rights in elective institutions, and peasant women sometimes functioned as household heads in village deliberations. At all levels of society and despite legal inequality, women were informally and, on occasion, formally integrated into public affairs.

Because organized civil society was small and fragmented in imperial Russia, the effective autonomy of individual households and communities represented a free space where the boundaries separating the state, public, and private spheres remained blurred.[50] The "private" domain was not confined to the female domestic hearth, but encompassed all unofficial, unregulated, and informal social interactions. When educated women demanded access to the professions and emancipation from parental controls and domestic duties, they endeavored to participate in formalized political life. By contrast, the general population, whether male or female, did not identify with the idea of a civil society. Peasants and workers rarely thought in terms of the proper relationship between independent public opinion and state power. Their goal was to avoid administrative controls and manipulate official structures whenever possible, in order to protect their families, communities, and informal freedom of action. The importance of local autonomy to the functioning of the imperial framework and the limited institutional links connecting the central government to individual communities meant that the public-private and state-civil society dichotomies, so crucial for the advocates of women's rights, carried little import for most people of either sex.

The nineteenth-century cult of domesticity, which women activists struggled to overturn, did much to neutralize the kind of public-private polarity that made the feminist message broadly meaningful. Images of the family as a moral ideal brought prestige and recognition to the bearing and raising of children, functions that invariably filled the adult lives of most women, physically and mentally. What women always had done and would continue to do, at least until the advent of safe medical abortions and effective mass-produced contraceptives, gained unprecedented public status. Domesticity became associated with virtue and service to society. Almost a century after Catherine II created the Smolny Institute for Girls of Noble Birth and introduced into public debate the theme of systematically educating mothers, N. I. Pirogov, a noted physician and reformer, explained why such women were important for social progress.[51] "Woman is already emancipated," he wrote, although

> she cannot, according to our laws, become a soldier, a bureaucrat, a minister. But can a man really nurse, raise and nurture children younger than eight years old? Can he really be society's bond *[sviaz']*, its flower and ornament? . . . And so, let women understand their high purpose . . . that they, by attending the cradle of man, setting up the games of his childhood, teaching his lips to babble their first words and first prayer, are the main architects of society.[52]

It is possible to interpret Pirogov's statement as a dominant male voice asserting its authority to confine women to a separate domestic domain, removed from official position and political power. Yet it is equally possible that he was acknowledging the dependence of husbands and children upon the wives and mothers who organized home and hearth and who imparted to family life its recently elevated moral value. The delineation and exaltation of the female domestic sphere derived from an idea of the family as an oasis of purity, a source of civility, and a refuge from official society. From the perspective of most women, including the educated, what has been said of the west European context also rings true for Russia: in France, the popularity of Rousseau, an early advocate of separate male and female spheres, was hardly astonishing, for "within the parameters of eighteenth-century culture, he offered women the better deal."[53]

The limited impact of the feminist message throughout the imperial period suggests that the idea of gender—defined as male-female relations or the social organization of the relationship between the sexes[54]—may be used not only to explain the persistence of sexual inequality or difference, but also to examine sources and patterns of societal integration. The concepts and characteristics attached to each gender surely implied difference, and historically, difference usually was defined and enforced by dynamic forms of patriarchal domination. Yet this difference also implied interdependence, and interdependence was essential to processes of integration. In Orthodox religious communities organized by women, the distinct gender roles and attributes of secular society were agglomerated and subsumed in self-sufficiency, celibacy, holiness, and service to God.[55] In descriptions of civil law, judicial decisions, peasant households, urban factories, professional organizations, and revolutionary or national politics, the ongoing presence and articulation of "feminist" goals became absorbed in governmental policy and public debates. Issues of central importance to the lives of women included marriage, divorce, childbirth, abortion, prostitution, sexual violence, access to education, legal equality, and voting rights; however, these gendered topics were neither discussed nor represented, even by women, from a uniquely female perspective.[56] Late imperial women writers and activists were themselves seriously divided over whether feminist goals should be secondary or even subservient to larger problems of social justice and political reform. More than a predictable distinction between radical socialists and liberal advocates of women's rights, this conflict revealed fundamentally different understandings of gender and its role in the organization of social life. Not surprisingly, the conclusions of scholars who theorize a distinct female mode of discourse, derived from a unique sociocultural position, are equally ambiguous. Questions of autonomy, education, abuse, and respect, as well as acts of accommodation and resistance, affected men *and* women, adults *and* children, at *all* levels of the social hierarchy in diverse historical and political settings.[57]

. . .

Whether one defines social identities in terms of state building (as in the chapters to follow) or in terms of family and kinship, "society"—and the people who comprised it—existed and operated on multiple levels in multiple roles, within the contours and constraints of multiple spheres and realities. Policymakers conceptualized functional legal-administrative categories in order to impose social control, but individuals and groups in society mastered and appropriated official formulas for their own purposes. Popular manipulation of the social order raises questions about how juridical definitions affected local existence—including, for example, their impact on structures of household life, their role in generating new social distinctions and definitions, and their economic and political consequences. The issue of societal reception is to some extent an artificial one, because it assumes a process of internalization, which itself assumes the existence of an autonomous inner self that can be distinguished from the outer world.[58] The importance of the legal-administrative categories to imperial Russian society did not depend on whether they were internalized as social consciousness. The categories were operative in the formulation of social policy and, until the end of the nineteenth century, in whatever empirewide institutional integration occurred. On the eve of the First World War, they continued to play a role in determining tax and service obligations; access to education, state service, and formal justice; and some occupational and economic opportunities.[59] However people defined themselves, and they did so differently in different contexts, these categories remained fundamental to life choices throughout the imperial period. The legal-administrative parameters of social life did not arise in an historical vacuum. To paraphrase Catherine II, lawmakers did not write on blank paper; they wrote on human skin.[60]

CHAPTER TWO

"RULING" CLASSES AND SERVICE ELITES

To define the characteristic parameters of imperial Russia's "ruling" and service elites, it is necessary to confront two seemingly contradictory realities: porous and indeterminate social boundaries, on the one hand, and hierarchical relationships and socioeconomic disparities, on the other. This is not an easy task, but it is an effective way to account for divergent interpretations of key historical issues. In an effort to accommodate conflicting historiographical images, this chapter examines the various components of the ruling and service classes—nobility, bureaucracy, military ranks, and clergy—with an eye to the broader problem of limited social differentiation. To stress the ambiguities of social delimitation is not, however, to overlook structures of power and dependency nor to deny the existence of entrenched elites: hierarchy, arbitrary authority, economic exploitation, and sexual subordination were very real conditions of social life.

The categories described here are grouped together either because, in their formal legal-administrative status, they served ruler and government directly and hence represented extensions of state authority into society (bureaucrats and military servicemen) or because they functioned as surrogates for state power in social and institutional contexts where effective administrative controls did not reach (nobles and priests). As will become clear, this was not the only socially significant attribute of these categories, but it was the primary factor defining their relationship to official society. All nobles—whether they were landowning or strictly bureaucratic, of ancient lineage or newly elevated—originally had acquired and frequently continued to maintain their privileges through service to the tsar. The army and bureaucracy were created as explicit instruments of governmental authority. The Russian Orthodox church, which also constituted an autonomous realm of institutional religious culture, was socially and economically delimited in secular law. Eighteenth-century reforms integrated the church into the state apparatus, defined the clergy in legal-administrative terms, secularized ecclesiastical lands, and transformed monastery into state peasants. Although the church retained authority over important dimensions of clerical and lay life, the state prescribed the relationship of the clergy to the imperial framework. In the shifting social territory where official and unofficial structures met, the incomplete differentiation of Russia's ruling classes and service elites was strikingly visible.

LANDOWNING NOBILITY

"Never and nowhere did the privileges of a noble estate rise so quickly, exist for so short a time, and crumble so completely as with us."—P. N. Miliukov[1]

Throughout the history of imperial Russia a small, powerful, and wealthy aristocracy of lineage and landownership remained closely identified with the ruler, upper bureaucracy, and highest military ranks. Exemplified by the service elite of 1730, a group of 179 officials occupying positions in the top four military and civil grades, the Petrine ruling class came overwhelmingly from seventeenth-century aristocratic families of princely, Moscow boyar, and Moscow noble ranks.[2] Despite the longevity and continuity of its Muscovite core, whose descendants could be found among the most influential officials and magnates of the early twentieth century, the imperial elite was still a "domesticated aristocracy," open to newcomers and never entitled to hereditary or proprietary control over a particular office, administrative domain, or "territorial jurisdiction."[3] Moreover, in contrast to the securely entrenched aristocracy, the vast majority of Russian hereditary nobles—whether landed or landless, lineal or bureaucratic—were neither fully nor clearly delineated from other groups in society, either before or after the Petrine reforms. Although the social consolidation of a landed nobility increased during the eighteenth and nineteenth centuries, it was not institutionalized in autonomous corporate structures extending to the level of national government until the early twentieth century. This limited differentiation of the nobility for most of the imperial period had important consequences, which merit careful examination. Ironically, it was at the close of the nineteenth century, at the very moment when rapid industrialization and urbanization began fundamentally to alter traditional social identities, that the landowning nobility came closest to representing a distinct interest group or class.

The relationship of social status to social category is crucial to understanding the formal and informal attributes of nobility in imperial Russia. In both Muscovy and imperial Russia, status honor was either customary (based on heredity) or legislated (based on service). Precedence or the "place system" *(mestnichestvo)*—the rank ordering of aristocratic families that mediated social and political conflict within the Muscovite elite from the early sixteenth century until its abolition in 1682—combined status honor and formal privileges by linking both to heredity and service. It is unclear whether legal privileges that derived from service were the source of status honor or vice versa. Repeated violations of the "place system" by sixteenth- and seventeenth-century tsars suggested the former, while aristocratic pretensions based on heredity suggested the latter. Peter the Great attempted to clarify the relationship between informal status honor, formal service position, and lineage; he made status honor a formal attribute of hereditary social category and required all groups in society to serve. Through a new "place system," the Table of Ranks (1722), Peter also regularized, bureaucratized, and institutionalized merit in promotion and ennoblement. Careful not to violate lineage, the tsar's reforms did not fully separate service position from heredity; both remained closely tied to informal status honor. Subsequent efforts to legislate (that is, regulate) status honor by creating the subcategories of "personal noble," "distinguished citizen," and "honored citizen" revealed the continuing lack of delineation between informal status honor and formal social category. Although the goal was to enhance security, legislated status honor only added to the ambiguities of social definition.

With the exception of aristocratic lineage—which existed independently of class (socioeconomic) situation, rank, office, or functional-occupational calling *(zvanie)*—the sources examined do not explicitly discuss Russian conceptions of status honor. They do, however, repeatedly suggest that such conceptions existed and that groups in society associated them with legal rights. When, in the instructions to Catherine II's Legislative Commission (1767), upwardly and downwardly mobile semi-elites sought marks of distinction and the right to possess serfs, their desire for formal privileges implied a notion of status honor. Similarly, when lineal nobles depicted new nobles or upwardly mobile commoners as interlopers, addressed them with the familiar "thou" instead of the formal "you," and reacted angrily to marriage across social boundaries, they, too, expressed an understanding of status honor. Even the designation of "noble," officially the most privileged status of the realm, frequently constituted a contested sphere. The phenomenon of status honor certainly deserves separate study; the very difficulty of distinguishing it from formal social category raises important questions about differentiation in Russian society.

Although one of the most accessible and best studied social groups, the Russian imperial nobility *(dvorianstvo)* continues to confound students and scholars alike with the variety of its images, life chances, and historical conditions. The Charter to the Nobility (1785) and the Digest of Laws (1832) identified six noble categories, all possessing equivalent degrees of legal privilege and formal status honor: (1) nobility granted by the sovereign, or "real nobility," (2) nobility achieved by reaching commissioned officer rank (rank fourteen) in military service, (3) nobility achieved by promotion to rank eight in civil service, (4) nobility derived from membership in foreign noble families, (5) titled (Russian) noble families, and (6) ancient wellborn (untitled Russian) noble families.[4] It is noteworthy that these seemingly straightforward categories pertained more to the original acquisition of noble rights than to any assumed way of life and thus symbolized the traditionally close relationship between lineage and service as well as the continual creation of new noble lines.

In contrast to the formalistic definitions of administrators, historians and the contemporaries whose voices they echo represent nobility more broadly, as a social and cultural milieu with meaning beyond ennoblement and legal privilege. An initial overview suggests the possibility of identifying the nobility with a ruling class of landowners, defined as

> a social group with a definite function to perform, which is to rule; with privileges giving it a status sharply different from the rest of the population; with a consciousness of its privileged status and leadership function; and one in which internal unity is maintained by de-emphasizing professionalism and occupational separateness and emphasizing the primacy of power unlimited by law, both between superior and subordinate within the ruling class and above all in relations between ruling class and dependent population.[5]

Although an accurate depiction of imperial Russia's noble landowners for any chronological period, this formulation minimizes a host of ambiguities generated by the very attributes that supposedly delineated the nobility: lineage, service to the sovereign, landholding, the possession of education and Western culture, and until 1861, the ownership of serfs.

To understand the full complexity of noble status, one can examine specific sources of privilege and identity, paying particular attention to the concrete manifestations of uncertainty and their consequences for long-term social development. A direct connection between elite status and personal service to the ruler can be found in Kievan Rus, Muscovy, and imperial Russia. As noted above, both the Muscovite order of precedence and the imperial Table of Ranks combined elements of lineage and service to define and regulate a ruling group. This dynamic interplay, particularly the role of service in legitimizing privilege and the ongoing possibility of ennoblement through service, continually blurred the parameters of the nobility and its relationship to the sovereign, the state, and society. At the same time, the importance of service to lineage neither negated the nobility's role as a local seignorial class nor accounted for its lack of interest in imposing formal limits on autocratic authority. The legal sources defining nobility highlighted the complicated, entangled connections between lineage, service, and the ownership of land. Landholding and service were so fundamental to noble life that it is impossible to privilege one or the other attribute in constructing a group identity. Service in and of it-self did not weaken local bonds. The nobility's commitment to family estates and close ties to serfs, reflected in its stubborn commitment to partible inheritance, actually helped to sustain its involvement in service.[6] Among established noble families of very modest means, service reinforced their role as landowners by providing sources of education and salaried employment, which then could be used to forestall impoverishment and hence preserve or possibly augment their estates. For new nobles, the relationship to service was even more straightforward: it represented the sole basis of their official elevation, which then permitted access to land and serfs.

True to the goal of remaking the traditional Muscovite elite into a "qualified elite"[7] capable of meeting the personnel requirements of an expanding army and bureaucracy, Peter the Great subjected all male nobles to a harsh regimen of forced education and lifelong service that began in the lowest ranks along-side commoners. To promote cohesion in this newly agglomerated category, he eliminated the distinction between estates granted for service and those held as patrimony, declaring all noble lands to be unconditional hereditary property. With the Table of Ranks, he linked social status to official position, which now derived from military or bureaucratic functions rather than wealth or ancestry, and he reaffirmed service as the primary justification for noble privilege. The result was not to displace the old aristocracy, but to regularize promotion in service and to create an administrative mechanism that allowed talented and meritorious individuals to rise regardless of lineage.[8] Although the purpose of the Table of Ranks was never to produce an entirely open nobility (hereditary nobles always enjoyed privileged access to service and its rewards), it did codify and bureaucratize the category's porous boundaries.

Throughout the eighteenth century, the autocracy continued to extend and define the formal rights of nobility. Peter the Great introduced two important marks of noble distinction, first by recognizing all noble lands as patrimony and later by exempting the nobility from the capitation. Preferential treatment in service, kept largely informal during the Petrine era, became institutionalized in 1730 with the founding of Russia's first Noble Cadet Corps, whose graduates were entitled to enter the army directly as officers, without first having to rise through the ranks.[9] Thus began a commitment, respected by all subsequent rulers of imperial Russia, to provide nobles, regardless of wealth, with the education they needed to secure advantages in appointments to service. This was followed in the 1760s with decrees giving them explicit preference over non-nobles in civil and military promotions.[10] Actual service requirements also eased from the second quarter of the century, beginning with a massive military demobilization in 1727, continuing with a reduction in the term of service from life to twenty-five years in 1736, and culminating in the nobility's emancipation from compulsory service in 1762, by which time only about one-quarter of the fifty thousand landlords were still actively serving.[11]

Economic privileges acquired by nobles during the eighteenth century included the right to engage in any type of trade when not in service (1711; limited in 1755 to the wholesale marketing of goods produced on estates, but then restored in 1807, when nobles were permitted to register in merchant guilds), the exclusive right to distill spirits (1716; confirmed in 1765), and a monopoly on the sale of liquor to government contractors (1754). Of equal importance, laws of 1730, 1743, and 1746 restricted the possession of serfs by non-nobles, though the ownership of populated villages and individual serfs became solely a noble right only after decrees of 1754, 1758, and 1760.[12] The capstone formulations of legal noble privilege came in the reforms of provincial government (1775 and 1778) and in the Charter to the Nobility. The provincial reforms established local noble assemblies, and the officials they elected, both as institutions of self-administration and as extensions of the state apparatus. Consequently, noble landlords not only exercised absolute authority over their serfs (theoretically, the latter had lost the formal right to petition against their masters in 1649, 1700, 1765, and 1767), but also were entitled to fill elective administrative and judicial posts in local government.[13] Soon thereafter, the Charter to the Nobility confirmed the status of the local assembly of the nobility "as a corporate organ with legal rights and powers," including the authority to elect local officials and determine whether individual nobles were eligible for membership and participation.[14] For the first time, nobles were exempted from corporal punishment and acquired full property rights over their estates, including the freedom to exploit all resources found therein for any economic or commercial purpose. In recognizing a noble's estate as a personal rather than imperial resource and in limiting membership in the provincial assemblies to landowners, the charter also officially defined the nobility as a propertied class "whose ownership of land and serfs had replaced state service as its essential attribute."[15]

After almost a century of formulating legal rights and privileges, the meaning of noble status nonetheless remained ambiguous. A major source of confusion was the relationship between the nobility and the bureaucracy—a relationship embodied but still inadequately clarified in the Table of Ranks. The 1762 emancipation from obligatory service, which on the surface seemed to promote delineation, only reinforced the ambiguity. It removed the primary justification for noble privilege, including that of owning serfs, by making hereditary noble rights unconditional. Although lawmakers clearly assumed that nobles would continue to serve, they were the only members of society not required to serve, at least until 1785, when merchants received an equivalent but not hereditary exemption. The emancipation of 1762 not only failed to delimit the nobility in a precise way, it made the nobility's boundaries and definition more indeterminate. Nor did the subsequent Charter to the Nobility seek to appease or elevate its putative beneficiaries; rather, the state prescribed service obligations and noble privileges, including recognition of landlords' power, in order to satisfy its own fiscal, administrative, and military needs.[16] In promoting the differentiation of a nonserving, landholding nobility, these acts of imperial recognition effectively separated the nobility from the state and thus marked important steps toward the development of a distinct stratum of bureaucratic nobles—nobles who, in their capacity as high-level officials, identified first and foremost with the monarchy and who, in the name of the general good, willingly violated the most vital interests of their landed counterparts.[17]

Even after the 1762 emancipation of the state from the nobility, the distinction between a landed, serf-owning hereditary nobility and a landless bureaucratic nobility was never absolute. This circumstance partly explains the persistent insecurity of noble status. Nobles continued to enter the army and bureaucracy long after business and professional careers became plentiful. They also served locally as serf-owning judges and administrators and following emancipation, as participants in all-class assemblies of provincial self-administration (zemstva; sing., zemstvo). Throughout the imperial period, the nobility constituted a crucial link binding the state to society. Even in the era of national parliamentary politics ushered in by the revolution of 1905, spokesmen for noble privilege, who strongly resisted bureaucratic intrusions into local life and sought to preserve the landowning elite's traditional domination of the countryside, justified their position in terms of the nobleman's time-honored role as servitor to the tsar.[18] The landed nobility never represented an autonomous ruling class, fully constituted in independent corporate bodies, but neither were they and the elected officials chosen from their midst passive instruments in the hands of the state. The government looked to nobles to do its bidding and execute its policies; in return, they expected the autocracy to protect their special interests and privileges.

The 1861 emancipation from legal bondage of twenty-two million serfs seriously eroded this informal understanding and represented yet another turning point in the relationship of service and landholding to definitions of nobility.[19] At a single stroke of the pen, the autocrat, encouraged by an energetic circle of reformist officials, removed former serfs from the informal administrative and judicial authority of their masters and made inevitable the eventual redemption by communal peasants of lands that nobles claimed as private property. To prepare the ground for this momentous act, Alexander II and his advisors consulted the nobility as a corporate group, through their local assemblies, but then unabashedly violated noble privilege and excluded noble delegates from direct participation in formulating the emancipation legislation. During the reform process of 1857–1862, the bureaucracy behaved as a distinct entity separate from the landowners, who themselves responded in similar fashion, as a serf-owning class seeking to protect its economic interests, social prestige, and political power. To some extent, the nobility always had been divided into landed and service elements. At no time since the death of Peter the Great had all eligible noble landowners been in service; nor were all noble servicemen necessarily landowners. Although the 1762 emancipation from compulsory service had marked the first formal separation into landowning and bureaucratic nobilities, no clear differentiation emerged before the mid-nineteenth century, by which time it had become lucrative for educated nobles to pursue alternative careers in business, literature, journalism, and the professions.[20] The emancipation of the serfs accelerated and solidified this process of delineation, even as it eliminated the nobility's most characteristic and cherished privilege vis-à-vis other groups in society.

In principle, the emancipation of 1861 implied dramatic and radical change, but its actual terms and implementation were ambiguous and inconclusive. Peasants remained bound to their communes, noble landowners continued to administer the countryside as elected and appointed officials, and until 1881 the redemption of village allotments was voluntary for former serf owners, though most proceeded to redemption because it brought immediate and substantial compensation in cash. On the other hand, the legal framework of social relationships was fundamentally altered, and the political authority of landlords, while still enormously discretionary, was mediated as never before through laws and formally constituted institutions encompassing all categories of the population. In their new role as provincial landowners serving in elected assemblies of local self-administration—assemblies that were distinguishable from the state apparatus in unprecedented ways—former serf owners became more thoroughly differentiated from noble officials. The emancipation of 1861 thus completed that of 1762, representing not the onset of the traditional nobility's political decline and economic ruin, but the onset of a clear demarcation between the landowning and bureaucratic elites. Even so, the delineation remained incomplete. Landowners, including magnates of pre-Petrine lineage, continued to dominate the highest levels of officialdom, and until the final collapse of the old regime, many of Russia's most powerful bureaucrats and the last Romanov ruler himself, Nicholas II, frequently acted upon local noble demands.[21]

The idea and sometimes the reality of a personalized relationship to the ruler did not prevent nobles from becoming closely integrated into the informal structures of provincial social life as serf owners, landowners, and neighbors; yet regardless of local bonds and familial values, access to the nobility depended almost entirely on the state. The government both controlled ennoblement and defined noble privilege. The only members of society able to achieve nobility through marriage were the widows and daughters of commoners; their sons and brothers could rise to noble status only in service or by special grant of the monarch. The centrality of service in defining nobility thus bolstered the traditionally close identification with the ruler, including belief in a good tsar who would defend the interests of the nobility.[22] The loss of faith in the myth of the tsar and the resulting disillusionment help explain the ease with which the nobility moved into opposition to the government in the late nineteenth and early twentieth centuries. Like their peasant neighbors and subordinates, landowning nobles continued to believe in a personal and benevolent monarch until, in the process of emancipating the serfs, it became clear that they no longer could expect the government to protect their rights and privileges. It was this political and moral betrayal rather than economic crisis that underlay both the acute social conflict in the countryside and the nobility's desertion of the autocracy in the revolutionary situations of 1905 and 1917.[23]

Controversy about the character of the imperial Russian nobility reveals the difficulties in defining and delimiting the group's boundaries. Images of alienation, absenteeism, economic torpidity, decline, and crisis derive from the multiple and malleable attributes of noble identity and from the scant attention paid noblewomen by scholars.[24] Regardless of how historians may characterize the impact of service on the psychology of noblemen or the relationship between landowners and officialdom, and regardless of whether they find evidence of inexorable decline and crisis or successful adaptation and evolution in the postemancipation period, it is certain that from the seventeenth century on, a sizable group of nobles of both sexes maintained close ties to the land, despite repeated changes in their prescribed obligations and privileges. Conflicting depictions of nobles, as either indifferent, economically inept servicemen alienated from the countryside or engaged landowners bounded by the mental and material structures of their estates, thus emanated from the lack of clear social parameters and the concomitant insecurity and uncertainty of noble status. Both depictions are in different ways correct: the first refers to the nobles of a given geographical locality and the second to nobles of the family estate. Unlike the aristocracies and nobilities of England, the German states, and the empire's Baltic provinces, Russian nobles lacked proprietary claims to authority beyond the family estate—claims that were historically articulated and politically constituted in the *local* laws, offices, and institutions of an identifiable territory.[25]

The most fundamental and legally secure privileges of nobility were similarly ambiguous. When Peter the Great introduced the capitation, he defined a crucial social divide between the unprivileged many who carried the full burden of taxation and the privileged few who remained exempt (though still subject to various levies on property transactions and land). By the end of the eighteenth century, nobles shared this exemption with a broad range of social categories, including active and retired military servicemen, ranked and unranked civil servants, state employees and specialists, clergy, and merchants.[26] Other prominent cornerstones of noble privilege—the exclusive right to own populated estates, preferential treatment in the army and bureaucracy, and freedom from obligatory service—did not become fully established in law, not to mention administration, until the 1750s and 1760s. Even then, a decree of 1758, not rescinded until 1814, allowed non-noble officials in ranks thirteen to nine (only rank eight granted nobility) to possess populated estates "on the basis of secretarial rights."[27] In practice, that most touted of noble privileges, the right to own serfs, never became exclusive. Through subterfuge and illicit arrangements, often carried out with noble collusion, commoners continued to acquire and exploit serf labor until the mid-nineteenth century.[28] With emancipation, nobles lost the fundamental source of their exclusivity and became simply landowners, a status threatened in turn by massive land sales in the final decades of tsarist rule and by persistent peasant demands for a radical re-distribution of rural private property—demands that received brief but serious consideration at the highest levels of government during the revolutionary crisis of 1905.[29]

The principle of personal inviolability revealed yet another restriction of noble privilege. Although it is generally assumed that Catherine II's Charter to the Nobility of 1785 firmly established security of person and property for nobles, the earliest guarantees against arbitrary search and arrest did not come to Russia until the judicial reform of 1864.[30] In the early eighteenth century, the wealthiest and most politically powerful members of the aristocracy regularly suffered personal disgrace and confiscation of estates at the discretion of the crown. Among the service elite *(generalitet)* of 1730, more than one-fifth (40 out of 179) had directly experienced confiscation either as the recipients or as the previous owners of seized properties. Of the twenty-nine who owned more than three thousand male serfs, ten suffered total confiscation of their property, and among those with over a thousand souls, one out of four experienced confiscation during his career. In addition, forty-seven of these powerful officials fell from favor at some time during their service and were stripped of rank and sent either to distant posts or into exile.[31]

In the Catherinean era and continuing in the first half of the nineteenth century, prominent intellectuals, public figures, and influential bureaucrats such as A. N. Radishchev, N. I. Novikov, E. R. Dashkova, and M. M. Speranskii faced similar punishments, as did ordinary civil servants and military officers convicted of crimes.[32] With some regularity, courts prosecuted landlords who cruelly abused their serfs: according to one estimate, between 1834 and 1845, 630 of 2,838 seigniors tried for mistreating peasants were convicted. The sources examined do not indicate what retribution the authorities imposed, but those nobles who were not convicted still received reprimands.[33] The Charter to the Nobility certainly enhanced personal security by granting immunity from corporal punishment and absolute rights of private property, but it also implicitly preserved the notion that state service was a necessary "accompaniment to the enjoyment of these advantages" and prescribed broad grounds for the deprivation of formal privileges, based on due process of law.[34] As one historian tellingly describes it, the charter was "a unilateral grant," not "a bilateral contract" in any way comparable to the Magna Carta.[35]

Preferential treatment in service similarly exemplified the limits to exclusive noble privilege. Despite increasingly strict rules giving nobles priority in appointments and promotions, personnel shortages in the lower rungs of the bureaucracy and army created continual opportunities for qualified commoners not liable for the capitation to rise through service. Real social mobility in the form of ennoblement remained exceedingly difficult, but in the nineteenth century formal education played a significant role in determining assignment to and advancement in service and also brought privileges associated with noble status, including exemption from corporal punishment, conscription, and the capitation. The government of Alexander I (1801–1825) tried in principle to make promotion to high office dependent upon successful completion of a civil service examination, though actual implementation of this measure was erratic and inconclusive until the 1860s and 1870s. Even as ennoblement through service became more circumscribed, requiring the attainment of ever higher office, the continual expansion of the bureaucracy and of educated cadres meant that growing numbers of commoners began their careers in a graded rank. While nobles were never displaced in this process and retained privileges in service until 1906, as educational requirements acquired greater stature and legal rights became more equalized across society, their special treatment became less exclusive.[36]

It is clearly also important to consider the role of downward mobility in the development of the imperial "ruling" class well before the postemancipation period, when significant numbers of déclassé nobles joined the ranks of the intelligentsia, the professions, and even the laboring poor. Changes in societal boundaries initiated by the introduction of the capitation and the establishment of a standing army did as much to exclude traditional categories of lesser nobles from the elite as they did to include new categories. Social groups such as the single householders *(odnodvortsy)* and, after 1831, the landless Polish *szlachta* possessed the right to demonstrate their noble ancestry. To regain these allegedly lost privileges, single householders had to document that the land grants received by their ancestors had been awarded specifically for noble service.[37] Relatively identifiable as a social category because of their geographical concentration in the former southern borderlands of the Russian state, single householders enjoyed special privileges in military service throughout the prereform period.[38] Their very existence shows that while many traditional ranks were absorbed into the simplified Petrine categories of the eighteenth century, others retained a distinct and indeterminate status until after 1861—when the elimination of serfdom, the standing army, and the capitation led to another fundamental restructuring of official social classifications.

In addition to single householders and déclassé *szlachta,* there were others whose claims to noble ancestry had been rejected or overlooked and who consequently had been enrolled in the poll tax registers, usually during the first half of the eighteenth century.[39] The ambiguous status of these claimants resulted either from a family's inability to document noble lineage or from an individual's failure to establish descent from a line recognized by the Heraldry Office. As late as 1767, both the Heraldry Office and the Senate complained about the absence of a complete register of nobles and requested an exact definition of whether the qualifications for nobility should be service rank, possession of an estate, or both.[40] Catherine II's Charter of 1785 did much to clarify the criteria for determining who was a noble, but throughout the century individuals of low birth moved successfully into elite status under various guises. In the nineteenth century, the often impossible task of documenting noble genealogies continued to place both unrequited claimants (at times close to half of the petitioners seeking recognition as nobles) and honest officials in a frustrating predicament. The questions raised in these cases and the inability to answer them testified to the very real uncertainties of noble status and the fundamental commitment of officialdom to protecting noble rights.[41]

The many legal-administrative vagaries of noble standing are more readily understandable when one remembers that the government did not seriously seek to delineate and hence elevate the nobility as a whole before the mid-eighteenth century. Until that time, neither broad distinctions based on service nor those derived from the ownership of populated estates had been clearly articulated, much less implemented. Censuses of graded civil servants from the 1750s underscored governmental indifference toward rigid delineation; the data identified officials according to service rank without indicating social category, and many respondents to the inquiries of the census takers did not even state their origins. S. M. Troitskii interprets these omissions as evidence of an effort by non-nobles to hide their humble roots.[42] But how then does one explain the hereditary nobles who also failed to refer to themselves as such? Furthermore, if officials were not required to provide this information, then perhaps it was of no great importance to the purpose of the census, which was to provide a general overview of the condition of civil servants. Nor was ancestry necessarily a concern within the bureaucracy, where in the formal relationships between officials in graded positions, current rank mattered more than heredity. Still, social distinctions were important to individual careers, which is why administrative personnel below the Table of Ranks were keen to proclaim their origins, either in order to improve their prospects for promotion, if they were noble, or to distinguish themselves from the poll tax population, if they were not.[43] In either case, personal insecurity and a desire for the rewards of service, rather than the existence of clear social boundaries, explain the interest in articulating the official designations.

Cultural and economic factors reinforced the numerous political uncertainties faced by nobles and further contributed to the underlying ambiguity of their status. Cultural stratification cut to the very heart of defining who was a noble, yet also clouded distinctions between the nobility and other groups in society. Already by the mid-eighteenth century, Russia possessed a socially diverse, self-conscious reading public identified by education, material comfort, and cultivated deportment. Composed of courtiers, aristocrats, lesser nobles, state officials, military officers, merchants, writers, artists, physicians, and scientists, the "honorable public" cohered around theaters, libraries, social clubs, literary societies, private salons, and Masonic lodges. Its members, who included both men and women, often served as courtiers and officials but still distinguished themselves from the dark masses (*prostaia chern'*) and the "corrupt" court and bureaucracy. Most important, the self-defined characteristics of the reading public derived neither from noble birth nor from economic and political power, but from culture, morality, civility, and virtue.[44] Increasingly, specialized knowledge and Western education represented vital sources of elite status, to which nobles enjoyed privileged but never exclusive access.

Despite the extensive penetration of European culture into provincial Russia during the eighteenth century, many nobles—among them persons of ancient and honored lineage—remained poor, uneducated, and steeped in custom. When Peter the Great institutionalized merit and performance as criteria for advancement in service, and when he set out to reform Russia's traditional aristocratic elite, he implicitly broadened the definition of nobility to include a cultural component based on education and Westernization. This cultural definition, which reinforced the traditional importance of service, is strikingly apparent in Sergei Aksakov's novel *A Russian Gentleman,* where the family of the heroine, Sophia, represents the post-Petrine urban, bureaucratic nobility, in contrast to her husband's ancestors, who are of ancient lineage. Sophia clearly regards her background as superior, not on the basis of birth or even service, but because of education and the possession of Western culture. By contrast, her patriarchal father-in-law, Bagrov, exercises unrestrained absolute authority over his dependents, and like his married daughters, who reside in filthy, rat-infested hovels, he lives in a manner that blends imperceptibly with peasant folkways. His son's marriage to Sophia, the daughter of a parvenu nobleman—who himself questions whether the Bagrovs, given their ignorance and boorish ways, offer a suitable match—reveals that more than ever before, Western culture, both spiritual and material, compensated for and, in the eyes of some, took precedence over lineage and wealth.[45]

The extent of economic differentiation and the presence of poverty among nobles also are well known. At the time of the tenth revision (1857–1858), serfs constituted about 40 percent of the empire's population with about four-fifths living on estates of at least one hundred male souls. Conversely, about three-fourths of serf owners possessed fewer than one hundred souls and together held less than 20 percent of the serfs.[46] Put another way, 44 percent of serf owners possessed properties with fewer than twenty-one souls; 81 percent of serfs belonged to the 22 percent of noble landowners who held estates of more than one hundred souls, and 29 percent of serfs were owned by the 1 percent of landowners with over one thousand souls. According to data from 1834, among the 106,000 nobles with fewer than one hundred souls, 17,000 had no land at all.[47] These statistics clearly illustrate the enormous differences of wealth found among nobles; even more important, they show that by far the largest segment of the serf-owning class enjoyed only the most modest material means.

The Russian nobility was by no stretch of the imagination a class of the idle rich. Until emancipation, most nobles with fewer than one hundred souls pursued careers in the army or bureaucracy, and many of those who stayed on the land appeared in lifestyle and manners closer to peasants than to the great landowning magnates.[48] Pronounced stratification continued in the postemancipation period, when noble landholdings remained highly concentrated, and the poorest landowners continued to live like their former serfs. In 1879 the radical populist A. N. Engel'gardt wrote of peasants who came to his estate in Smolensk province to purchase grain because their former lord was so poor he had gone to work as a manager for another landowner.[49] By 1905, 9 percent of estates accounted for 73 percent of the land owned by hereditary and personal nobles, and 61–62 percent of all nobles were landless.[50] According to the electoral law of June 1907, only about thirty-one thousand families—20 percent of all noble landowners and 12 percent of hereditary nobles—qualified for direct voting rights in the private landowners' curia.[51] Economic differentiation not only fragmented the nobility but also blurred the boundaries distinguishing it from other social groups.

As serf owners, even the most impoverished and uneducated nobles had been secure in their authority and social position, though theirs was a localized and personalized power that generally turned out to be inconsequential in encounters with the larger structures of state and society. This explains why, as a social group, noble landowners became most clearly defined in socioeconomic terms and politically dominant in formal institutional terms only in the final decades of the old regime, *after* the loss of traditional noble exclusivity. Despite the elimination of serf labor in 1861 and the spread of private landholding among commoners in the years following emancipation, the landowning nobility, more than ever before, could be distinguished both as a social elite and as a political force independent of the bureaucracy. Many accounts of the late imperial nobility convey images of economic ruin, political decline, and futile efforts to preserve anachronistic social and legal privileges. As evidence of this devastation, historians point to rising debt and land sales, movement into nontraditional urban occupations, loss of prestige and exclusive noble rights, aggressive bureaucratic intrusions into local affairs, and an official willingness to sacrifice agricultural interests to the needs of industry.[52] For some noble families these developments did indeed spell destruction. For others, who became effective modernizers of their estates, successful investors in commerce and industry, or trained specialists, professionals, scholars, and artists, the replacement of hereditary rights with social and political qualifications based on education, property, and wealth meant nothing more than change and adaptation.[53]

By the early twentieth century, the more prosperous elements of the rural nobility had been absorbed into "a class or interest group of intermediate and large landowners seriously devoted to agriculture."[54] The putative "decline of the nobility" referred to a changing relationship to the land and a broadening of employment opportunities due to economic modernization and the spread of education. In the postemancipation era, economically weak landowners and those who were not interested in farming their estates withdrew from the countryside, leaving in place a core of entrepreneurial noble proprietors who successfully adapted to the significant economic and social innovations of the late nineteenth century.[55] Although nobles were net sellers of land between 1861 and 1914 and although the proportion of individually held land owned by peasants increased substantially, former serf owners still could reap the rewards of plentiful and cheap labor, profitable sharecropping arrangements, rising land values, and high rents. Nor were land sales or mounting mortgage debts necessarily indicative of economic failure. Because of the dramatic increase in land prices, decisions to sell often constituted sound economic choice, especially if the annual income obtained from farming an estate was less than what a landowner could receive by investing capital in governmental or private securities. In addition, from 1893 on, land values rose as fast as, or faster than, the nobility's mortgage debt. The low interest rates offered by the Noble Land Bank (established in 1885) turned mortgages into an attractive source of capital. Most important, nobles remained dominant among the owners of middle and large estates, the very group that on the basis of tsarist electoral laws controlled the assemblies of local self-administration *(zemstva)* from 1864, the elected half of the State Council from 1906, and the national representative body, the Duma, from 1907.[56] No longer based on juridical privilege, the political power of noble landowners at the end of the old regime derived from their disproportionate hold over rural property in what was still an agrarian society.[57]

Given the revolutionary outcome of 1917, it is tempting to depict the late imperial nobility in terms of crisis and disintegration. On the other hand, if one views postemancipation conditions in the context of the entire imperial period, it is clear that the "new" uncertainties of elite status were traditional features of Russian society, not the consequences of a socioeconomic transformation that excluded nobles and undermined established identities. Even the underlying sources of social ambiguity, broadly defined, were similar to those of earlier times. While eighteenth-century nobles did not yet have to confront the social and economic volatility of rapid capitalization and industrialization, they were no more secure on their consumption-oriented estates, where crop failures, natural disasters, shortages of cash, and geographical isolation could bring ruin or at the very least make it difficult to maintain a lifestyle appropriate to their formally elevated status. Survival in a preindustrial economy, no less than in an industrializing one, required flexibility, dynamism, initiative, and entrepreneurial manipulations. What distinguished industrializing from preindustrial Russia was not inertia and stagnation but a modern conception of investment in production, strict methods of cost accounting, sufficient amounts of capital, and blind faith in technological innovation.

Political vulnerability and equivocation also were nothing new. The nobility had always depended on the autocrat to protect its formal privileges and ensure its traditional access to high office. Formal rights and service obligations were never contractual but discretionary and hence provisional. Nobles repeatedly adapted to changes by choosing either to comply with or ignore the legal prescriptions. Thus the aristocratic elite of the early eighteenth century selectively embraced the Petrine reforms in order to relegitimize their status. According to the dictates of the sovereign, they altered their lifestyle in matters of public appearance, material culture, patterns of service, and the education of their children. At the same time, in the intimate sphere of family life, they stood firm and absolutely refused to accept the 1714 law on single inheritance—a law that threatened familial relationships, time-honored custom, and the most deeply held values and expectations of the landowning elite.[58] In a complex relationship based on "privilege and compulsion,"[59] nobles readily submitted to the absolute political authority of the ruler. When he violated their trust in 1861, by depriving them of their serfs, the vast majority remained loyal. Prominent members of the nobility may have become embroiled in the kinship and patronage politics of the court and government and by the early twentieth century in the liberal political opposition, but the rank and file, not unlike their own serfs or peasant neighbors, resisted interference at the most immediate levels of private life. In the intimate sphere, and frequently in the larger local context, all were "free" to evade official obligations, disregard legal prescriptions, violate formal and informal social boundaries, and ignore corporate, *zemstvo,* and Duma politics.

In seeking to understand the nobility as a social category, it is important to distinguish between the minority of landowners who participated in public institutions, the educated minority who consciously abandoned the land to pursue alternative careers, and those ordinary nobles—poor, uneducated, politically inactive, and often déclassé—who chose disengagement over activism and thus rarely appear in historical accounts. Included in the above groupings were individuals who consciously shed their legal identity to join the ranks of the intelligentsia and professions, others who engaged in trade and manufacturing and sometimes registered in merchant guilds, and still others who blended imperceptibly into the general population as farmers and wage laborers.[60] These varieties of nobility also were not new to the postemancipation era of vibrant economic change and growing legal equality. They already could be found in the countryside and especially the towns of prereform Russia and among the unrequited claimants to noble status whose lack of formal recognition had become institutionalized degradation when Peter the Great introduced the capitation. Always an open, privileged, and hereditary elite—even at the highest levels—this was also an elite that continually experienced upward and downward mobility in terms of its internal composition, socioeconomic standing, and legal-political rights. A "boundless" social formation touching "the foot of the throne" at one end and the peasantry at the other,[61] the Russian nobility never constituted a secure, fully differentiated ruling class.

Visible moments of social cohesion, common expression, and potentially effective political mobilization did occur among nobles in response to specific events such as the succession crisis of 1730, the Legislative Commission of 1767–1768, the emancipation of 1861, and the liberation movement of 1904–1905. But these moments of cohesion exposed massive political apathy, as well as deep internal divisions, and so fail to impart the full complexity, dynamism, and ambiguity of the long-term, slow-moving daily realities of noble identity—realities that are better explained in terms of limited differentiation from other social groups. There was of course no question as to who were the masters. Whether or not landlords intervened directly in village affairs, they had the authority to do so at any time. By contrast, the nobles' relationship to the broader framework of society and to the autocracy contained numerous uncertainties and inconsistencies.[62] Michael Confino's conception of an integrated society of orders where the bond between master and serf derived from dynamic interdependence accurately describes the position of some noble landowners, just as Marc Raeff's description of the alienated state serviceman and the rootless noble intellectual describes that of others.[63] The ruined, déclassé former serf owner of the postemancipation era was no less an historical personage than the effective modernizer who belonged to an economically secure, politically powerful class of landed proprietors. Clearly, the imperial concept of the nobility *(dvorianstvo)* could not hope to accommodate the full range of economic, social, and political realities.

Civil and Military Servicemen

The legislation of Peter the Great posited a concept of the state as an abstract secular entity; however, the state's administrative apparatus and officialdom never took the concrete form of a truly professional bureaucracy with a unified outlook and ethos. Bureaucratic points of view crystallized around specific policies and projects for reform, but they expressed common intellectual influences and service functions rather than a characteristic mentality or collective vision.[64] The lack of cultural uniformity within officialdom, a pattern rooted in the social and political order, helps account for repeated failures to extend and complete significant reforms. In the reigns of Catherine II, Alexander I, Alexander II, and Nicholas II, enlightened bureaucrats sought in varying degrees to transform judicial, administrative, social, and economic institutions. In every instance, their efforts were truncated or reversed by opposition from within officialdom itself—opposition that also often found support in various segments of public opinion. To be sure, the sovereign could override any and all majority proposals, but time and again the politics of reform persuaded already reluctant tsar-reformers either to abandon radical change altogether or to temporize and introduce only partial measures.[65]

Because of weak institutional structures and inadequate personnel, policymakers could not always ensure adequate implementation of the legislative agendas they succeeded in adopting. The lack of constituted bodies in society and the incomplete administrative edifice emanating from the ruler created shifting and irregular spaces where state and society intersected.[66] Noble assemblies, peasant communes, and urban communities exercised administrative, judicial, and "legislative" authority only on a local, individualized basis and only to the extent that state law did not apply.[67] Elected noble officials thus represented both a point of societal contact with central and provincial government and an extension of the serf owner's private patrimonial power. Peasant and urban officials and even parish priests played comparable dual roles as spokesmen for their communities and as instruments of autocratic administration. In all of these relationships, the interfacing of state and society was imperfectly defined and tended to hinge upon particular officials or their surrogates—the serf owner, regimental commander, priest, town mayor, marshal of the nobility, land captain (after 1889), or village head—rather than upon formal institutions and bureaucratic links.

Another reason for the unsatisfactory execution of major legislative initiatives was the character of administrative personnel and the parameters within which they operated. Russian officialdom was enormously diverse in terms of education, levels of skill, service experience, economic well-being, social origins, and cultural background. This variety, apparent at all levels of the administrative apparatus, provided further evidence of the limited differentiation between state and society. It was possible for a core of aristocratic families to perpetuate their political power from the Mongol period to the twentieth century precisely because a hereditary bureaucratic elite fully distinct from the traditional landowning nobility did not develop.[68] Despite growing alienation from the government among some segments of the nobility in the postemancipation period and despite the impossibility of equating the service elite with serf owners and landowners, on the eve of the First World War, wealth, lineage, and high office remained concentrated in the hands of the most exclusive families, whose members nonetheless also could include landless individuals and fierce critics of the bureaucracy.[69] The ability of a few clans to maintain influence at the summit of the political system over several centuries was not, however, equivalent to personal security or oligarchy. Nonaristocrats also attained the highest offices, and all prominent officials were politically vulnerable in office. Powerless to pursue policy initiatives without the support of the tsar, even those who sought to realize liberal change were impelled to strengthen autocracy and rely upon discretionary authority.[70]

Active reformers were always a minority within officialdom, and at any given time only a very small group of high-ranking individuals actually guided policy and advised the monarch. The vast majority of bureaucrats, including many of noble origin, labored in lowly clerical posts in district, provincial, and central offices, with few opportunities to escape the endless drudgery of paperwork by achieving real power and influence. Those without graded posts generally received their training on the job, mastered only a handful of administrative tasks, and because of their limited skills and service experience, tended to resist change and thus proved ill-suited to carry reform to the localities.[71] The sons of poor nobles, merchants, unranked officials, soldiers, and churchmen, these ordinary servicemen had little in common socially, economically, or culturally with the increasingly educated and politically sophisticated civil servants who wielded direct administrative authority. The absence of a strong collective identity that could provide the basis for a professional bureaucracy resulted as much from the disparate fortunes and responsibilities of officials within service as from their diverse backgrounds. These social and cultural differences were most pronounced in the gap between upper and lower officialdom, but also could be found within the governing elite itself, in august bodies such as the State Council, and by the twentieth century, in the growing importance of "specialist and technically oriented ministries."[72]

Administrative fragmentation and varying degrees of organizational and professional development highlighted the bureaucracy's lack of cohesion. For much of the eighteenth century, the instability of supreme political power perpetuated the fluid institutional structures that had their roots in the seventeenth century, having been only partially reconstructed in the reign of Peter the Great. The process of stabilizing and standardizing the administrative apparatus began in earnest with the provincial and Senate reforms of Catherine II, continued with the military reforms of Paul and the ministerial reforms of Alexander I, and, after Napoleon's invasion, proceeded anew under Nicholas I with the expansion of specialized protoprofessional education, the compilation (not codification) of civil and military laws, and the elaboration of detailed rules for appointment to and promotion in service. Despite the greater predictability made possible by regularized rules and procedures, there was no point of comprehensive administrative integration beyond the person of the tsar before the cabinet and parliamentary reforms of 1905–1906. Even then, after the creation of a powerful first minister to coordinate governmental policy, the effective authority and influence of high officials continued to depend entirely upon the favor of the monarch, to whom they rendered sole obedience and remained directly responsible.

Together with atomized lines of authority extending from the ruler through various ministries, departments, and special commissions, the Russian bureaucracy also was characterized by extensive reliance on personalized power and the uneven development of professional expertise. Many officials in ministries such as finance and war exhibited high levels of technical knowledge, gave voice to professional concerns, and applied specialized criteria in evaluating general policy matters. At the same time, the autocratic system continued to uphold the principles of discretionary charismatic authority, thwarting full realization of impersonal bureaucratic rule. Given the empire's lack of administrative integration, modern specialization reinforced the traditional fragmentation of institutions and power, exacerbated intellectual and political differences, further limited the success of reform, and contributed to the paralysis of government in the revolutionary crises of the early twentieth century. Clique politics at court in the eighteenth century gave way to ministerial conflict in the nineteenth and early twentieth centuries. Although the autocrat theoretically united societal, bureaucratic, and military structures, the channels leading to and from the apex of the institutional edifice or between its various components were never precisely defined.[73]

Marc Raeff writes of the ongoing efforts to construct local administration that

> the realities of government were not those of society, and the languages expressing the two realities were never the same. The lack of an adequately codified system of law that would have provided one system of linguistic expression for common discourse is again a basic cause, as well as a telling illustration, of Russia's peculiar circumstance in this respect.[74]

Raeff views the indeterminate institutional structures and the absence of a shared and hence mediating legal-administrative language as the basis for a continuing separation of state and society. This is an accurate depiction, if by integration one means effective linkages. The Russian government never fashioned stable linkages, even in military administration, which was arguably the best coordinated and most professionalized of all official domains.[75] At the same time, the inadequate linkages also suggest a lack of clear delineation between state and society—manifested in the irregular interfacing of bureaucratic and social institutions and in the blurring of governmental and representative functions that characterized elected officials and bodies of local self-administration.

Corruption revealed yet another source of administrative inefficiency and illuminated once again the limited differentiation between state and society. Generally regarded by historians and contemporaries as endemic to Russian government, various forms of corruption (bribery, fraud, embezzlement, neglect of duty, abuse of subordinates) resulted from either blatant greed or pressing need. Nonexistent and inadequate salaries were a chronic problem but do not adequately explain the prevailing dishonesty, nor do timeworn references to low levels of education and culture or to the arbitrariness of autocratic authority.[76] Corruption often played an integrative role in the complex relationships binding state and society, particularly in contexts where the government sought to order social life or extract resources from the populace. One historian describes the broad social phenomenon of bribery as "the one point where the bureaucracy, the society, and, moreover, the entire population were closely interrelated, since corruption demands the agreement of both parties."[77] In addition to exposing the nebulous boundaries separating officialdom from the general public, corruption sometimes constituted popular resistance to governmental exactions, or in the case of civil and military officials, ad hoc measures taken in critical situations to ensure the fulfillment of service duties.

Archival research devoted to the army and bureaucracy illustrates this point. In the regimental economy of the early nineteenth century, commanders bore full responsibility for outfitting and provisioning their men and for ensuring the availability and good repair of all necessary arms and equipment. As early as the reign of Peter the Great, the central government began to supply the army with pay, equipment, ammunition, and weapons, with sources of food and forage, and with material for clothing and footwear. Sometimes these items came directly from grain magazines and state factories, but more often than not the troops were expected to satisfy their own physical needs, using resources extracted from civilian society and monies acquired from the government or through private contractual work. Although the law required that local communities provide quarters, fuel, and food and that the unit commander deliver to each soldier his allotted pay, provisions, and clothing, the central authorities could never guarantee that the prescribed goods were readily available. The government's unwillingness or inability to regulate the military economy fully caused much physical suffering and social conflict within the ranks. It also placed significant discretionary power in the hands of individual commanders, made subsistence largely a local affair, and clouded the boundaries delimiting institutional domains and separating military from civilian society. Leaving aside the very real possibility of venal commanders and contractors robbing the treasury and the troops, even the most honest officer could easily find himself in violation of the law. Given the unreliability of state and local supplies—and once again assuming integrity—commanders could ensure adequate support in two ways, either by rearranging resources already at hand (for example, using funds allocated for equipment to purchase food) or by pursuing private economic activities (for example, maintaining garrison farms or releasing subordinates to work for outside employers).[78] In either case, what in one context might constitute a justifiable response to economic exigencies, in another could be viewed as flagrant disregard for the rules of service.

The government generally tolerated improvisation of both sorts, which inevitably invited abuse and produced misunderstandings between officers and their men. It is no surprise that among officers subjected to formal investigation or court-martial between 1836 and 1855, economic offenses and neglect of duty, including failure to provide adequately for subordinates, represented the most common crimes.[79] Soldiers also collaborated with officers to "cheat" the state, if not by outright theft, then by neglecting service duties in order to engage in economically beneficial pursuits. The simple fact is that without extensive reliance on civilian society for housing and sustenance, including the quartering of the majority of troops in individual homes, the army was in danger of collapse. Without the economic violations habitually committed by commanders, but only erratically punished by the authorities, soldiers repeatedly would not have been fed. The difficulty of maintaining a standing army in a vast, sparsely populated empire with an overwhelmingly agrarian subsistence economy meant that the troops could never be completely separated from civilian society, nor could the goal of a regularized autocracy operating on the basis of laws and prescribed procedures ever be realized.

Late-nineteenth-century provincial governors similarly exemplified the ongoing tension between discretionary charismatic authority and standardized government based on the rule of laws. As agents of the ministry of internal affairs, governors were little more than powerful bureaucratic subordinates. But as emissaries of the tsar, they provided the means for bypassing the regular administrative apparatus and communicating directly with the general population. Further complicating these contradictory roles, they were also responsible for supervising and coordinating the diverse and diffuse branches of local government, including those under the authority of other ministries. Although in terms of service patterns, expertise, and political skills, governors became more clearly differentiated within the bureaucracy prior to the First World War, their effective power remained highly personalized due to inadequate resources, limited supporting staff, and legal and institutional confusion. Some clearly displayed professional attitudes and approaches to their duties. Still, the means available for fulfilling their responsibilities and the conditions in which they worked remained traditional. At most, it is possible to speak of a tendency toward professionalization within a transitional gubernatorial corps.[80]

The structural weakness of formal administration, together with paltry and poorly educated personnel, impelled governors to rely on their own personal authority and relationships in order to perform their service duties. The need to work effectively with elected officials, city councils, and noble and *zemstvo* assemblies—to persuade rather than coerce—made local government interactive and "pluralistic" but also fostered inconsistency and arbitrariness. Popular expectations of benign intervention reinforced the pattern of personalized rule, forcing governors to spend up to five hours a day receiving petitioners (who also might appear at any hour of the night). Like military commanders, governors sometimes violated the law in order to address immediate crises such as social unrest, crop failure, and famine. Decisive action repeatedly demanded that they ignore legal strictures, a practice that superiors in the ministry of internal affairs tolerated and even encouraged.[81] When in 1893 Minister of Internal Affairs I. N. Durnovo objected to proposals granting the Senate greater authority to reprimand governors and subject them to trial in regular courts, he noted that these changes "would give undue weight to 'purely legal considerations' and might inhibit the governors in meeting the many 'special circumstances' that required them to take technically illegal actions."[82] Given the meager human and material resources at the disposal of local officials and the limited coordination and support from the center, the goals of public welfare and well-ordered government rendered arbitrary personal rule as much a necessity as a source of abuse and illicit individual gain.

Together with institutional fragmentation, personalized authority, and persistent corruption, the social condition of servicemen and their families illustrated the incomplete separation of "state" and "society."[83] Because wives always occupied the current legal position of their husbands, and children that of their fathers at the moment of birth, the social consequences of service extended well beyond the formal structures of the bureaucracy and army, reaching into the most immediate levels of family, village, and urban community.[84] The categories of imperial society were incorporated into and transformed by bureaucratic and military structures. Whether voluntary or obligatory, service was at once the object and the subject of social identity. These intricate relationships and the dynamic interactions they produced affected all social groups and operated at all levels of the administrative hierarchy. Beginning with the introduction of the capitation (poll tax) in 1718–1727 and the Table of Ranks in 1722, and continuing until the collapse of the tsarist regime, official efforts to direct social development were closely related to the mobilization of resources for state needs. In the new Petrine order, inclusion in or omission from the poll tax registries defined a crucial aspect of legal-administrative status that brought downward or upward mobility. The process of ascription—of identifying who belonged to which social category or territorial community and who was or was not liable for the capitation—deeply affected and even transformed societal structures and customary relations. The actual dynamics and concrete results of this process are poorly understood, but the capitation's significance as a social barrier distinguishing the privileged few from the un-privileged many is undeniable.[85] Civil and military servicemen and their off-spring, regardless of social origin, were among the elite minority who enjoyed freedom from the capitation. It was this right that constituted the most effec-tive and all-embracing boundary separating the "lower ranks" of the army and bureaucracy from the rest of society.

The distinction between the poll tax population and non-noble officials (ranked and unranked) was in reality ambivalent and paradoxical. Until 1827, persons liable for the capitation, with the important exception of serfs, were permitted to enter state service. Their numbers were small, and such changes of status were not encouraged, but "educated" individuals repeatedly gained entry either illegally or as a result of official exclusion from the tax rolls. Dur-ing the eighteenth century, even a few runaway serfs managed to conceal their past and become state servicemen. State and church peasants and townspeople sometimes occupied a dual status, remaining registered to their original com-munities and continuing to fulfill tax obligations even after joining the bureau-cracy. Laws of 1744–1745 and 1771 banned persons who paid the capitation (including merchants) from holding official posts, but the practice continued: a decree of 1798 legalized these appointments with the Senate's permission, ex-empted all civil servants from the poll tax, and forbade them to participate in other occupations while in state service. Archival evidence convincingly shows that despite legal prohibitions, individuals subject to the capitation con-tinued to occupy administrative offices: 3,600 persons entered the bureaucracy from taxed social categories in 1810, including 600 who had not been ap-proved by the Senate. Effective measures limiting access to state service on the basis of social origin came only in 1827, but they too were quickly under-mined by the ever-increasing weight accorded formal education in the selec-tion and advancement of officials. Although social origin functioned nega-tively as a legal basis for determining appointments and promotions until 1906, throughout the eighteenth and nineteenth centuries, possession of the requisite skills could override any and all restrictions derived from birth.[86]

In contrast to ungraded civil servants, who in principle originated from seg-ments of the population already exempt from the capitation, the lower ranks *(nizhnie chiny)* of the Russian army, the noncommissioned officers and com-mon soldiers, came from the entire servile population of serfs, state peasants, and townspeople. At once the most unfortunate dregs of society and the mem-bers of the laboring classes most likely to achieve real social mobility, con-scripts became juridically "free"—free from the capitation and the authority of the landlord or local community—at the moment of induction. In excluding from the tax registers all military personnel and any sons born to them in ac-tive service, and in giving to former serfs legal rights and a civic identity, re-cruitment into the army formally represented upward mobility. Still, before 1874 it was imposed on those of inferior status liable for the capitation, and the freedom it brought could not be implemented until physical disability or com-pletion of the lengthy term of service ended a soldier's active military career.[87]

That military service meant much more than the incorporation of high- and lowborn individuals into a bureaucratic hierarchy was evident from the impact of recruitment on community life and from the status of veterans and soldiers' families.[88] In addition to welfare problems associated with subsistence, illegitimacy, and bigamy, conscription altered the social order by producing changes in juridical status—which in turn generated new social categories such as soldiers' wives *(soldatki)* and soldiers' children *(soldatskie deti)*—and generally increased the uncertainties of social classification and definition. While landlords, peasant villages, and urban communities might use conscription levies to rid themselves of economically weak or morally dissolute individuals, a significant trade in hired substitutes—supported by indentured servitude, illegal enserfment, trickery, concealment, and outright purchase—allowed some to escape military service altogether. The extent of evasion cannot be measured, but it is clear that most young men dutifully accepted the dreaded obligation to serve, the consequences of which lasted virtually a lifetime. Until universal conscription became the norm, the long term of service (initially for life but reduced to twenty-five years in 1793 and to twenty in 1834) permanently disrupted communities, families, and personal relationships. Villages and urban societies remained responsible for paying the taxes of conscripts until the next census; individual households lost not only a husband, father, or son but an able-bodied male laborer, and in the countryside, the recipient of a share of allotment land.

The wives of recruits were also emancipated at the time of conscription and thus lost their formal membership in the local community. Relatives, landlords, or the community as a whole sometimes provided for soldiers' wives, especially those whose male children represented potential taxpayers; but in rural areas, some of these legally free women were driven from their homes. Suspected of debauchery and denied a place in society, they were forced to make their own way, usually in a town, and only rarely managed to live with their husbands among the troops. Any children, legitimate or not, born to soldiers' wives after their husbands entered service, to unmarried soldiers' daughters, or to soldiers in active service belonged to the military command, and if male, were required to enroll in special schools that prepared them for careers in the army or bureaucracy. As free men with an elementary general education and some specialized training, soldiers' sons provided an important source of noncommissioned officers and were well positioned to rise through the ranks. Although most concerned with the whereabouts and welfare of soldiers' sons, the government also made some provision for the education of soldiers' daughters, who then were expected eventually to marry, thereby acquiring the formal status of their husbands, or to find employment as governesses. Privileged in their legal freedom, yet at the same time extremely vulnerable to poverty, unlawful enserfment, and forced marriage, soldiers' wives and children occupied an ambiguous position in the imperial social order.

Until a law of 1867 established that recruits, and hence also their families, would remain registered members of the communities from which they were drafted, discharged soldiers constituted a privileged category of freedmen. Still, as a result of their emancipation from servile status, they lacked ties to any formally constituted community, were unable to claim a share of allotment land, and repeatedly fell victim to poverty and destitution. The more fortunate among them either returned to their original homes or established themselves and their families on a new economic footing elsewhere. Regardless of financial vulnerability or domestic circumstances and despite legal freedom and exemption from the capitation, neither retired soldiers nor their wives and children necessarily became outcasts in society. The repeated appearance of these groups in the records of Moscow churches as parishioners, spouses, parents, godparents, friends, and employees makes the outsider image difficult to sustain. It seems that no matter how dire their economic straits, they generally found at least irregular employment, and a few even possessed houses.[89] The meager incomes of lower-class military families may have been painfully inadequate and their legal privileges may have led to the severance of all ties to the home community, but just because they were outsiders in official administrative terms did not inevitably mean they were people without a place in the local, informal structures of society. The Russian social order was sufficiently flexible to accommodate individuals and groups who did not belong to registered communities, lacked a legal status, or abandoned that status by choice or out of necessity.

Individuals and communities coped with recruitment levies in a variety of ways, yet regardless of time and place, all were forced to respond. In the process of selecting recruits and devising mechanisms to provide for their wives and children, customary and prescribed relations were challenged and transformed. Society's reactions to the draft affected both the organization of the army and the content of formal law. Deliberate evasion, self-mutilation, the general health of the population, and the delivery of physically unsuitable recruits all made it difficult for the military to meet its manpower needs. It also seems likely that the regulations governing apportionment of the service burden incorporated peasant practices. Recruitment levies simultaneously created and imitated custom in a relationship that illustrated the dynamic interfacing of state and society, as well as the blurred boundaries separating formal from informal institutions. After the military educational reforms of the 1860s and the introduction of universal conscription in 1874, the distinction between military and civilian society became still more confused and contradictory. Even as officers and military bureaucrats appeared increasingly career-minded and professionalized, Russia's "peasants in uniform," now drafted for six years of active duty, never joined a legally constituted citizen army.[90] With or without serfdom and the poll tax, with or without universal conscription, military ranks in both service and society remained only partially differentiated.

The army's role in the revolution of 1905–1907 raises important and still not fully answered questions about the boundaries distinguishing military from civilian society. It appears reasonable to attribute the troops' dual function as a source of revolutionary ferment—there were 413 mutinies beginning in October 1905 and continuing through 1906[91]—and an effective instrument of repression to a peasant mentality characterized by submissiveness and obedience to traditional authority. But if the soldiers were indeed revolutionary peasants, it is difficult to understand their isolation from the upheaval in civilian society. That military discipline ultimately prevailed when soldiers obeyed orders to suppress popular disorders indicates the relative success of training and socialization in the late imperial army. The same may be said of the high-level commanders who issued those orders and the officers who executed them, despite their own opposition to using troops for nonmilitary purposes.[92] As a result of military reforms following the Crimean War, the term of active service was greatly reduced, and conscription no longer brought a change in juridical status; yet the peasants who supplied the vast majority of recruits remained legally separated from other groups in society and the regimental economy continued to depend on improvisation and local resources.[93] Given these similarities to the prereform semistanding army and the still very vague delineation of the troops from civilian society, the decisive reality in 1905–1907 was not the spread of mutinies but their limited nature and the effectiveness of military repression. Without efficient socialization and training, bolstered by harsh discipline, this outcome would have been impossible.

Although the details of individual mutinies often are obscure, many known incidents repeated modes of disobedience found already in the first half of the nineteenth century (and probably earlier as well). Except for new demands related to parliamentary politics or the freedoms promised in the October Manifesto, soldiers' grievances were strikingly similar to those of the socially stable prereform period. In both eras, men in the ranks employed petitions, disobedience, and rebellion to articulate well-defined notions of what they considered just treatment from superiors. Failure to provide subsistence and clothing, to deliver pay and munitions, to impose fair and justified punishments, or to demand reasonable levels of performance and effort in drill—all led soldiers to complain against officers in legal and illegal ways. Throughout the prereform period, soldiers who were court-martialed for desertion, insubordination, and revolt repeatedly accused commanders of cruelty and economic crimes. Whether the lower ranks felt genuinely abused or sought to explain their own malfeasance, they spoke the normative language of formal law, military justice, and the social order.[94] It remains unclear whether mutinies among the troops in 1905–1906 were consciously, even spontaneously, revolutionary or whether they corresponded to traditional patterns of social conflict between officers and men—conflicts intensified and rendered more threatening by the broader context of societal rebellion and governmental breakdown. Similarly, in 1917 neither the soldiers' refusal to obey their superiors nor their determination to return home once land seizures began necessarily signified the failure of socialization. Rather it represented one dimension of a much deeper re-

volt affecting the essential instruments of tsarist rule at court, in the bureaucracy and parliament, and most important, at the highest levels of military
command.

Among civil and military servicemen of all ranks there were enormous socioeconomic, cultural, and political differences. Some derived from the branch
of service or the varied functions and hierarchies therein; others resulted from
personal inclinations and structural possibilities associated with social origin,
wealth, education, or family connections. Still others depended on geography
and chance circumstances. It was difficult for provincial officials to move into
central administration, even if they were nobles. By contrast, commoners possessing specialized or higher education could hope to find promising service
positions in the capitals. In the army, prestigious guards and cavalry units enjoyed better pay and living conditions, and artillery and engineering troops received the most technically advanced training, whereas ordinary line regiments coped with a range of physical and moral circumstances as diverse as
the vast Russian empire, and garrison battalions served as a dumping ground
for court-martialed, infirm, and incompetent officers and soldiers. Until the
late nineteenth century, when the forms of social advancement diversified, real
mobility, whether emancipation from servile status or the achievement of nobility, resulted almost exclusively from service. The Table of Ranks regularized ennoblement and, together with the capitation, bound social identity to
the state's administrative and material needs. For most of the imperial period,
the attainment of rank fourteen in the military and rank eight in the bureaucracy automatically brought noble status. Beginning in 1845, the government
repeatedly raised the ranks at which ennoblement occurred; yet in every era
conservative defenders of noble exclusivity arose to decry the harmful effects
of ennoblement through service, and in every era, too, the very desire to
tighten social boundaries testified to their actual porousness.

In civil and military service it was especially difficult to preserve distinctions between nobles and commoners, both because the bureaucracy and army
served as instrumentalities of autocratic rule and because their professional
functions tended to take precedence over hereditary attributes and privileges.
Non-nobles by birth could be found in the highest governmental positions already in the seventeenth and eighteenth centuries, and as the bureaucracy and
army expanded, so did the number of freedmen and new nobles. Because the
rank at which ennoblement occurred also rose consistently, the greater proportion of commoners at the end of the nineteenth century was at least partly attributable to persons who before 1845 would have been identified as nobles.
Service was important to social development not so much because it created
massive numbers of new nobles but because, however imperfectly, it formally
and firmly established merit, education, and performance as criteria for advancement. This was true at all levels of the administrative hierarchy for the
entire period under consideration, and it was also characteristic of the most

powerful aristocratic families. The merit principle, intensive state building, and the longevity of the traditional elite were in no way incompatible.[95]

Although official society defined social distinctions in law, it often failed to preserve them in practice. An imperial order of 1724 forbidding the assignment of non-nobles to secretarial posts without Senate approval was not enforced until the 1760s, when the senators reiterated that nobles should receive priority in appointments to these positions. It was but a short step from the rank of secretary to that of collegial assessor, which brought ennoblement. Apparently, commoners serving as secretaries behaved as if they were nobles, impelling the Senate to remind them that they did not possess noble rights, were forbidden to buy villages, and did not enjoy the same seniority in promotions as secretaries from the hereditary nobility.[96] Hereditary nobles may have enjoyed increasingly well defined advantages in service, but in reality it mattered little how an individual's father had achieved his status. The bureaucratic census of 1754–1756 did not even record the social origins of graded officials, and on occasion sons of personal nobles called themselves nobles.[97] Personnel data from the mid-nineteenth century did distinguish offspring of hereditary nobles from those of personal nobles (that is, of sons born to officers, graded civil servants, and unranked administrative office employees before their fathers reached hereditary noble status), yet paid absolutely no attention to how an official's father had acquired nobility.[98] For the sons of ennobled civil and military servicemen, the formal distinction between lineal and service nobles effectively disappeared.[99]

Local population and education statistics from the nineteenth century also failed to maintain the boundary between noble and commoner. Demographic data published by the ministry of internal affairs in the 1840s and 1850s repeatedly listed nobles (hereditary and personal) together with graded officials, regardless of whether the latter held a rank conferring hereditary nobility. Later in the century, more complete censuses took care to differentiate hereditary from personal nobles, though educational data frequently continued to pair nobles with ranked civil servants or hereditary with personal nobles.[100] Until 1841, church reports describing confessors employed vertical social groupings that amalgamated nobles and commoners on the basis of occupation and administrative hierarchies. The military rubric included generals, officers, noncommissioned officers, privates, soldiers, and sailors. The *raznochintsy* encompassed nobles, petty servicemen or gentry, single householders, coachmen, "police" troops *(razsyl'shchiki),* and monastery employees. And the category of state servicemen incorporated senior secretaries, secretaries, low-ranking civil servants, and unranked office employees.[101] The inconsistent delineations found in official statistics vividly suggested the central importance of institutional contexts and administrative applications in defining social distinctions.

The creation of juridical subcategories produced multiple statuses within a single family, a phenomenon that clearly undermined the precise delineation of social boundaries. The legal position of a soldier's wife was entirely different from that of her spouse or children, even though her husband was the direct source of her status. An unranked official, perhaps married to the daughter of an ordained priest or lowly church employee, might himself claim origins from an ecclesiastical family, having been driven into state service because of a dearth of positions within the church or because of personal shortcomings that rendered him unsuitable for a religious career. Especially among urban families, persons registered as merchants, lesser townspeople, nobles, peasants, or civil servants could also be inscribed in more than one category on legal or illegal grounds. In a suggestive example from the mid-eighteenth century, the wife of an employee in the Moscow police office deserted her husband and succeeded in marrying a church printer by posing as a soldier's daughter, one of the few free statuses available to an unmarried woman.[102] Persons of illegitimate and unknown birth were also not excluded from the fluid social territory produced by the structures of service. Foundlings, orphans, and other abandoned children who became wards of state institutions might receive education and training that prepared them for administrative and military service, for menial and artisanal labor in government-run factories and workshops, or in the case of girls, for employment as nannies and medical orderlies *(fel'dsheritsy)*.[103] Much nineteenth-century Russian literature depicts the lower-class urban milieu, peopled by many former and lesser servicemen, as a place of sordid degradation, poverty, and despair. Although service personnel and their progeny sometimes did experience downward mobility, returning to the poll tax categories of townspeople and state peasants, the social environment of the bureaucracy and army was also a place of opportunity.

CLERGY

"In a word, the farmer-priest is just a peasant, distinguished only by his literacy; otherwise he has a cast of thought, desires, aspirations, and even a way of life that are strictly peasant."—I. S. Belliustin, 1858[104]

Although the clergy of imperial Russia constituted the most castelike of social groups and the most completely sealed off from other categories, it nonetheless occupied an ambiguous, contradictory, and only partially delineated position in society—one that encompassed the characteristics of a service elite, a profession, and a lower class. The social condition of the clergy derived both from significant internal differentiation and from ambivalent relationships to the state and society. Legislation from 1721 and 1722 established an ecclesiastical domain *(dukhovnoe vedomstvo)* headed by a collegial body, the Synod, which controlled marriage and divorce, possessed the authority to impose penance upon the laity, and was responsible for education, administration, and justice among the clergy. Directly subordinate to the emperor, the Synod and territorial dioceses formed a structure that ran parallel to the domain of Senate and government. The intent and result of Peter the Great's ecclesiastical policy was not to incorporate the church "into state administration, but simply to superimpose the kind of good order and good rules that he already had prescribed for secular administration."[105] Even after the Petrine reforms and the confiscation of church lands in 1764 brought complete financial and virtual economic dependence on the state budget, the ecclesiastical domain still did not become absorbed into the monarchy's bureaucratic apparatus.[106] Throughout the imperial period, the church constituted an autonomous sphere of administrative authority, lawmaking, and social and cultural development with substantial influence over both religious and lay life.

Separation of the sacred church from the profane state was far more than an institutional arrangement; it was part of an ongoing process wherein the church sought to secure its authority over the laity by standardizing belief and elevating the status of the clergy. Whether one looks at church-state relations, popular religious belief, or the behavior of the clergy, full sacralization of the ecclesiastical realm was never achieved. Russian Orthodoxy was in reality "Russian Heterodoxy," consisting of an "aggregate of local Orthodoxies, each with its own special cults, rituals and customs."[107] Episcopal concern about the gap between popular belief and official canon was paramount in the Synodal period, yet only after the mid-eighteenth century were church administration and education sufficiently developed to launch a sustained effort to regulate, bureaucratize, and professionalize religious practice. Beginning in the 1760s, ecclesiastical authorities enforced educational standards in the appointment of parish clergy. In the 1770s they completed the Nikonian reforms of the mid-seventeenth century by distributing uniform liturgical books and by systematically removing the old surviving books that predated the great schism. In addition, the Synod defined the schedule and organization of church services in order to promote conformity with official teachings and to discourage both lay and clerical resistance to standardization.[108]

The ongoing failure to impose uniformity in Orthodox religious life was everywhere apparent. Like law, administration, and social organization, popular piety, belief, and religious practice continued to vary across parishes and regions. The early nineteenth century was a time of heightened concern about religious heterodoxy, fueled by the spread of Old Belief and by the government's reluctance, for fiscal reasons, to restrict drinking and commerce in the vicinity of churches on Sundays and holidays. At mid-century, roaming priests and monks still performed sacraments and liturgies outside of recognized places of worship, unauthorized religious processions and the local production of icons persisted, the Nikonian reform of church music remained only partly implemented, and allegedly pagan deities and supernatural forces lived on in Christian saints, demons, and rites. Popular worship of unofficial "miracle-working" icons, veneration for "fools in Christ," and the persistence of magic, superstition, and sorcery all revealed the diverse social and cultural meanings of Russian Orthodoxy. After a century of concerted centralization, successful "separation of the sacred and profane" was limited to the internal life of the church, and even in this relatively controlled context, the boundaries delimiting the clergy from secular society frequently seemed uncertain.[109]

The church's efforts to isolate "the sacred from the profane" also represented a response to the clergy's low social status. In order to elevate, dignify, and sacralize the clergy, it was necessary first to separate the parish priest from the laity. Thus the reforms of Peter the Great attempted to establish legal-administrative distinctions between the church and society by normalizing ecclesiastical administration, education, and appointments; by limiting the number of churches, priests, and unordained churchmen to ensure economically viable parishes; and by erecting social barriers that hermetically enclosed the clerical estate *(dukhovnoe soslovie)*. Like the nobility and other service categories, clergy of all ranks were distinguished from the general population by exemption from the capitation and conscription. The result was not, however, to create a visible and entrenched social elite. The outsiders who sought and continued, on a very limited basis, to enroll in the clergy, came from the servile categories of peasants and townspeople. Persons from the privileged population rarely pursued religious careers (even at the episcopal level).[110] For most of the eighteenth century, the legal privileges of the clergy and the delineation of the religious sphere from secular society were neither clearly fixed nor fully realized.

Despite the limits of effective reform, implementation of the poll tax provided a convenient mechanism for reducing the size of the clerical estate, barring access to outsiders, and excluding "excess" clergy and their progeny from the spiritual calling. Among clergy, lesser Muscovite and Petrine service categories, peasants, and serfs, the first, second, and third revisions brought both upward and downward mobility in the form of inscription in or release from the poll tax registries. Until the decade of 1764 to 1774, when legislation completely prohibited persons ascribed to unprivileged social groups from entering the clergy and similarly expelled individuals registered in the tax rolls from the ecclesiastical domain, it still was possible for actively serving clergy to remain liable for the capitation and even to become serfs.[111] Once the status of the clergy became firmly grounded in heredity in the mid-1770s, unprivileged outsiders were generally denied membership; yet arbitrary and sometimes demeaning exclusions from the ecclesiastical domain continued. Throughout the eighteenth century, and to a lesser extent during the first half of the nineteenth century, the government conscripted surplus and uneducated clerical youths into state service, factories, and the army. Although state and military service offered some opportunities for career advancement, these levies implicitly treated clergy as a servile category, undermined their special professional status, and caused social disruption and degradation.[112] Depending on occupational circumstances, priests' widows and children who left the clerical estate faced similar prospects of sinking into the servile population precisely because they, even more than their husbands and fathers, lacked a "personally inalienable status."[113]

Consistent with the government's broad effort to enhance the capacity and sociocultural prestige of its servitors, the imposition of higher educational standards accompanied the delimiting of the clerical estate. After the middle of the eighteenth century, the Synod established a stable educational system based on a curriculum in Latin and open only to the sons of clergy. The church schools played a central role in the formation of a hereditary ecclesiastical estate, while also raising the educational level of parish priests. By the end of the century, formal schooling at a seminary became an essential precondition for ordination, and by the first half of the nineteenth century, virtually all priests had completed a ten-year course of study. Formal education became the primary determinant of ecclesiastical career patterns, and entry into the clergy was effectively frozen precisely because the church schools successfully produced sufficient numbers of trained candidates. As a consequence, already in the 1840s there arose a surfeit of seminary graduates—a problem that impelled church and state officials to reexamine the clergy's hereditary foundations and legal parameters.[114]

Seeking to promote the institutional needs of the church without regard for the social needs of the clergy, the reformers of the 1860s allowed qualified students from any social category to receive an ecclesiastical education leading to the priesthood. As part of the "emancipation" of the clerical estate, the children of clergy also acquired a secular social status as personal nobles or honored citizens—a status that separated them from the church domain and facilitated their movement into alternative careers. In opening up access to the clergy, policymakers hoped to create a professional service class motivated not by hereditary rights and socioeconomic necessity but by a higher religious commitment. Like other educated segments of the population, the clergy did become intellectually, socially, and politically more active in the Great Reform era, though not necessarily in ways that accorded with synodal and governmental expectations. Moreover, while the dismantling of the clerical estate solved the problem of overpopulation, sending large numbers of ecclesiastical offspring into the universities, ecclesiastical reform failed to attract inspired outsiders to spiritual careers. Instead, the late imperial church faced shortages of educated seminarians, and endogamous social practices continued.[115] At the very moment when the legal boundaries segregating the clergy were removed, the functional character of the ecclesiastical calling, and the social and cultural isolation it brought, became more apparent than ever before.

Even though ascription to the ecclesiastical domain was virtually impossible for outsiders from the late eighteenth century until the 1860s, the boundaries distinguishing the clergy from the laity and the church from the state remained uncertain. The cultural gap and blurred distinctions between popular religion and formal Orthodoxy implicated parish priests in illegal marriages, paganism, and Old Belief. Nor did the endogamous insularity of the clergy prevent its members from becoming informally incorporated into societal structures and the intimate spheres of social life.[116] Appointments to ecclesiastical service, the clergy's internal structure and socioeconomic condition, and its relations with parishioners all revealed the dynamic interplay of separation and integration and the inability of eighteenth- and nineteenth-century reformers unambiguously to delimit and elevate the clerical calling. Official policies that aimed to sacralize the clergy through education and segregation also demanded uniform administration and the bureaucratization of the parish. Prior to the Petrine reforms, each parish existed as a self-governing community with legal-administrative, economic, and cultural functions, including responsibility for the construction and maintenance of its church and the selection of candidates for its clergy. During the eighteenth century, these traditional parish units were aggregated into larger, more economically viable entities and, as a result, ceased to correspond to the demarcations of local communities. Although, for administrative and geographical reasons, parish size continued to vary, the parish unit no longer represented a juridical and social collective but now constituted an ancillary link between the synodal command and the laity, as well as between the state and rural society.[117] While this change did not necessarily render meaningless the social and cultural bonds of the parish, it did make clear that the parish and the local lay community were no longer synonymous.[118]

Parish clergy served as state and church functionaries throughout the imperial period, often with unpredictable results. The government required priests not only to perform the obvious liturgical duties but also to read state laws in church, collect vital statistics, disseminate agricultural knowledge, assist in land surveys, provide medical services to parishioners, report dissenters, and dissuade peasants from rebellious acts.[119] The nonliturgical demands of the Synod were no less taxing, and from the mid-eighteenth century, church hierarchs stressed the obligation to provide parishioners with instruction in the catechism. Eager to counter secularism, radical philosophies, and Old Belief, the episcopal elite developed a distinct form of religious Enlightenment, insisting that faith and spiritual devotion could ensure salvation and the avoidance of sin only when derived from conscious awareness. Beginning in the late eighteenth century, the parish clergy, as the carriers of this cognitive Orthodoxy, were ordered to nurture lay understanding through sermons and the teaching of catechism. Beginning in the mid-nineteenth century, they were encouraged to participate in public education and the popular religious press. From the viewpoint of both church and state, the results of these activities were disappointing. The seminary education of priests did not prepare them to preach effectively, and popular religion remained rooted in emotion, "paganism," and "ignorance." Nor did the clergy avoid entanglements in social unrest, although most tried to refrain from either assisting or exposing peasant rebels. Their exceedingly limited success in ferreting out Old Belief was equally unsatisfactory, and their ability to impose canonical norms of marriage never complete.[120]

The nonliturgical duties placed upon the parish clergy surely undermined the proclaimed intention to elevate the ecclesiastical calling. So did the relationship of the clergy to the local community—a relationship that revealed the complex, contradictory dynamics defining the group's social condition. Although the assertion of episcopal prerogative in clerical appointments was central to the broad goal of ensuring church autonomy by separating the sacred and secular domains, actual control was not achieved before the end of the eighteenth century. The Petrine reforms may have desecularized and bureaucratized the traditional parish, but the laity's authority over the local church and clergy remained intact. Thus the episcopal elite continued to recognize the right of the parish or landlord to select candidates for church positions, with the important requirement that the nominees also pass the bishop's moral and educational examination. Although conflicts within the parish, manifested in the appearance of multiple candidates and forged election certificates, bolstered episcopal authority, bishops were unable to impose their own personal choices for local posts. The politics of ecclesiastical appointments was mired in the economics of ecclesiastical service. As a result, parishioners could by withholding emoluments readily starve out or evict any unwanted or unpopular priest.[121]

The effort to separate the parish from the lay community through administrative centralization and the expansion of episcopal controls fundamentally transformed the traditional parish, with its wide array of secular functions, but it did not entirely destroy the religious autonomy of local society. Rather, the parish ceased "to belong completely either to the Synodal or the secular command,"[122] and the desired distinction between it and the lay community remained tenuous. The social condition of the parish clergy, more than the uncertainties of episcopal authority, strikingly exposed these indeterminate boundaries. Although by the nineteenth century, parish priests constituted a professionally educated group, their pitiable material condition prevented meaningful social and cultural elevation. Like that other pillar of autocracy, the military regiment, the Orthodox parish was left to fend for itself in a variety of fluctuating local conditions. The very Petrine reforms that aspired to delineate the synodal and state commands also made the church financially dependent on the government. For the parish clergy, the implications of this dependence were profound, structural, and practically unchanging throughout the imperial period.

A central feature of the relationship between the clergy and the laity was the canonical rule that remuneration for religious services be voluntary. The result was an impoverished priesthood that rarely enjoyed the income required to ensure a predictable, much less a comfortable existence. State and church officials were keenly aware of this problem, which they repeatedly addressed by increasing the ratio of parishioners to clergy. The result, unfortunately, was that priests had to perform more rites, services, and sacraments to obtain equivalent means of subsistence. On those rare occasions when the government intervened specifically on behalf of the clergy, it either perpetuated or aggravated their economic vulnerability. In 1754 the state ordered parishes to apportion land for the use of local churches and clergy, a measure that not only antagonized townspeople, peasants, and noble landlords but also clouded the distinction between the parish and lay community. Far from promoting the social elevation of the parish priest, this policy required him to toil like a peasant at work he could complete successfully only by neglecting his spiritual duties.[123] Equally damaging, a 1765 statute defined normative rates for emoluments, but rather than encouraging more generous voluntary compensation, it suggested emoluments far below those already being paid. At no time did the treasury institute salaries for parish clergy. Reforms of 1829, 1842, and 1869 repeated the eighteenth-century solution of reducing the number of church positions and increasing the size of parishes, with responsibility to provide material assistance to the clergy continuing to devolve onto the local community. The "emancipation" of the clerical estate in the 1860s thus did little to alter the social and economic condition of those who remained within its ranks.[124] Throughout the imperial period, economic dependence on the lay community undermined the clergy's moral authority, created constant tension between individual priests and their parishioners, yet at the same time encouraged clergymen to participate in peasant rebellions and to ignore the sins and uncanonical practices of their spiritual underlings.[125] The tenor of relations between individual clergy and the laity varied from place to place, but clearly, administrative centralization and improvements in the educational level of the priesthood constituted ineffective weapons in the ongoing battle to reform Orthodoxy and eradicate local religious beliefs.

The government's inability or unwillingness to tackle forcefully the issue of clerical poverty deeply affected the social traditions and collective psychology of the clergy. Because Russian priests were generally married, the fees paid by local communities had to provide sustenance not only for clergymen but for wives and children as well. The need to support a family, the complete absence of state salaries and pensions, and the inadequacy of the pension funds created in the Great Reform era impelled priests and unordained churchmen to view their positions as an inheritance that could be passed on to sons or sons-in-law. Agreements between families turned clerical appointments into dowries, and those between individual priests and other clergymen guaranteed income for retirees and their families. Economic necessity promoted endogamous marriages within the clerical estate, preventing both the assertion of episcopal authority over appointments and the professionalization and social elevation of the priesthood.

Just as bishops remained reluctant to ignore the wishes of parishioners in approving candidates for parish priest, they also recognized the family claims of clergy as a substitute for pensions and welfare. The result was a socially isolated clerical estate, resistant to reform and demeaned by poverty, economic pressures, and the belief that the hereditary "right" to church positions was essential to a family's well-being. Seeking to eliminate hereditary claims as the primary basis for clerical appointments, a law of 1867 prescribed that qualifications take precedence over family needs in deciding placements, that vacant posts be filled immediately, that positions not be reserved for daughters, and that church authorities not enforce contracts requiring new clergy to share income with retired persons or their families. But because the abolition of endogamous practices and the hereditary order would have deprived clergy and their dependents of essential social welfare and would have forced priests, who could not afford dowries, to marry off their daughters to peasants, bishops continued to accept family claims as legitimate grounds for appointment. Endogamy persisted, as did the poverty and economic dependence of the parish clergy.[126]

Given the clergy's close economic ties to parishioners, it is no surprise that the social and material condition of individual priests varied widely. Still, internal distinctions within the clerical estate were not wholly attributable to economic circumstances. They also represented complex social and cultural phenomena resulting from the ultimate failure to elevate the clergy through law, education, and separation of the sacred from the profane. In Catholic countries and in pre-Petrine Russia, church hierarchs tended to come from the upper classes. In imperial Russia, bishops and parish clergy originated from the same clerical estate and shared a common seminary education. Within the ecclesiastical domain, the black monastic clergy produced the episcopal elite and remained distinct from the white clergy, who served local parishes. The Russian clergy's practice of marrying prior to ordination prevented priests from joining the ranks of their celibate superiors. Bishops attended ecclesiastical academies, followed a separate career path, enjoyed a comfortable material existence, and could not be deposed, though they could be transferred. Divisions within the lesser clergy were similarly pronounced. The introduction of formal schooling for parish priests meant that service among the unordained churchmen ceased to function as an apprenticeship, often reserved for relatives, preceding ordination. By the end of the eighteenth century, the successful development of clerical education created a permanent delineation between priests, who performed the sacraments, and sacristans and deacons, who rarely possessed a seminary degree and could not hope to rise in the church hierarchy. The internal structure of the clerical estate was thus frozen, as canon law barred mobility from the white to the black clergy and educational requirements, from the unordained churchmen to the priesthood.[127] Despite a high level of education, an organized administrative apparatus, and exclusive, if not elite, origins, the clergy never formed a cohesive social group capable of articulating collective interests.

A century after Peter the Great initiated fundamental ecclesiastical reform, the educational qualifications of the clergy had indeed improved, but their social status and incomes clearly had not followed suit. Especially from the 1820s, as desirable positions became increasingly difficult to obtain, parish clergy expressed feelings of painful insecurity and frustration—the result of their poverty, degrading dependence on parishioners, and subjugation to arbitrary superiors. Bishops possessed the power to discharge parish clergy from active service, transfer and imprison them without trial or investigation, and order them to stand trial without regard for rules of evidence. Not surprisingly, parish clergy, like peasants and soldiers, looked to the tsar and government to address their needs. Instead, the reforms of the 1860s served first and foremost the institutional interests of the church. In dismantling the clerical estate, the new order deprived clergy's sons of their automatic right to a seminary education and eliminated traditional forms of social welfare, without providing for pensions or dowries. Already in the mid-nineteenth century, parish priests such as I. S. Belliustin expressed open hostility toward monks and bishops, and in order to delimit and hence secure their own social standing, they demanded that deacons and sacristans be excluded from the clerical estate.[128] As happened throughout society, the hopes and expectations aroused in the Great Reform era crystallized into bitter disappointment, intensifying group consciousness, awareness of social distinctions, and political opposition.[129]

Whereas the servile and lesser service classes of society embraced in varying degrees the "myth of the tsar" and tended, whether emotionally or simply for tactical reasons, to presume that the tsar was "ignorant" and hence free of culpability for any wrongs, the "ruling" upper classes, including nobles and bishops, expected the autocracy to uphold their authority and privileges. The concerns of Orthodox hierarchs, who also emerged from the period of the Great Reforms as a socially conscious group, were quite different from those of the parish clergy. Bishops, who responded with hostility to the changes of the 1860s, which they viewed as an assault on episcopal authority, succeeded by the early 1870s in thwarting further innovations and began to advocate the creation of regional councils to ensure church autonomy and reduce state control. Always jealous of their prerogatives, though never unified in their political sympathies, they eventually agreed on the need for institutionalized church self-government (conciliarism). In addition, from the 1850s until the era of repression following the assassination of Alexander II in 1881, clergy of all ranks sought to revitalize the church through participation in secular affairs. Parish clergy and lay activists became involved in schools, charity, local government, and the popular religious press. Prelates and theologians preached the duty of the church to emulate Christ by entering "into this world" and consciously worked to establish more direct contacts with the educated elites. Early in the twentieth century episcopal conciliarism and "clerical liberalism" erupted in full force, as clergy of all statuses, while still politically divided, called for structural reforms and failed to defend the autocracy. Having ceased to regard the tsar as defender of the faith, the church at once helped to undermine the ruler's and its own sacred legitimacy.[130]

The church's continuing inability to eliminate state interference in religious affairs and to eradicate unofficial belief played a critical role in the unfolding revolutionary crisis. During the reign of Nicholas II, the politics of canonization provided evidence of the ruler's blatant intervention in the sacred realm; of intensified conflict between the autocracy and the church, and within the church between the Synod and subordinate clergymen; and of a popular piety that stubbornly defied canonical precepts. Whereas church law only required proof of miracles at the grave of a prospective saint, the faith of the common people also demanded that the saint's body be incorruptible. During the 1903 canonization of Serafim of Sarov, whose remains were physically decomposed, the Synod seemed to embrace the uncanonical expectations of popular belief and reluctantly undertook the necessary investigations, but then capitulated under direct pressure from the tsar and approved sainthood. The Synod's putative attention to bodily corruption may have been merely disingenuous tactics, for in 1913 it actively supported the canonization of another physically decomposed saint, Patriarch Germogen, despite the emperor's obvious indifference toward the case. Still further humiliation of the church occurred in 1916, when the bishop of Tobol'sk canonized Ioann Maksimovich without the knowledge of the Synod, which was then "persuaded" by Nicholas II and forced by the scandalous circumstances to approve the action.[131]

The autocracy's effort to use rites of canonization to enhance its waning spiritual and political authority had just the opposite effect. Together with proposals to liberalize divorce, reduce the number of religious holidays, adopt the Gregorian calendar, and secularize public education, the political theater of canonization bolstered traditional demands for greater autonomy within the church and so alienated clergy of all political persuasions that by February 1917 not even the conservative Synod defended the autocracy.[132] Neither the personal faith of Nicholas II nor the localized, particularistic faith of the pious multitudes was equivalent to the official Orthodoxy of the church. When the monarchy and church violated popular religious belief, both further damaged the already fragile linkages binding social life to formal institutions and thus contributed to the revolutionizing of political and social instability. At a time when the secular foundations of autocracy had been seriously weakened by a widespread loss of faith in the government's ability to ensure military security and societal well-being, the absence of a single Orthodoxy and the Synod's vulnerability to the whims of the imperial will became potentially menacing to constituted authority.[133]

In the revolution of 1905–1907 the relationship between the church and the autocracy, like that between the bureaucracy and the ruler, deteriorated to unprecedented levels of antagonism, as bishops openly demanded emancipation from state tutelage and restoration of the pre-Petrine patriarchate. Conciliarism also emerged among the parish clergy, who called for the democratization of ecclesiastical administration and the transfer of power from the bishops to locally elected boards of priests. Although the church sought to avoid political involvements during the revolutionary upheaval, social engagement by the clergy, as by all other groups in society, peaked at that time. Not surprisingly, the black clergy managed to stay aloof from the tumultuous events, while parish priests played the most visible role. The majority of priests in most dioceses did not participate in the liberation movement, and of forty thousand priests serving among workers and peasants, only a minority were drawn into social rebellion.[134] Among these, rural priests predominated over their urban counterparts, because of their closer ties to and greater dependence on parishioners. In the period 1907–1917, the clergy supported the October Manifesto and proposals for social reform, though together with most of the professional and cultural elite, they also moved to the right politically. Even so, from the government's perspective any clerical involvement in social and political unrest was dangerous. Given the traditional relationship between church and state, the silence of the clergy and its failure actively to defend the autocracy represented subversive actions.[135]

Among parish clergy, the experience of 1905–1907 intensified established patterns of social conflict and insecurity, reinforcing their ambivalent relations with lay communities and destroying the "myth of popular piety."[136] Although there were genuine social radicals among priests, many who participated in the revolution were forced to do so because of economic vulnerability. Most ominously from their perspective, parishes across the empire reasserted control over church finances and the appointment and support of clergy. Between 1907 and 1917, the real income of parish clergy declined as parishioners reduced emoluments and withdrew funding for ecclesiastical schools and libraries. The economic and social welfare problems that had dominated official discussions about the clergy throughout the nineteenth century—problems that the reforms of the 1860s had failed to redress—now loomed larger than ever. No longer could parish clergy look to their parishioners as a counterweight to episcopal arbitrariness, no longer could they attribute the religious shortcomings of the laity to ignorance and superstition, and no longer could they expect from the ruler any satisfaction of their grievances.[137] Rooted in traditional forms of economic dependence and functional duality, the status of the clergy grew less and less secure, even as institutionalized structures of authority were being transformed and unprecedented opportunities for civic involvement and professional organization had appeared.

In imperial Russia the nobility never became a securely constituted corporate entity, the military command and bureaucracy never evolved into distinct professional classes characterized by a common outlook and ethos, and the Orthodox clergy never shed the mantle of an atomized service estate for that of an autonomous spiritual calling. Although, within these categories, there existed subgroups that might have constituted an elite aristocracy, a professional officer corps and bureaucracy, or a religiously inspired clergy, on the whole, the "ruling" and service classes were only vaguely delimited from the rest of society. The clergy's scant cohesion and stunted professionalization resulted not from Peter the Great's administrative reforms, which created a separate spiritual domain headed by the Synod, but from the fragmented and immobile structure of the ecclesiastical estate. The canonical division between black and white clergy created an insuperable social divide, and endogamous marital patterns, which arose out of economic necessity, localized clerical identities and relationships. By the late eighteenth century, higher educational standards produced still another stark internal demarcation, that between ordained priests and the unordained churchmen who assisted them.

More significant in limiting professionalization and in defining the clergy's position in official society were the irregular, blurred boundaries separating priests from the laity. In institutional terms the church was not fully delineated from the state, nor the parish from the lay community. A secular procurator participated in, but neither supervised nor controlled, synodal deliberations; and the monarch, while generally deferring to canon law, could intervene in church affairs at any time. Only at the very end of the eighteenth century did the lay parish effectively cease to select its clergy, and after that time bishops continued to favor family claims over qualifications in making appointments—a practice that paralleled the persistence of personalized rule in the supposedly regularized bureaucracy. The most powerful force preventing full differentiation of the clergy from secular society, and one that often supplanted their hereditary origins and endogamous social traditions, was economic dependence on the laity. The priest's material condition hinged upon good relations with parishioners; his fate and life chances derived directly from theirs. Parish priests occupied an unenviable position as dependents of particular communities and as agents of the state and official church. Because their daily existence was so completely integrated into local societal structures, they were unable to uphold either secular or canonical law and order. Instead, they repeatedly became implicated in "paganism," Old Belief, and revolt, whether voluntarily, inadvertently, or under duress.[138] Nor did the clergy's seminary education necessarily segregate them from lay society. While it may have distinguished them from most parishioners and left them ill prepared to fulfill their spiritual duties, it also facilitated their movement into alternative service careers and the secular educated elites. Even after the dismantling of the clerical estate in the 1860s, the long-term result of the clergy's insularity and dualism was not rigid, secure, and precise boundaries but internal fragmentation, social isolation, and ambiguous delineation from other groups.

CONCLUSION

The "ruling" and service classes of imperial Russia occupied a wide range of formal and informal statuses, yet all functioned as mediating links in the spaces where state and society intersected and interacted, all occupied privileged positions relative to the servile population, and all experienced varying levels of economic and social uncertainty. The diverse and changeable roles of these groups revealed with particular clarity the dynamics and history of social categorization and development. Through the formal categories of juridical society, state building served as a force both for mobilizing human and material resources and for overcoming identities rooted in local particularism. The "ruling" and service classes of the imperial era represented mechanisms for achieving these goals. Not only did they overlap with and provide linkages to other groups in society; as functional groups, they themselves constituted unprecedented levels of social integration and standardization. Even as local circumstances continued to define social boundaries, processes of state building generated new subcategories of servicemen and specialists, and education produced larger, more diverse professional and cultural elites. Whether one looks at nobles, military and civil servitors, or clergy, the legal rights and sociocultural characteristics distinguishing these categories seemed to disappear in numerous institutional, societal, and intragroup contexts. The most immediate economic and social realities continually undermined distinctions between the privileged few and the servile many.

In contrast to the highest aristocratic, service, and episcopal elites—lesser nobles, lower military ranks, petty officials, and parish clergy blended imperceptibly into the general population. Regardless of their legal privileges and education, their material and cultural condition frequently differed little from that of peasants and ordinary townspeople. This ambiguity was not confined to the postemancipation era or the age of rapid industrialization beginning in the 1880s; it was a traditional feature of Russian society that revealed widespread social insecurity. For most of the imperial period the categories comprising the "ruling" and service classes played a central role in defining the social order. Service represented the only source of formal upward mobility, and the attainment of hereditary nobility was its highest achievement. Clergymen who left the ecclesiastical estate also could rise through service, though by the late eighteenth century there was no chance of upward movement from serfdom into the spiritual domain. In addition, formal downward mobility affected the "ruling" and service categories, primarily those whose proclaimed noble origins failed to receive official recognition and unemployed clerical youths who landed in the army and state factories.

From the mid-nineteenth century on, the importance of the "ruling" and service classes in determining the contours of the social order declined, and their privileges either were removed or lost their exclusivity. The end of serfdom in 1861 eliminated the most visible, though never absolute hallmark of nobility. Emancipation, the introduction of universal conscription in 1874, and the abolition of the poll tax in European Russia by 1887 eradicated crucial distinctions between lesser servicemen and the previously servile lower classes. Social status increasingly derived less from legal differences than from productive development and education, both of which had already provided essential sources of formal and informal categorization prior to the juridical changes of the Great Reform era. Economic relationships violated countless legislated barriers and produced just as many informal societal structures. Individuals crossed social boundaries out of necessity or in pursuit of profit, while military regiments and parish clergy, due to their economic dependence on local resources, remained deeply embedded in civilian and lay communities. Neither spontaneous productive development nor the failure of laws and institutions to accommodate its social consequences resulted solely from postemancipation patterns of economic modernization. Nevertheless, the pace and extent of change was unprecedented and led to the formation of entirely new groups in society.

CHAPTER THREE

MIDDLE GROUPS

hroughout the imperial period, the constituent elements of a "middle sort of people" encompassed elites and semi-elites of service, education, and wealth—persons who originated in the lower classes and might even remain liable for the capitation, persons who experienced firsthand the legal and socioeconomic channels of upward and downward mobility, and persons who also belonged to the sole elite of birth, the hereditary nobility. Because no description of Russia's allegedly "missing bourgeoisie" can adequately depict its social range and diversity, middle groups and subgroups neither were perceived nor necessarily conceived of themselves in broad collective terms. Individuals moved easily into and out of the protean categories generally identified as "the middle"—categories that formal social definitions failed to delimit in any clear manner.

This chapter explores the configuration of the Russian "middle" and its relationship to the larger framework of society. To account for the broad spectrum of middle groups—ranging from professional classes to peasant traders, and including groups such as the intelligentsia and "liberal educated society" (obshchestvo)—it presents Russia's middle as a search for social identity and for autonomous spheres of economic and legally recognized public activity. It sets aside continental notions of a third estate or bourgeoisie, as well as political criteria that equate the presence of a viable middle with capitalist institutions, organized civil society, and the struggle for liberal democracy. Instead, it offers a more inclusive definition derived from a sociocultural image of the Russian middle that emphasizes spontaneous development and self-definition rather than the formal organization of power.

"People of Various Ranks"

The conceptual predecessors to Russia's middle classes were the *raznochintsy,* literally "people of various ranks" or "people of diverse origins."[1] Conceived in the early eighteenth century as a legal-administrative, socioeconomic, and cultural category, the *raznochintsy* were defined less often by who they were than by who they were not. As outsiders or nonmembers of a given category or community, their ranks, depending on context, could include individuals from virtually any social group. Ranging from street vendors and serfs to graded bureaucrats and nobles, the *raznochintsy* occupied a shifting social space that sharply illuminated the porous boundaries of official society. The earliest recorded definitions of *raznochintsy* were legal, with societal usages following close behind. Often employed as an umbrella term, the designation applied to outsiders defined negatively, by exclusion, or to clusters of specific categories and subcategories. No single conception of the *raznochintsy* ever crystallized; nor did the evolution of the category follow discrete chronological stages of meaning.

Muscovite law employed the phrase "people of various ranks" *(raznykh chinov liudi),* but the first use of the term *raznochintsy* probably dates to 1701, when it referred very vaguely to persons who were not subordinate to the ecclesiastical domain. It was again defined by exclusion in the first certain legal usage (1718), which described *raznochintsy* as a lower-class group that was neither peasant nor registered in the taxed urban community *(posad),* and somewhat later in the records of Russia's first Commission on Commerce, which referred to all nonmerchant traders as *raznochintsy.*[2] Other groups identified as *raznochintsy* during the first half of the eighteenth century included ecclesiastical progeny who did not continue in the occupation of their fathers, low-ranking (non-noble) civil servants, unranked administrative employees in government offices, employees of the court and stables, retired soldiers, lesser Muscovite servicemen, children of service nobles born before their fathers achieved hereditary nobility, single householders, and children of the almshouse poor. By mid-century, officials also applied the term to Tatars and Siberian natives who paid the *iasak,*[3] as well as to non-nobles who claimed or illegally appropriated noble rights. Finally, in 1755, the year Moscow University was founded, the legal association of *raznochintsy* with educated commoners first emerged to describe non-noble students in state schools. Most eighteenth-century usages continued into the nineteenth century, and new subcategories also were added: free commoners exempt from the capitation; non-noble civil servants and children of personal nobles; scholars, artists, performers, and other protospecialists who were neither personal nobles nor honored citizens but who enjoyed comparable rights; and finally, persons who occupied a transitional status and were required to register in a taxed category within a prescribed period. With the exception of Tatars, tributary natives, taxed residents of Siberia and the city of Astrakhan, single householders, and persons in a transitional status, the vast majority of these *raznochintsy* were exempt from the capitation and thus occupied a semiprivileged status that in many cases indicated upward mobility. In central governmental sources of the 1880s and again in *zemstvo* statistics just prior to the First World War, the category referred to non-nobles and nonpeasants who settled in the countryside, purchased allotment lands, and participated in village assemblies. Legal-administrative usages thus combined a generalized notion of outsiders with specific social designations.

Frequently derogatory, the concept of *raznochintsy* as outsiders or nonmembers of a given group dominated societal usages in the eighteenth century. In *The Book of Poverty and Wealth* (1724), Ivan Pososhkov used the category to describe nonmerchants who engaged in urban trades but who, in his view, should have been barred from these activities.[4] In a similar fashion, instructions to the Legislative Commission of 1767 identified nonmerchants, nonmembers of the taxed urban community, non-nobles, and service nobles as *raznochintsy*. Disparaging societal usages of the nineteenth century usually applied to educated commoners in service and high society who were viewed as cultural inferiors and unscrupulous social climbers. Not all societal definitions were negative, however; in both the instructions to the Legislative Commission and nineteenth-century literature, one finds neutral descriptions of *raznochintsy* as lesser Muscovite servicemen, single householders, non-noble or unranked state officials, retired soldiers, the lower urban classes, and upwardly mobile educated commoners. Adding to the richness and multiplicity of meanings, radical publicists of the mid-nineteenth century associated *raznochintsy* with an enlightened, socially progressive milieu of right-thinking intellectuals. The literary critic Vissarion Belinskii led the way in this regard, identifying *raznochintsy* as one element in an educated, socially mixed company of morally and culturally advanced individuals. In the 1860s Alexander Herzen and Nicholas Ogarev compared *raznochintsy* to France's third estate, as the socially diverse, forward-looking segment of society that would lead the democratic struggle. The identification of *raznochintsy* with the non-noble, radical democratic intelligentsia of the 1860s—the definition that has had the greatest influence on subsequent historiography—appeared only in the early 1870s, penned by the populist critic N. K. Mikhailovskii. On the eve of the First World War, this usage was adopted and extended by the Marxist theoreticians G. V. Plekhanov and V. I. Lenin, who equated *raznochintsy* with the bourgeois-democratic element said to have dominated the revolutionary movement prior to its final proletarian stage. From here, the image of *raznochintsy* as political and social radicals entered both Soviet and much Western scholarship.

The concept of the *raznochintsy* originated in state policies that aimed to assign each and every individual, community, or status group to a juridically defined social category. The ongoing process of subordinating people to administrative domains generally determined who was included in the *raznochintsy* and under what circumstances, although a hereditary subgroup also existed as early as 1736 and as late as 1869. Prior to the local reforms of Catherine II, *raznochintsy* regularly appeared in connection with official efforts to implement the capitation and delimit the boundaries of the registered urban community. The tax and service obligations imposed on Russian society by Peter the Great required precise definitions of formal status, including assignment to specific categories and communities. Despite repeated enumerations of the taxed male population, the continuing presence of *raznochintsy* revealed the failure to achieve full ascription. Individuals from virtually all groups in society could in one or another context belong to the *raznochintsy,* suggesting that even among the primary social categories of nobility, clergy, urban "citizens," and peasants, membership was changeable and frequently uncertain. Church, census, and educational statistics from the eighteenth and nineteenth centuries also showed that, within a single ministry or administrative domain, the contours of the *raznochintsy* varied.[5] Until 1841, church confessional records employed their own functional delineation of social categories, identifying *raznochintsy* as nobles *(dvoriane),* petty servicemen or gentry, single householders, coachmen, *razsyl'shchiki* ("police" troops), and monastery employees. Similarly, although the law unambiguously identified retired soldiers as *raznochintsy,* local population data gathered by the ministry of internal affairs listed all military ranks separately and sometimes combined discharged soldiers with those in active service. The divergent usages strikingly revealed that social categorization was a tool of government rather than an autonomous indicator of concrete realities.[6]

The extension of administrative controls into society was accompanied by continual state and empire building, which created limited opportunities for upward mobility and broadened the developmental sources of *raznochintsy*. A growing bureaucracy and army, each requiring ever greater numbers of educated and semieducated personnel, produced a plethora of functional and occupational categories, reminiscent in their particularism of the numerous Muscovite ranks: university-educated scientists, scholars, and doctors; ranked non-noble officials and unranked office clerks; lower-class technicians, artisans, and workmen in state enterprises such as the mint and armory. In the case of commoners ennobled through civil or military service, the phenomenon of the *raznochintsy* embraced any children born to them before they became hereditary nobles. These professionals, specialists, servicemen, and laborers constituted a nebulous elite that generally lacked hereditary rights or guarantees of further social advancement. Real mobility depended on their remaining in service until retirement. For their children, further elevation and the prevention of downward mobility required that they obtain an official post. Only those non-noble servicemen who achieved hereditary nobility and only the children born to them after ennoblement were assured of retaining their newly acquired privileges. Still, even the lowliest among them was distinguished from the general population by exemption from the capitation and by greater access to education and the rewards of service.

Although, with or without formal education, there was both upward and downward movement into and out of the nobility, urban classes, and peasantry, education enhanced individual chances for promotion in service and helped define a host of social subcategories, each with specific legal obligations and privileges. The monarchy created primary, secondary, and higher educational institutions to meet particular military and administrative needs. Completion of a course of study could lead to a variety of careers both in and out of government. Before the second quarter of the nineteenth century, when private sources of professional employment began to expand significantly, the role of education in processes of social conceptualization related primarily to the redefinition of official categories and the creation of new ones. Well before the establishment of provincial *zemstvo* assemblies in the 1860s and well before the industrial takeoff of the 1880s and 1890s, Russian schools produced a significant protoprofessional, semieducated "elite," whose members occupied a particularly ambiguous social territory and often belonged, formally or informally, to the category *raznochintsy*.

It is often said that in the second half of the nineteenth century, the spread of education—brought on by the requirements of administrative, military, and economic modernization—contributed to a loosening of social barriers and a restructuring of social identities. Similarly, the first half of the century, particularly the reign of Nicholas I, appears as a time when educational policies rigidly reinforced traditional social boundaries, and the *soslovie* principle reigned supreme.[7] There is no question that prereform lawmakers attempted to order educational institutions based on the specific requirements and functions of clearly delineated social categories.[8] Their ability to do so was another matter. As late as 1837, in state, and particularly in private establishments, children of lower-class townspeople, peasants, and even serfs studied "higher philology" in violation of laws limiting their education to the technical subjects taught in parish and district schools. The government did not completely deny lower-class pupils access to the classical gymnasium course, which could lead to a university education. Although aspiring pupils liable for the capitation were ordered to obtain releases from their formal communities (and serfs from their lords), in 1845 these orders were not always enforced.[9]

Did the spread of general education, the socially diverse composition of student populations, and the proliferation of specialized courses actually undermine established social boundaries, or did the patterns of institutional development correspond to existing features of Russian society? Did education transform society, or did society and particularly its fragmentation shape education by modifying plans for reform at the moment of implementation? The 1828 regulation governing primary and secondary schools subordinate to St. Petersburg, Moscow, Khar'kov, and Kazan Universities designated specific institutions and curricula for specific social categories. Yet from the outset, lawmakers recognized the correlation between curriculum and social origin as "'a primary, but not exclusive function' of educational institutions." Minister of Education Prince K. A. Lieven vividly described the impossibility of applying "*soslovie* barriers" to the educational system:

> In states where social categories [*sostoianiia*] are strictly separated from one another; where movement from one to another, in particular from the middling into the noble, is extremely difficult and very rarely occurs; [in states] that grant nobility only [as a reward] for lengthy and superior services—in such . . . states it is very easy to introduce such an order [i.e., the organization of education on the basis of social origin]. But in Russia, where there is no middle category or citizenry; where only the merchant *soslovie* in some fashion represents such [a category]; where artisans are in all respects equal to farmers and almost always corrupt; where a prosperous peasant can at any time become a merchant, and often is both together; where the extent of the noble *soslovie* is so boundless that at one end it touches the foot of the throne and at the other is almost lost in the peasantry; where every year many [persons] from the urban and peasant *sosloviia* enter the nobility after receiving officer rank in military or civil service—in Russia such an arrangement of schools is difficult.[10]

Allowing that officials who sought to limit ennoblement exaggerated the actual prospects for social mobility, the important point here is that the minister of education considered the socially diverse character of Russian schools to be the result, not the cause, of porous social boundaries. More important, what distinguished Russia from other, presumably European, states was not the rigidity but the plasticity of social delineations.

Regardless of time and place, the development of education is closely related to the emergence of professional classes. In Russia, where education often brought changes in formal status, the exclusion of individuals from social groups subject to the capitation created a range of legal *raznochinnye* subcategories.[11] Official protoprofessional callings *(zvaniia)* such as teacher, artist, and dental practitioner gave individuals new legal rights, whether or not they were employed by the government.[12] By the 1860s, educated *raznochintsy* who abandoned civil service careers also could become self-sustaining writers and journalists. Others found work as specialists outside the framework of officially recognized degrees and certifications. When a dental practitioner *(dantist)* with a degree from Moscow University set up shop at the Nizhnii Novgorod fair in 1861, authorities fined him fifty rubles not because he was self-employed, but because he falsely claimed to hold a doctoral degree. With even greater audacity, he appeared before the local governor, wearing an official uniform of the sixth class, and requested a civil service appointment as a dentist *(zubnoi vrach)*.[13] This impostor had been released from the category townspeople after completing a recognized course of training, but he was not considered a dentist or *doktor*. His story and aspirations revealed both the development of protoprofessional activity (he was a certified dental practitioner in private practice) and the continuing importance of state service as the primary path to real upward mobility (he sought the more elevated post of official dentist).[14]

Alongside charlatans who deliberately misrepresented their credentials, there also were specialists whose skills and expertise failed to receive serious application and hence did not translate into productive development. Educated serfs, usually trained in the fine arts to meet the narrow needs of individual masters, sometimes were able to apply their skills more broadly and even attain freedom.[15] An example of potentially great economic significance was the self-taught mechanic and inventor I. P. Kulibin (1735–1818). The son of a townsman from Nizhnii Novgorod, Kulibin lacked formal education and had no great respect for the trained scholars he met in St. Petersburg. The fate of his most important invention, a self-propelling ship to transport salt along the Volga, illustrated the waste of technical know-how that slowed Russia's march toward modernity. Kulibin obtained governmental funding to build a single prototype and spent thirty-one years at the Academy of Sciences, yet he died a poor and forgotten debtor, and his prized creation received no further attention.[16] The monarchy did grant private concessions for the operation of steamboats in 1817 and 1823, but as late as 1843 transportation along the Volga depended almost entirely on vessels powered by men or horses.[17] In the life of Ivan Kulibin, one witnesses the potential for development that repeatedly appeared in imperial Russia, only to be overlooked or not taken seriously.[18] His career illuminates both the developmental sources of *raznochintsy* and the importance of this category in helping to explain the central paradox of Russia's socioeconomic evolution: the clear presence of entrepreneurial talent and abundant resources combined with technological backwardness and limited specialization.

The connection between the concept of the *raznochintsy* and spontaneous productive development appeared in a variety of contexts. One common eighteenth-century usage resulted from official efforts to limit and define the economic activities of urban residents who were not registered in the formal taxpaying community *(posad)*. In this setting, any person who did not belong to the legal "citizenry" but nonetheless engaged in urban trades was included in the *raznochintsy*. Probably the most open-ended meaning of the concept, this application could at once incorporate nobles, officials and servicemen, priests and deacons, serfs, state peasants, foreigners, and free individuals of any status whose economic activities encroached upon those of registered townspeople. Like the elites engendered by state service and education, illicit traders represented a significant source of middle-class groups. Their importance lies not in the handful of petty traders who became wealthy capitalists but in the extent and dynamism of Russia's informal, unregulated economy—a shadow economy that persisted and sometimes thrived beyond the confines of the official urban community.

Because the *raznochintsy* did not represent a socioeconomic class or perform an identifiable function in the organization of production, they draw attention to the microeconomies of imperial Russia and to the extensive network of entrepreneurial relationships that produced some of the most prominent capitalist dynasties of the late nineteenth century. Identified as factory owners, merchants, shopkeepers, artisans, and hired laborers, these economic *raznochintsy*—here defined as nonmembers of a given community or social category—avoided local forms of taxation and service. From the perspective of the registered townspeople in whose midst they lived and labored, they were "free men" who conducted their trades without interference and thus were "useless not only to the town, but also to the state."[19] If, for purposes of levying taxes and imposing service obligations, *raznochintsy* represented outsiders, this clearly was not the case in the context of informal economic structures. Despite the complaints of urban "citizens," they themselves hired *raznochintsy* as shop assistants, stewards, laborers, and transporters. In addition, they sold their economic rights without regard for social distinctions, signed promissory notes for persons forbidden to do so, and bought goods from *raznochintsy* and peasants rather than from other merchants. Business was the first priority, and whether it involved nobles, townspeople, *raznochintsy,* or peasants, the pursuit of profit continued regardless of juridically defined rights and boundaries.

Nowhere was disregard for socioeconomic legality more visible than in the phenomena of illegal enserfment and the ownership of serfs by *raznochintsy* (that is, non-nobles). Forbidden since the mid-eighteenth century to possess estates and serfs, non-nobles continued to acquire them at least until the late 1840s. Nobles, who enjoyed the right to own serfs, and non-nobles, who did not, repeatedly subjected free persons to illegal enserfment. One reason for the continued mobility into and out of bondage was the government's failure to apply the prohibitions against non-noble ownership of serfs retroactively. The legal confusion reinforced Russia's normally lax enforcement. Only in 1785, the year of Catherine II's Charter to the Nobility, did the Senate clearly deny rights of ownership to non-nobles who had possessed serfs at the time of the first, second, and third revisions. Implementation came slowly, and another two decades passed before local authorities strictly interpreted the prohibitions.[20] By then, non-nobles, abetted by their social superiors, had found ways to avoid the legal restrictions. Using letters of credit *(veriushchie pis'ma),* nobles "hired" middlemen to sell their serfs, in effect selling them outright. A law of 1816 forbade this practice and gave illegitimate owners one year to conclude any outstanding transactions. Even so, legal procedures were extremely cumbersome, and a decade or more could pass before an illegally held serf was set free.

It is well known that serf entrepreneurs could in the name of their masters become the illicit owners of other serfs. Less visible was the existence of similar arrangements between *raznochintsy* (here, free non-nobles) and nobles who, as legal middlemen, enabled unlawful owners to legitimize a deal. Thus it was possible for several generations of serfs, technically registered to nobles, to remain the de facto property of *raznochintsy.* Nor was it necessary for surreptitious owners or their serfs even to know or have direct dealings with the formal master. Nobles were permitted to hire out their serfs on a temporary contractual basis but did not always observe the legal requirement that the serfs receive a wage. Instead, serf owners used these relationships to repay debts and provide labor for non-noble friends and relatives. In some cases, as part of a loan agreement, *raznochintsy* also obtained illegal rights to sell the serfs who came under their control. Although the full extent of these illicit relationships cannot be calculated with any certainty, there is evidence that the unlawful serf owners included merchants, townspeople, officials, soldiers, and peasants. More important, it is clear that nobles—motivated by greed, need, or personal ties—readily ignored their own legal privileges.

Non-noble possession of serfs was aided and to some extent hidden by the phenomenon of illegal enserfment, which was in turn related to broader patterns of indenture and bondage. Until emancipation, free persons fell into servile status through employment or economic distress, just as they had in the Muscovite era before serfdom was legally fixed by heredity. Orphans, illegitimate children, and runaway wives were particularly vulnerable to the machinations of noble landlords, but studies of the army and working classes also reveal relationships, arising from poverty, that were tantamount to indentured servitude.[21] In the case of military service, these arrangements resulted from the need to purchase substitutes to avoid conscription, and among the working classes, they were the product of urbanization, migration from the countryside in search of work, and greater opportunities for employment in the towns. Both illegal enserfment and indenture suggest that relations of servitude not only were varied but also were present in a variety of social contexts both before and after the Great Reforms. Nor were the masters of these laborers, servants, and serfs confined to any one socioeconomic or legal category. On the contrary, they could be serfs, free peasants, lesser townspeople, merchants, or nobles.

If poverty facilitated illegal enserfment and indenture, economic vitality allowed individuals to escape lawful servitude. Significant geographical mobility even among serfs is well documented for the entire imperial period. Movement could be legal, illegal, or a combination of both; it could result from economic success or dire necessity. At the same time, the very ease with which runaways obtained employment made them and their children vulnerable to illicit reenserfment. Thus in 1803 the son of a runaway serf who had successfully registered as a townsman was at last set free after seventeen years of contractual and coerced labor, including efforts by a noble factory owner to claim him as a serf.[22] The serf entrepreneur Nikolai Shipov, who achieved emancipation in the reign of Nicholas I and ended his business career as a sutler in the Caucasus and Bessarabia, was forced to move legally and illegally and to change occupations repeatedly in the pursuit of his fortune—a fortune that could be lost overnight but then just as quickly regained.[23] Leaving aside the issue of noble privilege, as well as the sufferings and successes of specific individuals, it was precisely this movement in Russian society—be it social, economic, juridical, or geographical—that produced the phenomenon of the *raznochintsy* and, more important, that testified to the dynamism of informal and often extralegal productive development.

COMMERCIAL-INDUSTRIAL ELITES AND SEMI-ELITES

"Nowhere does property change hands as frequently as in Russia. In public service, in commerce, in manufacturing, and in the trades large fortunes are quickly amassed but are lost just as quickly."—August von Haxthausen, 1852 [24]

During the eighteenth and early nineteenth centuries social, economic, and geographical mobility could be equally characteristic of educated or wealthy elites, peasant entrepreneurs, and runaway serfs. The biography of F. V. Karzhavin (1745–1812), the son of a prosperous first-guild merchant engaged in European trade, illustrates Russia's lack of a clearly differentiated commercial-industrial class before the second half of the nineteenth century. Educated in France (his uncle was a linguist living in Paris) with practical training in medicine and architecture, Karzhavin moved rapidly and easily among a variety of occupations. Employed during the course of his career in Europe, the Americas, and Russia, Karzhavin worked as a translator, author, diplomat, teacher, private schoolmaster, assistant to a state architect, pharmaceutical assistant, field surgeon *(lekar')*, tobacconist, and purveyor of books, pictures, and curiosities.[25] Moreover, despite elite merchant origins, he experienced significant fluctuations in his social, financial, and occupational position. Not unlike the serf entrepreneur Nikolai Shipov, Karzhavin occupied a fundamentally uncertain social status, marked by chronic economic vulnerability and repeated changes in employment.

The fluid, changeable careers of both Shipov and Karzhavin, including their ability to recover from multiple misfortunes, were symptomatic of Russia's limited economic specialization and porous social boundaries—conditions that led many contemporaries to underestimate the dynamism of productive development, urban culture, and the commercial-industrial classes. August von Haxthausen, who in 1843 traveled extensively in the central and southern parts of the empire, appreciated both the precarious and the potentially creative nature of Russian social and economic life. In his description of Moscow province, Haxthausen describes the "talent for everything" that identified the "typical" Russian:

Of all peoples he may have the most practical sense for acquiring a suitable vocation. The attachment and love for his station, his trade and his work which is so characteristic of the German is wholly unknown to the Russian. . . . If he does not get anywhere in his trade, he immediately takes up another. How often does a man start out as a shoemaker or a tailor, give up his occupation, and become, let us say a *kalachi* vendor, roaming the streets of Petersburg or Moscow all day selling various kinds of baked goods. After he has made some money and bought horses and a wagon, he becomes a driver, traveling far and wide in the empire. He also engages in small business ventures and soon begins a peddler's trade. Finally he settles somewhere and, if luck is with him, he may become a powerful merchant. The careers of most of the wealthy merchants and factory owners, if one were to check into them, resemble this pattern.[26]

Although the aristocratic Haxthausen believed that commercial success quickly transformed Russian merchants into corrupt and wicked rogues, his attention to uncertainty, fluidity, and possibility as salient features of economic activity and urban existence helps to explain why contemporaries failed to discern the "missing bourgeoisie."

Both Muscovite and imperial law distinguished among various groups of registered merchants according to degrees of privilege and economic rights, but the composition of these groups was highly unstable. Few of the great merchant families of the seventeenth century maintained their position beyond the reign of Peter the Great.[27] Research in provincial archives reveals the presence of successful business dynasties, extending over several generations and even from the early eighteenth century into the twentieth, yet despite the presence of a stable and wealthy core, which paralleled the upper aristocracy, the general picture for the majority of merchants remains one of rapidly rising and falling fortunes.[28] Membership in the merchant category derived not from heredity or territorial citizenship but from the ability to pay an annual fee. Even after Catherine II secured the privileged status of merchants by exempting the members of all three guilds from the capitation and those of the first and second guilds from conscription and corporal punishment, the delineation of this category remained indeterminate. Because registration as a merchant continued to depend on yearly payments and because the conditions in which Russians conducted business could be so volatile, the composition of the commercial-industrial "elite" inevitably fluctuated.

Among registered merchants trading through the ports of St. Petersburg and Arkhangel'sk between 1772 and 1804, only 10 of 289 families remained regular participants in the foreign trade of the capital. Of the 42 merchant families active in 1804, 20 appeared in earlier records, while 22 were entirely new to the St. Petersburg trade. In Moscow, 26 of the 382 first-guild merchant families registered in 1748 remained in the last two decades of the century, and only 10 of the 235 families registered in 1766–1767. The high rates of turnover continued in the first half of the nineteenth century, when in St. Petersburg, Moscow, and other cities, estimated membership in merchant guilds changed by 54 percent each year. Of 137 first-guild Moscow families identified at the end of the eighteenth century, 21 maintained that position in 1815.[29] In 1873, only 108 of 623 first-guild Moscow merchants traced their origins to eighteenth-century merchant families, the ancestors of 185 had entered the guild from other social categories between 1800 and 1861, and as many as 330 had first joined the guild between 1861 and 1873.[30] Even allowing for ennoblement, lateral geographical mobility, increases in fees and capital requirements, the possession of undeclared capital among second- and third-guild merchants, and the registration of previously illicit traders, these data reveal a striking instability in the composition of the merchant category.[31] This social instability goes a long way toward explaining why it was so difficult to discern significant commercial-industrial activity before the second half of the nineteenth century.

The failure to perceive Russia's productive potential already was apparent in the reign of Catherine II, when high-level officials attributed economic backwardness to a lack of urban development, manifested in the absence of a European-style "third estate" or "middle sort of people." Discussions in the Commission on Commerce and the Legislative Commission directly related economic prosperity to a properly organized society that would include a middle estate characterized by sound behavior, industry, and hard work, employed in the arts, sciences, navigation, trade, and crafts. Excluding nobles and farmers, the Catherinean notion of the middle estate also encompassed graduates of church and state schools and children of low-ranking state officials and unranked administrative employees.[32] The Charter to the Towns (1785) and the Digest of Laws (1832) formally associated the "middle sort" with all registered city residents, who were further divided into legally differentiated subcategories occupied in trade, manufacturing, the arts, sciences, and crafts.[33] The legal consistency was deceptive, for during the 1820s policymakers again expressed concern about a perceived absence of commercial vitality.

The guild reform of 1824 and the introduction of the title "honored citizen" in 1832 both represented efforts to delineate and stabilize an urban elite based on economic or educational achievement. In order to regulate, tax, and delimit urban society more effectively, the guild reform extended the formal boundaries of commerce, making it easier for peasants and other *raznochintsy,* who were not registered "citizens" of a town, to legalize their economic activities. The purpose was not to enhance merchant privileges or expand peasant trade but to establish a closer correspondence between legal-administrative definitions and socioeconomic facts.[34] Nor was the title "honored citizen," clearly a form of legislated status honor, designed to elevate the merchant elite. On the contrary, officials sought to tighten social boundaries as part of a larger effort to restrict access to the nobility.[35] Descriptive sources from the reign of Nicholas I reveal that a lack of clear socioeconomic differentiation also blurred the boundaries of middle groups. In a series of reports submitted to the emperor between 1827 and 1830, the chief of the imperial gendarmerie (the third section), Count A. Kh. Benkendorf, first described the "middle class" (here the singular was used) as the loyal patriotic "soul of the empire," including in its ranks landlords who lived in towns, nonserving nobles, first-guild merchants, the educated, and literati; later he defined the "middle classes" as petty nobles, bureaucrats, and merchants.[36] A similar conflating of categories appears in the memoirs of V. N. Karpov, who divided the population of Khar'kov in the 1840s into two sharply differentiated halves, the ruling minority of nobles, graded civil servants, and merchants (defined by exalted birth, formal social privileges, and wealth) and the exploited majority, possessed of only "the most meager rights to the blessings of life."[37] The government's fruitless search for an identifiable "middle sort of people" shows very clearly that the relatively small number of registered urban "citizens" corresponded neither to the actual size of city populations nor to the occupational profile of imperial society as a whole.[38]

In contrast to official depictions of Russia's putatively absent middle, tales and proverbs from the late seventeenth and early eighteenth centuries place honorable and intelligent merchants, together with their chaste and competent wives, in a setting that values trade, money, and profit making and that energetically transmits business skills and capital to respectful and worldly sons.[39] Similar portraits abound in literature and memoirs of the eighteenth and nineteenth centuries.[40] Historians also have reconsidered traditional images of urban stagnation that deny the presence of a vital business class before the mid-nineteenth century and now insist that the absence of a visibly differentiated and financially stable commercial-industrial elite should not be equated with economic dependency, political inertia, and cultural conservatism. Their findings indicate that Russia's "absent" bourgeoisie formed its social identity in the central Moscow region, long recognized as the commercial hub of the empire, the source of a native capitalist class, and the birthplace, already in the 1840s, of an industrial transformation based on cotton textile production. If in the early nineteenth century, the entrepreneurial elite consisted almost entirely of actual merchants and Old Believers, by the second half of the century, it encompassed industrialists and financiers engaged in a wide range of business activities and originating from a variety of social-administrative categories, including peasants. From the 1880s and throughout the 1890s, the Russian empire experienced unprecedented industrial expansion, which along with continuing development in textiles, now encompassed mining and metallurgy, machine construction, and chemical products.[41] Increasingly aware of their economic importance, established Moscow businessmen, joined by regional groupings of entrepreneurs, began to play an ever greater and more visible public role.

The assumption that economic power translates automatically into a defined set of political (that is, liberal) attitudes repeatedly led critics to attribute pre-1905 bourgeois quiescence to the government's heavy involvement in industrial development. Traditional scholarship focusing on the relationship between state policy and productive evolution from the seventeenth century to the present also centers debate on the consequences of governmental involvement (or indifference), and particularly on whether tsarist policy hindered or stimulated progress toward a modern industrial economy. There is general agreement among historians that the eighteenth century was a time of steady economic growth followed by relative decline in the early nineteenth century, culminating, as a result of the Crimean War, in greater official and societal awareness of Russia's technological weakness and inadequate infrastructure.[42] Consequently, under the last three tsars, Ministers of Finance M. Kh. Reitern

(1862–1878), N. Kh. Bunge (1882–1886), I. A. Vyshnegradskii (1887–1892), and S. Iu. Witte (1893–1903) presided over a program of economic development that incorporated active state involvement in mining, metallurgy, and the building of railroads; the use of protectionist tariffs and indirect taxes to encourage domestic manufacturing, maximize grain exports, and ensure favorable trade and payments balances; and finally, the creation of an economic climate attractive to foreign investment and loans.[43] In many accounts of Russian modernization, these policies rather than the activities of private entrepreneurs receive credit for an industrial takeoff beginning in the 1880s.

Of all the modernizing ministers of finance, S. Iu. Witte was the most aggressive in pursuing foreign investment and promoting railroad construction. In a monetary reform undertaken between 1894 and 1897, he established a fully convertible ruble based on the gold standard and well before becoming minister of finance, committed himself to winning support for the proposed trans-Siberian railway.[44] Throughout the 1890s, industrial output grew by more than 8 percent a year, spurred by state policies that created markets and provided foreign capital and expertise.[45] This unprecedented industrial boom, which ended in the depression of 1900 to 1906, was then followed by another period of growth, this time under the leadership of Russian as opposed to foreign entrepreneurs.[46] According to this chronology, Russia experienced no significant economic development before the late 1880s. When that development came, it depended heavily on foreign investment, technology, and personnel, brought to Russia through governmental stewardship, and on the growth of heavy industry, fueled by state-sponsored railroad construction and military contracts. Thus, just as industrial expansion resulted from governmental policy, so did the stature and success of Russia's commercial-industrial elite.

Disputing this characterization of the agents and patterns of Russia's economic transformation, recent scholarship (1) dispels persistent images of urban stagnation derived from the relatively small size of towns and business elites; (2) questions prevailing notions of economic backwardness prior to extensive state involvement in industrial development; and (3) provides evidence of considerable intellectual sophistication and involvement in public affairs on the part of Russia's "missing bourgeoisie." One provocative study rejects outright the myth of backwardness and concludes that by the late eighteenth century Russia had joined the ranks of a very few advanced, urbanized premodern societies, including England, France, Japan, and China.[47] Although Russia generally lagged behind England, France, and Japan in measures of efficiency in the mobilization of resources to sustain city populations, the empire's rate of urban development exceeded that of any other country at the time. Thus, in a global preindustrial context, eighteenth-century Russian society was unusually dynamic; neither the absence of constitutional self-government, nor the disorderly physical condition of towns, nor the large number of serfs engaged in urban occupations necessarily indicated backwardness.

The inclusion of Russia in a worldwide premodern framework reconstitutes the meaning of urban development and conveys the dynamism and productive potential of eighteenth-century imperial society. Given the slow tempo of urbanization from the mid-eighteenth to the mid-nineteenth centuries, it is possible to recognize the significance of entrepreneurial activity only by abandoning a purely economic definition of the city. Using statistical factor analysis, another recent study classifies Russian cities according to levels of economic evolution—ranging from administrative to agrarian to commercial and industrial—and finds that economic differentiation was extremely limited. The presence of a few highly developed cities, such as St. Petersburg and Moscow, amid a mass of primitive ones, then provides evidence of Russian "backwardness," defined as the slow formation of a distinctly urban culture. Not until the 1850s did sharply delineated urban economies based on manufacturing and trade become characteristic of Russian cities.[48] Ironically, the lag in urbanization, manifested in the lack of separation between city and village, resulted from productive factors rather than economic backwardness. Throughout the eighteenth century and until the 1820s, rising agricultural prices generated an expansion of production, which, given the absence of technological innovation, kept labor on the land. At the same time, the peasant market failed to stimulate the urban economy, because unrestricted handicraft production minimized the demand for manufactured goods. Dispersed industrial progress, plentiful land, a sustained need for agricultural labor, and the viability of peasant handicrafts provided a firm basis for limited differentiation and continuing mobility back and forth between city and countryside.[49]

The extent to which official policy stimulated productive change remains a major source of controversy. Even if state initiatives were responsible for the onset of full-blown industrialization—and the very notion of an industrial "takeoff" has been questioned—there is no doubt that private economic activities were also significant. Although the scale of private entrepreneurship was often small and its impact uneven—at least before the mid-nineteenth century—there is substantial evidence that spontaneous productive change and even industrial modernization occurred "naturally" in response to an empirewide, consumer-based, and self-sustaining (as opposed to state-created and directed) market.[50] This is illustrated by the great fair at Nizhnii Novgorod, which served the predominantly peasant, national consumer market, and by patterns of foreign investment in the Russian economy, which illuminate the state's role in promoting industrial development. Both reveal the strength of autonomous forces in the Russian economy and thus point to factors beyond serfdom and official policy to explain the seemingly slow pace of economic transformation prior to the late nineteenth century.

As a "transitional institution in the development of a modern capitalist market,"[51] the Nizhnii Novgorod fair, the largest of the nineteenth century, belonged to an extensive commercial network consisting of periodic markets, permanent urban markets, and itinerant traders. Scheduled to allow for travel, Russia's web of fairs served the entire empire and increasingly involved peasants in the money economy. Beginning in the 1860s and 1870s, railroad construction, not the abolition of serfdom, transformed commerce at Nizhnii Novgorod, dominated until then by merchants and industrialists active in the trade with Persia and Central Asia. Rapid advances in transportation and textile manufacturing[52] brought an influx of peasant consumers and traders. The fair began to function both as an enormous wholesale market for domestic manufactured products and as a commercial center where entrepreneurs arranged transactions, settled accounts, and acquired information about business conditions. During the second half of the nineteenth century, the organization and economic functions of the fair, the makeup of its participants, and the business practices they employed all changed in response to dynamic market conditions.[53] The volume and nature of the Nizhnii Novgorod trade consistently indicated that the national consumer market was absorbing larger quantities of goods and that the primary brake on Russian economic development was technological: the expense and inefficiency of communications across the vast imperial territories.[54]

Responsiveness to economic opportunity was equally characteristic of foreign participation in Russian industry. Despite the touting by tsarist officials of policies designed to attract European capital, British involvement in the Russian economy revealed that spontaneous market conditions rather than calculated state initiatives drove investment. As early as 1839 and continuing into the early twentieth century, foreign participation in Russian industry resulted from "the opportunities intrinsic to a large, increasingly integrated market with steadily rising aggregate demand."[55] To be sure, tariff policies encouraged British entrepreneurs to establish Russian operations, and the government's role in providing legal services, maintaining a monetary system, and developing transportation was crucial to the creation of "a wider effective market area."[56] But on the whole, the importance of foreign capital and protective tariffs in stimulating Russian industrialization has been exaggerated. Tariffs served state fiscal needs more than they promoted economic growth, and foreign investment was "a response primarily to the potential of the Russian mass market, not to government enticements."[57] Whether one examines Russian consumer industries, trade at the Nizhnii Novgorod fair, or the activities of foreign entrepreneurs, there is striking evidence of the "robustness of the nongovernmental or autonomous sector of the Russian economy."[58]

If one places Russia's industrial revolution in a global rather than strictly European context, it is possible that the rate of development (like that of urbanization in the eighteenth century) was not unusually slow. Excluding Britain, which despite its exceptional status set the standard for economic change, European industrialization was primarily a nineteenth-century phenomenon. Given the size and geography of the Russian empire, one might reasonably expect that a thoroughgoing transformation of society would take longer, that its progress would be less even, and its initial results less generalized, than in the more concentrated markets of western and central Europe. That said, it is nonetheless also the case that educated Russians placed themselves in a European framework, measured their achievements against those of their western neighbors (even when they rejected the latter), and, from the reign of Peter the Great until the present, defined Russia's future in European or counter-European terms. It is therefore important to consider why economic modernization did not occur more rapidly and why there was no visible commercial-industrial elite before the mid-nineteenth century. If chronology is the crucial variable, then Russia most certainly lagged, but if the substance and quality of the transformation are the more important factors, then Russian development closely paralleled that of western Europe.

The very same lack of differentiation that made it difficult to identify a significant commercial-industrial class before the mid-nineteenth century also accounts for the seemingly slow pace of economic transformation. Throughout the imperial period, individuals from all social categories, including nobles, officials, state peasants, and serfs, engaged in a broad range of economic activities dispersed over wide-ranging territories.[59] Both the irregular composition of the merchant elite and the geographical conditions of the empire reinforced the limited specialization. Despite enormous entrepreneurial energy, substantial natural resources, and an intermediary location between east and west, Russia's commercial environment was fraught with danger and risk. Leaving aside the question of whether autocratic authority was truly patrimonial or tsarist rulership truly proprietary,[60] as a result of administrative corruption, attacks by marauders, and climatic and navigational problems that made the transport and preservation of goods expensive and uncertain, Russian traders and businessmen frequently experienced enormous financial losses. Ruin came easily to even the most successful merchants, at least until the 1860s, when railroad construction, modern banking, and laws facilitating incorporation began to ensure a more stable and predictable business environment.[61]

In Russia's preindustrial economy and in the earliest phases of industrial modernization, the absence of insurance, an inadequate legal framework, and sparse credit facilities did not always translate into a shortage of capital, although they did contribute to the high incidence of nonfulfillment of contractual obligations. The institution of serfdom, which denied civil rights to substantial entrepreneurs, and the limited development of contract law, provisions for bankruptcy, and formal property rights made it difficult to take legal action in cases of failure to repay loans or deliver goods. To stay afloat in this volatile commercial environment, entrepreneurs diversified their operations by investing "in many different kinds of activity in widely separate parts of the country." Such a rational response to uncertain market conditions surely testified to "flexibility and a willingness to take risks when profit lay in prospect."[62] Nor did governmental assistance in the form of land grants, exploiting rights, contracts, and loans lead to economic subjugation. Rather, it highlighted the ability of Muscovite and imperial entrepreneurs to take advantage of the economic opportunities that became available.[63] Responsiveness to the market and accommodation to official policy, not passivity and dependence, ensured economic success while also perpetuating limited specialization.

Local self-sufficiency further contained specialization, keeping resources and entrepreneurship scattered and individualized. Throughout the Muscovite and imperial periods, long winters, short growing seasons, unpredictable agricultural surpluses, and sparse population density encouraged peasant involvement in handicraft production, which in turn blurred the boundaries between town and country and between social-occupational categories. The absence of traditional guild structures permitted free craftsmanship and created a vast, undifferentiated space for entrepreneurial activity. Thus, despite social and residential restrictions on urban trade and manufacturing, individuals from all classes of the population could readily be found among both small- and large-scale operators. The variety of this activity and its frequently illicit character reinforced the lack of clear socioeconomic differentiation.[64] At the same time, "generations of such activity provided a pool, not only of artisanry, but also of entrepreneurial aptitude and experience."[65] The result was not a "missing bourgeoisie" but an indeterminate, ambiguously delineated one.

Clearly, Russia possessed a vibrant entrepreneurial tradition, yet there remained formidable obstacles to economic modernization. Limited specialization was at once both symptom and cause of the dispersion and easy dissipation of resources. Sudden losses, expensive transport, the absence of a well-defined legal framework, and the lack of modern banking and credit facilities preserved traditional business practices, including poor record keeping and secret, personalized deal making. That was to change in 1836 with the legislating of clear principles of company registration and limited liability; Russia began to develop modern capitalist institutions and hence also a discernible commercial-industrial class.[66] As Russians adopted standardized business techniques, pricing and other market conditions became sufficiently stable or predictable to allow modern specialization to supersede broad-based, fluid, transitory, and often illegal mass entrepreneurship. Nevertheless, industrial and preindustrial forms of production and business organization continued to coexist at the time of the 1917 revolution, even after more than half a century of rapid economic growth and substantial modernization in both agriculture and industry.[67]

The spontaneous societal development documented by urban and economic historians undermines the thesis that the political passivity of the business elite can be traced to the heavy hand of state regulation, made palatable by material assistance. Indeed, among industrialists in St. Petersburg, a group that included high-level officials, reliance on state orders brought financial instability and frequent individual bankruptcies, conditions that could lead just as readily to disaffection.[68] If one looks carefully at the public roles of prominent capitalists already in the eighteenth centuries, their alleged social and cultural backwardness consisted of an inability or unwillingness to spearhead a united democratic opposition to the autocracy. It is important to examine this political failure in light of recent scholarship that emphasizes the rich cultural life of provincial towns and the significance of peasant and urban self-government or self-administration (not to be confused with legislative authority or constitutional government) in the age of serfdom.[69] Attention to the local arena suggests that eighteenth- and nineteenth-century merchants and business leaders not only actively participated in public affairs but exhibited a pattern of social, cultural, and political evolution comparable to that of the educated and professional classes.

The political evolution of Russia's commercial-industrial elite also indicates a need to employ less formalistic definitions of institutionalization and to examine informal societal structures, which, in the absence of formally constituted bodies, acquired special importance as integrative mechanisms of resistance and mediation in the relationship between state and society.[70] With the exception of the nobility (and excluding the fleeting dialogue of the Legislative Commission of 1767), businessmen represented the first social group to consult formally, though not institutionally, with the government about policies affecting their interests.[71] This occurred as early as the seventeenth century, continued in the reign of Peter the Great, whose top advisors included trading men, and in various commissions until the 1760s, and again became significant in 1857 and throughout the 1860s, when outspoken entrepreneurs publicly defended their interests in official discussions of tariffs. Even before these debates revealed the political sophistication of business leaders and inspired them with new confidence in their public stature, they had served in elected city offices and on the exchange committees of St. Petersburg (established in 1703), Moscow (established in 1839), and Nizhnii Novgorod (established in 1848). This involvement continued in the 1860s and 1870s with the reform of urban government and the creation of elected provincial assemblies (zemstva; sing., zemstvo).[72] In addition, from 1867 the Russian Industrial Society, composed of capitalists, intellectuals, and bureaucrats, gave the business elite a permanent public forum for debating economic policy. In 1870 the first Commercial-Industrial Congress convened in St. Petersburg, and the Moscow stock exchange committee received the right to submit unsolicited recommendations to the ministry of finance. Thus, after 1855, leading representatives of trade and industry acquired a privileged position as consultants to the government on economic affairs—a position they maintained until the collapse of the tsarist regime.[73]

Nor was the regular participation of industrialists in official deliberations a simple case of co-optation.[74] Already in the sixteenth and seventeenth centuries, merchants avoided overt political demands and accommodated themselves to governmental policy. Rather than passivity in the face of tsarist claims to absolute proprietary rights, such behavior revealed an ability to influence official policy and in some contexts represented effective resistance. In the words of one historian, "rather than confront established institutions, traditions, and forces, the Russian merchants maneuvered around, over, and between these obstacles, to maximize their opportunities, status, and security."[75] Even the apparent indifference of urban "citizens" toward institutions of local self-administration could constitute noncompliance, a viable form of counteraction. When the establishment of the Nizhnii Novgorod exchange committee introduced a limited merchant role in fair administration, traders perceived it as a mechanism for bureaucratic interference and were on the whole reluctant to participate. Rather than provide the government with information on the volume and value of goods bought and sold, they preferred private transactions, concluded in their shops or in restaurants and taverns, outside the framework of formal authority.[76] Many reacted in similar fashion to the institutional reforms of the 1860s and 1870s, which created a fair committee (distinct from the exchange committee), elected by an assembly of merchant delegates. Once again, the majority of traders avoided involvement and its attendant administrative duties, seeking instead to remain free of bureaucratic ties. Although a small elite seized the opportunity to articulate business interests through greater self-administration, and by the 1890s was participating regularly in representative bodies and reform commissions at the fair,[77] most traders had no time for public service or sought to protect their informal autonomy through evasion and privacy. Indeed, evasion and manipulation of the law pervaded imperial society, giving the general population a means to define itself socially, in order to avoid and hence refashion formal authority without becoming openly oppositionist or revolutionary.[78]

In the Moscow business community of the late imperial period, it was also a relatively small and financially secure elite, composed of two generations from about twenty prominent families, that chose to seek a visible public position. The older generation—born to fathers of humble, sometimes even serf, origins between the 1830s and 1850s—acquired their stature through economic success (often rooted in the networks of Old Believer communities), philanthropy, patronage of the arts and sciences, and participation, however reluctantly, in local government. As early as the 1840s members of this generation attended secondary schools and went abroad to study European business techniques and technology. Already early in the century, their parents, the founders of leading industrial dynasties, displayed attributes of cultural Westernization in their dress, manners, and hygiene and in the forms of entertainment they supported. Even so, the education of their children did not extend past age fifteen or sixteen and was designed to provide practical training for a business career.[79] The younger, more formally and generally better educated generation, born into wealth and security between the 1860s and 1880s, continued their fathers' involvement in civic life, while also seeking more individualized social roles. As graduates of gymnasia and universities, many in this age cohort abandoned business for careers in the arts and professions. It was representatives of this second generation who presented themselves as spokesmen for an all-Russian business elite *(kupechestvo),* participated in government-sponsored conferences and commissions to discuss economic policy and labor reform, and in 1905 provided the leadership for the bourgeois opposition to autocracy.[80]

The civic and intellectual activities characteristic of Moscow and provincial commercial elites already at the end of the eighteenth century challenge stereotypical images of isolation and backwardness.[81] In Tula and Moscow provinces, nobles and wealthy merchants participated in the same educational, cultural, philanthropic, and social organizations. Involvement in secular, literate theater was popular among bourgeois groups, and as early as 1786, the

Moscow Merchant Club sponsored balls, literary evenings, and card games, where privileged families socialized and interacted.[82] Membership in the business elite required not only wealth but service to society and a high level of cultural achievement, the very values traditionally identified with the intelligentsia and Westernized nobility.[83] Thus merchants paid twenty-five rubles an hour to read A. N. Radishchev's *Journey from St. Petersburg to Moscow,* after it was banned by Catherine II. In the reign of Alexander I, Moscow and St. Petersburg entrepreneurs criticized the government and maintained contacts with leading Decembrists. Writing in Siberian exile, the Decembrist A. N. Murav'ev extolled the elegance and cultural accomplishments of the Irkutsk merchant V. N. Basnin and described the rich merchantry *(kupechestvo)* he met as "a local aristocracy in education and manners."[84]

In the late 1850s and early 1860s, individual merchants collaborated with Slavophile journalists and intellectuals to campaign for higher tariffs, privately owned railroads, and state sponsorship of industrial development. Nor was this involvement in policy debates confined to narrow issues of economic self-interest; merchants also organized and attended banquets and dinners in support of emancipation and contributed financial backing to Slavophile periodicals that criticized bureaucratic interference in the economy. In adopting the language of the Slavophile intelligentsia, representatives of the business elite accepted an ideal of national economic self-sufficiency that until 1905 fully meshed with devotion to the autocracy.[85] Clearly, the reluctance to embrace abstract principles of political transformation did not mean that Russia's commercial-industrial classes failed to connect their immediate "life-context"[86] to a larger societal arena. Although in the early twentieth century, business leaders proved unable to attract a mass following or establish stable political and organizational ties with other middle-class groups, the very same can be said of Russia's educated elites, who despite their artistic originality and world-class cultural accomplishments, also failed to sustain ongoing civic activism.

Beginning in 1846 and culminating in the municipal statutes of 1870 and 1892, reforms of urban government gave elite merchants, defined as always in terms of wealth, a preponderant role in selecting mayors and city councilmen.[87] The equivalent of the noble-dominated elected rural assemblies *(zemstva),* city councils *(dumy;* sing., *duma)* enforced imperial laws, levied taxes, and administered a broad range of municipal services. Although frequently subjected to the arbitrary authority of police and provincial officials, the councils served as a locus of community autonomy and a forum for national political debate. Thus, while the Moscow city government failed to advocate the extension of representative institutions before the revolutionary upheaval of 1905, it nonetheless objected to bureaucratic intrusions, such as occurred in 1883 when the liberal jurist B. N. Chicherin was forced to resign his post as mayor.[88] It happened that throughout the 1880s and 1890s, the state's economic policies generally corresponded to the expectations of the business leaders who served in local government.[89] Like the eighteenth-century court aristocracy, which effectively changed governmental personnel through palace coups and hence had no reason to seek formal limits on autocratic authority, the nineteenth-century commercial-industrial elite also successfully influenced policy and thus before 1905 experienced no need to lobby for constitutional reform.[90] That business leaders did not use official deliberations and institutions of local self-administration as rostrums from which to demand political change in no way indicated civic backwardness. Rather, it suggested a misguided perception of social stability, overwhelming optimism and confidence in Russia's future and in the role these leaders would play henceforth, and most important, an assumption that the government would continue to accommodate their basic needs. Once their faith in the autocracy—to guarantee the security of their property or even the integrity of the empire—was shaken, the representatives of trade and industry quickly became oppositionist. This occurred initially in 1905 and again during the First World War, though the seeds of politicization already were sown in the labor reforms of the early 1880s.

Between 1859 and 1880, three governmental commissions examined but failed to produce legislation regulating labor conditions in the factory. Although industrialists generally objected to such legislation in the name of patriarchal values and the paternalistic ideal, the real reason for official inaction was the quiescence of the labor force. Once serious worker unrest erupted in the 1870s and 1880s, the autocracy moved rapidly toward reform. In addition to legislated limits on child labor and the length of the workday, a factory inspectorate was created in 1882 to enforce laws, monitor working and living conditions, and review worker grievances.[91] The actual impact of these reforms on the lives of workers was negligible.[92] Their primary importance lay in having brought the state directly into the factory—a policy that politicized the commercial-industrial and working classes by making the government responsible for ensuring social peace, whether through repression or further regulation.

By the early years of the twentieth century, involvement in elected institutions of local self-administration, well-established patterns of labor protest, and increased bureaucratic intervention in factory operations produced a politically active core of moderate conservative and liberal entrepreneurs who expressed a growing sense of alienation from the government and seemed increasingly receptive to constitutionalist demands. Stunned and sobered by the autocracy's rejection of societal initiatives during the famine and cholera epidemic of 1891–1892,[93] by the introduction of police-sponsored labor unions in 1901–1903, and by the losses of the Russo-Japanese War, they, like other middle groups, were ripe for opposition.[94] As early as February 1905, the Moscow city council called for societal participation in the legislative process through elected representatives.[95] This classic bourgeois liberalism was never a broad-based movement in Russia, nor was it universal within the business community, whose members occupied political positions spanning the ideological spectrum from constitutional democrat to loyal monarchist. Nevertheless, the experience of revolution and working-class radicalism in 1905–1907 hastened the consolidation of a national (though not all-Russian) political bourgeoisie, a development already underway in the context of local government. Locked in a two-pronged struggle against labor and the monarchy, politicized representatives of the business elite publicly began to attribute economic backwardness to bureaucratic interference, and worker discontent to the absence of civil rights and legal equality.

The presence of a conscious bourgeoisie ensured neither political unity nor the ascendancy of republican values. Indeed, by intensifying social fragmentation and conflict, heightened political consciousness and activism may have weakened liberal opposition to the autocracy. Throughout the revolutionary crisis of 1905, only a minority of the business elite supported parliamentary institutions (in contrast to an elected consultative assembly) or the right of workers to organize unions and peaceful strikes. Still, even in the absence of a consensus concerning the extent and pace of political reform, the vast majority of businessmen welcomed the October Manifesto, with its promises of civil rights and limited constitutional monarchy.[96] At the same time, they embraced the government's use of violent force, administrative exile, military courts-martial, and summary executions to suppress worker and peasant unrest. For the commercial-industrial elites, as for virtually all groups in society, the revolution of 1905 represented a turning point both in societal relationships and in attitudes toward the autocracy. Forced to defend their vital interests in the face of worker radicalism, a minority among them openly advocated fundamental political reform. Whether they spoke for the mass of petty traders and manufacturers was of no consequence. They, along with other educated and propertied groups, played a crucial role in changing the foundations of government, something that generations of enlightened bureaucrats had tried and failed to do. Nor were the representatives of trade and industry necessarily motivated by abstract constitutionalist principles, but rather by the traumatic perception that their persons and property, and indeed even Russia's national existence, were seriously threatened.

Having once adopted the language of classical liberalism, crossed the line into political opposition, and then subsequently participated in almost a decade of parliamentary politics within the Duma system, Russia's commercial-industrial elites moved easily from the economic and military crisis of the First World War to direct involvement in the overthrow of the monarchy. In 1909–1910, Russia entered a new period of industrial expansion, characterized by shortages of key commodities, rampant inflation, and growing labor militancy. By 1912, leading industrialists once again became convinced of the need for further reforms to ensure a broad program of economic development that, in their view, was vital to Russia's security and independence. Although business leaders continued to support the autocracy, especially after the outbreak of war in July 1914, their awareness of the crucial role played by the economic rear in modern warfare also led them to expect that they would work in partnership with the government to confront the national crisis. The bureaucracy, by contrast, questioned their political intentions, accused them of speculation and profiteering, sought to exclude them from wartime planning, and stubbornly relied on state enterprises to meet emergency needs.[97]

In early 1915, the Russian economy was experiencing severe declines in the production of coal and metal, as well as shortages of rolling stock and disruptions in transport services. The army, too, was suffering from a dangerous shortfall in the supply of arms and munitions. Industrialists attributed the deteriorating economic conditions to disorganization in the railroad system caused by official ineptness and corruption, and to labor shortages caused by conscription. Ministers blamed the manpower problem on employers who subjected their workers to low wages and inhumane living conditions. The Duma and military leadership both responded to the emergency by calling for the mobilization of private industry to increase production for the army, a position fully consistent with the aspirations of industrialists. Efforts to cooperate with the government culminated in the establishment of war industries committees in May 1915, after which official actions quickly dampened the hopes of industrialists to participate in the formulation of wartime economic policy. From September 1915 until the final collapse of the autocracy in February 1917, confrontations between the government and business leaders escalated, political divisions among the representatives of trade and industry became steadily more pronounced, and the economic emergency continued to worsen.[98] At the end of 1916, labor radicalism and political and economic crisis persuaded many of the government's supporters that it was too feeble to guarantee either security of property or the uninterrupted flow of manufacturing and commerce, both of which the business elite deemed essential to the war effort.

Throughout the revolutionary situations of the early twentieth century, the political posture of the commercial-industrial elite often seemed narrow and selfish, especially with respect to the worker question.[99] Yet there was more at stake than simple self-interest. Business leaders rightly associated themselves with the further progress of economic modernization, and thus could honestly conclude that what was good for industry also was good for Russia. They could even argue that the empire's future prosperity, the well-being of its people, the integrity of its borders, and the very foundations of its national security depended directly on their continued entrepreneurial success.[100] In assuming political positions advantageous to their personal interests and in seeking to avoid revolutionary action, the business elite did not fail to develop a public identity beyond the confines of their immediate economic needs. On the contrary, their cultural sophistication and civic involvement were clearly evident already in the late eighteenth century, well before they emerged as a distinct interest group. Regardless of the mutual disdain that nobles and business leaders sometimes expressed, by the end of the nineteenth century, they belonged to the same clubs, dined in the same restaurants, lived in the same neighborhoods, married the same women, cultivated the same friends, supported the same charities, and patronized the same artistic endeavors.[101]

In Russia, as elsewhere in Europe, the development of bourgeois values resulted from "practical experience with the necessities of the business world,"

not from religious dissent, Protestantism, or the desire of outsiders to overcome persecution and prove their worthiness.[102] Self-respect, hard work, hon-
esty, temperance, thrift, and the responsibility of wealth were characteristic
traits of Russia's mature business class.[103] By the mid-nineteenth century a socially and economically distinct businessman appeared in Russian society. At
century's end, the modern bourgeois was fully discernible in all his political,
cultural, social, and economic dimensions. Having at last become securely and
functionally separated from the fluid, undifferentiated, mass entrepreneurship
of preindustrial Russia, he articulated a commercial-industrial point of view
that revealed awareness of both his personal dignity and his historic importance. In an 1894 press interview, S. I. Shchukin, member of a prominent business dynasty, was asked whether industrialists performed a disservice to society in stimulating peasant demand for high-quality manufactured goods.
While admitting that factory production created such a desire without regard
for the financial means of its satisfaction, he nonetheless concluded that

> the expansion of personal demands is the natural result of any progress. Industry
> and trade always and everywhere have introduced and will introduce this vice.
> This is the natural course of things and to demand from industrialists and from
> merchants that they should deliberately give up regions of their sale with the
> goal of not accustoming the village to luxury would be . . . very naive.[104]

In the course of a half century, an elite core of Russian entrepreneurs had
achieved a measure of wealth and security previously reserved for an equally
small group of aristocratic landowners. More important, they had done this on
their own initiative, independently of state service and official largesse.

THE PROFESSIONS AND INTELLIGENTSIA

Only from the 1860s did industrial development and the creation of elected
assemblies of local self-administration provide ample employment opportunities to permit the differentiation of specialists and technicians into professional
and semiprofessional classes. That this process was never completed was due
in part to official distrust of societal initiatives, though administrative repression is not a sufficient explanation. In 1905, when the autocracy was brought
to its knees and effective governmental authority crumbled, societal organizations also disintegrated, into acute political acrimony. Underlying this fragmentation was the same lack of social and economic differentiation that de-
layed the appearance of a stable commercial-industrial elite until the
mid-nineteenth century, with an activist political bourgeoisie following only
decades later. Despite a broad-based tradition of public instruction dating back
to the school reforms of Catherine II, and despite the continual growth of educated cadres from at least the early eighteenth century, Russia's recognized
professionals and semiprofessionals—including physicians, medical orderlies,
psychiatrists, pharmacists, attorneys (created by the judicial reform of 1864),

scholars, journalists, teachers, and engineers—were neither clearly differentiated within elite society nor fully distinguished from their informal, frequently unlicensed, and at times illicit premodern prototypes.

In imperial Russia the traditional free professions or "great person professions" of law, medicine, the ministry, and university teaching never achieved sufficient autonomy in their "essential work" or control over the regulation of their membership to be regarded as anything more than "aspirant occupations" or "semi-professions."[105] With the partial exception of sworn attorneys (who were organized into bar councils after 1864, but still excluded from participation in significant areas of the judiciary), none of the established or newer technical professions ever gained authority over training, licensing, employment, and ethics.[106] According to modern sociologists, the possession of specialized knowledge, group consciousness, and occupational aspirations is insufficient to attain professional status. Nor is employment in a bureaucracy or close cooperation with the state—a widespread condition in Russia—of crucial importance to the presence or absence of professional standing. Rather, recognition as an organized profession hinges on societal acceptance and "the relationship between administrative and professional authority."[107] While Russian historians have barely begun to explore the extent of public recognition, it is certain that before 1905 the political and institutional conditions of autocratic rule did not permit the mechanisms of professional self-administration to evolve.

Given the empire's economic uniformity and the absence of autonomous guild structures, the emergence of professional classes resulted primarily from state-directed occupational training and specialization. For this reason historians of the professions generally take as their point of departure the establishment of public schools to train specialists for the army and bureaucracy, a line of research that allows them to explore the connection between the tradition of state service and the formation of professional identities emphasizing service to society. In addition, protoprofessional training and work took place outside of state institutions.[108] Private medical practitioners, informal legal experts, and unlicensed teachers operated throughout the imperial period. By the 1830s, settled artists, journalists, and writers—as opposed to the traditional itinerant purveyors of oral and print culture—could maintain themselves by producing for wealthy clients and the periodical press.[109] From 1864, in connection with the judicial reform and the creation of assemblies of local self-administration, specialists such as attorneys, physicians, medical orderlies, midwives, agronomists, engineers, architects, statisticians, and teachers acquired institutionalized nongovernmental bases of employment. Traditional specialists and protoprofessionals continued to operate illegally, blending imperceptibly into the populations they served, but increasingly, certified experts worked within a rapidly expanding network of formally recognized societal structures. The new opportunities for private employment and social engagement encouraged self-conscious professionals and semiprofessionals to pursue organizational ties outside of state service and to demand autonomy within legal institutions on grounds of expertise. When the government disappointed these expectations, denying specialists a role as expert consultants to policy-makers, they joined *zemstvo* and business leaders in political opposition.

The evolution of public sector physicians (about three-fourths of all physicians) illustrates this pattern.[110] Before emancipation, physicians constituted a distinct, official medical category *(soslovie)* trained and employed by the government. Only in the period of the Great Reforms did physicians coalesce into a corporate group, acquire a professional consciousness, and seek to play a more independent role in society.[111] Professionalization began with the appearance of medical associations and the ideal of service in the 1860s, and throughout the later part of the century physicians claimed authority over public health on the basis of scientific knowledge. Frustrated by official interference and popular indifference, medical professionals entered the opposition movement by 1902. Moving beyond traditional efforts to address public health issues, they also criticized social inequities and articulated political demands for broad civil rights. Ultimately, however, physicians failed to realize the transition from an ascribed category with specific legal obligations to a Western-style profession with control over licensing, medical ethics, education, employment, and association. Limited in their autonomy by the ethos of state service and by dependence on public employment, physicians emerged fragmented and demoralized from the revolutionary crisis of the early twentieth century. The shattering of professional bonds in 1905 suggests that the liberal physicians, active in the medical press and in organizations such as the Pirogov Society, probably exaggerated the group's unity of outlook prior to the revolutionary upheaval. Most physicians did not identify with the radical intelligentsia or become involved in politics for abstract ideological reasons. Their search for professional recognition and independence was more than a political issue rooted in notions of public service; it was a social issue as well, an expression of "status-inconsistency"[112] and of the need for delimitation and identity in a society of amorphous structures.

While historians document in great detail a broad range of professional achievements in public health, primary education, law, science, scholarship, culture, and the arts, depictions of the social condition of professional people derive almost exclusively from a desire to explain the revolutionary events of the early twentieth century.[113] Thus the existing historiography emphasizes relations with the government and relies heavily on the experiences of articulate, usually elite minorities within each specialty. Scholars readily admit that most recognized professionals and semiprofessionals were neither politically involved nor openly oppositionist, yet concrete knowledge of the rank and file is exceedingly limited. There are two historical reasons for this conundrum: (1) professional identities, when publicly expressed, tended to become politicized; and (2) the ambiguous social differentiation found throughout Russia was equally characteristic of the professions.[114] Because only a very small proportion of specialists ever coalesced into aspirant professional classes, it is no surprise that the available documentation gives undue weight to activist, self-conscious subgroups who propagated images of political struggle and social commitment.

It is the undeniable politicization of these subgroups that makes it so difficult to distinguish the professions from the intelligentsia. Indeed, in the effort to achieve professional status, particularly the authority to fulfill a self-defined service ideal based on expertise, many individuals became politicized and radicalized and hence joined the ranks of the activist intelligentsia.[115] Although the absence of fully institutionalized, autonomous professions by no means prevented the growth of voluntary association and public services, it did contribute to the fragility of professional unity. Police repression also played a formidable role in thwarting impulses to organize professionally and in politicizing society's more liberal elements.[116] Still, the relationship between governmental policy and limited social organization is difficult to assess.[117] When the societal fragmentation of the revolutionary era exposed the weakness of professional associations and identities, it also revealed that just as the "woman question" in late imperial Russia tended to be subsumed in larger issues of social justice, such as the peasant and worker questions, the articulation of professional relationships became absorbed into the concept and ethos of the intelligentsia. Both the politicization of the professions and the sociocultural concept of the intelligentsia are best understood as part of a more general process, wherein educated Russians sought to delimit and define for themselves a recognized public identity.[118]

For historians, the most problematic and elusive of these self-constructed identities is the category "intelligentsia." Michael Confino regards the intelligentsia as a creation of intellectuals, which "conveyed at one and the same time a sociological concept, a psychological characterization, and a moral code." Recognizing the ambiguity of the concept and contradictions "between the outlook and self-image of those who used it and the social and intellectual reality it is supposed to represent," he nonetheless describes the intelligentsia as "a group of sorts," though neither an estate nor an economically delineated class nor a category defined by the professions of its members, their level of education, or a precise "set of ideas." Still, "the aggregate result" of the category's characteristic features was "the delineation of a group (of sorts) in a state of potential or actual dissent (not necessarily political)."[119] Confino's approach is fully consistent with historiographical tradition; but if this group's most stable trait was "potential or actual dissent," then the notion of a sociological entity can be understood only in terms of subjective and constantly shifting definitions. Thus the intelligentsia as "self-image" clearly must take precedence over the intelligentsia as "group" and "moral code."

The notion of "self-image" implies multiple conceptions of the intelligentsia that undermine attempts to formulate a sociological or "objective" scholarly definition. Some Western and Soviet historians seek to overcome this difficulty by eliminating the subjective element. Noting that diverse conceptions of the intelligentsia "accurately reflected the self-image of various groups of writers and politically active men in Russian society," Daniel R. Brower concludes that "the very subjectiveness of the definitions should have precluded their use in historical research." In his view, a sociological interpretation is needed to provide "a socially valid and neutral definition," so that "the term intelligentsia as a historical concept would no longer be tied to subjective criteria of consciousness or belief, nor to a particular class," becoming instead "an objective tool of analysis for the study of the history of Russian society." Even so, he repeatedly refers to "the concept of the intelligentsia," treating it as a subculture of values in conflict with societal norms.[120]

When defined as a social group, the intelligentsia becomes difficult to delineate satisfactorily. Otto Müller finds in the contradictory meanings and usages of the term an alternative and ultimately more successful conception.[121] After tracing the Latin and European origins of the concept intelligentsia, including its transformation from an abstract notion to one of collective intelligence, Müller turns to detailed analysis of textual usages (linguistic, literary, and publicistic). He identifies psychological (abstract) and sociological (collective) meanings of intelligentsia, but argues that in Russia the term first developed as a political concept in the context of the Great Reforms of the 1860s.[122] Hence it is impossible to understand the divergent meanings found in the sources without reference to the political and philosophical debates of the nineteenth century. Individual writers applied the term in different ways with varied meanings, all the while seeking to define the "true" and "best" intelligentsia or deride the "so-called" intelligentsia.[123] Noting that political polemics and theoretical reflection undermined the collective notion of intelligentsia, Müller examines numerous distinctions within the category—distinctions based on ethnicity, geography, chronology, social status, politics, and philosophical-ethical values. Repeatedly, the subjective conceptions of individual authors represented ideological or ideal types, dooming any effort to delineate a sociological entity or develop a value-free definition. Müller's scrutiny of nineteenth-century texts and his willingness to embrace a multiplicity of conceptions show conclusively that there was not, nor can there be, a single definition of the intelligentsia.[124]

Precisely because the intelligentsia constituted a subjective, normative category that cannot be delineated either sociologically or philosophically, it is difficult to formulate neutral scientific terms of analysis that adequately describe the group's historical significance. Only by defining membership in the intelligentsia as a form of conscious identification or positive self-identity is it possible to incorporate the shifting legal, socioeconomic, and intellectual differences. Once this is done, distinctions between the intelligentsia and the educated elites and professions become easier to maintain. This did not mean that the democratic social composition of the intelligentsia and its formation as a self-defined, self-proclaimed subculture resulted solely from radical political views. Although such views promoted voluntarism and an egalitarian disregard for accepted social distinctions, the category originated in the flexible social boundaries and incessant social intermingling characteristic of Russian society since earliest times. Composed primarily of educated individuals, the self-conscious intelligentsia shared with other elite groups—including the professions, the nobility, and even the autocracy itself—the need to secure its identity through staged and ritualized displays of cultural values. The imperial court's ceremonial "scenarios of power," the pleasure palaces and theatrical troupes of wealthy aristocrats, the affected peasant dress of Slavophiles and populists, and the nihilist subculture of the 1860s all sought to project authority, where in practice it was limited, or to affirm social status, where in reality it was indeterminate and uncertain.[125]

If a clear distinction between the intelligentsia and professions is to be maintained, it is necessary to account for the common patterns of politicization, which cannot be blamed entirely on an archaic system of government. Despite the autocracy's relentless penchant for bureaucratic regulation and centralization, its policies did not preclude spontaneous development, societal initiative, or autonomous professional activity. Local achievements in primary schooling, public health, charity, and social services are well documented from the late eighteenth century, as is the persistence of traditional values, attitudes, and practices in the emergent professional fields of the late empire. In order to avoid adopting the perspective of an articulate, politically conscious minority, historians focus on interactions between formal institutions and unofficial local structures. These interactions then help to explain the relationship of the professions to the intelligentsia, the radicalization of an activist professional core, and the latter's failure to establish stable organizational links with rank-and-file colleagues and with the populations they served. A national movement for political liberation began to appear among professionals in August 1903, reached a peak with the formation of the Union of Unions in early 1905, and encompassed the organization of local unions and all-Russian congresses, as well as demands for constitutional and social reform. Throughout the revolutionary crisis of 1905–1907, only a minority of professionals actually spoke out, joined organizations, entered politics, and opposed the tsarist regime.[126] At the height of its influence in 1905–1906, the All-Russian Teachers Union had thirteen or fourteen thousand members, many of whom neglected to pay their dues.[127] Similarly, when membership in the Union of All-Russian Medical Personnel reached its high point in August 1905, it numbered no more than twenty-five thousand out of nearly seventy-nine thousand certified medical practitioners.[128] Even among medical professionals, whose greater social stature and institutionalized roles in the formulation of local health policy produced higher levels of political participation, the consciously oppositionist element never predominated.

If so few professionals, semiprofessionals, and paraprofessionals were in fact politically engaged, then why did the impulse to organize so often assume an oppositionist character? One reason is that the intellectuals writing for the periodical press were more likely also to be radical activists seeking to mobilize the rank and file and "the people." What historians know of professional organizations comes largely from the pens of this group or from officials who detected dangerous political intentions lurking behind every societal initiative. A second reason is that in repressing local activities and programs, the government unwittingly encouraged the consolidation of minority political oppositions among professionals, *zemstvo* deputies, and elite entrepreneurs. A third reason for the politicization of professional societies was that ordinary specialists, living and working in local contexts, were integrated into a variety of community structures and hence were not sufficiently differentiated from the populations they served to maintain all-Russian ties on an organized basis. Membership in professional organizations, including mutual aid societies, was generally confined to a politicized minority or to the better educated, more clearly delimited elites within specialized fields. Ultimately, however, given the very real danger of popular and official reprisals, including dismissal and arrest (which surely suppressed the appetite for political activism), one cannot rule out the possibility that many nonradical, nonoppositionist individuals quietly sympathized with their more articulate cohorts.

In the absence of detailed local studies, it is difficult to resolve the problem of political attitudes and consciousness or to understand the complex relations between university-trained specialists and the more numerous but less educated auxiliaries or paraprofessionals. Still, it is possible to explain why Russia's educated elites failed to sustain a politically effective civil society and why organized professional ties were so fragile. Geography clearly played a role, making communications and transportation throughout the empire, and even between major cities, extremely slow and arduous.[129] Despite astounding progress in railroad construction during the second half of the nineteenth century, Russia's communications network was wholly inadequate to meet the empire's vast administrative, economic, and military needs—rural schoolteachers and medical practitioners faced daunting journeys in order to exchange information and to attend professional meetings, and, in the case of the latter, even in order to serve their patients. The poverty of teachers made it so difficult to obtain books and subscribe to periodicals that the issue of subsidies for these materials became a major focus in their relations with *zemstvo* employers.[130] Another important factor slowing professional organization was internal conflict, exacerbated by political efforts to define independent public roles and delineate recognized areas of expert competence. Because professionalization invariably involved a struggle to achieve autonomy within formal institutions, specialist and political issues tended to become inseparable. This occurred even when the real source of acrimony was not relations with the government, but the acceptance of professional services in society or the delimitation of elite and lesser specialists within a particular field. Thus, during the revolutionary crisis of 1905–1907, when ideological boundaries were pitilessly exposed, professional unity easily disintegrated into social and political conflict.[131]

Closely related to problems of internal differentiation within broad areas of expertise was the traditional disjuncture between the structures of central administration and those of society—a disjuncture intensified by increased professional specialization and by the expansion of local self-administration in the reforms of the 1860s. As long as societal institutions remained largely informal (or nonjuridical), and as long as the government did not commit itself to bringing standardized education and health care to the countryside, there was no pressing need to integrate state and community structures. Once rural self-administration was extended and formalized in institutions such as the *zemstvo* assemblies and the peasant cantonal *(volost')* courts, it became necessary to incorporate the newly constituted bodies into the larger bureaucratic framework. The institutional interfacing of "state" and "society" was a difficult process occurring in a variety of contexts on an ad hoc basis. It was not a new problem, but in the postemancipation period, the rapid proliferation of legally recognized associations facilitated politicization by making it more difficult to express social opposition and alienation through passive resistance and simple evasion. As discontent was increasingly articulated and confronted in formal institutional channels, it inevitably became politicized and hence more easily directed against the government. To the extent that professionals, semiprofessionals, paraprofessionals, and protoprofessionals worked within the framework of these new structures, their activities also were more likely to assume a political character. Clearly, such politicization contributed to professional fragmentation by undermining incipient associations, but it was neither the sole manifestation of professional consciousness nor the primary reason for the failure to establish stable organizational ties.

Beneath the radicalization of an articulate minority lay larger patterns of protoprofessional development that deserve greater emphasis in general depictions of late imperial society. The universally acknowledged achievements of tsarist education and public health resulted from the labors of trained specialists, working effectively in their respective fields, who delivered much-needed services to the general population. Although their activities rarely extended to national programs or policymaking, and as modern professional classes, they never became fully differentiated, these specialists nonetheless played a paramount role in the integration of state and societal structures. At the same time, the lack of clearly delineated professional functions and the continuing viability of illicit local practitioners, frequently also the associates of certified personnel, encouraged conflict among specialists and between experts and the government. From the differing perspectives of both official and educated elites, widespread popular disregard for enlightened guardianship and expertise not only slowed the march of progress but also represented an open challenge to their common expectation that professionals and semiprofessionals would serve as carriers of modern values and social control to the countryside.[132]

The legal profession, brought to life and officially recognized in the judicial reform of 1864, is widely understood to have been the most modern, autonomous, and securely organized of Russia's professions. Constituted in formal bars consisting of a general assembly and an elected council, the university-educated sworn attorneys *(advokatura)* of any city were entitled to receive a professional monopoly when their number exceeded twenty. Implementation of the judicial reform was exceedingly slow, however, and in 1874, when the government suspended the establishment of new bar councils for thirty years, only three had been created—in Moscow, St. Petersburg, and Khar'kov. Nor did the ministry of justice ever grant monopolies to the sworn attorneys of any region. Practicing only in major cities and higher courts, their numbers remained small. Outside the main urban centers, private attorneys and street advocates, many of the latter unregistered, served the general population.[133] In the prereform period, any citizen not expressly forbidden to do so by law had enjoyed the right to represent clients in court. The street advocates thus belonged to a tradition of legal practitioners *(striapchie)* extending from the reign of Peter the Great into the Soviet era. Although generally of low birth, their ranks sometimes included nobles with higher education and, in the postreform period, qualified attorneys who preferred not to join the bar. Thus the new legal profession, the pride of liberal reformers in the Great Reform era, was effectively "swallowed up" by the traditional "underground advocates."[134]

The government responded to these ambiguous realities by seeking to legalize and hence regulate unauthorized practitioners. In 1874 it recognized "private attorneys," who regardless of education were allowed to practice law by purchasing a license and registering with the local court. In addition, only registered private and sworn attorneys were permitted to appear in court as legal counsel. Enforcement remained lax, and the street advocates survived. Official and professional pronouncements to the contrary, the government tolerated their presence and limited the number of registered attorneys. The latter also continued to work with their illicit counterparts, pleading cases for them in court and relying on them to refer new clients. Societal reception represented yet another factor, particularly among peasants, who did not clearly differentiate between sworn attorneys and underground advocates. Moreover, because the separate peasant courts often operated on the basis of customary law, which educated attorneys did not know, the street advocates provided a crucial link between newly formalized societal institutions and state structures, which is to say, between customary justice and the larger judicial edifice. Although frequently accused of corruption and blamed for causing legal chaos, the underground advocates were effectively integrated into both peasant society and the recognized legal profession. As one critic described the situation in 1885, the moral standards of sworn attorneys had become so compromised that the boundaries between them, private attorneys, and the petitioners of times past had disappeared.[135]

Studies of primary education find comparable evidence of illicit specialists performing an important social service. Private instruction in informal literacy schools dated back at least to the seventeenth century and continued to provide an autonomous source of learning throughout the imperial period. Both church and community-sponsored schools outside the official framework of public institutions contributed significantly to the high rates of rural literacy discovered in the early twentieth century.[136] Not until the mid-1890s did the central government and local elites commit significant public resources to the goal of universal primary education. Until that time the expansion of schooling depended almost entirely on peasant initiative and funding. This was officially admitted in 1882, when limited revenues, a chronic shortage of teachers, and the pragmatic educational expectations of peasants led to the legalization of village schools, where uncertified instructors taught reading, writing, and counting.[137] Primary education illustrates both the importance of spontaneous development and the potentially effective integration of state and societal institutions, central and local administration, and formal and informal structures.

Although there were obvious gaps between the performance of local schools and the goals of elite educators, these resulted from successes in adapting rural education to the needs and expectations of parents. Whereas officials and intellectuals viewed the village schools as purveyors of enlightenment and modernity, peasants were interested in acquiring the basic knowledge needed to survive in conditions of rapid economic change. Whether as an educator in the broad moral sense or as a source of vital information and skills, the primary schoolteacher represented a crucial link between the general population and the educated and ruling elites. Although traditionally characterized as social and cultural outsiders, rural teachers were well suited to meet the needs of peasant society. That they failed to transform the village, as intellectuals and bureaucrats had hoped, cannot negate their daily successes. Nor did their own complaints of intellectual isolation indicate an absence of functional integration. The "outsider as insider" was a traditional feature of imperial society. In the postemancipation period, rural teachers, many of whom actually came from the peasantry, joined parish priests and prereform retired soldiers as informally incorporated and fully efficacious nonmembers of the local community. Within villages, these nonmembers played recognized social roles and in an age of limited communications and widespread illiteracy, transmitted important information to the countryside.[138]

Accounts of the medical profession reveal similar gaps between local realities and the expectations of an articulate, activist minority. Once again less-educated, paraprofessional personnel, together with unofficial healers, provided the connection between formal and informal structures. Developments in public health fit nicely with Peter Burke's analysis of cultural change in early modern Europe, where newer elite forms of culture served as additions (rather than displacements), which were absorbed into and transformed by more traditional popular forms.[139] In late-nineteenth-century Russia, the medical orderlies (fel'dshery) represented elite culture, carried professional knowledge to local society, and linked traditional to modern medicine. While fully trained physicians denounced practitioners for illegally performing operations and prescribing treatments outside their recognized areas of competence, they employed their services to offset chronic shortages of funding and qualified personnel. The medical orderlies were so instrumental in promoting public health that in the 1860s and 1870s, zemstvo assemblies expanded their numbers by establishing formal training programs at provincial hospitals. Clearly, the extension of health services to rural Russia resulted less from the development of professional elites than from the traditional practices of medical orderlies, who combined folk with modern medicine and adapted methods of treatment to the expectations of their peasant constituents.[140]

Rather than undermining the authority of physicians, as the medical elite claimed, the orderlies probably facilitated the penetration of modern medicine into the village, a place where licensing was not an issue nor the benefits of medical expertise clearly discernible. Like street advocates and rural school-teachers, they served well the requirements of a peasant society that failed to distinguish traditional from modern modes of medicine and thus consulted physicians, medical orderlies, nuns, monks, witches, sorcerers, and faith heal-ers without discrimination, believing that each was useful in a different way.[141] Despite the frustrations of physicians who sought more rapid and comprehen-sive change, the problem of "two Russias" or "two societies" derived more from disappointed elite aspirations than from society's acceptance or rejection of modern medicine. From the perspective of the general population, the per-sistence of traditional healers reflected not the clash of elite and popular cul-tures but a pluralistic integration of the available modes of understanding. (Truly effective medical progress in the form of sulfa and antibiotics had not yet arrived.) Peasant responses to public health, as to education, were emi-nently sensible: discriminating use based on a rational but culturally condi-tioned assessment of real needs. That their choices did not correspond to the expectations of elite physicians revealed both the significance of professional development and the still very limited delineation of modern professional classes and functions.

It is clear from the history of Russia's emerging legal, educational, and medical professions that with the exception of highly educated or politically conscious activist minorities, there was only minimal differentiation between certified rank-and-file professionals and their unrecognized prototypes. Partly the result of limited resources, the lack of delimitation did not prevent signifi-cant progress in public services or the effective integration of traditional, in-formal practices and their more modern, formally institutionalized counter-parts. Neither the failure to satisfy the hopes of elite professionals nor the persistence of premodern, protoprofessional structures precluded concrete public successes. The relentless imposition of modernity continued, as the emerging professions, semiprofessions, and paraprofessions were co-opted, not always smoothly, into a preexisting framework, where they both initiated change and were themselves transformed. If this mingling of old and new ele-ments slowed progress and professionalization, it was not because of irrecon-cilable conflict but because of societal initiative, institutional flexibility, and spontaneous integration based on daily interactions and experiences.

TOWARD A DEFINITION OF THE RUSSIAN MIDDLE

Given the role of the urban middle class in the expansion and capitalization of European commerce and manufacturing, it was natural for observers such as Catherine II to relate the problems of middle-class formation to those of ur-ban development and economic modernization. In the case of Russia, how-ever, the association was less illuminating and generally led contemporaries to underestimate levels of economic dynamism, entrepreneurial activity, and cultural development. With the exception of a very few urban centers, the distinction between town and countryside remained indeterminate for much of the imperial period. The empire's urban-rural geography, like that of the physical environment, was characterized by uniformity, monotony, and the absence of clear delineations. The putative weakness of the Russian middle thus reflected a larger blurring of social boundaries, rather than societal passivity, political immaturity, or economic stagnation. The patterns of social structuring outlined here reveal that by the mid-nineteenth century, the legal-administrative and socioeconomic dimensions of the *raznochintsy* had become more clearly differentiated into commercial-industrial and emergent professional and semiprofessional classes. On the whole, however, Russian society remained relatively undifferentiated, or only ambiguously so, which then helps explain why there was no clearly discernible civil society or political bourgeoisie.

In contrast to the limited consolidation of social and political associations, the empire's rich cultural life exhibited extraordinary sophistication; by the nineteenth century, it was easily incorporated into, and often at the forefront of, pan-European artistic developments. Within Russia, the appearance of a mass circulation press and the vitality of popular boulevard culture also offered striking evidence of a dynamic and distinct middle.[142] By focusing attention on Russian society's limited differentiation, it is possible to understand why, despite enormous entrepreneurial, professional, and intellectual achievements, imperial Russia was slow to produce a massive political and industrial transformation comparable to that which had fundamentally altered much of west and east-central Europe by the time of the First World War. Most important in this regard were the traditional fragmentation of Russian society, including its mobility and porous boundaries; the limited development of formal (though not necessarily informal) societal structures; and the accompanying dispersion of resources and cadres. Underlying these social factors, a geographical setting of vast distances and harsh climatic conditions discouraged specialization, the hallmark of economic modernity, requiring, instead, undifferentiated flexibility, mobility, and self-sufficiency.

That there was no broad-based political bourgeoisie, nor a mass reform movement led by clearly delineated capitalist and professional elites, did not mean that Russia lacked a middle-class culture, including such values as education, industry, respectability, belief in private initiative and individual rights, and commitment to public service. It meant simply that there was no organized, all-encompassing middle-class movement. Ordinary entrepreneurs and protoprofessionals, together with the general population, sought to resist the regulatory proclivities of the autocracy by avoiding participation in formalized institutions. Better-educated and financially secure businessmen, fully trained elite professionals, and liberal landowners active in the politics of local self-administration struggled to define for themselves a legitimate public role that would ensure independence from the bureaucracy and clear delineation from their lesser cohorts. What bound these groups together was their engagement in an ongoing process of legal, economic, social, and cultural self-definition either within or in opposition to society's official framework. If one discards a narrow political definition of the bourgeoisie and focuses instead on the interfacing of informal societal structures and officially constituted bodies, it becomes clear that Russia's diverse and only partially differentiated middle was indeed a formidable social presence. That this middle failed to form an organized civil society capable of sustained political action revealed not social and cultural isolation but dynamic, flexible, and effective integration into traditionally fragmented societal structures. In this, the middle differed little from other categories in Russian society—a society where social groupings can be understood as contiguous relationships in specific contexts and where the shifting, changeable boundaries between such groupings represented contingent moments of cohesion in response to concrete conditions and events.

The relationship between the middle classes and civil society in nineteenth-century Europe illuminates the issue of social bonds and when applied to the Russian case helps to explain the problematics of the middle and the meaning of sociocultural concepts such as the "honorable public," "liberal educated society" *(obshchestvo),* and intelligentsia. Jürgen Kocka defines civil society as a political program or plan calling for representative constitutional government and an autonomous, legally equal citizenry. In England where the elements of civil society were most fully institutionalized, the concept itself was insignificant. In Germany, by contrast, where the ability to realize the civil society project was limited, the idea developed in conjunction with a well-defined economic and cultural elite, the *Bürgertum,* a group consisting of educated and professional classes, businessmen, and civil servants, which distinguished itself from the nobility, petty bourgeoisie, peasants, and workers. Coalescing in a supralocal identity based on education, achievement, secular values, family relationships, a strong work ethic, self-reliance, and the possession of relative economic security and leisure time, the *Bürgertum* constituted itself as a social formation from the late eighteenth to the early twentieth century. Combining Enlightenment thought with traditional corporate autonomy and a clear delineation between town and countryside, the German concept of an independent civil society hinged upon official position, education, or private property and thus excluded women and the laboring classes. Although in Germany liberalism and bourgeois culture initially converged, by the twentieth century they had grown apart, as ever more heterogeneous groups demanded inclusion in the universalist civil society plan.[143]

In Russia, where economic security, corporative structures, and the separation of town and countryside were largely absent,[144] distinct middle classes associated with the idea of a civil society did not cohere until the late nineteenth century. Although present by the second half of the eighteenth century, the advocates of the principles of civil society remained socially and geographically atomized, and neither in practice nor in theory did they embrace all elements of the political plan. Their ranks included enlightened rulers such as Catherine II, the reading public, Freemasons, men and women who organized private charitable societies, liberal bureaucrats and noble landowners, educated, artistic, and urban economic elites, and after 1864, *zemstvo* professionals (known as the third element).[145] Instead of crystallizing in a social group comparable to the German *Bürgertum*, Russia's idea of a civil society was most closely identified with the flexible cultural and political concepts of the "honorable public," "liberal educated society" *(obshchestvo)*, and intelligentsia. Through these transcendent sociocultural categories, educated Russians from diverse social and occupational backgrounds sought to overcome societal fragmentation. In the process, they articulated cultural and intellectual identities that represented discursive ideals but that rarely achieved a secure, organizationally independent existence. However one defines "civil society" or the "public sphere" (and the historical and philosophical sources offer multiple possibilities), the important question is not whether the groups and ideas constituting civil society existed in Russia. The language of civil society was present by the mid-eighteenth century. What is important to note in the Russian case—and both Peter I and Catherine II represent early examples—is that the constituent elements of the emergent civil society were at once official and unofficial. Not until the second quarter of the nineteenth century did a clear distinction between the official and unofficial public spheres appear.

CHAPTER FOUR

LABORING PEOPLE

Don't run away from anything,
but don't do anything.

—*Russian popular proverb*

"It takes two people to make you,
and one people to die. That's
how the world is going to end."

—William Faulkner, *As I Lay Dying*

Numerous categories of rural inhabitants and urban residents constituted the laboring classes of imperial Russia—classes that were identified by enormously complex and only vaguely differentiated boundaries. Generally defined in the policies of Peter the Great as groups obliged to pay the capitation and provide conscripts for the army, the laboring people were no less heterogeneous than more privileged social groups. At the same time, despite legal, occupational, and cultural diversity, they shared a common function in society: whether servile or wage laborers, ordinary men and women devoted the bulk of their time and energy to producing and obtaining the means of subsistence for their families and superiors. Thus it was they who made possible the development of civilization.[1] The preferred subject of Russia's "new social history," the laboring classes rarely expressed themselves in writing and, as a result, are extremely difficult to bring to life. Scholars, forced to rely overwhelmingly on secondhand information reported by administrative, religious, and educated elites, can achieve a satisfactory understanding of this population only through painstaking specialized research. Even after decades of intensive archival work, historians of Russia have yet to reach a level of empirical knowledge comparable to that found in the historiographies of England, France, Germany, or the United States.

Historians of the unprivileged classes have demonstrated in rich detail the essential value of local and group studies, which can reconstruct the dynamics of social institutions, economic relationships, and cultural practices in individual households and larger communities. While the varied patterns of interaction and development discovered in these careful reconstructions serve to discourage imposing well-defined models on messy and murky realities, they cannot in themselves explain how society functioned as a *whole,* how it fit together and was integrated in its conceptual, administrative, economic, social, and cultural dimensions. That there was no idea of society as an abstract entity before the late eighteenth century does not in any way negate the existence of a social order that can be defined *functionally.*[2] One way to overcome the confusion and contradictory results produced by micro- and macrolevel investigations is to focus on the intersection of these two realms of experience, on the interfacing of immediate and particular with more distant and formalized relationships.[3] Because of the difficulty in drawing general conclusions from countless microrealities, this chapter does not directly explore the psychologies and mentalities of the common people, as expressed in the intimate spheres of everyday life. It presumes neither to know what went on in the heads of peasants and workers nor to understand the thoughts and feelings of husbands, wives, fathers, mothers, and children, who left few accounts of their experiences and reactions to events. Rather, it is concerned with the sum of the parts as the whole, with the broad integrated framework of society in the abstract, and with the parameters of individual and community lives.

PEASANTS

In 1897, Russia's first-ever empirewide census identified 84 percent of the male population of fifty European provinces as peasants. Although the census included in this category single householders *(odnodvortsy),* state armorers, Caucasian mountain peoples, veterans, colonists, and Cossacks, as well as most non-Russian minorities *(inorodtsy)* of the eastern and southeastern borderlands, there is no question that at the dawn of the twentieth century the overwhelming majority of tsarist subjects remained agrarian.[4] That segment of the population described by historians as "peasants," lawmakers called "rural inhabitants." This is no simple semantic discrepancy. Throughout most of the imperial period, official categories of free farmers incorporated a variety of state peasants and semiprivileged lower-class agriculturalists, but did not include privately owned serfs, who came under the jurisdiction of noble landlords. In 1857–1858, the tenth revision identified 49 percent of male peasants as serfs, 46 percent as state peasants, and 4 percent as appanage peasants belonging to the royal family.[5] Although the emancipation of 1861 did much to erase the sharp legal distinction between former serfs and free peasants, important differences remained, and at no time did the official designation "peasant" necessarily denote farmer or even agricultural worker. In addition, rural inhabitants, state peasants, private serfs, and former serfs all occupied a broad spectrum of unofficial statuses, ranging from millionaire entrepreneurs and a "serf intelligentsia" to the most impoverished laborers and abused domestic servants.[6]

Rural Russia's consistent ability to defy uniform standards of definition and measurement revealed the resilience and vitality of peasant institutions. Precisely because peasant "ways of seeing"[7] were so diverse and variable, and because many identifiable features of village culture were also found in other social milieus, it is important to view these institutions dynamically, as process. In various forms, the patriarchal values characteristic of patrilineal family relations existed at all levels of society, extending from the throne to the village hut.[8] Peasants also labored in a variety of geographical and economic environments, participating in agricultural, commercial, protoindustrial,[9] and industrial forms of production, both rural and urban. When one focuses on how peasants functioned in the greater economic, social, and political order, it quickly becomes apparent that the notion of village society as an isolated and insulated "little community"[10] is problematic, except perhaps in connection with "survival strategies" and communal self-government. Peasants may have formed little communities, which they effectively and fiercely defended and preserved, but these communities developed in direct relation to the "big community" of official society. To highlight these interactions, the following analysis focuses on two themes: (1) the pragmatic malleability of the boundaries and institutions defining imperial peasant societies; and (2) the relationship of individual peasants and rural communities to the larger formal and informal structures of economy, society, and state.

Family and Community

M. M. Gromyko defines peasant culture in functional terms as "the totality of the results of knowledge about nature and society," including what can be understood "by artistic means." Noting that specific customs and beliefs may lose their original purpose over time, she calls for local studies of concrete historical situations and urges scholars to examine the various components of peasant culture in the aggregate.[11] Edward L. Keenan is close to Gromyko in describing peasant political culture and community norms as collective "wisdom based upon shared experience and expectations concerning human behavior."[12] In his view, the harsh environmental conditions of northeast Europe prevented the individual and the nuclear family from achieving self-suffi-ciency; consequently, in order to ensure physical survival, cohesive village in-stitutions and collegial patterns of decision making evolved to limit risk and maximize resources.[13] Stressing peasant self-exploitation, patriarchal famil-ism, and especially the household or family farm as the essential features of village life, Steven Hoch writes that "peasant goals in Russia were less to es-tablish freehold control over the land (as in France) than to establish distribu-tive mechanisms which reduced risk in an uncertain environment and limited the numbers of those most vulnerable to crisis by providing more equal access to productive assets."[14] The need to survive in Russia's dangerous and inhos-pitable climate thus produced a matrix of practices and relationships that co-hered to form the peasant commune, an institution nearly universal in its exis-tence, though by no means uniform in its organization.

Despite enormous variations, all peasant societies in Russia shared impor-tant cultural and institutional features.[15] The commune, whether organized on the basis of repartitional or hereditary land tenure, consisted of patriarchal households of one or more families. Each head of household, except in rare cases where the head was a woman,[16] voted in the village assembly, the locus of peasant self-government, which made basic economic, administrative, and judicial decisions affecting the community as a whole. Within the house-hold—variously described as a center of production, consumption, family con-tinuity, and social control—gender, age, material conditions, and occupational opportunities combined with marital and filial bonds to define labor functions, hierarchies, and emotional divisions. As long as the eldest adult male was not incapacitated, he wielded virtually absolute authority as head of the house-hold. All family members owed him unquestioning obedience and could nei-ther leave the village nor establish a separate homestead without his permis-sion. As the family's representative in village affairs, he also was responsible for controlling the behavior of his dependents. Sons, nephews, younger broth-ers, uncles, and unmarried daughters, sisters, and nieces who left to work in nearby towns remained theoretically under the patriarch's authority; without his approval, which was needed to obtain a passport, their absence from the village became illegal. Abused wives sometimes fled, sometimes received the village assembly's permission to leave a profligate husband, or in rare cases successfully petitioned church authorities for a divorce.[17] Married sons, en-couraged by their wives and perhaps also by their adult children, sometimes sought to separate from the extended household and become masters of their own conjugal domain. In most situations, however, the senior male exercised full control over several generations of family members either until his sons became grandparents or until his own death, when property divisions normally occurred. Succession to the headship was usually patrilineal, passing to the oldest son or, if there were no adult sons, to a younger brother; property, by contrast, belonged to the entire household and was distributed according to need and custom.

Nineteenth-century ethnographic descriptions of rural society record lurid

details of infanticide, wife beating, sexual abuse of daughters-in-law, and conflicts among brothers, nephews, and uncles—all indicative of the economic
pressures and patriarchal hierarchies governing peasant life. Wives clearly
were subordinate to husbands, and daughters and daughters-in-law were at the
mercy of both. Yet women still possessed personal property and enjoyed considerable authority by virtue of their essential productive and reproductive duties, which included bearing and caring for children, performing field work,
raising small livestock, cultivating kitchen gardens, carrying water, working
for wages, preparing meals, producing food products, clothes, and other handicraft items for sale and household use, and generally overseeing the organization of home and hearth. In some special circumstances, women, particularly
those with male children, fulfilled the functions of deceased or absent husbands, and in individual cases they participated in the village assembly (not always with voting rights) in place of the missing spouse. The ability of women
to survive and occasionally thrive on their own or as heads of households during their husbands' absence—a phenomenon that became more visible as increasing numbers of late imperial peasants left the fields for work in factories—illustrated the pragmatic flexibility of village institutions.

The biological cycles and vicissitudes experienced by a family, together
with the behavior and occupations of its adult members, determined economic
functions and position within the household and village community. Too
many young children, too many female children, the presence of elderly parents, or too few able-bodied adults entitled to land allotments could undermine
a family's subsistence. Some weak households became extinct, as individual
members left home voluntarily or found themselves excluded and ostracized;
other households received assistance from the commune or landlord. Redivi-
sions of land, the adoption of heirs, ritualized forms of mutual aid and cooperative labor *(pomoch')*, and subsidies for orphans, widows, single women, the
aged, the disabled, and the indigent promoted village cohesion and physical
security. The extent and form of these measures varied: cooperative labor was
not always available as a form of social welfare, and not all needy persons
were considered worthy of help. At times, assistance was forthcoming only after the intervention of landlords, state officials, and clergy.[18] Whether a household prospered, survived, or completely disappeared depended on chance circumstances, material conditions, individual personalities, and collective
behavior. Families, rural communities, and landlords—and after 1864 *zemstvo*
assemblies—performed vital welfare functions, but their efforts could not
guarantee stability and continuity for all.

Even when it contained multiple or divided villages, the peasant commune
was a community that met the needs of its members—including some who
lived outside the framework of the patrilineal family—by providing essential
welfare and organizing cooperative labor. In addition, it served as the basic administrative unit through which the state and noble master exercised varying
degrees of coercion and control.[19] Official statistics from 1905 indicate that in
fifty European provinces, 77 percent of peasants belonged to repartitional

communes that maintained a customary and statutory right to redivide arable fields periodically, based on the number of male souls, husband-wife work teams, or persons per household. Communal tenure was nearly universal in the mid-Volga, lake, trans-Volga, Volga-Don, southern steppe, northern, central, and Dnepr-Don regions (with the exception of Poltava and Chernigov provinces). Hereditary possession prevailed in parts of Siberia and the Urals and in the non-Russian western borderlands (for example, in the Baltics, Belarus, Ukraine, and Bessarabia, excluding the provinces of Mogilev and Vitebsk). Even in these areas, the commune continued to regulate agricultural production, allocate common resources (such as the use of pastures, meadows, forests, ponds, and mills), and distribute the burden of taxes, feudal dues, rents, and military conscription.[20]

The origins of repartitional and hereditary tenure are far from certain. Historians believe that communal farming practices arose in areas where land became scarce due to population growth or where the extension of a landlord's authority brought new obligations and exactions. State demands generated similar results, although in most settled areas noble or church proprietary rights would have preceded any effective governmental presence. In Siberia, where the manorial system did not develop and old settlers held large amounts of land, the government actively replaced individual with communal ownership from the mid-eighteenth to the mid-nineteenth centuries and encouraged repartitions during the 1890s.[21] Although Siberian peasant communes also carried out repartitions as early as the 1780s, there was no significant development in this direction until the nineteenth century.[22] Evolution from individual to group forms of tenure is consistent with the predominance of patrilineal succession[23] to the headship of the household and with seignorial and governmental reliance on collective responsibility for the fulfillment of all monetary, labor, and military obligations. Even the custom of land repartitioning was not entirely alien to principles of hereditary tenure; redistributions were temporary, and when circumstances changed, every household could "repossess" land that previously had been "appropriated."[24] In some areas, the repartitional commune eventually succumbed to private property and "modern" capitalistic development; in others, it was the more recent institution imposed by state decree or in response to economic necessity.

Eclectic farming practices and forms of landownership represented ongoing adaptations to geography and the sociopolitical order. The structure of the repartitional commune revealed a clear and close connection between collective arrangements and environmental conditions.[25] A study of seven late-nineteenth-century communes in the northern province of Arkhangel'sk, where there had been no estate system before emancipation and where no repartitions were recorded before the 1830s, illustrates the evolution of individual farmsteads, communal villages, and patterns of land use that were highly variable and dependent on environmental conditions. In this area, not all peasants enjoyed equal access to collective resources, not all households voting in communal assemblies actually held land allotments, and not all village residents belonged to the commune. In addition, individual farming coexisted with communal harvesting, carting of wood and manure, and aid in the event of theft, fire, marriage celebrations, births, and deaths. Together with general divisions of land, repartitional communes carried out partial redistributions and allowed individual households to arrange temporary exchanges of parcels. These flexible relationships, characterized by dynamic and complicated "resource management," at once determined and were in turn reinforced by the needs of specific families and communities.[26]

That peasant communes worked cooperatively and tended to present a collective face to administrative, economic, and educated elites did not preclude deep internal tensions. Families and communities were patriarchal, hierarchical, and socially differentiated. Peasants assumed that each member of the commune was entitled to a fair allotment of common resources, but fairness did not mean that all deserved equal shares or authority. The possession of land was not a right; it was conditional on the ability to work the soil effectively. In important ways, the community functioned as "an arena in which individual households or factions clashed and competed over access to communal resources, or, more often, over distribution of collective obligations: taxes, rents, and military conscription."[27] Local power structures that hinged upon wealth, kinship, and patron-client relations were concretized in elected communal officials and, on private estates, in generally appointed stewards or bailiffs.[28] During the first two decades of the nineteenth century, on the Lieven estate of Baki in the non-black earth province of Kostroma, two factions headed by the richest timber dealers practically controlled a commune of twelve villages. Poor households tended to provide recruits, sometimes losing their only adult male, because the "oligarchs" were able to purchase exemptions or substitutes for their own sons and for the barge workers they needed to transport timber. Access to forest resources also was unequal, as wealthier peasants bribed estate clerks to allow them to gather wood in excess of the prescribed amounts.[29]

In the years before emancipation, similar conditions prevailed on the Gagarins' prosperous black earth estate of Petrovskoe in Tambov province. Under the authority of a bailiff, estate officials violently abused field serfs, consistently supported senior males in domestic disputes, and—despite instructions from the landlord that recruits be taken from large families—used conscription to rid the commune of thieves, disobedient or undesirable individuals, and households with only one husband-wife work team *(tiaglo)*.[30] Bribery, patronage, a desire to settle old scores, and collective economic interests all combined to thwart seignorial and governmental desires that tax and conscription obligations be distributed equitably, over the maximum number of labor units. While the state and landlords tended to insist that entire villages shoulder the burdens of weaker members, with the goal of preserving and eventually elevating impoverished households, at least some communes preferred to exclude families and individuals who could not provide for themselves in order to reduce welfare obligations and tax liabilities and to reclaim land allotments and other resources for stronger, more independent members.

Nineteenth-century changes in the size of peasant households exposed ongoing conflicts between individual aspirations and family or community needs.[31] Throughout the imperial period, officials and masters assumed that large families were best equipped to pay taxes and rents, perform labor services, and provide recruits. Multigenerational extended families were likely to be better endowed with sons and hence also with allotment land, so that the loss of an adult male to the army would not spell economic ruin.[32] The patriarch generally upheld the authority of the commune, which in turn bolstered his power over dependents, yet in many cases it was the seignior who prevented family divisions. Illegal separations suggest that neither the household head nor the community necessarily accepted the restrictions of landlord and state. Communes permitted divisions when the village assembly believed that the new homesteads were economically sustainable; peasants used disguised divisions to rid themselves of orphans and the disabled or mentally ill; and heads of households, however reluctant they were to give up control over family members, were more likely to accommodate individual aspirations if a division could save a son or relative from the draft.[33] Beginning in the 1870s, official reports noted with alarm that divisions were on the rise, and a law of 1886 sought but failed to restrict the practice. The implications, extent, and speed of the reported upsurge in household separations remain unclear; not only did unauthorized divisions occur without the commune's consent, divided households sometimes continued to share land, farm buildings, tools, and livestock. The ability to live in a separate home, even while cultivating fields as an extended family, represented a significant, and perhaps sufficiently satisfying step toward greater independence for younger men and their wives. Regardless of governmental policy, peasant communities—or rather the patriarchs who controlled them—made their own decisions about living and working arrangements, and they did so for their own purposes, according to their own customs and personal proclivities.

Two deep-seated changes in the postemancipation countryside help to explain the apparent growth of nuclear families. The most immediate consequence of emancipation was to remove the seignior's authority over communal decisions. Given how little masters directly intervened in village affairs, however, if there was indeed a trend toward smaller units, it was most likely the result of increased migration, off-farm wages, and new economic opportunities in agriculture, trade, and industry, which made smaller families viable and thus permitted the satisfaction of long-suppressed individual aspirations within the framework of communal life.[34] By allowing greater personal choice, increased labor mobility and the creation of single-*tiaglo* households could only change community structures. Initially, migration buttressed patriarchal and communal authority through the removal of discontented and less deferential individuals. It promoted economic stability by allowing able-bodied adult men to contribute cash earnings to their village families and perhaps also purchase the land and tools needed to establish a separate household.

Over time, however, as women became heads of households in their husbands' absence, and as possibilities for employment outside the village expanded, it became easier for wives and children to defy the authority of husbands and parents. Traditional hierarchies of age and gender inevitably weakened when it became clear that women, children, young men, and various social misfits could successfully pursue alternative occupations beyond the local community.[35] These opportunities were not entirely new, but they had never before existed on such a large scale.

Peasant Society and Economic Development

There is abundant work describing the relationship of peasant society to the empirewide market, but recent advances in empirical knowledge have yet to produce a generalized understanding of the rural economy. One fundamental problem with almost any study of village life is that conditions documented for one place may not be documented for another.[36] The numerous microstudies needed to establish basic social and economic facts do not always add up to certainty about macrolevel developments. Given the present state of research and the vastness of the imperial lands, statistical studies measuring poverty, stratification, economic innovation, productivity, and demographic trends pertain primarily to local particularistic conditions. Larger realities also are discernible but lack universal applicability. Keeping both the micro- and macrospheres of experience in sight is crucial; while it may not produce definite answers to long-standing debates, it illuminates the patterns of change that affected peasant lives.

Although Russian agriculture was remarkably uniform in its emphasis on grain production, local processes of development, even within a single geographical area, could be strikingly different.[37] Historians have long divided agrarian society into three or more economic regions characterized by distinct forms and relations of production.[38] The central industrial region or non-black earth provinces served as the commercial and manufacturing center of European Russia; here quitrent *(obrok)* paid in money and kind defined serf-landlord relations, and peasant involvement in commercial farming and nonagricultural production was widespread. In the central agricultural region of black earth provinces, labor dues *(barshchina)* prevailed in the days of serfdom, and both before and after emancipation, peasants tended to be economically dependent on farming their allotments. To the south and southwest lay New Russia and Ukraine, where large-scale grain production for the domestic and international markets was highly evolved and where, in the postemancipation period, modernized plantations employing hired agricultural laborers dominated the agrarian scene.

Familiar images of the serf economy correspond most closely to conditions on estates in the central black earth and Volga provinces, where peasants performed labor services for the lord and supported themselves from their own allotments. Beginning in the mid-eighteenth century, relatively high yields, rising prices, and growing market demand encouraged serf owners to exploit their lands directly and to increase production by expanding the demesne.[39] Given the lack of technological innovation in the eighteenth and early nineteenth centuries, greater productivity depended on the ability to bring new fields under cultivation. Yet despite similar geographical and economic conditions in this heartland of servile labor, patterns of development varied significantly. Seigniors who lacked land reserves put their serfs on quitrent, and these peasants, like their counterparts in the northern provinces, were more likely to participate in nonagricultural activities. Some owners of prosperous farming estates also combined labor dues with quitrent payments, and peasants who worked the demesne continued to maintain outside sources of income.[40] On the Sheremetevs' central black earth estate of Rastorg (Kursk province), serfs grew hemp, which they sold in raw form or as woven sackcloth, and during the winter months they further supplemented their earnings with transport work.[41] The central industrial region was similarly diversified: in Tver province 60 percent of privately owned serfs reportedly worked for the demesne in 1858. Estate economies based on both labor services and quitrent existed in black and non-black earth areas, and in any of these settings peasant production for the market could be found. Clearly, the economic structures of the central industrial and central agricultural regions did not represent divergent paths of development but complemented and reinforced each other. Without the grain surpluses produced in the south, the expansion of rural manufacturing in the north might have been impossible. Whether the serf economy depended on farming or on trade and manufacturing, it was dynamically integrated into larger processes of market formation and specialization.[42]

The entrepreneurial achievements of millionaire serfs were notable, and while economic successes of such magnitude constituted exceptions, they nonetheless pointed to broader patterns of commercial and protoindustrial development. In the late eighteenth and early nineteenth centuries, serfdom accommodated and in some cases encouraged economic specialization and capitalist enterprise. Varied productive activities were characteristic of farming estates in the central agricultural region, but diversification was particularly pronounced in the non-black earth provinces, where peasants were more likely to pay quitrent than work the master's fields and where opportunities for earnings in commerce and industry were well established. Many peasants also obtained extra money as small-scale producers and petty traders who periodically traveled to rural markets and towns to hawk agricultural and handicraft goods. On the Lievens' Kostroma estate of Baki, peasants were self-sufficient in grain production but also heavily involved in nonfarming occupations. They worked as timber and horse traders, craftsmen, fishermen, and wage laborers, while maintaining a weekly fair where fish and baked goods were sold. The fact that Baki could feed itself is important, because it suggests that economic diversification resulted from opportunity and choice rather than agricultural vulnerability.[43]

Protoindustrial development, frequently concentrated around clusters of villages in parts of Moscow, Vladimir, Kostroma, Tver, Nizhnii Novgorod, and Iaroslav provinces, also revealed the economic vitality of rural society. In Nizhnii Novgorod province during the 1850s, over 15,000 peasants on two Sheremetev estates worked in metalworking operations that produced locks, knives, scissors, and surgical instruments. Similarly, in four districts of Vladimir and Kostroma provinces, rural cotton weaving and dyeing enterprises employed more than 135,000 peasants in the mid-1850s. Textile production, the most widespread industry in the countryside, displayed a wide range of organizational forms. Each stage of flax production and linen weaving could be found in single households, whereas cotton and silk weaving depended on capitalist structures such as the importation of raw materials and the expansion of wage labor. Of particular importance was the development of factory-related cottage production (the "putting out" system), which often arose independently of state and landlord in response to interregional trade in raw materials and semifinished goods.[44]

Protoindustrial capitalist production for the market was distinct from but also overlapped with the manufacture of decorative, household, and religious objects for personal and local consumption. Across the empire, entire villages and individual artisans and artists were famed for the quality and beauty of their work. Their ranks included communities and craftspeople whose connections to merchants, towns, monasteries, and seasonal fairs drew them into more centralized market relations, as well as legions of specially trained serfs who produced luxury items for the manor houses and pleasure palaces of wealthy nobles. Lords and peasants benefited from the commercial exploitation of these valuable skills and in some cases extraordinary talents. Potentially, the seignorial economy served the needs of large-scale serf industrialists and traders whose prosperous masters provided capital, legal guarantees, natural resources, and a controlled labor force. The mingling of "traditional" and "modern" manufacturing survived into the early twentieth century. Some handicrafts for both noble and peasant consumption died out or were appropriated by elite entrepreneurs and art exhibiters; others flourished within the framework of the changing agrarian economy. Small-scale industry remained viable, buttressed by better and cheaper semifinished products—for example, cloth, iron, and timber—produced in mechanized factories.[45] The relationship between traditional crafts, protoindustrial cottage production, and the modern factory, like that between farming and manufacturing, was complementary and interactive.[46]

It is virtually impossible to measure the macroeconomic significance of peasant trade or protoindustrial development. According to one estimate for the 1850s, cottage production in non-black earth provinces may have accounted for 23 percent of Russia's total industrial output.[47] Whatever the statistical realities, each protoindustrial web could involve hundreds of villages and thousands of peasants who, if they did not work directly in manufacturing, might be employed in transportation and other related occupations as stevedores, carpenters, and blacksmiths. The village of Mstera in Vladimir province exemplified the potential for growth. By the mid-nineteenth century, Mstera contained no full-time farmers, and although the villagers (not unlike many townspeople) continued to keep milk cows and gardens, already in the mid-eighteenth century and continuing into the twentieth, the village produced icons that were peddled all over Russia. An illustrating business was established in 1844, followed by a lithography shop in 1858, and later by a paper mill on a nearby estate. Thus a small operation that initially hired girls and women to color purchased monochrome lithographs helped to generate a more complex, multifaceted production and distribution network.[48] While serfdom certainly thwarted individual entrepreneurs and foreclosed specific lines of development, it did not entirely prevent personal economic success or commercialization and industrialization.

The emancipation settlement of 1861 ensured that peasants would retain access to land resources, but it reduced their prereform allotments significantly and required them to redeem their plots at rates well above actual market value. In some villages, peasants may have received more land than they held before emancipation, while in others redemption payments exceeded prereform quitrents.[49] Nor were the former serfs immediately freed from obligations to their masters. They continued to fulfill labor or monetary dues on the basis of written agreements until 1881, when redemption became obligatory for all.[50] Once the redemption process began, the government compensated nobles for land assigned to peasant communes, which then became responsible for making annual payments to the treasury.[51] While emancipation clearly did not undermine the agrarian economy, its financial and material terms were hardly favorable to the twenty-two million liberated serfs. All were saddled with new forms of monetary dues, and those who faced reduced ratios of land to population were forced to rent additional fields at inflated rates. In some areas, this led to economic and social arrangements (for example, sharecropping) not unlike the relations of serfdom. Just as peasants could not survive on the plots they now possessed, landlords could not continue to farm their estates without the labor power of their former serfs.[52]

Most disturbing from the peasant point of view, especially given the rapid population growth of the late nineteenth and early twentieth centuries, the emancipation statute allowed seigniors to "cut off" allotment land customarily held by the village and to curtail rights to valuable nonarable resources. Peasants continued to plant in the landlords' fields, graze livestock in their pastures, fish in their rivers, and hunt and gather fuel in their forests; but now such use was either illegal (fines or prison sentences were faced if caught) or dependent on labor contracts and lease agreements. In the eyes of the former serfs, the economic provisions of 1861 dramatically undercut their new legal freedoms. They were forced to pay for fields that, in their view, rightfully belonged to them and for access to resources that in the past had been readily available, even if regulated and restricted. In denying them the maximum allotments allowed by the emancipation legislation, seigniors deprived these peasants of land that, again in their view, they should have received.[53] Finally, any moral obligation that the masters once had felt to assist peasants in case of crop failure or other natural disaster evaporated. The universal unpredictability of farming incomes, the financial burden of redemption, local *zemstvo* levies, indirect consumption taxes, and the Petrine capitation—abolished in European Russia only in 1883–1887 and in Siberia only in 1899 [54]—seriously hampered the peasants' ability to save and thus limited the purchase of nonallotment lands. Conditions improved somewhat with the opening of the Peasant Land Bank in 1883 and the organization of credit cooperatives beginning in the 1890s. Still, in the final decades of tsarist rule, it also became evident that the perceived injustices of the emancipation settlement consistently informed and eventually radicalized the social attitudes of peasants. [55]

Although it coincided with a period of accelerated growth, the emancipation did not constitute a fundamental break in Russia's economic development. The basic indicators of progress were all present in the prereform era: technological advances in industry, small-scale manufacturing, regional specialization, wage labor, and corporate business organization. [56] Nor did the reinforcement of the commune's authority, manifested in collective responsibility for redemption and in the legal binding of the individual to the community under the new cantonal *(volost')* administration, prevent steady agricultural and industrial expansion throughout the nineteenth century. This was so despite the persistence of the three-field method of farming, which dominated among peasants in central Russia from the sixteenth century until the onset of forced collectivization in the Soviet period. [57] In the three-field system, two parcels were planted and one remained fallow in a given year; in addition, most communities also divided their fields into strips that were apportioned among individual households. During the late nineteenth and early twentieth centuries, outside observers viewed the communal system of strip cultivation as inherently backward and inefficient. Collective controls, it was believed, stifled individual initiative, limited profit-oriented commercialization, and thwarted technical innovation, causing stagnation and impoverishment. By the time of the 1905 revolution, official and intellectual elites of all political persuasions argued either that the commune was fundamentally flawed and hence an impediment to modern progress, or that it was disintegrating under the impact of capitalist development and hence a blighted source of human misery and suffering.

Recent scholarship shows that the realities of communal farming were considerably more complex and ambiguous than appeared to most contemporary commentators. Peasant economic strategies, like family and community structures, derived from the need to survive in a potentially dangerous and unpredictable environment. In its economic, social, and cultural functions, the commune was dynamic and adaptable. The division of arable land into strips provided members with parcels of equivalent quality and thus, peasants assumed, with a greater measure of security. According to some scholars, joint plowing facilitated the ability of each household to sow its fields and meant in effect that individual strips were farmed as "consolidated" plots, without, however, eliminating the wasteful pathways crisscrossing allotments. Although repartitions and collective decisions about land use clearly limited personal ambitions, not all resources and productive activities were subject to communal controls. Peasants who purchased private land and transferred their property to the repartitional commune did so in return for rights to common pastures, which they could not afford to maintain individually. Families owned their houses and garden plots and were free to dispose of the products of their labor without interference. Adult females also accumulated earnings from the sale of food products and handicrafts. Communal farming may not have encouraged individual profit making but neither did it prevent entrepreneurial success. Before and after emancipation, significant income differentials existed in all geographical regions and were especially pronounced in nonagricultural protoindustrial villages.[58] As economic institution and patriarchal social unit, the commune was never egalitarian; its purpose was to ensure not equality but continuity, security, and resource conservation.

It was precisely their shared means of survival that led peasants to attempt innovation. Slow change and cautious adjustment were ongoing features of peasant life. In the late nineteenth century, "modern" improvements in agricultural techniques arose within the communal framework, usually in the more economically diversified regions. Already in the 1870s, groups of communes in Moscow province began to plant grass on fallow lands. By the end of the century, multifield systems that rotated industrial or cereal crops with forage crops and cultivated grasses dominated in the northwest and Poland and were spreading in the central industrial and northern black earth area. Some communities introduced grass and clover after years of experimentation, others postponed innovations until all households were able to purchase the improved seeds, and still others designated special parcels outside the three-field system for growing fodder. Forage crops allowed peasants to support more livestock and thus increased the supply of manure, while roots and clover actually improved the fertility of the soil. Additional improvements included the production of potatoes, a nutritious supplement to peasant diets, and the use of farming tools with metal parts.[59] In the 1890s the agricultural sector consumed more of Russia's iron output than railroad construction. From the 1860s to 1911–1913, peasant grain yields grew 1.5 percent per annum.[60]

Beginning in 1906, the Stolypin land reforms sought to eliminate the commune and promote "modern" production by granting peasants title to their plots, allowing them to consolidate allotment parcels, and encouraging them to establish individualized farms separate from the collective.[61] Much to the government's chagrin, when peasants petitioned to rearrange their holdings, they generally did not intend to leave the commune but used the provisions of the Stolypin legislation to continue experiments with new methods of land redistribution already begun prior to the reforms. These advances included consolidating parcels and reducing the number of strips, exchanging or dividing common fields, disentangling plots intermixed with the holdings of other landowners, and in general working out intercommune land settlements. As undeclared "modernizers," peasants carried out inexpensive, small-scale improvements that represented pragmatic responses to material constraints and the opportunity or need to make deliberate choices. Although the changes were piecemeal, sometimes harmful, and at the time of the revolution, did not add up to fundamental "progress" in the system of peasant farming, they indicated effective interaction with local conditions and the demands of a growing domestic market.[62]

It is unclear whether small producers or individuals who held land in private tenure were more likely to initiate change, but when communes adopted new methods, they spread more rapidly over larger areas. In the postemancipation countryside, communes punished members who failed to comply, forced peasants to use their manure for fertilizer instead of selling it, and limited the planting of flax, which required enormous work and which, without proper fertilization, crop rotation, and use of fallow, exhausted the soil.[63] In addition, they drained swamps, irrigated fields, and cleared land—all labor-intensive projects that individuals could not afford to undertake—and pooled resources to cut timber or rent quarries, bogs, mills, and fields. Independent innovators also received rewards; in repartitions they were compensated monetarily, allowed to keep their plots, or granted similarly improved parcels. Because direct assistance from landlords tended to disappear after emancipation, collective resources, including support for welfare and education, became ever more crucial for survival. Even noncommunal peasants joined with neighbors to mow hay and share meadows, forests, and pastures. Given Russia's limited infrastructure and credit facilities, communes sometimes could innovate more easily than individual peasants; and as commune members, individual peasants could better absorb the calamities of climate, fire, illness, and untimely death.[64]

The commune's willingness to accommodate individual enterprise and its ability to adapt to economic change were nowhere more visible than in the growing importance of labor migration.[65] Because the farming, protoindustrial, and modern industrial sectors of the economy were so closely intertwined, it is difficult to determine whether off-farm work indicated choice, ambition, and opportunity, or necessity, poverty, and crisis. Both situations existed, and both were the result of local and personal circumstances. There is no question that Russian peasants lost land in emancipation—a loss that in individual cases represented the difference between economic security and dangerous marginality. It also is possible that in some places, inflated redemption rates and new *zemstvo* levies increased the overall weight of taxation and hence the need for cash. Although the elimination of prereform feudal dues, including labor services and payments in money or kind, may have neutralized the impact of greater direct taxation, redemption payments required cash, and peasants whose reduced allotments forced them to rent noble lands sometimes remained effectively subject to "servile" obligations. It therefore is conceivable that growing migration resulted from shortages of cash and land, which could be overcome by working off the farm or selling agricultural and handicraft products on the commercial market.

Even assuming that intensified economic pressure caused by emancipation sometimes forced peasants to seek outside employment, there is convincing evidence that the cash income it provided also improved the well-being of individuals, households, and entire villages. Peasants induced by poverty to work off the farm boosted the local economy and helped to sustain the rural commune. Both their earnings and their absence enhanced the resources available to the home community. Migrants paid departure fees to cover their financial obligations, sent wages to their families in the village, and on occasion transferred their allotments to the collective. In return, any relatives left behind could rely on the commune for basic security, and migrants themselves could reclaim a place in local society—including access to collective resources—in times of illness, disability, old age, unemployment, and political upheaval.[66] Outside wages also allowed peasants to buy land and livestock, build larger and cleaner homes, and adopt urban consumer culture. By the end of the nineteenth century, observers in the central industrial region noticed suggestive changes in consumption patterns: the appearance of fashionable dress, the drinking of tea, and the use of beds, candles, and samovars. In the early years of the twentieth century, the provinces of Iaroslav, Tver, and Kostroma registered both the highest levels of out-migration to work in urban centers and the largest proportion of individually owned peasant land.[67] Between 1883 and 1914, over two million peasants purchased land with assistance from the Peasant Land Bank.[68] The status of women also may have risen in areas of substantial male out-migration: reportedly, female rates of literacy increased and matriarchs enjoyed greater independence. Unmarried women could improve their standing as well, with earnings in towns and factories that allowed them to escape rural life entirely (not always a path to happiness and prosperity) or provide themselves with a dowry and a position in the village.[69] Not all women benefited from the absence of their husbands; the assumption of male agricultural responsibilities also could lead to mental and physical breakdown.[70]

Given the significant movement between the countryside and towns throughout the eighteenth and early nineteenth centuries, growing numbers of late imperial migrants pointed less to a change in the direction of development than to a broadening of its effects. Although during the 1890s over six million peasants in European Russia left their villages for outside employment, the vast majority preserved their ties to the countryside and eventually returned home.[71] Nor did industrial employment necessarily mean flight from rural life. In the early years of the twentieth century, 65 percent of workers and 65 percent of factories in the non-black earth region were still located outside urban centers.[72] The impact of off-farm work on peasant survival strategies and cultural values was in most places slow-moving, incremental, and often imperceptible. The one large regional exception was right-bank (western) Ukraine, where beginning in the 1860s capitalist plantations based on wage labor produced a peasant "proletariat" and radically transformed the agrarian social order.[73] The cumulative effects of out-migration, off-farm labor, and new nonagricultural occupations were potentially dramatic, but the question of when, where, how, and whether peasants experienced any momentous or disorienting change remains open. Such outcomes were most likely limited to particular localities and to the small minority of migrants who became fully urbanized hereditary proletarians. Even the permanent flight of a defiant wife, daughter, or son did not fundamentally alter the patterns of village life, at least not in any broad societal sense. Only after several generations of both evolutionary and revolutionary transformation would the underlying structures of rural society become characteristically modern.

In late-nineteenth-century conditions of rapid "modernization" (characterized by capitalist market integration, industrial development, urbanization, demographic growth, state-sponsored education, and the spread of scientific medicine), "traditional" peasant society remained viable. Its strength derived not from insularity or the ability to prevent change, but from the successful incorporation of new economic, social, and cultural experiences into existing relationships and customs. Russian peasants possessed extensive firsthand knowledge of entrepreneurship and wage labor, yet massive urbanization—the most telling marker in the transition from "traditional" to "modern" society—was still a long way off. The complexity of late imperial productive development helps to explain why it is so difficult to evaluate the economic condition of peasants, even allowing for significant local and regional variations. Most official and intellectual commentators painted a dismal picture of a collapsing agrarian economy and dissolving peasant institutions, and for decades images of crisis and despair dominated discussions of prerevolutionary society. In recent times, however, historians and economists have modified this characterization by directly examining specific communities and series of economic and demographic data. Although their conclusions cannot yet be accepted as universally valid across the vast Russian empire, they have shown without a doubt that there was no evidence of pervasive patterns of impoverishment or disintegration. Change there clearly was; massively disorienting crisis there clearly was not.[74]

Original studies of indirect tax receipts, land purchases, and grain production, consumption, and marketing all suggest that on average late imperial peasants did not suffer from growing poverty caused by economic stagnation and that some actually may have experienced a rising standard of living. The exact meaning of these variables still is controversial.[75] Three factors suggest that growing revenues from consumption taxes did not always indicate greater prosperity: (1) the urban market was expanding and might account for the increase; (2) peasants who engaged in nonagricultural work were sometimes paid in consumer goods, such as sugar, soap, tobacco, vodka, grain, kerosene, and matches; and (3) changing market conditions may have induced peasants to purchase products previously made at home or considered unnecessary. If peasants spent less time producing handicrafts and more time farming, this development, like the increase in off-farm work, could signify either worsening or improving conditions. Nor did significant land purchases by peasants or overall growth in per capita grain output and retention provide adequate measures of economic well-being. Higher land prices and a shift in distribution from nobles to peasants revealed only that a "rising effective demand for farm land . . . was being exercised by one segment of the peasant population."[76] In the traditional agricultural center of central black earth and middle Volga provinces, where outside earnings often depended on plentiful harvests, per capita cereal output and livestock numbers actually declined from the 1880s until the First World War. The official view that growing arrears in redemption taxes represented economic crisis and an inability to pay is equally problematic: between 1886 and 1899, former serfs met 96 percent of the total redemption debt owed to the state. Whatever the implications of the aggregate economic patterns, the data needed to establish reliable indices of living standards—for example, comprehensive figures on real wages and personal or household incomes—simply do not exist for any period of imperial history.[77]

Despite good evidence for upward macroeconomic trends and for the absence of universal distress, regional fluctuations and local production crises still occurred, peasants increasingly were unable to subsist solely from farming, and intensified methods of cultivation could over the long term prove detrimental to particular areas. Agricultural dynamism was most visible in Ukraine, the north Caucasus, the Urals, Siberia, and the southern steppe. In the Moscow and St. Petersburg regions, the Baltic provinces, and the northern non-black earth belt, declines in grain production were cushioned by industrial development, market gardening, and livestock husbandry. In contrast to these areas of greater productivity and relative prosperity, the central black earth and middle Volga provinces suffered periodic crises and decreasing agricultural yields, without any corresponding upsurge in manufacturing. A four-year production crisis, lasting from 1889 to 1892, contributed to the famine and cholera epidemic of 1891–1892, which hit these provinces the hardest. A similar concentration of four relatively low harvests, also related to climatic conditions, occurred in 1905–1908. Because emancipation left the former serfs of the farming center with reduced land resources and a burdensome debt, they endured still another economic blow between 1875 and 1895, when international grain prices fell as rents and land prices were rising.[78] It is doubtful that the international grain market affected all Russian peasants in the same way. Continuing crop failures generated higher prices, which benefited entrepreneurial peasants with surpluses but spelled ruin for underemployed rural laborers, including those who continued to farm their own plots.[79] Economic stagnation punctuated by severe crises tended to be geographically and socially limited, yet even in the most dynamic and productive conditions, cereal output fluctuated from year to year. Although economic diversification made significant strides in the nineteenth and early twentieth centuries, peasant grain production continued to dominate the agricultural economy.[80] While growth and even prosperity did not guarantee long-term security and predictability, neither was famine solely an economic phenomenon. When administrative incompetence and political considerations prevented the implementation of effective relief measures, "marginal subsistence" easily became hunger and mortality.[81]

Peasants and the Legal Order

With the exception of nobles, clergy, and retired soldiers, all imperial subjects were formally registered in and legally bound to specific communities, which were in turn subordinated to particular administrative domains *(vedomstva;* sing., *vedomstvo)* or in the case of serfs, to private landlords. Peasants also paid the capitation, remained liable for conscription, and delivered feudal dues to the landlords, monastery, or state in money, kind, or labor. State peasants, who enjoyed the most desirable terms, owed a fixed annual rent to the treasury, readily obtained passports to work outside the village, and (in the first half of the nineteenth century) received rights to engage in wholesale and retail trade and to own factories and unpopulated lands.[82] At any moment the government might demand that they resettle or provide labor for public works, but they were able, with much greater ease than serfs, to change their official social classification by acquiring specialized skills or entering a taxed urban category. In addition, they possessed limited access to state schools and thus to the rewards of the civil service, from which serfs were expressly, though in practice not completely, barred.[83] Catherine II included state peasants in the Legislative Commission of 1767–1768 and herself drafted a "Project on Structuring the Free Village Inhabitants." Only partially enacted in Ukraine, the project illustrated Catherine's belief that state peasants, in contrast to serfs, belonged to the corporative "constitutional" order envisioned in her provincial reforms and charters to the nobility and the towns.[84]

At the time of emancipation less than half of all peasants and just over 37 percent of the total male population were privately owned serfs, their numbers were declining,[85] and although they lacked a civic identity, they nonetheless possessed significant legal rights. The Law Code *(Ulozhenie)* of 1649 firmly established serfdom as a formal institution; yet in binding the peasant to the land rather than to the person of the lord—a step taken later by the Petrine inheritance law of 1714—it stopped short of defining the precise relationship between master and serf.[86] Two features of that relationship—the "right" of peasants to complain against masters and the authority of landlords to exile serfs to Siberia—illuminated the malleable social bonds and ambiguous legal boundaries defining the institution of serfdom. Although a decree of 1700 forbade all imperial subjects to address the emperor directly, except to appeal decisions rendered in the course of formal judicial proceedings, popular refusal to abide by these prohibitions led to new legislation, which in 1765 prescribed punishments for violators, including proprietary peasants, and thus implied that serfs were permitted to petition the ruler through the proper channels. The assumption that serfs enjoyed a right to complain was consistent with seventeenth-century practice and earlier Muscovite laws, though it clearly contradicted the 1649 Law Code, which forbade denunciations against a master in any court or state office, except in cases of treason. When news of the Legislative Commission stimulated an alarming upsurge in peasant petitions, Catherine II's government issued still another decree, repeating the provisions of

1649 and 1765.[87] After the 1767 ruling, peasants continued to complain against seigniors, encouraged by specific laws appropriately cited in their petitions and perhaps also by twenty judicial prosecutions conducted against cruel landlords during Catherine's reign.[88]

Similar legal uncertainties abounded in connection with the seignorial right to exile serfs. A law of 1760 allowed landlords to send peasants to Siberia in return for recruit quittances; the purpose was not to bolster the master's authority but to serve the government's economic, administrative, and military needs by promoting settlement.[89] Local officials and free urban and rural communities exercised comparable powers. Abrogated in November 1773 in connection with the Pugachev revolt, but evidently restored in 1775, the landlords' authority to exile peasants under age forty-five was explicitly reaffirmed in 1787. A law of 1802 once again halted the local reception of deported serfs, and an imperial ukase of 1811 made clear that only the courts could impose exile to Siberia. A seignior, by contrast, could without trial sentence peasants to detention in workhouses and houses of correction for minor theft, drunkenness, and "willfulness."[90] This legal precision disappeared in the 1820s, when Alexander I permitted landlords to bypass the courts and exile serfs of all ages by applying directly to provincial boards of government.[91] For close to a century, the laws regulating the imposition of exile by serf owners remained changeable and contradictory. While one should not underestimate the abusive arbitrariness these laws encouraged, seigniors certainly enjoyed neither absolute authority nor unlimited powers of punishment.

It is unclear how administrators implemented the rules defining landlord-serf relations or treated peasants who submitted illegal petitions. Much depended on local officials, who could themselves be serf owners and whose actions might never be reviewed by higher authorities. Exposure of the abusive Daria Saltykova occurred only in the summer of 1762, after twenty-one petitions became waylaid in provincial bodies and the twenty-second one finally reached the hands of Catherine II.[92] During the eighteenth century, very few laws directly prescribed the mutual obligations of lords and serfs. In the decades leading up to emancipation, governmental interference in these relationships began to increase, culminating by 1861 in the removal of the seignior's explicit judicial and administrative powers.[93] A decree of 1773 forbade punishment with the knout in cases of petty theft, instructing landlords to punish their serfs with lashes instead. In addition, the 1775 provincial reform empowered governors to sequestrate and place under guardianship the estates of nobles who cruelly abused their peasants.[94] The two most significant legal changes in the prereform period were a decree of 1797, limiting labor services to three days a week, and another of 1845, restricting the physical punishment of peasants (masters still could send them to the army or to exile in Siberia) to four months of imprisonment or forty blows with the rod.[95] Although there is little evidence of effective enforcement, all peasants—both state and proprietary—were to some extent able, on the basis of formal laws, to negotiate their position in the social order.

Archival records show that during the eighteenth century and the first half of the nineteenth, peasants of all categories regularly attempted to use the courts and laws to lighten feudal obligations, reallocate the distribution of collective resources, demand assistance from the commune, protest cruel treatment, and seek emancipation. In petitions submitted from the 1720s to the mid-1770s, monastery and proprietary peasants requested moratoriums on new requisitions *(pobory)*, reduced dues in money and kind, an end to the exactions of traveling officials in need of quarters, and unlimited access to passports for persons who left the village in search of work. In addition, they expressed a desire for emancipation and complained of excessive and illegal obligations, hostile officials, and arbitrary landlords. Their statements contained repeated references to the Law Code of 1649, the inheritance law of 1714, the 1722 Table of Ranks, prohibitions against the ownership of serfs by non-nobles, Catherine's Instruction to the Legislative Commission, and a variety of statutes and legislative acts, including a series of Petrine decrees defining the obligations of state peasants. This is no surprise, given that Peter's church reforms had placed ecclesiastical resources under governmental supervision, and that privately owned serfs sometimes shared the same village with state and crown peasants who lived under different social and economic regimes.[96] In the second half of the century, poor peasants and retired soldiers in state villages also invoked legislated norms to obtain land allotments and direct economic aid. Whether peasants themselves wrote the petitions or relied on the assistance of scribes, clerks, and priests, they consistently cited the same laws, and they did so from geographically dispersed communities that had no known contacts with one another. Drawing upon the abstract formulations of absolutist legislation, they demanded justice, material assistance, and official protection from arbitrariness and abuse.[97]

Both formal law and judicial practice allowed peasants of all statuses to sue on strictly prescribed grounds. State peasants, because they were freemen, enjoyed access to special courts and also served with nobles on the elective conscience courts and lower land courts created by the Catherinean reforms.[98] The most telling suits brought by serfs in district courts involved demands for emancipation on grounds of unlawful servitude. The numbers and outcomes remain uncertain, but these cases reveal much about the relationship of peasants to formal institutions of justice and about the ambiguities of serfdom as a "system." Although legislation from the 1750s prohibited the ownership of populated estates and serfs by virtually all non-nobles, it took decades to establish relatively strict enforcement, and as late as 1847, the government issued new legislative measures to address continuing violations and abuses.[99] Laws of 1816 and 1823 allowed serfs who were illegally possessed by non-nobles to sue for freedom. These statutes generated so many petitions and caused so much confusion that in 1837 and 1840 the State Council forbade all such suits from peasants currently residing with nobles. Litigation demanding emancipation also came from illegitimate soldiers' children, who belonged to the military domain but could not always escape the clutches of local landowners, and from persons who fell into servile status as a result of economic distress or employment based on relations of indenture.[100] A study of thirty cases heard in the Perm district court during the reigns of Alexander I and Nicholas I revealed only four that were decided in favor of the serf; all of these involved the illegitimate children of women who belonged to the state domain. Among the rejected suits, many were based on claims of hardship and seignorial abuse, including excessive work burdens and unjust or life-threatening punishments. Authorities were instructed to take measures to prevent such abuses, but the courts imposed no punishment on the landlords and in general did not treat moral issues as legitimate grounds for emancipation. Persons legally entitled to freedom also repeatedly failed in their suits for a variety of reasons, most notably, local misunderstandings about the law, expiration of the statute of limitations (sometimes caused by a landowner's success in delaying proceedings), and an inability to document descent from a free ancestor. Others were dissuaded from seeking liberation by their masters' use of intimidation, fines, and seizures of property.[101] Between 1835 and 1858, the Senate reviewed 15,153 cases of unlawful enserfment or illegal bondage, and the provincial *(guberniia)* courts handled more than twenty thousand suits.[102] There is little evidence that serfs could sue successfully; but effective or not, the suits showed how peasants interpreted the laws broadly for their own purposes.

The desire of peasants for freedom—defined explicitly as freedom from obligations to the landlord and state—appeared time and again in response to specific laws, the provisions of which were embellished by rumors and aroused expectations. Legislation of 1829 and 1831 permitted state peasants to escape regular military conscription by settling in the strategically important north Caucasus. Serfs also seized the opportunity to flee into the area, and local officials mistakenly registered them. The government's long-standing toleration of runaways in borderlands must have been familiar to these peasants, who conveniently interpreted the legal prescriptions. Peasants used an 1847 decree in similar fashion; the law granted serfs belonging to estates sold at public auction the right to redeem themselves with land, and on this basis they petitioned for liberation from new masters, alleged to be exploitative and repressive. Finally, in 1854, when the autocracy appealed for volunteers to join a naval militia to serve in the Crimean War, peasants once again employed imperial law in a search for emancipation. Although the legislation specified that upon discharge volunteers would return to servile status, serfs responded to the call on the assumption that they would be freed after three years of service and also would avoid much-dreaded conscription into the regular army for twenty years, a fate that actually did bring legal emancipation.[103] The peasants' yearning for emancipation was consistent with their understanding of legal statutes and official justice. In accordance with tsarist legislation, they expected fairness, reasonable obligations, and protection from abuse, and they loosely applied laws "to achieve what seemed possible in a given situation."[104]

Serf involvement in judicial institutions is crucial for understanding the

well-publicized issue of "legal consciousness" in the postemancipation countryside. The ongoing and direct relationship between state law and village customs raises questions about the dualistic notion of a fundamental conflict between elite and popular values. Customary practices and expectations certainly
affected encounters with formal authority, yet already in the seventeenth century, peasants possessed detailed knowledge of specific legislation affecting
their status and employed this information to offset the abuses that serfdom and
economic subordination so readily permitted. In the early eighteenth century,
monastery peasants in central Russia occasionally appealed to administrative
superiors to mediate internal disputes and to overturn the terms of communal
repartitions.[105] Peasant attitudes toward tsarist justice exhibited the same pragmatic flexibility characteristic of family and community relations. If politics is
defined as the exercise and negotiation of power, then the relationship of peasants to the state-imposed social order, including their use of laws and courts,
constituted a form of political behavior that offers significant insight into the
massive societal mobilization of the early twentieth century.

The late imperial perception of bifurcated legal cultures resulted not from
any new interaction between two essentially autonomous spheres of elite law
and popular custom but from the introduction of new judicial arrangements
and channels of administrative integration in the Great Reforms. Officially
sanctioned and legally regulated elective courts had existed for state peasants
since the reign of Catherine II; the Kiselev reforms of 1837–1841 reorganized
these bodies, which the emancipation acts again restructured and extended to
former serfs. After the reforms of the 1860s, all peasants became subject to
cantonal administrative units and courts of elected peasant judges, who rendered decisions on the basis of customary and statute law. Together with informal village and formal cantonal bodies, peasants also had access to district
boards for peasant affairs (until 1889), justice of the peace courts and assemblies (until 1889), land captains (from 1889), district assemblies (from 1889),
circuit courts (with or without juries), and higher appellate courts and administrative bodies. From 1906, all rural commoners came under the cantonal
courts, which in 1912 were linked to the general judicial system under the authority of the Senate. In thirty-five provinces, superior rural courts composed
of peasant judges and revived justice of the peace courts and assemblies appeared to hear appeals from the cantonal courts. Given the availability of multiple legal processes, reviewed separately by the Senate and by the ministries
of justice and internal affairs, postemancipation peasants chose whichever
court appeared convenient and accessible, least harmful, and most likely to
work for them. While most reportedly tried to avoid officials and formal
courts, some appealed village decisions to cantonal courts and cantonal decisions to boards for peasant affairs, land captains, district assemblies, superior
rural courts, and justice of the peace courts and assemblies.[106]

Historians have barely begun to examine how imperial courts functioned or
what their proceedings reveal about social relationships and peasant attitudes.
The courts were crucial to the social order because they represented an arena

where formal and informal structures met, where peasants individually and collectively intersected with official society. The blending and clashing of local customs and tsarist statutes became more visible in the postemancipation period because the new cantonal and justice of the peace courts operated on the basis of both. In cases where village practice and state laws were contradictory, the latter were supposed to take precedence. This legal ambiguity already existed in the courts for state peasants created by the Catherinean reforms, and since that time, bureaucratic regulation had made ever greater inroads into village life. As imperial legislation and government became more regularized and coherent, the impact of state power on social life increased; the Great Reforms further promoted administrative control. Yet this enhanced authority by no means meant that the autocracy had its way in local arenas. The bureaucracy formulated legislation in response to conditions in society, and peasants used formal law selectively for their own purposes. Russian legal culture remained a mixture of local customs and state judicial institutions, neither of which can be understood except in combination with the other. During the eighteenth and nineteenth centuries, the government repeatedly was forced to abandon efforts to codify imperial laws, settling instead for periodically updated digests. Formal statutes and informal practices were so interdependent and societal structures so porous and fragmented that it proved impossible to integrate the empire administratively without also accommodating local hierarchies, traditions, customs, and beliefs. In law and in life, indeterminate definitions were necessary to ensure that the institutions and tools of governance functioned and that individuals, families, and communities survived.

Resistance and Rebellion

In addition to manipulating and evading tsarist legislation, peasants challenged the social order through direct negotiation, passive resistance, and open rebellion. Without attempting to explain the revolutions of 1905–1907 and 1917, it is important to examine social conflict, which, even when it lacked revolutionary implications, constituted a crucial aspect of relations in rural society. From a conservative, liberal, or socialist perspective, peasant radicalism resulted from legal-administrative and economic conditions; but in the relationship of village culture to the social order, both quiet opposition and violent unrest were "natural" occurrences, rooted in the experiences of everyday life and defined by formal and informal institutional structures. In the absence of constitutional rights, acts of disobedience and rebellion were no less functional and immediate than the need to cope with environmental constraints, material insecurity, and the exactions of superiors. Peasants did not conceive of their revolts in the abstract; what officials, intellectuals, and local elites called a "revolt" was for peasants one concrete event in a series of concrete events, one of many possible outcomes in a specific historical situation.

Flight, evasion, and the assumption of false legal identities represented effective tools for peasants struggling to forestall physical insecurity and the demands of officials and seigniors. Although impossible to measure with any certainty, these survival strategies persisted throughout the imperial period. During the 1720s and 1730s, authorities discovered more than 37,000 runaway peasants in the middle Volga region, and local administrative records from the 1780s and 1790s report that among male and female fugitives, some had lived in forests and peasant villages or found employment in factories and towns for as long as thirty years.[107] In the eighteenth century and the first half of the nineteenth, the demand for military manpower provoked similar acts of passive rebellion. Outright flight remained an effective means of escaping the army, and although officials were reluctant to admit that imperial subjects might be less than eager to serve "the faith, tsar, and fatherland," they could not avoid this conclusion entirely. Self-mutilation to avoid the draft was a chronic problem that the government was powerless to combat. The real extent of the practice is not known, but an 1848 report of the Recruitment Committee is suggestive: in the four preceding levies, out of 100,000 recruits, 34,000 were rejected for height, 20,000 for chronic diseases, and 31,000 for other physical inadequacies.[108]

The ability of peasants to negotiate feudal obligations and conditions of labor provides further insight into society's power structures. Even the most actively interventionist seigniors could not always impose their will on serfs or achieve administrative order on their lands. In the early nineteenth century, the Lievens tried but failed to break the hold of the communal hierarchy on their Kostroma estate, where wealthy serf entrepreneurs simply ignored their collective responsibilities, refusing to pay the dues owed by their poor neighbors and, in direct defiance of the master's regulations, employing outside laborers instead of peasants from their own village. Ultimately, landowners could enforce discipline by appealing to local authorities, which is exactly what the Lievens did when they sent a gendarme officer to collect three years of arrears in 1836.[109] The arrears issue was problematic for serf owners and officials because economic difficulties sometimes caused peasants to fall behind in their payments. To exert too much pressure would only bring further hardship, which undermined the goal of ensuring revenues and flew in the face of the paternalistic ideal upon which tsar and lord based their claims to legitimate authority.

On N. S. Gagarin's Manuilovo estate (Tver province), serfs engaged in an ongoing struggle with an absentee lord, who vigilantly guarded his income. Beginning in 1810, Gagarin repeatedly increased the assessment collected from his peasants, and by 1814 arrears began to mount. He then ordered that labor details be sent to other estates and that the wages earned be applied toward the uncollected dues. In response, the Manuilovo serfs, who were anxious to avoid the loss of valuable labor at home, assigned boys as young as fourteen and men over fifty to the work parties. This stalemate continued through four years of crop failure in 1821–1824; the peasants incessantly complained of poverty, hunger, and administrative corruption and abuse. Inspectors sent by Gagarin in 1826 countered these reports, accusing the peasants of neglecting to plant and fertilize arable fields. As a result, the seignior sent workers to St. Petersburg, deported twenty-one households to a Moscow estate, and placed the remaining families on labor dues under the supervision of an appointed clerk. (Previously, the estate administration had been in the hands of elected peasant officials.) These intrusions and controls still did not eliminate the debt, and two years later Gagarin restored feudal payments in money and kind. Such chronic, low-intensity conflict between master and serfs persisted until the mid-nineteenth century, with crop failures producing arrears once more in 1832–1833 and again in the early 1850s.[110] It is impossible to say whether the peasants could not pay because of economic distress or refused to pay because they thought the levies unfair. Even given the apparent connection between poor harvests and arrears on the Manuilovo estate, either scenario is possible. Peasants may have thought that rents should be lowered in times of scarcity; but with or without a crop failure, they repeatedly exploited opportunities to lighten their obligations.

Throughout the eighteenth and nineteenth centuries, local uprisings and disturbances connected with the murder of a landlord tended to melt away when confronted by military force or by a visiting official who warned of such action. Before the nineteenth century, large-scale peasant and minority rebellions occurred with some frequency, though once regular army units arrived on the scene, they too were relatively easy to contain, and their political repercussions were limited. The Pugachev rebellion—the last and best known of the massive popular revolts prior to 1902—began in September 1773 to the east of the Volga river, among the Iaik Cossacks, Bashkirs, and Ural factory workers in the provinces of Orenburg and Kazan. Claiming to be the murdered Tsar Peter III (husband of Catherine II), Pugachev quickly gained a mass following, which did not, however, include serfs until July 1774. By November, all vestiges of the uprising had been suppressed. For about a year, the military danger presented by Pugachev was a very real one. The long-term psychological effects were even more significant. The rebellion exposed the weakness of governmental authority in the empire's borderlands and left serf owners everywhere fearful of peasant revolts. Although Pugachev's forces never truly threatened the centers of state power, the rebellion represented the largest popular uprising anywhere in eighteenth- or nineteenth-century Europe, with estimates of the number of participants ranging from two hundred thousand to three million.[111]

Smaller serf rebellions and riots also repeatedly occurred when new rulers ascended the throne and expectations of beneficial change were aroused. After nobles were emancipated from obligatory service in 1762, it was natural, according to some historians, that serfs would expect their own liberation.[112] When this came a century later, the results were disappointing and ultimately revolutionizing. The emancipation settlement of 1861 was first and foremost a political act, which gave rise to a comparably political peasant reaction, framed by the culture of the tsarist myth. In the heady years prior to the reforms of the 1860s, all groups in society, including the relatively educated nobles and clergy, looked to the ruler to protect their interests and redress their grievances. When the actual terms of emancipation and various other measures became known, disillusionment set in, seriously eroding the covenant between tsar and people, and opposition began to crystallize, first among nobles and cultural elites, but eventually across society. Peasants clung most tenaciously to their belief in the monarch's good intentions, assuming that landlords and bureaucrats had thwarted the true emancipation.[113] As time passed and as economic relationships and conflicts continued to evolve within the framework of 1861, peasant hopes turned to bitter resentment, and the myth of the good tsar began to unravel.

The provisions of emancipation created material conditions that fueled the persistent mass demand of late imperial peasants for "black repartition" *(chernyi peredel)*, a general expropriation and redistribution of large private landholdings, to be carried out within the communal framework. The exact meaning of peasant "land hunger" remains controversial. It is difficult to reconcile productive dynamism and population growth in the countryside with a dearth of land, unless one defines "land hunger" in broad moral and political rather than narrow economic terms. In 1905–1906, peasants from Vladimir province demanded the return of lands "cut off," which they defined variously as the difference between pre- and postemancipation holdings, or between the maximum allotment allowed by the emancipation act and the actual share received; as lands allotted or subsequently sold to other communes; as lands owned by neighboring communities in excess of the 1861 maximum; and as "adjacent or intermingled private and state lands." They distinguished lands "cut off" from the private holdings of persons within their own communities. When moderate peasant deputies to the first Duma called for a redistribution of private lands, they also did not intend to confiscate the noncommunal property of individuals from their own villages.[114] It seems then that "land hunger" did indeed result from the terms of emancipation, but not for the reasons frequently cited: Malthusian demographic pressure, formal immobility, communal constraints, lack of economic innovation, or the burden of taxation and redemption. Although these factors may have operated in specific localities, in the peasant revolution of 1905–1907, "land hunger" clearly emerged as a political phenomenon engendered by expectations of what emancipation would bring and by village norms of fairness, justice, and "moral economy."[115] There remains a need for detailed examination of local patterns of rural rebellion,[116] including possible differences between former serfs and state peasants. On a general level, however, it is possible to explain the peasant revolutions of the twentieth century as the outcome of two political developments: the settlement of 1861 and the desacralization of the tsar.[117]

The postemancipation countryside was a place of open disputes over land use and boundaries. Peasants continued to plant fields that had been cut off by their former masters and refused to recognize that forests, pastures, meadows, fishing ponds, and watering-holes constituted the lawful property of landlords, tsar, or state, which they might be allowed to access for a fee. The government and seigniors had restricted the exploitation of these resources already in the days of serfdom, but never consistently; only after 1861 did the modern meaning and implications of private property become readily apparent. The commercial market in real estate expanded in an unprecedented fashion, and while peasants themselves became major purchasers of nonallotment lands, both as individuals and collectives, they ignored the formal property rights of outside owners, who were more likely to enclose fields, deny access to nonarable resources, charge higher rents for plots crisscrossing those of the commune, and fine villagers whose livestock wandered onto intermixed private holdings. At the end of the nineteenth century, the courts were clogged with land disputes resulting from the peasants' unwillingness to accept the emancipation settlement as just and fair. Villagers rarely received judicial satisfaction in conflicts with the government or large landowners, and their ongoing refusal to abide by court decisions repeatedly led to imprisonment or violent, sometimes deadly, clashes with forest guards, police, and military authorities.[118]

During the 1890s the government also employed repressive measures, such as property seizures, mandatory labor, arrests, and fines, to enforce the payment of redemption dues. This pressure began to ease in 1903, when peasants at last were freed from corporal punishment and collective responsibility for taxes, and in 1904, officials began to lose control over rural taxation altogether. In the revolutionary summer of 1905, peasants rose up against the agrarian order, pillaging estates, destroying records, setting fires, felling trees, and seizing grain, lumber, livestock, and poultry. Across the empire, three thousand incidents of rural unrest were documented in 1905; in European Russia 75 percent of the disorders were directed against landlords.[119] Peasants of all categories, conditions, and socioeconomic statuses joined in these actions. Young males of average means were the most visible participants, but older villagers and women also lent their support. As one peasant correspondent from Novgorod wrote in response to a 1907 survey concerning the disturbances: "the women too sympathized with the movement—they live in the same huts as their husbands."[120]

The government reacted to the revolution in the countryside with severe repression and halting reform. The popular expectation that the tsar would deliver the land, still evident in petitions sent to Nicholas II in 1905, was neither an expression of naive monarchism nor mere dissimulation designed to forestall punishment. It represented an effective posture in the greater social and political order—a posture that was at once consistent with formal institutions and informal practices. The Russian monarch remained the linchpin of governmental power, the undisputed source of state laws, and the final arbiter of official justice at least until 1906, when the new legislative assembly, the elected State Duma, began to share this responsibility. Throughout 1905, peasants evoked the image of the benevolent tsar to press for radical land reform and secure recognition in the expanding arena of public debate. After February 1906, they ceased to direct their petitions to Nicholas, turning instead to the Duma, which they expected to implement the desired black repartition. By May, both the autocracy and the legislature had explicitly rejected any notion of compulsory expropriation, dashing peasant hopes for a true emancipation. While those who continued to address the Duma called for political reform, legal equality, and a radical reallocation of private lands, most withdrew from national politics, especially after peasant representation in the Duma was drastically reduced in June 1907.[121]

The final blow to the peasants' desire for "land and liberty" came with the Stolypin reforms of 1906–1911, which defined property rights according to formal laws and encouraged individuals to leave the commune with consolidated allotments. Official enactment of these measures was flexible, and the results were mixed. Some communities successfully transformed specific provisions to suit local economic needs; by 1916, an estimated 27–33 percent of Russian peasant households farmed arable land in enclosed tenure outside the communal framework. The rural revolution of 1917 reversed this process; separators were forced to return to the commune, or did so voluntarily, and their lands together with those of private estates were subjected to the long-awaited village-based black repartitions.[122] It is ironic that while peasants frequently opposed departures from the commune, the most obvious economic outcome of the separations may have been to increase per capita landholdings within individual communities. Further study of local developments is required, but once again, it appears that peasant volatility was rooted in moral and political rather than economic conditions. Approximately one-half of able-bodied men in rural villages were mobilized during the First World War. In their absence, entire communities resisted efforts to continue officially sponsored land reorganization, forcing the government to suspend all reform operations in November 1916.[123] The perceived injustices and accumulated grievances arising from the administrative process of implementing the Stolypin program, like those associated with the lands "cut off" by the emancipation, effectively explain the "land hunger" embodied in demands for black repartition, popular hostility toward separators, and the rapid dispersal of the army in the summer of 1917. At last, the time had come when individual households and villages could hope to right the wrongs of state-imposed land reforms that for decades had clashed with customary practices and expectations of fairness.

Having ceased to believe that tsar, Duma, or (after February 1917) Provisional Government would provide a just solution to the explosive land issue, rural people took matters into their own hands. In conditions of war and revolution, peasants remained deeply committed to the village community, the traditional guarantor of collective security and physical survival. Such loyalty did not mean they would preserve the commune indefinitely or that their prerevolutionary interest in acquiring private property was superficial and insignificant. Peasants, as they always had in the past, sought to restructure collective landholding for a variety of moral, political, and environmental reasons. The theme of immiseration thus reflected a broad range of issues, attitudes, and relationships: (1) the peasants' lingering, almost instinctive sense of physical insecurity, intensified by the real threat of scarcity in years of crop failure; (2)

their firm belief that the terms of emancipation were fundamentally unfair and that the true emancipation lay in the future; (3) disputes over boundaries and nonarable resources, which repeatedly brought them into conflict with landlords and officials who sought to impose new and stricter definitions of private property,[124] and (4) bureaucratic attacks on the integrity and autonomy of the commune, manifested in more effective judicial and administrative intrusions, including the potentially offensive Stolypin reforms.

Like all groups in society, peasants sought to limit the demands and controls of those who exercised authority over them. For most of the imperial period, this meant landlords and an occasional state official or military unit sent into the countryside to suppress disturbances, collect taxes, and retrieve recruits. In borderlands, it also meant the burdensome quartering of troops. Overall, direct contact with the government was fairly limited until the Great Reforms significantly increased the channels and mechanisms of intervention. Elected *zemstvo* assemblies levied taxes, introduced scientific medicine, and (from the 1870s) organized public primary education. Through the offices of these provincial bodies, the educated classes extended their reach into peasant society. Statisticians, physicians, teachers, trained artists, and a variety of other semiprofessional specialists—as opposed to the unofficial experts generally consulted by peasants—joined with the clergy in seeking to impose their own ideals of cultural enlightenment and moral edification on a people perceived to be backward, ignorant, and benighted.[125] Universal conscription, introduced in 1874, meant that larger numbers of people experienced military service, the continual contact with state power that it brought, and the disruptions of war. Furloughed soldiers remained subject to wartime call-up, which left wives and children without a source of income and thus increased the welfare responsibilities of the commune. Equally important, universal conscription reduced local autonomy in selecting recruits, who prior to 1867 were often permanently excluded from the peasant community.[126] It was no accident that the revolutions of 1905–1907 and 1917 erupted at moments of military conflict and failure that had weakened the government's credibility and intensified the pressure to deliver manpower and horses. Judicial reforms in 1864 and 1912, the appointment of noble land captains beginning in 1889, and the commercial market in private land also brought formal courts and state laws into peasant life in ways previously unthinkable. Perhaps the greatest attack on indigenous freedoms came with the Stolypin land reform of 1906, which explicitly aimed to transform the organization of agricultural production by destroying the commune. For some individuals these developments offered a means of escape from patriarchal village norms and hierarchies, but for the family and the community as a whole they constituted heightened interference and concrete losses of independence.[127]

At the time of the 1917 revolutions, the advantages of urban industrial life were only just becoming visible in rural Russia. The willingness of peasants to embrace public elementary education, albeit on their own terms, and their taste for urban art forms, print culture, and the material conveniences of the emerging consumer society offer ample evidence of an ability both to initiate development from within and to incorporate change from the outside. Peasants created their own literacy schools as early as the seventeenth century. Beginning in the 1870s, they flocked to *zemstvo* and state-sponsored institutions, taking from them whatever knowledge proved useful and remaining enrolled only long enough to acquire it.[128] Their approach to agricultural innovation, scientific medicine, and formal law was similarly pragmatic. They used these tools if they discerned tangible benefits; otherwise, they ignored the unsolicited intrusions of officials and experts. A few peasants went on to secondary education and joined the ranks of officialdom, the professional classes, or the revolutionary intelligentsia. On the whole, however, peasants clung to long-standing structures of family and community, not because they corresponded to essential folk values and cultures but because, for several centuries, these institutions had provided a workable framework for physical survival and social relationships.

TOWNSPEOPLE

Townspeople *(posadskie, meshchane)* probably represent the least studied and most poorly understood of all imperial social categories. Constructed as a legal-administrative unit in the Law Code *(Ulozhenie)* of 1649, the townspeople paid taxes and rendered services as members of the official urban society *(posad* or *posadskaia obshchina)* while also occupying a broad range of formal and informal socioeconomic statuses. There is very little research devoted to this group, a fact that at once reflects and perpetuates the difficulty of definition. Among the questions raised in the existing historiography is the relationship of the townspeople to peasants, merchants, and urban residents who did not belong to the legal community of registered "citizens," and in the late imperial period, also to commercial-industrial elites and the emergent working classes. The features of Russian society highlighted throughout this book—porous boundaries, indeterminate definitions, and flexible structures—were strikingly visible among the lesser townspeople, the largest and most amorphous segment of the taxed, officially recognized urban community. Called *posadskie* or *kuptsy*[129] before 1775, and *posadskie* but more frequently *meshchane* after that date, this group has been described as "a residual, juridically defined social category of subjects, who belonged neither to the nobility nor to the peasantry and who also were not in a position to rise into merchant status through economic achievement."[130] Although correct in its broad outlines, this image requires some modification in light of research that emphasizes the vitality of local institutions and the potentially fluid economic and legal condition of virtually all imperial social groups.

The status of lesser townspeople depended on legal-administrative definitions, taxation, service functions, economic development, and the bonds of neighborhood and parish. The Law Code of 1649 eliminated the distinction between the taxed *posad,* now equated with the city, and the untaxed *slobody* (suburbs or "white places"), establishing the former as the locus of central state administration, trade, and urban manufacturing. Within the official town, the code limited commerce to designated social categories; prescribed who could trade, where they could trade, and what they could sell or produce; and forbade untaxed residents to maintain shops, cellars, and saltworks. Privately owned suburbs became state property, and large populations of peasants and petty servitors bound to landlords and monasteries were forbidden to conduct business, unless they registered in the official urban society, paid local taxes, and performed the service obligations of townspeople. Various categories of state military personnel—musketeers *(strel'tsy),* Cossacks, and dragoons—also continued to pay customs duties and enjoy commercial privileges on untaxed lands. Filled with exemptions and ambiguities, the code established a definition of urban "citizenship" based upon official registration and taxation rather than economic monopolies or simple residence.[131] At no time did the legal city correspond to the geographical, social, or economic city. Nor did the legal townspeople correspond to all town residents, a group that included permanent or semipermanent settlers and temporary visitors who lived and worked within the law or whose status and means of subsistence lay outside of it.

As a result of the Petrine reforms, which reorganized urban government and introduced the capitation, the city emerged as a juridical and social unit with a prescribed structure of local self-administration and an official population defined by heredity, occupation, and tax and service obligations. The failure of seventeenth-century policies to secure an adequate financial base for local and central government was strikingly apparent in Moscow, where in 1701 only 6,800 of 16,500 households belonged to the taxed urban community.[132] Not surprisingly, Petrine policymakers were less interested in ordering the urban population on the basis of legislated criteria than in increasing the size of the taxed community. Full enumeration of urban society began with the poll tax reform of 1718–1727, which substantially increased state revenues but also disrupted the configuration of formal statuses, caused downward legal mobility, and failed to eliminate the large numbers of unregistered town residents. Diverse groups of the lesser Muscovite ranks who no longer actively served in the army, bureaucracy, or church fell into the taxed population; former townspeople who had fled the official community were forced to return; and newly identified city dwellers tried to escape their obligations by registering as peasants, clergy, or military and state servicemen. Peter's legislation also divided "townspeople-merchants" *(kuptsy)* into three subcategories or "guilds," based on wealth and occupation, and created craft organizations *(tsekhi)* to regulate artisans and incorporate them into the taxed population. Because the new definitions and structures represented administrative mechanisms designed to extract resources and ferret out evaders, they did not fundamentally alter the legal status of the subgroups making up the registered urban community. The vast majority of official townspeople continued to fulfill lower-class tax, conscription, and local service obligations. Not until the Catherinean reforms of 1775 and 1785 did merchants *(kuptsy)* acquire special privileges distinguishing them from ordinary townspeople *(meshchane)*.[133]

Although eighteenth-century legislation established a relatively precise delineation of the city and its inhabitants, effective control over urban populations remained minimal. The government itself contributed to the problem by legally recognizing peasant traders who registered properly and paid the required fees; by redrawing territorial boundaries and designating rural villages as administrative cities, especially in the wake of Catherine II's provincial reforms and in the ongoing process of imperial expansion; and by employing the category "townspeople" *(meshchanstvo)* as a repository for unattached individuals, such as retired soldiers, vagrants, orphans, foundlings, and persons of illegitimate birth, regardless of whether they possessed sufficient capital or an appropriate occupation.[134] Although laws of 1812 and 1824 were purported to protect the economic rights of townspeople, their real goal was to regulate unregistered traders and increase state revenues by facilitating enrollment in the official city. Instead of equating social categories with specific occupations and service functions—a policy that never had been realized in practice—the law permitted nobles, peasants, merchants, and townspeople to purchase certificates granting prescribed rights to trade. Each category of urban resident and each type of certificate carried specific economic privileges. Trading peasants, for example, could choose from six different certificates that legalized their productive pursuits without, however, changing their formal social status.[135] Ironically, in granting ascendancy to "liberal" economic criteria, these measures did not effect a loosening or leveling of juridical society. On the contrary, they aimed to assert control over social life by institutionalizing traditional violations of official boundaries.

Before and after emancipation, any man with adequate economic resources, who obtained a release from his master or community of origin was free to enroll as a townsman. Members of the formal urban community constantly complained of resident outsiders and peasant traders who did not pay the taxes or fulfill the service obligations of official "citizens." At the same time, they welcomed productive individuals who could be expected to share the burdens of local self-administration and meet the fiscal demands imposed by the central government. Just as landlords sometimes facilitated the illegal ownership of serfs by non-nobles for economic gain, townspeople also did not eschew profitable dealings with illicit entrepreneurs. The pursuit of profit in defiance of juridically defined social boundaries continued until the Great Reform era, when property became the sole criterion for participation in city government, and formal status generally disappeared as a legal basis for economic rights.[136] The lesser townspeople—who like peasants had borne the tax, service, and legal obligations of servile status—were also exempted from the capitation and corporal punishment, in 1863, and from special military obligations, when the government introduced universal conscription in 1874.[137] The category "townspeople," with its local bodies of collective self-administration, survived these changes, but its legal distinctiveness was diluted, and the term *meshchanstvo* itself began to acquire new cultural and political meanings.[138]

More than other sociolegal entities, the official urban community always had served first and foremost as an administrative-fiscal unit.[139] Its social meaning was fundamentally ambiguous and unstable, its institutional manifestations limited. To understand the place of townspeople in the Russian social order, it is important to emphasize the lack of urban-rural differentiation, the blurred boundaries delimiting all groups in society, and the flexibility of formal and informal institutions. Throughout imperial history, popular survival strategies and entrepreneurial ambitions led peasants and townspeople to administrative, commercial, and manufacturing centers where large and often illegal migrant populations could be found. These transient migrants must be distinguished from the large numbers of unofficial town dwellers, who in social, economic, and cultural terms could be well established and integrated into neighborhoods and local communities.[140] Migration did not necessarily imply rootlessness. Whether it was temporary or permanent, movement between individual towns and between towns or cities and countryside was a widespread phenomenon well before the period of heightened mobility encouraged by emancipation and urban industrial development.[141]

Town censuses are problematic and contradictory, although it seems clear that Russia experienced slow urban growth from at least the 1760s and significant urbanization in a handful of cities after 1870.[142] Historians generally attribute this expansion to rural immigrants rather than to natural increase, but migration was not unidirectional. Just as there were significant numbers of peasants living in cities—one-third of the urban population, according to the 1744 revision, and three-quarters of the population of Moscow and St. Petersburg in 1914—there also was a sizable group of townspeople who lived in villages.[143] During the reign of Nicholas I, reports from St. Petersburg indicated that out of 21,700 registered townspeople, 5,000 would be excluded from the city rolls in the next census for failure to pay taxes.[144] Similarly, in 1851, officials in Kashin (Tver province) were unable to account for more than 30 percent of registered townspeople; their passports had expired, and they could not be located in the city.[145] Significant mobility continued in the postemancipation period. In the mid-1880s the townspeople of Schlüsselburg (Shlissel'burg) numbered 12,500, but only 500 actually lived in the community; the rest, including 3,250 women, reportedly wandered about Russia without passports.[146] Between 1900 and 1910, 65 percent of St. Petersburg's registered townspeople died or departed, at a time when the category constituted almost 16 percent of the city's population.[147] It is impossible to determine whether these elusive souls had disappeared into the countryside or moved to other towns. Although legal movement clearly increased after 1861, many migrants were "missing persons" who had not applied for residency permits and whose whereabouts were unknown. Like the peasants who fled landlords, conscription, and state taxes, these people were lost to juridical society. One wonders just how many "lost" individuals were thriving or barely surviving across the vast imperial lands.

The occupational structure of the category "townspeople" was no more stable than its legal and geographical boundaries. Much depended on whether a particular town arose for administrative, military, or commercial purposes. At no time did formal social affiliation fully correspond to occupation or economic position. Like peasant migrants, townspeople made a living as merchants, shopkeepers, petty traders, hawkers of secondhand goods, artisans, transport and factory workers, casual laborers, and domestic servants. They also farmed, cultivated gardens, raised livestock, and fished. In the middle of the eighteenth century, a few owned serfs, some entered servile status through indebtedness, and still others sought ascription to state factories in order to escape the military draft. Serfs or registered residents of a city could enroll on a hereditary or temporary basis as members of craft guilds, created in the 1720s. Although Catherine II's Charter to the Towns established legal and occupational distinctions between merchants and townspeople, merchants by vocation could remain townspeople in their formal status.[148] A listing of industrial enterprises, compiled from data reported by provincial governors in 1817–1820, identified factory owners who were third-guild merchants, lesser townspeople, peasants, and members of other nonurban categories.[149] According to official sources from 1845, only 42 percent of Moscow townspeople possessed a demonstrable trade.[150] A fluid mosaic of legal-administrative categories and socioeconomic groupings, urban society defied the juridical parameters and conceptual structures of the tsarist state.

The criteria that distinguished cities or towns from villages, that is, urban settlements from rural, were equally ambiguous. Not only did officials repeatedly reclassify commercial centers as villages and rural settlements as towns, old cities might be urban in name only. The provincial reforms of Catherine II corrected some anomalies by downgrading existing towns to villages and elevating state settlements to the status of district centers. What emerged was a territorial definition of cities fixed by law for administrative purposes.[151] While discussions of migration in Russian society normally depict peasant laborers, traders, and artisans moving to cities for work in the factories, townspeople also migrated to villages in search of work. In some parts of northern Russia and the Ural region, where the decorative painting of household interiors was customary, hundreds of master painters from Viatka and Tiumen traveled to the countryside every year, finding jobs along familiar routes.[152] Given the disjunction between economic profile and formal designation as a "city," it is no surprise that many "cities" retained an agrarian character or that farming remained an important feature of urban life well into the twentieth century. Registered urban "citizens" received plots of communally owned city land, which could be bought, sold, rented, and exchanged. Individual families grew crops for consumption and sale, enjoyed access to common hay, and reduced their fuel expenses by gathering wood in city forests. Although the true extent and significance of these resources varied locally, these preindustrial urban economies clearly paralleled the more diversified peasant villages discussed above.[153]

In the cities of the central agricultural region, numerous townspeople and merchants earned their living primarily from farming. Together with their peasant neighbors, they also followed time-worn paths to seasonal labor in the countryside and the central industrial region. In thirty of sixty-nine southern and southeastern cities investigated in the early 1860s, residents earned a significant proportion of their income from agriculture, which could be a supplementary activity for household consumption or a profit-oriented commercial enterprise. Townspeople in Bessarabia specialized in the cultivation of vineyards, those of Tauride province in the produce of kitchen gardens, and in Samara and Astrakhan provinces cattle breeding was an important "urban" occupation. In the Volga provinces of Simbirsk, Kazan, and Saratov, many townspeople worked in fishing and transport. In the cities of the north—for example, in Arkhangel'sk province—hunting and fishing were widespread. Of 553 district capitals and medium- to small-sized cities studied in 1862, one-third engaged in some form of agriculture, horticulture, and vegetable cultivation; in nearly one-sixth, a sizable number of inhabitants engaged in farming. Across European Russia—excluding provincial capitals and the cities of Finland, Poland, and the Baltic lands—about half of all cities were barely distinguishable from villages.[154] Agrarian cities remained visible in the late nineteenth century, when what one contemporary journalist called "urban land communes" still could be found in Riazan province and in the northwest, southwest, Siberia, New Russia, Don Cossack region *(oblast')*, and north Caucasus.[155]

At the end of the nineteenth century, as Russia began to experience significant urban growth, the absence of a decisive demarcation between some cities and villages continued to highlight the undifferentiated socioeconomic diversity of townspeople. On the eve of the First World War, St. Petersburg and Moscow—with populations of 2,118,500 and 1,767,700 respectively—outstripped all other imperial cities in size and degree of modern development. The third and fourth largest cities under tsarist rule were Warsaw and Riga, which numbered 885,000 and 558,000 respectively. Across the empire, 29 cities contained more than 100,000 inhabitants, and according to data from 1910, 31 percent of urban residents lived in cities with fewer than 50,000 people. These figures in no way suggest a broad-based process of urbanization, yet it is significant that in 1856 only 4 cities—St. Petersburg, Moscow, Warsaw, and Odessa—exceeded the 100,000 mark.[156] As migrants flocked to large cities and as the legal and institutional parameters of the official urban community eroded, townspeople looked increasingly like a segment of the growing and variegated working class. Even though few of them actually joined the industrial labor force, if one stresses differentiation within social groups, defines the working class as "working classes," and incorporates into its ranks nonfactory laborers, then the differences between these groups fade in the late imperial context of urban industrialization.[157]

Heightened migration, urbanization, and industrialization destroyed important structures of economic, social, and cultural life, erecting new ones in their stead. But indeterminate definitions, fluctuating identities, and insecure legal moorings were abiding patterns in Russian society. Peasants and other outsiders had long pursued—and in some places had dominated—the urban trades of juridical townspeople. Late-nineteenth-century townspeople continued to work as petty traders, artisans, shop workers, hired hands, farmers, and agricultural laborers. The rapid expansion of railways undercut the role of city dwellers who had made their living in long-distance transportation, and factory production rendered specific categories of artisans obsolete. For other townspeople, market integration brought new sources of employment as middlemen between the peasant producers of raw materials and merchant-manufacturers. In any of their traditional or new occupations, urban "citizens" might, as they had in the past, live permanently in one city or wander between cities.[158] On the whole, very little is known about earnings and living standards among urban laboring people, and even less about specific groups of artisans. Much depended on regional development and on the extent and pace of demographic growth and industrial transformation. As cities grew, municipalization also proceeded unevenly, and the position of some social classes clearly deteriorated. Improved infrastructure in the form of safe and sanitary housing, mechanized public transportation, paved roads, street lighting, sewage systems, and water purification often failed to reach outlying and poorer districts or simply remained financially inaccessible to the working population that occupied such a large part of the urban landscape.[159]

There are few studies of how towns and cities actually functioned before the late nineteenth century, and even for that period scholars understandably focus on the most visible and important centers.[160] At the same time, it is difficult to explain the spectacular development and rich cultural achievements of late imperial cities such as Moscow and St. Petersburg without first recognizing the extent of economic and social dynamism prior to the Great Reforms. Although the wealth created by productive modernization clearly contributed to the transformation of the empire's major cities, historical geography also shows that urbanization and industrialization were distinct processes and that the former did not necessarily result from the latter.[161] Nor did the creation of effective institutions and a vibrant collective culture derive from economic modernization and artistic recognition. However impossible it may be to delineate the townspeople in socioeconomic terms, and however vague, contradictory, and changeable the legal attributes of the category, lower-class urban "citizens" nevertheless enjoyed a clear sense of community, custom, and sociability.[162]

The longevity of local structures even in the face of aggressive governmental action revealed that urban communities formed, evolved, and survived in interaction with and sometimes without regard for state institutions and pre-scriptions. Prior to the provincial reforms of Catherine II, towns were "orga-nized" into fragmented territorial units and juridically defined social cate-gories that functioned as fiscal-administrative mechanisms for collecting taxes, delivering conscripts, and maintaining order. The formal urban commu-nity also elected local officials, though it is unclear whether all its "citizens" participated or whether political rights required the possession of capital or knowledge of a craft.[163] Catherinean legislation attempted to integrate the di-verse components of urban society by delimiting administrative tasks and es-tablishing elected city councils and courts, chosen by representatives of the registered merchants and townspeople. In practice, these redesignated local communities, whether former rural communes or "reorganized" towns, adapted and altered the juridical definitions as it suited them. The resultant in-stitutions, internally fragmented and minimally connected to larger adminis-trative structures, were not civil societies, political organizations, or bureau-cratic bodies in the modern European sense. But like peasant communes, they cohered as communities in a specific historical context and developed in re-sponse to particular conditions and needs.

Two cases from the late eighteenth century illustrated the strength of col-lective ties, despite decades of legal-administrative restructuring. In 1782, thirty-one petitioners from the city of Vasil (Nizhnii Novgorod province) iden-tified themselves as the descendants of petty Muscovite servicemen and resi-dents of Kozmodem'iansk, where they fulfilled the service obligations of townspeople. Although they had once served as "police" troops attached to the provincial administration *(voevodskaia kantseliariia)*, in the second revision (1743–1747), they were registered to the "plowing soldiers" of Vasil, where they now paid the capitation and manned the frontier force. Having been or-dered to relocate to Vasil, they sought to remain in their homes—a position the local governor endorsed when he ruled that in the next census, they should be registered in Kozmodem'iansk.[164] An even more striking case occurred in the city of Nizhnii Novgorod, as a result of the secularization of church lands in 1764, when former peasants *(bobyli)* of the Dukhov monastery lost their for-mal community and were subordinated to the College of Economy.[165] In 1799, twenty-nine petitioners asked local authorities to return property that, accord-ing to a registered deed of 1686, had become part of Kunavinskaia suburb near Nizhnii Novgorod. Officials considered the demise of the Dukhov community to be final, yet its previous members—some of whom lived in Kunavinskaia and others in Nizhnii Novgorod—insisted on the legitimacy of their self-defined collective.[166] Here, as in Kozmodem'iansk, urban residents preserved the memory of their formally abolished communities in defiance of the autoc-racy's impulse to standardize and agglomerate.

The Catherinean reforms of 1775 and 1785 did much to impose uniform ad-ministrative structures throughout the empire, yet local adjustments even at the center of political power were common. A fascinating and all-too-brief study of the 1785 Charter to the Towns in St. Petersburg province shows that it

provided a basic framework for city government even though its specific legislative norms could not always be fully realized. This framework was dynamic, flexible, wide-ranging, and probably reflective of the population it
served.[167] Specially elected six-councillor *dumy,* consisting of one councillor
from each of the six social categories in the general town *duma,*[168] dealt with
economic affairs, infrastructure, food supplies, the condition of buildings,
town revenues and expenditures, welfare, education, city contracts and tax
farms, military conscription, labor obligations, passports, and registration in
the formal urban society. Attendance at meetings was good, and when the
membership of a *duma* did not correspond to the provisions of the charter, it
usually was because the specified social categories did not exist in a given
city. At the same time, the legislation itself was vague, territorial jurisdictions
and areas of competence often overlapped, and the relationship of the *duma* to
the magistracy, police, governor, provincial board, and courts was not always
apparent. Much duplication and practical interference occurred at all levels of
local government; consequently, particularistic and idiosyncratic interpretations of the law arose within a small geographical region and among district
towns of comparable size. Across the empire, six-councillor *dumy* performed
similar duties but also functioned differently, depending on the needs and circumstances of particular communities. Institutional ambiguity, legal fluidity,
and conflict between town governments and the individual societies comprising a city remained characteristic of administrative and judicial practice
throughout the tsar's domains.

Somewhat less democratic than its Catherinean antecedent, the 1870 reform of city government and urban "citizenship" broadened the definition of
the town society by incorporating important social groups, previously excluded from the registered community: nobles, state officials, clergy, military
servicemen, educated elites, and wealthy peasant entrepreneurs.[169] Investing
administrative authority in a city council *(duma)* elected on the basis of property qualifications, this "liberal" reform replaced ascribed social statuses with
"class" divisions based on wealth and, thus, also restricted the role of juridical
townspeople in urban self-government. As political power became concentrated in the hands of a small activist elite and as postreform city governments
became more centralized and reformist, communities of townspeople, like
their peasant counterparts, suffered losses of local autonomy, as well as attacks on the economic foundations of collective life. Farming townspeople
were particularly vulnerable. In actions reminiscent of eighteenth-century
English enclosures, city councils increasingly asserted control over urban
lands, auctioning them off to commercial bidders, who then leased subdivided
plots to local residents. Because of the high rents charged for fields previously
distributed on a cooperative basis, townspeople lost the supplementary income
they had received from the sale of produce; some were forced to reduce the
size of their holdings, while others abandoned agriculture altogether.[170] As in
England, where propertied individuals, backed by the courts and Parliament,
pressed legal claims to commons, in Russia, city governments joined wealthy

landowners to deny traditional rights of usage. This did not mean that the goals of large property owners and local governments always coincided: in 1912, for example, Moscow officials opposed plans to build apartment blocks on Sheremetev lands that were inhabited by thousands of tenants paying rents far below market rates.[171] Careful research is required to explain the complicated redefining of property rights in individualistic commercial terms.

The restriction or elimination of common rights to city lands represented one aspect of a larger postreform tendency to limit the institutional bases of the society of townspeople. In practice, the pattern of change was neither unidirectional nor everywhere unfavorable to unprivileged groups. Legal prescriptions were vague; city governments consistently sought to extend their authority, yet townspeople continued to meet in assemblies, elect elders, and maintain collective financial resources. In 1871 the village *(selo)* of Ivanov and the town community *(posad)* of Voznesensk were reorganized into the city of Ivanovo-Voznesensk, a move that reportedly benefited the commercial-industrial elite but was opposed by the general population. The very same year, however, the State Council upheld the principle of local independence when it thwarted an effort by the St. Petersburg city authorities to incorporate the adjacent settlement of Okhta. A series of circulars issued by the ministry of internal affairs followed in 1877–1878, forbidding urban governments to interfere in the affairs of townspeople. Still, city councils repeatedly confiscated the real property of societies of townspeople, and superior state courts rendered contradictory decisions when these seizures were appealed. Although the statute of 1870 affirmed that the common properties of the separate categories of merchants, townspeople, and craftsmen were distinct from the economic resources of the city as a whole, it did not create social institutions *(obshchestva)* to accommodate the new groups now included in the urban "citizenry" and increasingly prominent in local government.[172]

In 1878 the Stavropol city council claimed the cooperatively owned shops of townspeople, and the circuit court *(okruzhnoi sud)* approved the action on the grounds that the 1857 Digest of Laws made no mention of common property belonging to specific categories of the urban community. A few years later, in 1881, the court contradicted its earlier ruling and upheld the townspeople's ownership of a house purchased at auction, as well as the land on which the house stood—land that the city council had given to the society of townspeople.[173] The status of self-defined communities that were not recognized as juridical entities was even more confusing. In the early 1880s the Senate twice rejected suits from the old residents *(starozhily)* of Novokhopersk (Voronezh province), whose seventeenth-century ancestors had received fields and forests when they were sent there to establish a fortress. The old residents belonged to the urban "citizenry" but used these lands, recently seized by the city government, as a separate collective. Although the Senate had confirmed their property rights in 1812, it now refused to interfere in the conflict, insisting that the self-proclaimed community of old residents did not constitute a distinct legal entity and that in order to press their claims, the four hundred affected families would have to submit individual cases to the courts.[174] By contrast, in Rostov-on-Don propertyless residents had settled on city lands in the early 1870s and again in 1882. As a result, new communities had formed within the town, one containing 1,500 homes and the other 850. Unable or unwilling to prevent these popular appropriations, the city government accepted the settlements and collected rent for the occupied land.[175] Competing interests, diverse conditions, and ambiguous legal formulas produced inconsistent responses from local officials and the central government—responses that could destroy, preserve, or create individual communities.

It is not known how many disputes arose between townspeople and city officials, how societies of townspeople fared in the courts and in practice, or how these conflicts evolved in the early twentieth century. The legal-administrative confusion suggests, however, that interactions between informal communities and formal structures were crucial to urban social development. Although recent scholarship employs cultural categories such as the public sphere, hooliganism, and moral community to explain the social volatility of late imperial cities,[176] scholars have not as yet explored the equally important role played by societies of townspeople and merchants, some dating back to the seventeenth century, that formed, endured, and coexisted alongside the legally recognized components of the urban society.[177] Crisscrossing the formal and informal entities were urban parishes, which did not always correspond to official or historical definitions. Juridical townspeople appeared in all of these communities whose cultural significance is belied by their legal and economic amorphousness.

Policymakers and political activists sought to integrate urban society and culture through law, administration, public education, literacy committees, Sunday schools, temperance societies, consumer and mutual aid cooperatives, parish brotherhoods, people's clubs, literary readings, and the mass circulation press.[178] Their failure to overcome pervasive social and institutional fragmentation resulted not from an insuperable gulf separating Westernized elites from unprivileged laboring people but from the strength and durability of countless, practically invisible microcommunities—communities that are well documented in peasant Russia but largely ignored in the urban context. The formation, preservation, manipulation, realignment, and overlapping of formal and informal, legal and illegal, contingent and lasting networks, hierarchies, and communities provided the framework for urban society. Localized relationships and fragmented structures defined the city environment, where, in the final decades of tsarist rule, capitalist labor conflict and organized party politics would take shape.

WORKERS

The question of whether the working classes of imperial Russia constituted a distinct social group has long occupied a prominent place in the historiography. At every turn, the boundaries delimiting factory workers, lesser townspeople, and peasant migrants appear indistinct and changeable. The controversy continues at least in part because scholars know so little about the categories of lower-class townspeople and, to a lesser extent, migrant peasant laborers. Until the parameters of these categories and the connections between them are better understood, there can be no comprehensive discussion of the formation of a Russian working class. How, then, are scholars to define the working classes? Are only factory workers to be included? Where do skilled artisans, already dependent on an employer or at risk of losing their independence, fit? And what about unskilled or semiskilled employees in small commercial and manufacturing shops? Perhaps, following the lead of some English historians, scholars should define the working classes as wage labor?[179] If so, how should they characterize relations of indenture and domestic labor arrangements (outside of serfdom)—arrangements that existed before and after emancipation but that have not been studied beyond the reign of Peter the Great? Keeping these problems in mind, it seems justified to treat the working classes separately for two reasons. First, there is an extensive body of scholarship devoted to Russian workers, mainly in St. Petersburg and Moscow, in the late imperial period. These workers probably represent the most deeply studied segment of Russian society and hence constitute a crucial element in the analytical models of the "new social history." Second, Russia's working classes played a decisive role in the revolutions of the early twentieth century, with many workers in the capitals supporting the Bolsheviks in October 1917. Whether passively or actively, spontaneously or consciously, by choice, default, or deceit—some groups of workers moved to the center stage of world history in the context of the disintegration of the tsarist regime and the Bolshevik takeover of the Russian empire.

The degree of social differentiation implied in notions of a working class or labor movement was only just beginning to appear in Russia at the time of the 1917 revolutions. Division into distinct socioeconomic and professional classes and a clear demarcation between city and countryside characterize a particular phase in the development of modern industrial society, which was barely visible in only a few urban and manufacturing centers scattered throughout the Russian empire. Equally important, historians have established beyond any doubt that there was no single Russian working class:

> *The* Russian working class is a fiction. The Russian working class on the eve of World War I, like all classes everywhere, was neither homogeneous nor monolithic. It was internally differentiated by gender, skill, ties to the land, generation, ethnicity, structure of opportunities for employment and mobility, and the historical "conjunctures" it faced. The Russian working class was also internally differentiated by the consequences of these widely varying circumstances.[180]

Scholars who move beyond description and attempt to interpret the implications of this diversity in relation to social and political processes tend to focus on the development of working-class consciousness and the role of factory workers in the revolutions of the early twentieth century. Although derived from this extensive and readily accessible historiography, this discussion takes a more general, long-term view. Instead of examining the internal evolution and eventual radicalization of Russia's industrial workers, it emphasizes broad patterns and continuities in their interactions with the factory regime, the legal-administrative order of the tsarist state, and the structures of officially defined society.[181]

Industrial Development and Social Boundaries

In the absence of systematic reporting on urban artisans and small workshops, most labor historians necessarily limit their accounts either to workers employed in factories or to those, including some artisans, who joined trade unions and party organizations.[182] Since relatively few workers left memoirs, wrote letters to the mass press, or participated in the labor movement and elected soviets, broad information about the working classes comes most often from city censuses and the records of the factory inspectorate, an administrative agency created in 1882 to supervise the implementation of labor laws and investigate workers' complaints against employers. However arbitrary and inadequate the categories and definitions applied by the factory inspectorate, they were relatively consistent across time and space and thus represent an important source of generalized data. Eighteenth-century officials made no attempt to distinguish small workshops from factories, and as late as 1867, governmental documents failed to employ any standardized definition of a factory. Only after inspections and the collection of statistics became regular administrative functions did officials define factories as manufacturing enterprises that employed at least fifteen workers or used engine-powered machinery. In 1901, the government broadened this definition to include any manufacturing operation with twenty or more workers, regardless of the type of machinery. Even with improved and more predictable reporting, ambiguities and contradictions remained. Local city censuses did not necessarily incorporate the criteria of the central authorities, and within each urban or factory district, administrative personnel on the ground might not interpret the prescribed formulas in a uniform manner.[183]

Confusion about whom to include in the category of "factory workers" revealed more than a cognitive lapse on the part of bureaucrats and census takers. Concrete differences between types of workers and between factory workers, artisans, and other laborers were not always easy to discern. Blurred boundaries were endemic in Russian society and the contours of the working classes were no exception. The tempos and characteristic features of development varied greatly, as did the experiences of the men and women laboring in factories. During the first quarter of the eighteenth century, over two hundred manufacturing enterprises were established in Russia, the majority as state operations producing for military needs. Also evident by the early 1720s, privately owned establishments officially numbered 25 in 1750, and 110 by

1797. As noted above, eighteenth-century data did not distinguish small workshops from factories, yet the overall trend was one of growth. When a Scotsman introduced the manufacture of steam engines to Russia in 1794, industrialization—that is, change in production technology, the rise of the factory system, and increased specialization—clearly was under way.[184] At century's end, 1,200 large-scale enterprises employed about 200,000 workers.[185]

Whatever the criteria adopted to identify modern industry or the onset of self-sustaining industrial takeoff, Russia's economic development was ongoing, uneven, and (after 1890) frenetic. The absence of an empirewide railway network before the late nineteenth century slowed the formation of an all-Russian market based on interdependent specialization and interregional trade.[186] Commerce was extensive and dynamic, but productive integration was not necessarily national in scope. Instead, factory workers and agriculturalists blended into a single laboring class, handicrafts remained widespread, and diversified territorial economies incorporated urban and rural industries that processed local raw materials for nearby markets. In Moscow province, center of the oldest and most developed commercial-industrial region, an estimated 90 percent of registered households residing in their native villages in 1899 had at least one member working outside of agriculture for all or part of the year. Among those earning supplementary wages, 41 percent did so in their home communities.[187] Data from 1900 revealed that 37 percent of Moscow workers were located in Moscow city and 63 percent in other parts of the province.[188] According to the 1897 census, just under half (48 percent) of the tsar's subjects who were employed in manufacturing actually worked in cities.[189] Similar figures for 1902 showed that only 41 percent of 1.9 million factory workers (excluding miners) labored in urban areas.[190] In short, industrialization was at once urban and rural, with industrialization and urbanization constituting separate, sometimes localized processes.

As a country of locational economies combining agriculture and manufacturing, the Russian empire contained distinct industrial regions with their own characteristics and chronological patterns of development. Toward the end of the eighteenth century and continuing in the nineteenth, southern Ukraine, tsarist Poland, the Baltic provinces, and Baku (Transcaucasia) joined Moscow, St. Petersburg, and the Urals as centers of industry.[191] Although by mid-century large and mechanized factories had appeared, and more than half a million workers labored in ten thousand manufacturing enterprises, industrial development did not begin to accelerate until the 1860s. Between 1850 and 1890, the number of factories in the empire grew to thirty thousand, with close to 1.5 million employees. By 1914, the factory population reached 3 million. The most intensive change occurred in a few places: (1) in the cities of Moscow and St. Petersburg, which represented pockets of atypical urban industrialization and in 1914 accounted for 15 percent of the country's factory workers; (2) in Baku, which by 1900 produced half of the world's oil; and (3) in the Donbass (Donets Basin) of southern Ukraine, which in the late 1860s arose from the barren, inhospitable steppe to become the empire's single most important source of fuel and metal, delivering 70 percent of its coal and 67 percent of its iron on the eve of the First World War. In all of these areas, rapid population growth resulted in deteriorating living conditions, overcrowding, poor sanitation, epidemics, high death rates, and ever more frequent outbreaks of labor unrest.[192]

At the risk of oversimplifying, one may compare conditions in Moscow, St. Petersburg, and the Donbass in order to illustrate the varied worker profiles that resulted from the distinctive patterns of economic evolution. Until the First World War era, textiles dominated Moscow's industrial landscape, even though the industry's relative importance declined from 84 percent of the factory workforce in 1850 to 36 percent in 1913.[193] The second largest and the fastest growing sector was metalworking, which employed 21 percent of the city's industrial workers in 1913. St. Petersburg displayed a similar path of development, except that in the capital, metal production quickly became predominant. In the mid-nineteenth century, textiles accounted for nearly one-half (47 percent) of the industrial labor force and metalworking for only one-fifth. Still, compared to Moscow, St. Petersburg was home to almost twice the number of metalworkers; by 1913, its factory population included 78,000 metalworkers and 44,000 textile workers. Labor concentration reached high levels in both Moscow and St. Petersburg. At the turn of the century nearly half the factory hands in the two capitals worked in firms employing between one hundred and one thousand people, about one-third in enterprises with more than one thousand employees. Centralized production was a general feature of Russian industry, and although modern mechanized factories tended to be large, size was not commensurate with technological sophistication. On the contrary, Russian manufacturing remained characteristically labor-intensive and diversified within a single enterprise, which meant that even the most advanced plants continued to employ significant numbers of unskilled manual laborers. Interdependent production required substantial cadres of managerial personnel and auxiliary companies to provide specialized parts and services, neither of which was broadly characteristic of the late imperial economy.[194]

At moments of mass unrest, Russia's high concentrations of workers may have facilitated social cohesion and political mobilization. On the whole, however, large-scale production translated into an internally differentiated and correspondingly fragmented factory population. This population was more likely to express the localized allegiances of "craft consciousness" (tsekhovshchina) and "patriotism" to enterprise or district than "class consciousness," defined as the "awareness of belonging to a broad collectivity that is different from, and often perceived to be antagonistic to, other social groups."[195] In the early twentieth century the metalworking industry was divided into five branches: munitions, shipbuilding, railroad construction, machine production, and electrical. Individual plants included both artisanal and factory forms of manufacturing and as a result were compartmentalized into numerous small workshops. Textile mills were somewhat less atomized, but they, too, contained multiple subunits specializing in spinning, weaving, and dyeing, as well as large numbers of women workers.[196] The textile industry also incorporated cottage production and peasant workshops, although increasingly giant factories that combined all phases of the manufacturing process overshadowed the small operations.[197]

Functional and occupational diversity within enterprises further accentuated established distinctions between unskilled or semiskilled laborers *(rabochie)* and skilled workers or artisans *(masterovye)*. For the latter—who were more likely to be literate, well paid, urban in appearance and manners, and involved in trade union or political activities—maintaining the differences was important.[198] However much skilled workers sought to separate themselves from ordinary laborers, in virtually every industrial and service sector, employees with varying levels of training and expertise mingled in private and public spaces. Among construction workers, a small permanent core of expert artisans—carpenters, masons, plumbers, marble and granite carvers, and decorative plasterers—labored alongside unskilled seasonal migrants. Plumbers and carpenters were often also metal fitters and pattern makers, who moved freely between the building and metalworking trades. In transportation, skilled and unskilled railroad workers were joined with temporary dockworkers and freight haulers. In the service sector, cooks and waiters underwent semiprofessional training in formal apprenticeships, while janitors, maids, barbers, laundresses, gardeners, and chimney sweeps possessed no particular skills. White-collar telegraph, telephone, and postal workers included low-level clerical personnel as well as educated specialists. Reinforcing this extensive and fluid differentiation within the broad categories of labor, individual family members and workers in general moved between multiple occupations.[199]

Workers in the mining and metallurgical settlements of the Donbass-Dnepr bend displayed similar patterns of intrasector diversity. Second in its concentration of workers only to the industrial centers around Moscow and St. Petersburg, this region contained large numbers of transient miners and unskilled factory workers and day laborers, together with skilled factory and railroad workers, and literate, stable, and politically active Jewish artisans and traders. Miners, who lived in squalid isolation around individual pits, tended to be younger, less educated, single, and seasonal workers. By contrast, the metalworkers employed in steel mills constituted a fairly permanent and increasingly hereditary labor force that was better paid, relatively skilled, older, and more likely to be married. Ethnic differences also were important in the Donbass, where working people of Russian and Jewish origin represented an alien, colonial element in the Ukrainian peasant countryside.[200] In 1917 the mining and metallurgical center of Iuzovka, the most important of the company towns, was home to a population of 54,000 that included 34 ethnic groups. In Donbass mines as a whole, 137 of 267 technical experts were foreign.[201] Alongside cultural and religious heterogeneity, social distinctions between miners and factory workers intensified over time. Turnover among the region's working classes was always high, and chronic labor shortages continued into the Soviet period; but increasingly it was miners who migrated on a seasonal basis, while mill hands began to settle, break their ties to the village, and raise families in the new urban environment. In 1913, only about one-third of Donbass workers lived with their families, although there was significant variation between enterprises—in the Iuzovka factories of the New Russia Company the figure reached two-thirds—and by the mid-1880s the transition to a more stable industrial labor force was evident.[202]

Across the empire, the late-nineteenth-century development of a permanent factory population, reflected in growing numbers of male and female workers with families and in the trend toward year-round employment, still did not indicate the presence of a fully delineated, self-conscious working class. With the exception of a small minority of militant activists and highly skilled artisans such as master printers,[203] the boundaries delimiting factory workers from other laboring groups remained indeterminate. Very rapid industrial and urban expansion in the last decades of the old regime was one reason for the limited differentiation. Between 1879 and 1902, the number of workers in small factories (100–499 employees) grew by 75 percent, in medium-sized factories (500–999 employees) by 116 percent, and in large factories (1,000 or more employees) by 280 percent.[204] This growth resulted from the in-migration of peasants, who dominated the populations of Moscow and St. Petersburg. In the period from 1870 to 1914, immigration accounted for more than four-fifths of the total demographic increase in the two capitals. By 1914, three-quarters of the inhabitants of these cities were legally classified as peasants, most of whom retained ties to the countryside.[205]

Peasants were inundating urban centers and industrial settlements, but migration often was temporary. Transience and seasonal labor were pervasive and not limited to peasant workers, although the majority of migrants were peasants. As was noted above, townspeople also migrated. Of those arriving in St. Petersburg between 1896 and 1900, close to 60 percent were no longer resident in 1910. Among migrants in general, 65 percent departed the city or died between 1900 and 1910. In 1900 and again in 1910, only 32 percent of the total population of St. Petersburg had been born in the capital.[206] Geographical mobility, movement between town and countryside as well as to and from factories, and the accompanying processes of "exchange proletarianization" (Austauschproletarisierung),[207] were not new to postemancipation industrializing Russia. The size of the migrant population increased significantly in the late nineteenth century, but the tradition of migration and the lack of clear demarcations in society were long-standing features of Russian life. It therefore is useful to examine the dramatic changes associated with the urban-industrial revolution by focusing on continuities in the social relationships and cultural values of Russia's working classes, including the multiple trajectories of evolution from peasant to proletarian and sometimes back again.

As of 1917, only a minority of peasant workers had undergone the transformation to conscious proletarian, "conscious" in the sense of being politically active and aware of belonging to a distinct social group beyond the immediate neighborhood, workshop, or factory. Most people employed in manufacturing retained strong rural ties, and factory workers, like the peasant traders and migrant laborers of preindustrial times, carried village traditions, including that of labor migration *(otkhod)*, into the city and workplace. Whatever the economic, and on occasion political, reasons for high levels of turnover among workers, this phenomenon indicated how easily peasants moved into the urban-industrial setting and how readily they returned to rural life. In 1895, when Semën Kanatchikov began an apprenticeship at the List machine construction plant in Moscow, skilled workers derided him as a "country bumpkin"; yet within four months, a foreman assigned him to a joiner's bench and raised his daily wage from twenty-five to forty kopecks. A year later, he had learned to draw and design simple patterns and had himself become an "aristocratic" pattern maker.[208] Together with economic mobility and the opportunity to acquire a specialized skill, personal relationships also facilitated Kanatchikov's transition to the factory milieu. Although eventually he severed his ties to the countryside and became a Bolshevik activist, Kanatchikov, like many other radicalized and nonradicalized workers, initially found employment through a fellow villager and lived in an informal cooperative *(artel')*, where he shared room and board with "countrymen" *(zemliaki)* from his home community.[209]

Village relationships expedited successful moves to the city, preserved existing social bonds, and served as the foundation for novel community structures in the urban setting. Cooperatives varied in form and function and were not necessarily based on informal housekeeping arrangements. Some were organized by employers on factory premises to provide room and board. Others were created as legally recognized work parties, composed of peasants from a particular village or locality who collectively contracted to complete a specific job. Over time, joint work units, which had originated in preindustrial practices of seasonal off-farm labor, gave way to household cooperatives whose members lived outside a specific enterprise and were not always from the same village.[210] Whatever the precise nature of these associations, they demonstrated the workers' sense of community as well as the effective transmission of village or regional ties to the factory context. The patterns of labor migration and the role of "countrymen" in workers' lives challenge images of industrial workers as disoriented peasants, suggesting stable relationships, rooted in customs and experiences that were passed on from generation to generation.[211] The frequent concentration of migrant "countrymen" in particular factories, divisions of plants, and occupations highlighted the strength of local identities. Cushioning the psychological and physical impact of the factory environment, networks of peasants from a single village, district, or province actively mediated "between agrarian traditions and urban-industrial structures."[212]

Although the collective work crews hired by manufacturers and subcontractors tended to be village-based and peasant-initiated, they provided convenient administrative mechanisms for officials and bosses. Some potential employers actually sent recruiters to particular districts each year, so that trades and skills (like rural handicrafts) became locally specialized. In agreements

with subcontractors, serf owners and peasant officials arranged to deliver laborers whose rents and taxes were in arrears. Such peasant work crews were
not generally found in large factories of the Moscow region by the end of the
nineteenth century, although the role of contractors and organized production
units remained significant among the floating population of Donbass miners.
The government encouraged these practices as a form of social control. Some
industrialists imposed "mutual responsibility" *(krugovaia poruka)* to ensure
the completion of a job or to regulate groups of peasant workers. With or without the formalities of group contracts and collective responsibility, factory
managers and foremen generally preferred to hire individuals whose fellow
villagers they already employed. Workers themselves seemed to welcome this
practice.[213] When trade unions in St. Petersburg and Moscow sought to organize central labor exchanges after the February revolution, most job seekers
continued to find employment through personal connections and networks of
"countrymen."[214]

Institutionalized consumer cooperatives and mutual aid societies also carried the stamp of governmental and employer approval and so served to mediate relations between workers, factory owners, and officials. Employees who
joined consumer cooperatives purchased shares, operated retail stores, and received dividends. Mutual aid societies accumulated capital through regular
contributions from members and then lent out or invested the funds. From the
monies that accrued, they provided lump sum payments to members or their
survivors in case of disability or death. Although closely watched by the police
and factory administrators, these organizations sometimes were allowed to
elect officers, and within limits, they represented a form of direct popular participation in workplace and community affairs.[215] In numbers of persons involved, nonpolitical sources of urban working-class association far surpassed
socialist parties, trade unions, and soviets.[216] For example, insurance boards
composed of industrialists and elected representatives of labor, "became the
largest associations of workers in the country's history."[217] Established in
1912 to provide accident and illness insurance for factory, transport, and mining workers, the boards administered funds collected from compulsory contributions made by employers and employees. The insurance law, a product of P.
A. Stolypin's repressive "third of June system," covered about one-fifth of the
3 million workers in European Russia and the Caucasus. By June 1914,
Moscow province had 344 boards, representing 378,000 workers, and St. Petersburg province had 176 boards, representing 164,000 workers.[218] In January
1916, 77 percent of workers supervised by the factory inspectorate in the city
of Moscow belonged to insurance funds.[219] By contrast, at the height of union
organizing from March 1906 to December 1907, 904 legally registered labor
unions claimed an estimated membership of 300,000 workers in *all* of Russia.
From March 1906 until June 1907, only about one-tenth of the total workforce
in Moscow and St. Petersburg joined a union.[220]

Whether formal or informal, the perpetuation of village ties in the urban-
industrial milieu and the appearance of new forms of worker organization an-

swered the needs of labor, industry, and government. Employers and officials used these institutions to exercise control and impose administrative order. Workers used the possibilities for association to pursue their own goals. The vitality of these structures, relationships, and communities is crucial to understanding how workers responded to the factory order, state policy, and large-scale economic and political developments. When transposed to the factory, feelings of group loyalty among migrant "countrymen" created a potential basis for social action and collective protest. Rural ties and traditions of migration softened the blow of city life by providing continuity into the urban context, as well as the promise of village support in old age and in periods of unemployment, illness, and political upheaval. Familiar social bonds also were likely to foster a sense of security that prompted workers to seek redress of grievances. Letters and other channels of communication between relatives and neighbors could facilitate the spread of labor unrest by offering encouragement and news of conditions and strikes in other localities.[221] There are few sources documenting these microinteractions, yet one aspect of worker mobilization in late imperial Russia seems clear: it resulted from immediate circumstances and dynamics in a particular place at a concrete historical moment.[222]

The Factory Regime

In the factory setting, novel forms of small-scale association, originating within individual enterprises and in specific neighborhoods or administrative districts, combined with established village-based bonds to preserve traditional patterns of collective resistance and reinforce localized identities among workers. Framed by the factory regime, the labor policies of the tsarist government, and the organization of the production process, these new relationships represented responses to a rapidly changing urban-industrial environment. They also were consistent with long-standing social behaviors and popular expectations of the "moral economy." Because so few workers acquired radical proletarian or Marxian class consciousness and because the boundaries separating pogrom violence from political action or hooliganism from calculated defiance were so tenuous,[223] it is possible to explain the experiences of late imperial workers, including the massive strikes and revolutionary mobilizations of the early twentieth century, in terms of underlying continuities and the mingling of old and new values, relationships, and institutional structures.

Drawn by the prospect of cash earnings and the amusements of city life, workers from the villages soon found that the repressive restrictions and physical hardships of the factory regime contrasted sharply with the urban freedom they had imagined. There is no need to describe here the squalor, dangerous working conditions, and abusive administrative practices that were everywhere characteristic of factories and rapidly growing urban centers in the early stages of industrialization.[224] Polluted environments, material deprivation, and backbreaking labor were hardly new to the men and women who entered the industrial labor force. Yet, unlike the village, where seasonal variations, numerous holidays, and the centrality of the household permitted relative autonomy in structuring work and some variation in economic activities, the factory regulated work and time spent on the job in unprecedented and intrusive ways. Many people continued to labor on a seasonal basis, returning to the countryside for religious holidays and summer field work (hence the high rates of transience). Skilled workers, who often were trained artisans employed in large factory complexes, retained much greater control over the production process, although in the years prior to the First World War, technical modernization threatened their status and independence as well. Among metalworkers, one of the most politically active and highly educated occupational groups, changes in the methods of production and management were major sources of social discontent and labor conflict after 1905.[225]

Of broader and more immediate importance to the majority of workers were issues of pay, hours, breaks, holidays, fines, and human dignity. Medical examinations for venereal disease, body searches upon entering and leaving factory premises, locked gates, and the ringing of bells to signal the start and end of work—all revealed the heightened levels of direct control imposed on industrial labor. Fines for tardiness, absenteeism, and unsatisfactory performance lowered earnings and made workers painfully aware of the ongoing administrative surveillance. Plant foremen and supervisors insulted and beat their subordinates, demanded bribes in the form of vodka treats, and sexually assaulted women workers. They possessed the power to hire and fire employees, set wages on an individual basis, and—bolstered by the presence of private police and guards—impose corporal punishment and confine workers to factory jails and drunk tanks for one or two days. Not surprisingly, by the 1880s, demands for respectful treatment and the elimination of fines were common during work stoppages and periods of serious labor unrest. Although workers could appeal against excessively abusive administrators to the directors and owners of individual enterprises, factory inspectors (after 1882), and even provincial governors, collective actions such as the organization of strikes and trade unions to defend the interests of labor remained illegal until 1905–1906.

From the perspective of individual employees, enlightened bureaucrats, and concerned intellectuals, the factory regime often appeared inhumane. In practice, however, it extended a measure of protection and security to workers. While historians are not likely to resolve Russia's "standard of living debate" or penetrate the subjective consciousness of the vast majority of laborers, research shows that imagined—and to some extent institutionalized—concepts of paternalism, justice, and the good tsar prompted ordinary people to negotiate with superiors in a variety of social settings. Equally significant, laborers sometimes were able to win concessions that ameliorated the worst aspects of administrative arbitrariness and economic exploitation.

Representatives of the government frequently criticized capitalists for their treatment of workers, yet the broad outlines of official policy meshed nicely with managerial practices at least until 1905. By the 1880s, both groups exhibited a strong commitment to industrial development and accepted some responsibility for meeting the material and spiritual needs of workers. The government assumed that it would play an active role in defining these needs, and employers acquiesced to the idea of tutelage or guardianship put forth by officials. In addition to organizing cooperatives and mutual aid funds, some industrialists supported prayer meetings, schools, libraries, and artistic performances on factory premises.[226] A small "entrepreneurial intelligentsia" in the printing industry very consciously sought to create an enlightened atmosphere of "moral community," based upon patriarchal images of a "social family." Akin to the myth of the father-tsar, the metaphor of the benevolent father-employer caring for his obedient and grateful worker-children mediated social relationships and expectations among factory owners and laborers.[227] However much the paternalistic ideal served the economic interests of capitalists and legitimized their authority, until 1905 it remained consistent with state policy and reinforced patterns of social resistance that had been evident since the early eighteenth century.

Official recognition of workers as a distinct category dated from an 1835 law regulating relations between factory owners and hired laborers. The law required that the conditions of employment be specified in writing, that financial transactions between employers and workers be recorded in a labor booklet, and that all the obligations of employees be posted on a factory wall. Although implementation was negligible, because local police were authorized to decide disputes over alleged violations of the terms of employment, it is possible that workers submitted complaints against employers, just as peasants did against landlords and common soldiers against officers in the same period.[228] Subsequent legislative acts included an 1845 prohibition on employing children under age twelve in factories between midnight and six in the morning and an 1866 law requiring industrial and mining enterprises to provide health care for a fee and free medical services in case of work-related injuries and illnesses. Factories with more than one hundred workers were ordered to hire a doctor and medical orderly and to maintain five hospital beds for every one thousand employees.[229] In the absence of adequate provisions for prosecution, the extent and precise meaning of official regulations remained ambiguous. Nonetheless, they revealed the government's clear intention to intervene in internal factory life and established two important principles of labor policy: the state's role as arbitrator and the employer's responsibility for health and disability insurance.

Serious enforcement of existing regulations began only after an unprecedented wave of labor disturbances swept St. Petersburg during the 1870s. A series of laws enacted in 1882–1885 established a system of factory inspection subordinate to the ministry of finance and limited working hours for women and minors.[230] In the mid-1880s, additional strikes impelled policymakers to restrict the imposition of fines and to require that the monies collected be put into sickness and disability funds for workers. The "labor code" of June 3, 1886, also bolstered the authority of factory inspectors, who were authorized to approve rules governing the internal organization of individual enterprises.

In addition, it created new supervisory offices for factory affairs in major industrial centers; again required that the terms of employment, including wage schedules, be specified, this time in a labor booklet; prohibited payments in kind and the charging of interest on advances made to workers; and detailed the punishments that would apply when employers and employees violated the law. Finally, after yet another cluster of strikes in St. Petersburg in 1896–1897, new legislation banned work on Sundays and holidays and introduced workdays of eleven and one-half hours and night shifts of ten hours. In his autobiography, Semën Kanatchikov reported that following the 1896 weavers' strike in St. Petersburg, his "sagacious employer," G. I. List, introduced a ten-hour workday, although he earlier noted that in the fall and winter, when factory orders increased, forced overtime was common and refusal to comply meant dismissal.[231] Such practices continued, and despite official admonitions to shorten the length of the workday, an 1898 circular issued by the ministry of finance allowed unlimited overtime work. Nor did authorities address the contentious issue of wage rates or permit workers to organize collectively to defend their rights and express their grievances.[232] The labor legislation of the 1880s and 1890s did not alter the essential conditions of industrial employment. It did establish the tsarist government's responsibility for controlling abuses, ensuring justice, and maintaining order in the workplace. Like other nondominant groups in Russian society, workers responded to the legal possibilities for amelioration by suing employers in court and filing complaints with factory inspectors.[233]

Beginning in 1901 and continuing to some degree until 1914, official policy included an orientation known as "police socialism," which sanctioned the creation of mass labor organizations under strict governmental control to provide workers with legal channels for satisfying their economic and cultural needs. The Zubatov societies in Moscow and the Gapon Assembly in St. Petersburg encouraged workers to challenge employers who violated their rights; sponsored public lectures that reinforced religious values and expectations of tsarist intervention on behalf of ordinary people; and exposed the factory labor force to district-based organizational models, which trade unions and soviets would later emulate.[234] Although direct links are difficult to establish, there is some evidence that the new associations encouraged labor militancy; in a few places, most notably St. Petersburg, their leaders openly advocated political change. During 1902, Moscow workers deluged local courts with suits against employers, and factory inspectors reported 2,146 complaints concerning abusive treatment and beatings. This represented a huge increase over the 161 comparable grievances submitted in 1901. Massive strikes involving Zubatov-like organizations broke out in Odessa and the Donbass in the summer of 1903. In January 1905, the Gapon Assembly organized a peaceful demonstration to petition the ruler, which ended in the massacre of 130 participants by troops and triggered Russia's first revolution.[235] As an "experiment in controlled mobilization,"[236] police-sanctioned labor organizations were a failure: precisely because popular faith in the monarchy assumed that official intervention would bring concrete benefits, actual experience led to bitter disillusionment. The government continued to repress collective worker actions and refused to regulate wages or limit management's authority over hiring and firing.[237]

Despite the autocracy's failure to recognize the implications of the popular response to "police socialism," it pursued a legislative course that, if fully implemented, would have significantly extended the legal protections available to workers. Always seeking to promote social control without compromising the fiscal interests of the treasury, legislators enacted disability insurance for accident victims in June 1903, to be paid for by the owners of factory and mining enterprises. But employers could deny benefits to individuals whose disabilities resulted from "gross negligence" or "intentional" injury, and there is no evidence that substantial numbers of workers actually received the prescribed pensions. Equally limited was the impact of the law on factory elders, which legalized the election of worker delegates, who henceforth had the right to represent the concerns of labor before plant administrators. The election of elders and the time and place of meetings occurred at the discretion of the factory owner, who also appointed the representatives from a list of candidates put forth by the workers. Although some manufacturers and local officials previously had allowed illegal elections of worker delegates, before 1905, the law on elders was applied formally in only thirty to forty enterprises across Russia.[238] More important, the government continued to ignore issues of adequate pay and the right to strike.[239]

The combination of repression and reform that characterized the autocracy's approach to labor was a traditional feature of social policy. Given the regime's institutional weakness, its ability to impose administrative order remained extremely limited. Well-intentioned laws that might have ameliorated the most exploitative aspects of the factory system barely saw the light of day or were applied haphazardly in response to popular unrest. Once the bureaucracy began to supervise the conditions of employment, and especially after officials created the factory inspectorate to enforce regulations, the government accepted practical and moral responsibility for the well-being of workers. While one should not judge the tsarist factory regime by the standards of the modern welfare state, it is necessary to highlight the contradictions and ambiguities in official policy. The monarchy insisted on presenting itself as the guardian of industry and labor. In reality, it failed to finance a system of social insurance, blamed industrialists for mistreating workers, and refused to allow employers and employees to settle their differences freely through democratic mechanisms such as independent trade unions, collective bargaining, strikes, and arbitration.

The effective integration of modern manufacturing into the larger structures of Russian society required that workers be able to evade or negotiate the constraints and demands of the industrial order. In the factory setting, evasion still was possible when foremen left the shop; skilled workers enjoyed relative autonomy in an artisanal production process, and laborers of all sorts could pick up and leave their jobs. But because wages were tied to productivity and tended to come from a single economic source, it was much more difficult for a worker to ignore a plant manager than for a peasant to elude the watchful eye of a steward or landlord. In the urban-industrial milieu, tangible improvements in living standards and working conditions depended on participation in public institutions. Because the government preferred to develop a bureaucratic presence in the factory, rather than allow free organizing among workers (and in society more generally), it became the immediate guarantor of security and justice, as well as the object of popular outrage when processes of social negotiation ended in disappointment. In denying the legitimacy of open political conflict and in seeking to ensure social harmony through strict administrative control, the monarchy replaced the distant idea of the good tsar with direct experience of state police and factory inspectors. By associating officials and the emperor himself with daily arrangements and unsatisfied demands, it promoted the identification of economic needs with political change.[240]

Labor Mobilization

What distinguished factory turmoil in the late imperial period from already existing patterns of peasant and soldier protest was not class consciousness, effective organization, or the substance of popular grievances but rather the historical context in which social conflict erupted and the tools and solutions that were available to workers who moved to redress perceived injustices. Workers were no different from peasants and soldiers in their awareness of legislated rules and specific points of law. They demanded that employers observe legal codes, insisted on recognition of their formal rights, and complained to factory inspectors about concrete conditions that came under the inspectorate's jurisdiction. When their social and economic security was threatened by changes in the status quo, they took defensive action. When they sensed the possibility of extending their rights, altering the factory regime, and improving their position in the workplace, they were capable of mounting offensive challenges as well.[241] These challenges had little to do with whether workers were peasants or proletarians. They were fully consistent with long-standing practices of tsarist justice and with local traditions of community autonomy, "moral economy," and collective self-administration.

Official strike statistics, which did not appear before 1895, are incomplete and difficult to interpret. However one counts and categorizes the various forms of labor mobilization, it is clear that worker agitation, especially in St. Petersburg and Moscow, was crucial to the revolutionary crises of 1905–1907 and 1917. Between 1895 and 1916, almost 10 million factory workers across the empire went on strike, an average of one-quarter of the industrial labor force each year. Strike activity peaked in 1905–1906 and again in 1912–1914, when the average proportion of factory workers who walked off the job each year was close to three-quarters. In 1916, the last year for which official statistics are available, there were 957,000 strikers, the largest number since 1906. Relying upon press reports, historians estimate that 2,441,000 strikers partici-

pated in 1,019 strikes between March 3 and October 25, 1917. More important
than the propensity to strike, however, was the fact that mass worker actions
directly contributed to empirewide political changes. The revolution of 1905
began when 160,000 workers in the capital struck in response to the shooting
of peaceful petitioners on Bloody Sunday, January 9. The labor movement
ebbed and flowed throughout that year, reaching a dramatic climax in the October general strike, which brought the autocracy to its knees and induced Tsar
Nicholas II to issue a manifesto promising basic civil rights and the convocation of an elected legislative assembly. Despite these concessions, strike rates
remained high during 1906, abating only in the repressive atmosphere of 1907.
A second upsurge in factory disturbances occurred in 1912–1914, after hundreds of strikers were killed or wounded at the Lena gold mines in Siberia.
Worker monarchism and patriotism revived after the start of war in July 1914,
but a year later, the strike movement again intensified in response to price increases. In February 1917, massive strikes in the capital, initiated by female
textile workers in search of bread, fueled the already existing political "crisis
at the top," which ended with the tsar's abdication on March 2.[242]

   Regardless of the actual intentions and goals of workers, their repeated
willingness to act and their physical concentration in the centers of governmental authority made them leading players in the epic developments of the
early twentieth century. Although at no time did the vast majority of workers
become either radicalized or politicized, the cumulative consequences of their
common actions were undoubtedly revolutionary, especially when interpreted by officials and party leaders who themselves sought to maintain or
gain political power. One way to illuminate the crucial importance of workers
in the Russian revolutions, and concomitantly in world history, is to focus on
social relationships of the long duration. Beginning with Russia's first modern industrial strikes in the 1870s and 1880s and continuing until the February revolution of 1917, the patterns and dynamics of labor mobilization and
social radicalization may be explained in terms of broad continuities in the
development and organization of imperial society. The public attitudes and
deeds of workers appear to be the outcome of localized allegiances and identities, immediate economic needs, preindustrial traditions of popular protest
and community organization, and the possibilities for social amelioration
provided by formal justice, the idea of the good tsar, and the teachings of Orthodox Christianity. Integration into urban lifestyles, together with exposure
to the political propaganda and secular culture of educated elites, also played
a role; yet at the time of the revolution these had deeply affected only a small
minority of workers.[243]
   Russia's earliest strikes revealed that labor mobilization could be well ordered and disciplined, depending upon the institutional framework and the results that accrued. The Kreenholm strike of 1872 followed months of negotiation involving elected worker delegates, factory management, local police, the
governor of Estland province, and authorities in St. Petersburg. The unrest

began when a group of masons requested permission to leave the factory temporarily during a cholera epidemic that began in July. More generally, workers sought to restore previous conditions of employment that had been altered in the late 1860s, when the factory administration extended hours, reduced piece rates, and increased fines for insufficient productivity and damage to machinery. With the governor's mediation, workers accepted an initial agreement that allowed them to nominate three candidates for the post of elder and granted concessions on issues such as fines, deductions from pay, wage rates, hours, leaves to return to the countryside, and unpopular administrative personnel. Serious defiance and rock throwing began more than two weeks later, after workers became convinced that the head factory manager intended to renege on the signed protocols, and after the district police chief arrested six "instigators" who had appealed to local officials concerning their employer's betrayal. Throughout this confrontation, and later during a similar incident in 1882, the Kreenholm workers demanded fair treatment by supervisors, adequate earnings, and a reasonable workload that accommodated personal and cultural ties to the village. They also insisted that their chosen delegates, usually identified as the "instigators" by authorities, not be fired or singled out for punishment. In their concern for basic subsistence, human dignity, and just retribution, they carried traditional themes of peasant and soldier disturbances into the modern factory setting.[244]

The government's reaction to the Kreenholm strike also was consistent with established practices of tsarist justice. Officials readily blamed the factory administration for exploiting the workers, recognized some popular grievances as legitimate, and pressured management to make concessions. At the same time, authorities increased the visibility of state police at the factory, sent troop reinforcements to the area, and arrested and tried a core of "instigators." In the aftermath of the 1872 strike, twenty-one of twenty-seven workers charged with criminal offenses were convicted, and the ministry of internal affairs established a special commission to investigate the entire affair. The government legitimized the claims of labor when it concluded that management was responsible for provoking the disorders but then punished the convicted workers and immediately took steps to tighten discipline and adherence to existing labor legislation at the factory.[245] Order with justice was the hallmark of the monarchy's response to industrial conflict and popular disaffection in general. Here as elsewhere, officials emphasized the need to observe legal norms, although they did not always act consistently or in concert, and until social discontent threatened to get out of control, they did little to enforce the law effectively. The result was to antagonize employers, whose authority was permanently weakened by the state's ongoing presence, and to arouse workers' expectations without actually satisfying their most essential demands. Thus the minister of internal affairs refused to accept the governor's position that labor should participate in setting payment schedules for the replacement of damaged equipment, and in the end no action was taken on fines or deductions from wages.[246] In its pursuit of social control, the government inadvertently intensified the sources of disorder. Official policies and practices sanctioned the expression of popular grievances, while encouraging workers and factory owners to hold the monarchy responsible for the increasingly unsatisfactory solutions to labor disputes.

In the eyes of Russia's workers, and of society more generally, the events of Bloody Sunday irrevocably shattered the myth of the good tsar. Whether or not a majority of workers ever really expected satisfactory restitution from above, the gunning down of peaceful petitioners seeking to address the sovereign made it painfully clear that the efforts of ordinary people to use paternalistic images to protect themselves and effect positive improvements in their lives had come to naught. During the months and years of upheaval and repression that began in January 1905, modern labor protest was born, as working men and women sought new tools with which to negotiate the factory regime and the reality of their own social subordination. The revolution of 1905–1907 was a time of massive societal organizing and broad-based "unionization" among economic, educated, and administrative elites, as well as among peasants, artisans, workers, and common laborers.[247] In this environment of relative political freedom, workers continued to rely upon the traditional mechanism of elected delegates—firmly sanctioned by the 1903 law on elders and now constituted more permanently in factory or workshop committees—to present their demands to management. Yet, even though workers created factory committees, called strikes, and joined trade unions and political parties as never before, only an activist minority participated in citywide, not to mention all-Russian, associations. In general, the impulse to organize remained temporary, fragmented, and localized; consequently, the possibility of sustained social and political cohesion proved ephemeral.[248]

The history of the trade union movement between 1905 and 1917 clearly illustrated the inability or unwillingness of workers to replace immediate parochial allegiances with national political goals. This did not mean that workers failed to think formally or theoretically. Rather, it meant that they did not conceive of politics as the realization of a set of abstract principles but practiced politics in the organic, evolutionary manner described by the conservative critic of the French Revolution Edmund Burke.[249] In 1905, the most immediate form of labor organization was the factory committee, composed of worker representatives elected in accordance with the 1903 law on elders; among artisans and salesclerks, trade unions also began to appear in the spring and summer. In the factories, activists (who often possessed experience with political parties), the Zubatov societies, and the Gapon Assembly initiated the movement. Although radical intellectuals sought to establish industrywide unions, workers preferred to organize associations on the basis of craft and occupational subgroups within a trade. Thus the bakers' union included separate sections for bread bakers, pastry makers, *pirog* makers, *prianik* makers,[250] and others. In a few sectors (printing and baking, tea packing, perfume making, and plumbing and heating), the proportion of organized laborers was over 60 percent. On the whole, workers pursued their economic and social goals through enterprise-based committees and councils of elders. By the second half of 1906, apathy set in even among workers who had initially supported unions. Attendance at meetings dropped, dues payments fell into arrears, and membership rolls registered high rates of turnover. While employer hostility and police repression also weakened the impact of legal trade unions, the most important reason for their limited success was the gap between the large-scale political goals of organizers and the immediate needs of workers. When workers perceived that to join a union could bring real benefits, such as unemployment assistance, disability payments, loans, and help with funeral expenses, they readily participated, just as they did in government and employer-sponsored mutual aid societies and insurance boards.[251]

Social fragmentation and the weakness of institutional structures capable of mediating labor conflict intensified the destructive violence that so easily materializes when administrative paralysis, even if momentary, accompanies an upheaval in society. Recent work on hooliganism in St. Petersburg and labor mobilization among Donbass factory workers and miners shows that "conscious" social action, wanton pogromist behavior, and petty criminality could be intermingled and indistinguishable.[252] Bloody attacks against ethnic and religious minorities, especially Jews and Armenians, were concentrated in the south and southwest, but some historians believe that, on the whole, labor violence has been underreported in accounts of strikes and other forms of worker protest.[253] Throughout the 1880s and 1890s, riots and anti-Jewish pogroms accompanied strikes in the Donbass-Dnepr bend. In the first two decades of the twentieth century, particularly in 1905, strikers in Moscow, St. Petersburg, Ukraine, and the Caucasus used intimidation and armed force against workers who hesitated to act. Massive melees could occur when the authorities intervened, when workers tried to defend their factories against rioters, and when violent crowds attacked intellectuals, revolutionaries, and strike leaders.[254] There is no question that in the capitals and the periphery, criminal behavior and disciplined labor action repeatedly were joined in a multifaceted process of worker mobilization.[255]

Historians of the Donbass generally attribute labor violence to the presence of large numbers of unskilled immigrant workers who flooded the raucous industrial boomtowns of the south and imparted to the region's factory population its "backward" character. There were, however, also institutional factors that may explain this putative lack of consciousness. In the central areas of European Russia, and particularly in Moscow and St. Petersburg, more effective and firmly established administrative-judicial structures contributed to the greater order and discipline of labor protest. Although ultimately politicizing in its effects, protective legislation, implemented by factory inspectors, provided workers with institutional channels for the expression of social discontent. Other sources of stability included generations of migratory experience, personal bonds rooted in family and geography, and the varieties of formal and informal worker associations created in the new industrial milieu. All of these mediating mechanisms were more extensive and secure in older manufacturing centers than in borderlands and newly settled factory towns. Throughout society, the crucial factor in determining how ordinary people pursued their social goals was not consciousness or the lack thereof—all were and always had been conscious of their legal rights and human dignity—but the tools that were available to workers in negotiating their relationship to superiors, political authority, and the economic constraints of the market.

The workers of Iuzovka, like those in the capital, displayed an ongoing willingness to resolve disputes with employers and officials through legally recognized means, whenever and wherever these existed. However, in Iuzvoka the absence of preexisting social and governmental institutions meant that the laboring population was ruled directly by tsarist police and the foreign-owned New Russia Company, which successfully resisted formal municipalization until August 1917. Because the town lacked a long-standing tradition of peasant migration as well as juridically defined communities or civic bodies that cushioned the impact of capitalist exploitation, social fragmentation was exacerbated, and high levels of destabilizing violence accompanied mass worker actions.[256] In central Russia, increased contact with state power tended to radicalize workers (and peasants) by threatening local autonomy, arousing expectations, and exposing the limited benefits of the paternalistic ideal. At the same time, relatively independent societal structures, both formal and informal, offered possibilities for evasion and the collective or individual pursuit of just redress. Tsarist institutions interacted with customary communities to make organized social mobilization the norm. Studies of peasants and soldiers clearly reveal that nonviolent petitioning, orderly protest, and judicial practice were well established and functionally operative in preindustrial lower-class cultures. By contrast, in the factory settlements of the Donbass, workers and unusually large numbers of transient migrants met the managerial and governmental regimes head-on, without the mediating possibilities of traditional mechanisms and relationships. The result was a particularly volatile and fluid social structure.

The vitality of urban societies *(obshchestva)* in the prereform period and of rural communities throughout imperial history suggests that worker radicalism and proletarian identity may also have had institutional sources. The minority of workers who became conscious of and identified with the concept of class were also those whose ties to constituted communities were most tenuous or had been severed altogether. In contrast to peasants and lesser townspeople, workers lacked collective status as a juridically defined social community. Once their links to established rural communes or urban societies were broken, they began to live outside the formal social institutions that traditionally had provided the framework for adapting to imposed social and political relationships. As workers, they were denied access to customary-legal arenas of local autonomy and collective self-administration. To be sure, leaving the village brought its own forms of personal emancipation, cooperatives and mutual aid societies offered limited means of social mediation and independent living, and factory work sometimes led to the acquisition of specialized skills and upward economic mobility. After 1905, trade unions and political parties were relatively free to organize prospective constituents. On the whole, however, urban industrial workers experienced community in informal associations based on geography, occupation, place of work, boarding arrangements, self-education circles *(kruzhki),* parish, and neighborhood taverns and clubs. Reforms of local administration that began with the 1861 emancipation and national Duma politics, launched only in 1906, tended to exclude workers, who as peasants and townspeople had participated in community institutions that were formally linked to the official structures of society and government.

Given that peasants were no less conscious of their legal and moral rights than workers, and given that historians have recognized the inadequacy of a "typology that places Russian workers along a peasant-proletarian continuum" extending from backwardness to consciousness,[257] it seems possible that the feelings of exclusion, alienation, and class hatred expressed by some politicized workers reflected, at least in part, the degree of their separation from formal and informal mechanisms capable of mediating labor conflict and cushioning social subordination. These alienated workers—for whom flight, strikes, and legal appeals to officials no longer promised amelioration—became permanently radicalized, joined educated elites in a "quest for public identity," and eventually found new sources of community and tools of adaptation and just redress in the social representations and political organizations of the socialist intelligentsia.[258] For the vast majority of workers, labor mobilization was an immediate offensive or defensive response to perceived possibilities or injustices. The spontaneous, changeable, and sometimes pogromist nature of these actions did not render them unconscious or subconscious. That workers did not seek, preconceive, or organize for political change did not mean that they failed to think abstractly. They understood, protected, defended, and promoted their rights and needs in ways that seemed appropriate and feasible the moment connections were discerned and judgments and choices had to be made.[259] However morally reprehensible, self-destructive, and tribal it could be, popular violence had little to do with "reactionary" or "progressive" politics; it was the product of human consciousness in desperate or advantageous circumstances. Like other forms of lower-class resistance to inequality, poverty, and oppressive or humiliating authority, it could be defensive or offensive in nature.

Regardless of the subjective motives of participants, labor mobilization in Russia proved crucial in bringing down the monarchy and its immediate successor, the Provisional Government. In the revolutionary year of 1917, when workers aggressively demanded higher wages and an eight-hour workday, their growing insistence on direct control in the factory and their support for changes in government, including the Bolshevik takeover, resulted from the perceived need "to defend their economic existence," threatened by "the multiple crises of power, food, production, and war." Their brief collective identity as workers represented a view of themselves as "common partners" in a struggle to ward off economic collapse. When they challenged the authority of management and monarchy, they did not seek "a more just distribution of goods and profits"; rather, they remained loyal to their factories—the source of their immediate livelihood—and acted first and foremost to keep them operating.[260] Eventually, in the wildly fluctuating conditions of war and revolution, political change became the only visible alternative to total economic breakdown.

For a few weeks during the fall of 1917, large numbers of workers in key urban locations supported the Bolshevik idea of soviet power, which they expected to bring reliable economic organization, peace, and a new political order, to be inaugurated by the election of a Constituent Assembly.[261] Responding to the imperative of physical survival and the confusingly fluid realities of daily life, workers either returned to the countryside or vigorously defended the immediate workplace and their position in it. In a context of economic crisis and governmental incompetence, this paralleled the actions of peasants who retreated into the collective autonomy of the village commune and soldiers who initially attempted to administer military units by regulating their officers but then deserted the front for the greater security of the rural society and the long-awaited black repartition.[262] Keeping in mind the disorderly, fluid situation on the ground, it becomes clear that the Bolshevik seizure of power and the workers' role in it were neither cynical nor inevitable nor accidental.[263]

CONCLUSION

With the exception of the most skilled, educated, or politically conscious workers living in urban centers and factory towns, the distinction between "traditional" peasants and "modern" proletarians remained blurred even after large-scale industrial development got under way in the late nineteenth century. Throughout the imperial period, taxation, conscription, economic rights and restrictions, and the legal-administrative controls and protections, provided by local communities and the government, defined the relationship of laboring people to the official social order. In their dealings with formal society and superordinate authority, peasants and workers consistently focused on issues of the "moral economy" and fair treatment. Their increasingly strident protests during the final decades of the old regime did not necessarily suggest the emergence of a qualitatively different "modern" consciousness rooted in notions of human dignity and self-worth. Popular objections to excessive obligations and cruel treatment were visible already in the early eighteenth century. In the first half of the nineteenth century the assumption that the lower classes were entitled to basic subsistence also appeared in "negotiations" between serfs and landlords over the burden of feudal dues and in soldiers' complaints against officers who failed to provide the legally prescribed equipment, clothing, and provisions. It was but a short step from these protests to the twentieth-century insistence on polite and respectful address, now expressed in the language of the elite's Enlightenment culture.[264]

In the late nineteenth century, readers' letters to the penny press joined state-mediated petitions, complaints, and lawsuits as legal means of popular protest. Unlike long-standing official channels for expressing grievances, boulevard journalism was generated for and by the people. It represented a new sphere of social action, created a cultural bridge between writers and the urban population, and encouraged a generalized, rather than personalized, sense of injustice.[265] Changed responses to the social order did not require a cognitive transformation. New tools of adaptation and survival, new choices of occupation and lifestyle, and new perceptions of the possibilities for re-dressing old grievances were sufficient to undermine obedience. Because this heightened awareness coincided with an extension of governmental power into the factory and village, giving ordinary people ever greater contact with the actual functioning of autocratic authority, it was not surprising that popular dissatisfaction with official action or inaction would extend to the monarchy. Expectations based on custom and the precepts of tsarist justice combined with new experiences, problems, and possibilities, including a more pro-nounced official inclination to equate popular protest with revolutionary sedi-tion. In the absence of secure institutional links integrating local communities with the political-administrative order, governmental breakdown and eco-nomic crisis produced complete societal disintegration. Peasants and workers responded by withdrawing from the imperial framework to defend their homes and sources of livelihood in whatever way seemed viable at the moment. In the process, they rejected the autocracy and eventually the Provisional Govern-ment, adapting as immediate circumstances required to the economic, politi-cal, and military realities that enveloped them.

CONCLUSION
INTEGRATION AND DISINTEGRATION

Nonconformist artists occupied a peculiar
position within Soviet society. Not simply
unambiguous outcasts, they were, for the most
part, able to carve out a fragile space between
the forbidden and the compulsory.

—*Art in America,* February 1996

In France, recorded images of the society of orders emanated from prominent medieval theologians, struggling to preserve the political and cultural
prestige of the church in relation to increasingly powerful kings and new feudal classes.[1] In Russia, it was eighteenth-century rulers and administrators who
first imagined secular "society" and its constituent groups. Explicit efforts to
articulate an inclusive conception of Russian society dated from the reign of
Catherine II and were embodied in the abstract notion of a corporative, "constitutional" order.[2] Before that time there was no attempt to define an all-
embracing earthly social realm, distinct from the divine realm. In the early
eighteenth century, lawmakers and intellectuals imagined the social landscape
as part of the great chain of being,[3] rather than as an integrated "society." Despite the ultimate failure fully to conceptualize, much less to realize, a coherent

"system" or "structure," the government continually formulated legal-administrative categories, which not only helped to define social identities but also
functioned as instruments of "integration" and "stability." Through the dynamic prism of juridical society, it is possible to explain the long life of the imperial Russian (autocratic) regime as well as its sudden and well-nigh total collapse in 1917.

The great prerevolutionary historian V. O. Kliuchevskii recognized long
ago that social boundaries in imperial Russia frequently depended on negative
definitions. He viewed the concept of *soslovie* (legally defined social status) as
a series of political institutions *(uchrezhdeniia),* independent of economic, intellectual, moral, or physical characteristics and conditions. He explained social differentiation as unequal obligations, which corresponded to unequal
rights; thus lighter obligations represented a negative "right" in relation to
other groups.[4] The phenomenon of social demarcation by negative definition
and exclusion is consistent with the broad role of "otherness" in imperial society, culture, and politics. Scholars of gender, race, nondominant ethnic
groups,[5] religious minorities, workers, peasants, and colonial subjects consistently focus attention on the problem of otherness in order to explain myriad
and persistent forms of inequality. By "others" they mean subjugated communities and peoples who possess a distinct cultural voice and historical experience that must be understood outside of the normative institutions and values
imposed by governing hierarchies, classes, nations, and states. At the same
time, cultural and political historians demonstrate that the identification of
"others" is essential to the self-definitions that allow rulers and elite groups to
elevate themselves, legitimize their power, and control their subordinates.[6]
Thus the Enlightenment's articulation of the idea of "Eastern Europe" made
possible the self-perception of a progressive and liberal "Western civilization," which was immanent in the countericon of a backward, barbaric, and inferior "East,"[7] and which, together with Christianity, justified the increasingly
aggressive and global imperialism of the nineteenth century.

In Russia as well, foreignness was central to the mythologies of the monarchy and court nobility. The multiethnic peopling of Kievan Rus, the forced territorial consolidation of Muscovy, and continual imperial expansion beginning
in the mid-sixteenth century produced an image of the ruler as victorious con-
queror, defender of Orthodoxy, and bearer of civilization—an image that highlighted the foreign sources of the sovereign's divinely sanctioned status. Thus
the Kievan princes appeared as descendants of Varangians or Vikings, who
originated in Scandinavia, and the Christian Muscovite tsars became heirs to
the Byzantine emperors, who combined Orthodox holiness with imperial
power. Peter the Great's secular style of rulership preserved the traditional
military and religious symbols but added to them human agency and Western
education, etiquette, and culture. Throughout the imperial period, the ruler's
foreignness symbolized sacred distance, legitimate authority, and the common
good, which stood above and beyond the parochial interests and perspectives

of his or her subjects.[8] When in 1865 the Moscow nobility appealed to Alexander II to reorganize central government, the Tsar-Reformer brusquely proclaimed that "no single social group [soslovie] has the legal right to speak in the name of other groups. No one [other than the ruler] is called upon to accept . . . a petition concerning the general benefits and needs of the state."[9] As official patterns of social categorization always had implied, the emperor made no clear distinction between society and government, yet set himself apart from both. His words did not represent the Russian equivalent of "I am the state" ("L'état, c'est moi") but rather suggested "I am, my state-society is, and my subjects in their particular statuses, communities, and institutions are as well."

Parallels to the otherness of the sovereign and court existed across society, where negative definitions contributed to the formation of positive identities and thus constituted a source of integration. When Muscovite lawmakers identified non-Christian natives under the tsar's suzerainty as "other believers" (inovertsy), and when imperial officials and ethnographers described foreigners and ethnic minorities as "non-Russians" (inozemtsy or inorodtsy),[10] they were defining themselves in terms of relations between the Russian/Orthodox "community" and groups outside of it. Eighteenth-century scholars who attempted to classify the numerous peoples of the tsarist empire also frequently applied "a negative mode of description" based upon "a growing collection of absences," or specific customs, virtues, and traits that various minorities supposedly lacked. Even official histories, designed to glorify the state and nation, presented civilized Russia as foreign in origin. Before Prince Rurik arrived from Scandinavia in the mid-ninth century, historians claimed, the "Russians" themselves belonged to a lesser species of human beings who did not yet possess "politics, history, religion, and Enlightenment."[11] As Peter the Great's Russia assumed the military and political mantle of a European empire, intellectuals began consciously to divide their country into European and Asiatic halves, separated by the Ural mountains. To the east lay Siberia, part of Russia since the sixteenth century, but from the 1730s depicted as a "non-European geographical Other." In imagining Siberia as a foreign Asiatic colony, educated Russians eagerly embraced the long-standing reality of imperial power, while securing their own identity as Westernized and European.[12]

From this association with Europe the very idea of Russianness and Russian nationality emerged as a positive identity formed by negative definition and future reality. The literary elite who created Russian national consciousness defined the nation in opposition to the "antimodel" of an idealized West. They viewed Western values as universal and applied Western standards to Russia, while insisting upon the uniqueness of a superior Russian soul, the site of real inner freedom. From the start, their concept of the true nation was rooted in an image of the people (narod) as blood, soil, and rabble. Thus "the people" were of the same essence as the elite literati themselves (blood and soil) but also separate from, inferior to, and other than themselves (rabble).[13] In a juxtaposition of pride and anxiety, caused by the incessant interplay of new knowledge and dynamic aspirations, Russian intellectuals discovered that "for every Western vice . . . [Russia] had a virtue, and for what appeared as a virtue in the West, it had a virtue in reality, and if it was impossible to see these virtues in the apparent world of political institutions and cultural and economic achievements, this was because the apparent world was the world of appearances and shadows, while the virtues shined in the world of the really real—the realm of the spirit."[14] Thus common identification cohered as difference from "less well-known people," foreign and Russian, who were "not quite like themselves."[15]

Within Russian society similarly negative usages and antitypes arose. As early as 1724, Ivan Pososhkov contrasted the usefulness of registered merchants and artisans to the "people of other ranks" *(inochintsy),* who were excluded from the juridical community of townspeople but continued to engage in urban occupations.[16] In legal-administrative society the "people of various ranks" *(raznochintsy)* also represented nonmembers of a given category or community, including persons who illegally owned serfs or traded in towns. Polite (cultured or high) society often depicted *raznochintsy* as educated, upstart commoners; and while some intellectual circles associated them with the positive identity of the right-thinking democratic intelligentsia, the "people of various ranks" nonetheless appeared as new arrivals and hence former outsiders.[17] Negative delimitation continued in the early twentieth century among professionals, who sought to ensure their own elite status by establishing monopolistic control over specialized services.[18] During the revolution of 1905–1907, peasants from Vladimir province displayed a similar tendency to secure local ties by excluding others. In petitions sent to Nicholas II and the Duma, villagers called for the expropriation of private lands, *except* for those held within their own communities. In "demanding additional lands from nonmembers," they made no distinction between "private owners, the state or crown, or peasants from other communes."[19] The crucial distinction, at least with respect to the land issue, was between the immediate community and all outsiders.

More explicitly positive forms of negative identity developed among people who chose to be "others"—that is, among people who lived or defined themselves, legally or illegally, outside the particular parameters of Russian society or in overt opposition to imperial institutions. Their numbers included ethnic and religious minorities, as well as Orthodox Old Believers or dissenters who rejected the new "purified" rites introduced by Patriarch Nikon in the 1650s. Old Belief represented an unauthorized, informally tolerated, and either entirely voluntary or locally induced liminal state within Orthodox Russia. In their rituals, religious dissenters remained outside official structures, but in order to survive, they either lived within formal society or willingly withdrew from it. Constituting a multitude of "cultural systems" and attracting "support among many social groups,"[20] the meanings of Old Belief were embedded in local contexts and in conflicts between the monastic elite and central church that predated the introduction of the reformed liturgy.[21] Old Belief also functioned as a language of social rebellion, and prior to the declaration of religious freedom in 1905–1906, dissenters lived with serious legal liabilities.[22] At the same time, the monarchy's traditional toleration of local particularism and community autonomy allowed Orthodox religious sects to flourish and diversify.[23] From the early nineteenth century, even radical dissenters such as the priestless "people along the sea" *(pomortsy)* accepted the legal requirement of ritual support for political authority and prayed for the health of the Antichristian tsar. A 1909 council of *pomortsy* defined the appropriate prayer as "Lord save and have mercy on our sovereign tsar," while a liturgical book published by the priestly Rogozhskoe center in 1912 asked for the "mercy and remission" of his sins.[24] Flexible rites—which in the case of prayers for the ruler still implied that he needed God's forgiveness for his apostasy—and tacit official acceptance of dissent made political and spiritual accommodation viable and effective.

The relationship between the state, official church, and religious dissenters was fluid and changeable throughout the imperial period. The degree of governmental repression fluctuated, and at no time did authorities consistently enforce legal restrictions or even know with certainty the size of the dissenting sectarian population.[25] In 1800 the church itself created a "unified faith" *(edinoverie)* that allowed dissenters who accepted synodal authority to practice the old ritual. Nor was there a single community of Orthodox dissenters or a standard set of Old Believer texts. Organized Old Belief represented pre-Nikonian Russian Orthodoxy, and dissenters, like the adherents of official Orthodoxy, preserved local cults and practices. They also maintained varying degrees of pragmatic liturgical association with the established church. "Half-schismatics" *(polu-raskol'niki)* received some sacraments such as baptism and marriage from priests in recognized churches, but then conducted prayer services led by laymen and -women in private homes. Priestly Old Believers *(popovtsy)* accepted no sacraments from any Orthodox church, yet their religious leaders came from the ranks of officially ordained fugitive priests. Only the priestless schismatics rejected all clergy and sacraments from the legal church.[26] What united dissenters was not necessarily positive identification with Old Believer church fathers such as Archpriest Avvakum, but rejection of the liturgical reforms of Nikon.[27] Religious dissent blended into formal society with relative ease, both because community independence was an essential feature of the larger imperial framework and because widespread religious localism or heterodoxy blurred the boundaries between all forms of official and unofficial Orthodoxy.[28]

Like religious dissenters who denied the legitimacy of state and church, intellectuals who conceptualized the "honorable public," "liberal educated society" *(obshchestvo),* or the intelligentsia also employed negative definitions in order to delineate new identities.[29] As a "discursive entity" consisting of the periodical press and "physical sites where sociable interaction was possible," the late-eighteenth-century reading public consciously distinguished itself from uncultivated groups in society, though usually not from the court and government.[30] By contrast, the nineteenth-century ideas of *obshchestvo* and intelligentsia, which also represented political and cultural concepts or spheres, implied opposition to social barriers as well as separateness from the state and monarchy.[31] Depending on the context, the relationship between positive identity and negative definition by exclusion often meant that the outsider in official society also was an insider.[32] Whether they occupied an outsider status because of economic necessity, legal uncertainty, religious practice, political conviction, or assumed moral virtue—*raznochintsy,* Old Believers, and self-proclaimed members of the public, "liberal educated society" *(obshchestvo),* and the intelligentsia defined for themselves social roles that were incorporated into official and unofficial visions of society. In becoming "outsiders," they effectively altered formal structures and thus functioned as "insiders" who lived within the evolving social order.

Throughout the imperial period, local forms of Orthodoxy and magic created generic cultural bonds that transcended social difference and united individuals from all walks of life. Glorifications of saints, mass pilgrimages to the shrines of miracle-working icons, supernatural visions, almsgiving, the protection of holy fools, and observance of religious holidays and rituals attested to a genuine realm of shared Christian belief that regularly encompassed ruler and ruled, rich and poor, noble and peasant, factory worker and capitalist employer. The faithful attended church services, observed prescribed fasts, and maintained icon corners in their aristocratic palaces, middling homes, proletarian workshops, or peasant huts. In the countryside especially, the privileged and the subordinated prayed together, received offices from the same priest, and celebrated local festivals before and after emancipation. During the great Pugachev uprising of 1773–1774, clergy and parishioners cooperated to protect their churches. Even people who sided with the rebels and seized the financial resources of local parishes continued to respect actual places of worship.[33] The relevance of customary and Orthodox traditions to individuals of all social stations, in urban and rural settings, was striking and indisputable.

Beginning in the late seventeenth century and particularly in the reign of Peter the Great, Russia's nebulous cultural amalgam of custom and religion encountered the secular values of neoclassicism, the scientific revolution, and eventually the Enlightenment. As had occurred in the earlier process of Christianization, the state aggressively propagated a new Western rationalism, which service elites and urban groups quickly embraced. Much has been written about the incorporation of European ideas into the Russian context and about the resultant cleavage between the traditional, though never stagnant, local folkways of the general population and the relatively homogeneous Western culture of the educated classes.[34] Secularization did indeed make rapid progress in Russian educated society, and by the mid-eighteenth century, the country's cosmopolitan elites moved easily in pan-European cultural circles. But secularization did not mean the elimination of belief in religion and magic. In the early nineteenth century, members of literary society consciously employed both mathematics and cabalism to cope with the chance and chaos of the outside world.[35] Whether viewed in scientific or traditional terms, chance could bring success or catastrophe, and as a result people lived in constant expectation of the unexpected and irrational. To overcome nagging uncertainty, the literate and illiterate alike found solace in fortune-telling, divination, and witchcraft. Even among the highly educated, what they knew of science and the supernatural appeared fully compatible.[36] Religious and secular values originated in multiple sources and cohered in diverse syncretic patterns that challenge simple distinctions between Christianity and paganism or between elite and popular culture.[37]

Beyond the world of the spirit, at every level of formal society, people judged whether constituted authority met the needs of the family or community. When they perceived formal controls as unjust or threatening to their individual or collective security, they did all in their power to evade them. This was no less true of nobles who ignored Peter the Great's 1714 decree on single inheritance than it was of peasants who chose to apply customary rather than canonical or statutory laws. Although state-imposed social categories were tools of administration that served an integrative function from the government's point of view, they were sufficiently malleable to accommodate informal, sometimes illicit relationships and to be incorporated into unofficial society's legal, socioeconomic, and cultural self-definitions. Individuals moved easily between the social modalities of formal structure and informal community—sometimes legally and sometimes illegally, sometimes in the name of autocratic authority and sometimes with reference to juridical norms and relationships. These fluctuating definitions and porous institutions surely promoted bureaucratic arbitrariness, but they also integrated society by allowing people to violate official boundaries and change legal identities in order to survive, define a social position, and perhaps even prosper. Russia's revolutionary outcome of 1917 has encouraged an historiographical emphasis on social conflict and coercion. Attention to sources of integration is equally important for understanding how the empire collapsed. The socioeconomic transformation underway in late imperial Russia surely intensified the search for new public identities, yet aggressive "self-fashioning" had deep roots in established processes of social development and delineation. Russian society was traditionally fragmented, and those identities that supposedly were crumbling had in fact never been firmly fixed.

. . .

The social and institutional effectiveness of the old regime to a large degree derived from ambiguity, uncertainty, and personalized authority. Tsarist justice, like Christian salvation and Russian national superiority, lay "in the world beyond the apparent."[38] The God of heaven, His divinely ordained ruler, and the latter's government were at once distant and virtually invisible yet also ubiquitous. Social control and the legitimacy of the monarchy depended upon the idea of autocracy, which could be sustained only if direct interaction between society and administration remained limited. As contact increased in connection with state building, emancipation, and economic modernization, the gap between the idea and the reality of tsarist rule—between the imagined expectation of what was or should be and actual experience—became evident to ever greater numbers of people. By the end of the nineteenth century, the ruler had been desacralized and the legitimacy of the regime undermined by the government's failure to ensure military security, political stability, the autocracy's religious sanctity, or the justice and protection expected by privileged and ordinary people.[39] Lacking a charismatic tsar, the myths of imperial rule were quickly abandoned. Even conservative monarchists were unable to conceptualize a national autocracy independent of the personal qualities and failings of the reigning emperor and his spouse.[40] The absence of institutionalized national politics before 1906 radicalized and politicized protest by limiting the sphere of public opinion to private conversation, local self-administration, and the periodical press and by channeling the articulation of grievances directly toward the tsar, in his role as the font of divinely sanctioned authority.

In accordance with a "non-rights-oriented" legal culture and with "the notion of the state as a nonteleological network of multiple interconnected sources of social and political power,"[41] imperial Russia can be described as a society of formal privileges and obligations—economic, social, and political—imposed by the monarchy on its subjects yet limited by the government's institutional weakness, which prevented effective implementation. Throughout the imperial period, new state demands and administrative structures disrupted collective and individual lives. In the process, the informal ties of local community were bolstered, and lawmakers were forced to compromise with societal adaptation and resistance to official prescriptions. After the emancipation of 1861, social arrangements began to move very slowly in the direction of legal equality. This did not mean that society was breaking out of the putatively rigid structures of a particularistic "estate" *(soslovie)* order. Rather, formalized institutional life, especially state bureaucracy, was spreading, and people in society were reacting to heightened levels of administrative interference and the loss of local autonomy. Growing alienation from the autocracy, bolstered by a traditional mistrust of the bureaucracy, intensified social conflict. Society's localized and fragmented institutions could neither replace the desacralized monarch nor mediate mass discontent.

If the history of legal-administrative society sheds any light on the Russian revolutions, it is to underscore the limited development of secular social organizations capable of channeling disaffection and negotiating conflict. The extension of governmental authority, or at least of official pretensions to exercise control, was accompanied by a growing desire among educated and socioeconomic elites to extend the boundaries of independent civic activity beyond traditionally recognized structures. The impulse to form free associations first appeared in private charities, learned societies, Masonic lodges, and the cultivated public of the mid- to late eighteenth century. Among the educated classes, a commitment to public society *(obshchestvo)* and organization was clearly established by the second quarter of the nineteenth century.[42] Despite impressive results, efforts to construct autonomous civil institutions eventually collapsed under the weight of social fragmentation, the crisis of the First World War, and a ruler who opposed meaningful political reform.[43] Medical relief operations during the war emergencies of 1904 and 1914 demonstrated both the limits to effective social organization and the potential for cooperation between the tsarist regime and civil society. Centralized initially in the General Zemstvo Organization and subsequently in the All-Russian Zemstvo Union, relief initiatives emanated from provincial assemblies and depended entirely on local sources of funding. Both the government and the army recognized the *zemstvo* program as an important contribution to the cause of national security. By 1915–1916, however, officials expressed alarm over the growing authority of the All-Russian Zemstvo Union. *Zemstvo* activists consciously sought to broaden their sphere of civic competence, the professionals employed by *zemstvo* assemblies demanded a more direct role in local self-government, and the Duma and *zemstvo* leaders who spoke for society's liberal forces repeatedly clashed over the legislature's indifference to administrative reform. As they participated in large-scale public action and the effective coordination of medical relief by societal institutions and officialdom, the various groups comprised by incipient civil society became embroiled in acrimonious conflicts with each other and with the state.[44]

Social distinctions were also hardening in the late nineteenth century. Whether nobles identified with officialdom, local corporate assemblies, or elected *zemstvo* bodies, they occupied institutional bases from which to venture into the larger political arena. As a result, the differences between provincial landowning nobles and high-level bureaucratic or military servicemen became more pronounced than ever before. The social characteristics of commercial, industrial, and financial elites also became firmer, as they consolidated their economic power in the capitalist marketplace and their political power in elected city governments and the Duma. The emerging professions remained more vaguely defined in a social sense, not so much because of their diverse origins or political passivity—periodicals, informal networks, and constituted societies mushroomed in this period—but because of their economic dependence on *zemstvo* employment, their limited acceptance among the general population, and police restrictions on their ability to form free associations. In contrast to the greater delimitation of these relatively small and privileged groups, which also could be found among many national minorities, the vast majority of rural and urban Orthodox Russians remained socially and economically diffuse, ambiguously delineated, and tied first and foremost to local institutions and communities. The dynamic, fluid quality of imperial Russia's multiple social "structures" or "systems," and the tenuous linkages connecting the center to the localities or periphery, produced a fragmented "society," separate from immediate community or neighborhood, that consisted of bundles of amorphous, changeable, and often contradictory legal rights and social identities.

Popular participation in elections to the first Duma and the receptiveness of late imperial peasants and workers to the church, formal education, and urban print culture indicate that the perceived gulf separating ruling and intellectual elites from the general population was largely institutional, a problem of linkages in a society that lacked stable structures and mechanisms of integration beyond the person of the monarch. Bruce W. Menning argues that the military failures of the early twentieth century, including the inadequate pace of modernization, were neither purely technological nor purely economic. They represented a failure to establish and maintain "intellectual and procedural linkages"—linkages between means and objectives, supporting base and fighting front, tactics and operations, offensive-defensive correlations, and concentration and dispersion.[45] The issue of linkages also appeared in the populist current of Russian social thought. In its radical, liberal, and conservative forms, the populist orientation attempted to establish (or imagine) bonds across the breadth of society, either through the transmission of Enlightenment civilization to the people or through submersion in local folkways. Chief Procurator of the Holy Synod K. P. Pobedonostsev's vision of a popular autocracy, emancipated from legal formalities and the manipulations of the intelligentsia, addressed the government's relationship to ordinary Russians and its duty to protect them from capitalists, Jews, and rich peasant usurers.[46] The same concern for cementing social relationships appeared in the first issue of the constitutionalist periodical *Osvobozhdenie,* published in June 1902, which editor Peter Struve hoped would provide "the crystallization point of the national liberation movement."[47] The absence of linkages implied in voluntaristic social identities may have peaked in Leninist revolutionary tactics, which called upon peasants first to play the historical role of the missing bourgeoisie—that is, to become the bourgeoisie—and then to accept the Bolshevik party as the dictatorship of the proletariat and poorest peasants. Beginning in the 1860s intellectuals of every possible political persuasion explicitly confronted the problem of forging ties to ordinary people. The question of how these connections would or should evolve remained at the center of tactical and ideological debates among bureaucrats, politicians, and revolutionaries.

The revolution of 1905 painfully exposed the elusiveness of large-scale societal cohesion even as virtually the entire population rose up against the social order or was mobilized in an "all-nation movement" against the autocracy. The articulation and pursuit of new social models led by the intelligentsia—a process that Leopold Haimson considers a sign of crisis and instability on the eve of the First World War[48]—also represented a redefinition of elite identities in an ongoing search for links in society. Throughout most of the imperial period, the categories of official society and the myths of tsarist rule provided important mechanisms of integration. Gradually after emancipation in 1861 and then altogether in the legal changes of 1906 and 1912,[49] the disappearance of Petrine juridical definitions—together with the monarchy's lost sacrality and the exclusion (or withdrawal) of peasants and workers from Duma politics—eliminated the empirewide structures that traditionally had mediated or potentially could mediate massive class conflict. The result was greater social particularism and weaker organizational ties in increasingly chaotic political and economic conditions. Even before the outbreak of war in the summer of 1914, hooliganism appeared in St. Petersburg as a street phenomenon, a form of working-class protest, and an artistic creed. Characterized by the public, deliberately offensive and shocking, and increasingly violent and destructive defiance of authority and established culture, hooliganism revealed that, at the center of state power, traditional social fragmentation easily hardened into intractable alienation, which precluded hopes of legitimate redress for the laboring population or cultural integration for the educated elites.[50]

The enduring viability of the Russian empire as a multiethnic, multiconfessional, multicultural, and multinational polity, as well as its ultimate failure to ensure political and social stability through fundamental reform, are best understood in terms of long-standing institutions, values, and patterns of behavior that changed very slowly from the seventeenth century until the early twentieth century. The Western model or antimodel, which educated Russians embraced as their own, was central to the relationship between society and state, but until the very end of the tsarist period, it was not the model of western Europe's protracted nineteenth century. Clearly, the history of imperial Russian "society" and its ultimate demise cannot be understood solely as a linear progression from one set of structures and relationships to another. Old and new characteristics certainly coexisted, overlapped, clashed, combined, and disappeared; but the linear transformation from agrarian to urban-industrial society had barely begun in the early twentieth century. More suggestive were the ongoing and dynamic tensions and accommodations between the idea and the reality, the imagined and the experienced, the desired and the attained. Such tensions could be found in all facets of community and individual life. The meeting of the social and administrative regimes—the central subject of this book—was just one of the places where these interactions occurred. As much as any structural, functional, or objective parameter, the moral universes of individuals and groups—their understanding of what should have been and their rationalizations for the choices they made, the behaviors they exhibited, and the actions they failed to carry through—powerfully defined social identity and experience. These imagined relationships were also a fundamental condition of social stability.[51]

ABBREVIATIONS

AHR	*American Historical Review*
BPIV	Conze and Kocka, *Bildungssystem und Professionalisierung in internationalen Vergleichen*
CASS	*Canadian-American Slavic Studies*
ch.	*chast'*
CMRS	*Cahiers du Monde russe et soviétique*
CRR	Belliustin, *Description of the Clergy in Rural Russia*
d. (dd.)	*delo (dela)*
DNGUAK	*Deistviia Nizhegorodskoi gubernskoi uchenoi arkhivnoi komissii*
EIRSU	Guroff and Carstensen, *Entrepreneurship in Imperial Russia and the Soviet Union*
E&S	Edmondson and Waldron, *Economy and Society in Russia*
ES	*Entsiklopedicheskii slovar' F. A. Brokgauz–I. A. Efron*
f.	*fond*
FIR	Ransel, *The Family in Imperial Russia*
FOG	*Forschungen zur osteuropäischen Geschichte*
GARF	Gosudarstvennyi arkhiv Rossiiskoi Federatsii
IR:SSO	Mendelsohn and Shatz, *Imperial Russia, 1700–1917: State, Society, Opposition*
IZ	*Istoricheskie zapiski*
JGO	*Jahrbücher für Geschichte Osteuropas*
JMH	*Journal of Modern History*
kn.	*kniga*
l. (ll.)	*list (listy)*
LCPC	Bartlett, *Land Commune and Peasant Community*
op.	*opis'*
PECP	Kingston-Mann and Mixter, *Peasant Economy, Culture, and Politics*
PIIIR	Raeff, *Political Ideas and Institutions in Imperial Russia*
PSZ	*Polnoe sobranie zakonov Rossiiskoi imperii*
RGADA	Rossiiskii gosudarstvennyi arkhiv drevnikh aktov
RGB	Rossiiskaia gosudarstvennaia biblioteka

RGIA	Rossiiskii gosudarstvennyi istoricheskii arkhiv
RGR	Ekloff, Bushnell, and Zakharova, *Russia's Great Reforms*
RGVIA	Rossiiskii gosudarstvennyi voenno-istoricheskii arkhiv
RMMC	Balzer, *Russia's Missing Middle Class*
RO:BRS	Pintner and Rowney, *Russian Officialdom: The Bureaucratization of Russian Society*
RR	*Russian Review*
RS	*Russkaia starina*
SEER	*Slavonic and East European Review*
SIRIO	*Sbornik Imperatorskogo Rossiiskogo istoricheskogo obshchestva*
SR	*Slavic Review*
SRHG	Bater and French, *Studies in Russian Historical Geography*
st.	*stat'ia*
SZ	*Svod zakonov Rossiiskoi imperii*
t.	*tom*
TsGIAgM	Tsentral'nyi gosudarstvennyi istoricheskii arkhiv goroda Moskvy
V. N. Karpov	itself
ZMVD	*Zhurnal ministerstva vnutrennikh del*
ZR	Emmons and Vucinich, *The Zemstvo in Russia*

NOTES

CHAPTER 1: THE INSTITUTIONAL SETTING

1. Michael T. Florinsxky, *Russia: A History and an Interpretation,* 2 vols. (New York, 1947 and 1953), 1: 324; Richard S. Wortman, *Scenarios of Power: Myth and Ceremony in Russian Monarchy,* vol. 1, *From Peter the Great to the Death of Nicholas I* (Princeton, 1995), 61–64.

2. Marc Raeff, *The Well-Ordered Police State: Social and Institutional Change through Law in the Germanies and Russia, 1600–1800* (New Haven, 1983).

3. Most recently, "in June of 1988 an official [church] act of canonization was issued, recognizing 'the blessed, pious Grand Prince of Moscow, Dmitrii Donskoi,' as a saint who selflessly 'lay down his life for his friends' . . . and who was gratefully remembered and emulated by his countrymen." Gail Lenhoff, "Unofficial Veneration of the Daniilovichi in Muscovite Rus'," in *Culture and Identity in Muscovy, 1359–1584/Moskovskaia Rus' (1359–1584): Kul'tura i istoricheskoe samosoznanie,* ed. Ann M. Kleimola and Gail Lenhoff (Moscow, 1996), 17. On the veneration of rulers, see as well Michael Cherniavsky, *Tsar and People: Studies in Russian Myths* (New Haven, 1961). On pagan ancestor worship, syncretism, and the glorification of princes, see Gail Lenhoff, *The Martyred Princes Boris and Gleb: A Socio-Cultural Study of the Cult and the Texts* (Columbus, Ohio, 1989), 34–37, 79–87.

4. Works that shed light on these issues include Isolde Thyrêt, "Life in the Kremlin under the Tsars Mikhail Fedorovich and Aleksei Mikhailovich: New Perspectives on the Institution of the *Terem*" (unpublished paper presented at the conference Private Life in Russia: Medieval Times to the Present, University of Michigan–Ann Arbor, October 4–6, 1996); Wortman, *Scenarios of Power;* Adele Lindenmeyr, *Poverty Is Not a Vice: Charity, Society, and the State in Imperial Russia* (Princeton, 1996), 99–119; Brenda Meehan-Waters, "Catherine the Great and the Problem of Female Rule," *RR* 34 (1975): 293–307.

5. E. R. Dashkova, *The Memoirs of Princess Dashkova: Russia in the Time of Catherine the Great,* trans. and ed. Kyril Fitzlyon, reprint (Durham, N.C., 1995).

6. Ibid. On the Muscovite situation, see Nancy Shields Kollmann, "Ritual and Social Drama at the Muscovite Court," *SR* 45 (1986): 486–502.

7. Marc Raeff, "La Noblesse et le discours politique sous le règne de Pierre le Grand," *CMRS* 34 (1993): 33–46; Cynthia H. Whittaker, "The Reforming Tsar: The Redefinition of Autocratic Duty in Eighteenth-Century Russia," *SR* 51 (1992): 77–98.

8. The practice of consulting society was exemplified by the Muscovite Assembly of the Land *(zemskii sobor)*, Catherine II's Legislative Commission, M. M. Speranskii's proposals for political reform in the reign of Alexander I, the role of noble committees in the emancipation process of 1857–1862, P. A. Valuev's 1863 plan for *zemstvo* representation to the State Council, M. T. Loris-Melikov's "constitutional" project on the eve of Alexander II's assassination, and a host of late imperial reform commissions that included nobles, businessmen, and professionals.

9. For overviews, see Marc Raeff, ed., *Plans for Political Reform in Imperial Russia, 1730–1905* (Englewood Cliffs, N.J., 1966); David Saunders, *Russia in the Age of Reaction and Reform, 1801–1881* (New York, 1992). For more specialized references, see chap. 2.

10. Examples include the service elite's "constitutional" projects of 1730, the instructions to the Legislative Commission of 1767, the proposals for emancipation and governmental reorganization composed by noble assemblies in 1857–1862, and the demands for a national body that would unite delegates from provincial assemblies of self-administration *(zemstva;* sing. *zemstvo)* prior to the 1905 revolution.

11. Raeff, *Police State;* David A. Bell, "The 'Public Sphere,' the State, and the World of Law in Eighteenth-Century France," *French Historical Studies* 17 (1992): 912–34.

12. Stephen Velychenko, "Identities, Loyalties and Service in Imperial Russia: Who Administered the Borderlands?" *RR* 54 (1995): 189.

13. The fiscal and service obligations of minorities varied.

14. Historians identify three phases in the development of national movements: (1) scholarly interest in the cultural, linguistic, social, and historical characteristics of nondominant ethnic groups; (2) patriotic agitation by minority elites who seek to win over the masses to the ideal of national autonomy by convincing them that their national identity has special value; and (3) the development of broad-based mass support for the ideal of national autonomy and the emergence of national movements. See Gerhard Brunn, Miroslav Hroch, and Andreas Kappeler, "Introduction," in Andreas Kappeler, ed., *The Formation of National Elites* (New York, 1992), 1–10.

15. Hans Rogger, "Nationalism and the State: A Russian Dilemma," *Comparative Studies in Society and History* 4 (1961–1962): 253–64; idem, "The Skobelev Phenomenon: The Hero and His Worship," *Oxford Slavonic Papers* 9 (1976): 46–78.

16. On soldiers' wives and children, see Elise Kimerling [Wirtschafter], "Soldiers' Children, 1719–1856: A Study of Social Engineering in Imperial Russia," *FOG* 30 (1982): 61–136; Elise Kimerling Wirtschafter, *From Serf to Russian Soldier* (Princeton, 1990), 35–40; idem, "Social Misfits: Veterans and Soldiers' Families in Servile Russia," *Journal of Military History* 59 (1995): 227–32; Beatrice Farnsworth, "The Soldatka: Folklore and Court Record," *SR* 49 (1990): 58–73. For further discussion, see chap. 2.

17. A law of 1841 required that among state peasants, the wives of recruits be allowed to farm their husbands' plots. In addition, they continued to pay the rents and taxes associated with the land, unless the village freed them from their share of the burden. It is possible that this regulation simply codified existing practices; if not, then it is not known at this time whether enforcement followed. Wirtschafter, "Social Misfits," 228–30.

18. Obviously, a soldier's widow did not need spousal permission.

19. David L. Ransel, *Mothers of Misery: Child Abandonment in Russia* (Princeton, 1988), 3–61, 176–221, 256–93. Provincial public welfare boards, created in 1775, also maintained orphanages and foundling homes. Lindenmeyr, *Poverty*, 32–36.

20. Just such a collective identity seems to have played a role in the Kreenholm strike of 1872. See Reginald Zelnik, *Law and Disorder on the Narova River: The Kreenholm Strike of 1872* (Berkeley, 1995).

21. The description of women's inheritance and property rights is based upon a very limited body of concrete research, which in the case of peasants repeatedly has yielded contradictory information. This is to be expected, given the local variations characteristic of rural society and the dearth of in-depth microstudies. Ironically, perhaps, historians of the nobility and propertied elites devote more attention to the economic rights of women than to the general development of property relations. Thus there are no full-scale studies of Russia's first general land survey in the mid-eighteenth century or of the chronic litigation over estate boundaries and inheritance rights that occupied the landowning nobility. The information presented derives from V. A. Aleksandrov, *Obychnoe pravo krepostnoi derevni Rossii: XVIII–nachalo XIX v.* (Moscow, 1984), 206–33; Rodney D. Bohac, "Peasant Inheritance Strategies in Russia," *Journal of Interdisciplinary History* 16 (1985): 23–42; idem, "Widows and the Russian Serf Community," in *Russia's Women: Accommodation, Resistance, Transformation,* ed. Barbara Evans Clements, Barbara Alpern Engel, and Christine D. Worobec (Berkeley, 1991), 95–112; Beatrice Farnsworth and Lynne Viola, eds., *Russian Peasant Women* (New York, 1992); Lee A. Farrow, "Peter the Great's Law of Single Inheritance: State Imperatives and Noble Resistance," *RR* 55 (1996): 430–47; Steven L. Hoch, *Serfdom and Social Control in Russia: Petrovskoe, a Village in Tambov* (Chicago, 1986), 120–22; Daniel H. Kaiser, "Women, Property and the Law in Early Modern Russia," unpublished paper (Grinnell, Iowa, 1988); Valerie A. Kivelson, "The Effects of Partible Inheritance: Gentry Families and the State in Muscovy," *RR* 53 (1994): 197–212; Michelle Lamarche Marrese, "A Woman's Kingdom: Women and the Control of Property in Russia, 1700–1861" (Ph.D. diss., Northwestern University, 1995); N. A. Minenko, *Russkaia krest'ianskaia sem'ia v zapadnoi Sibiri (XVIII–pervoi poloviny XIX v.)* (Novosibirsk, 1979), 156–70; William G. Wagner, *Marriage, Property and Law in Late Imperial Russia* (New York, 1994); George G. Weickhardt, "Legal Rights of Women in Russia, 1100–1750," *SR* (1996): 1–23; Christine D. Worobec, *Peasant Russia: Family and Community in the Post-Emancipation Period* (Princeton, 1991), 42–75. Nancy Shields Kollmann, "The Seclusion of Elite Muscovite Women," *Russian History* 10 (1983): 170–87; Dashkova, *Memoirs;* David L. Ransel, *The Politics of Catherinian Russia: The Panin Party* (New Haven, 1975). See also chap. 4.

22. See chap. 4.

23. In some communities, widows were exempt from feudal obligations.

24. Barbara Alpern Engel, "Women, Men, and the Languages of Peasant Resistance, 1870–1907," in *Cultures in Flux: Lower-Class Values, Practices, and Resistance in Late Imperial Russia,* ed. Stephen P. Frank and Mark D. Steinberg (Princeton, 1994), 34–53.

25. Although the law allowed Muscovite testators some discretion in assigning property to heirs, relatively few landowners wrote wills; as a result, most inheritance rights derived from the rules of intestacy. Kaiser, "Women, Property and Law," 3.

26. Service lands *(pomest'ia)* were held in temporary tenure and their possession theoretically remained conditional upon active service. Service estates *(vysluzhennye*

votchiny) were granted for service already rendered and legally approximated patrimony. Daniel H. Kaiser, "Women's Property in Muscovite Families, 1500–1725," unpublished paper (Grinnell, Iowa, 1988), 10–11; idem, "Women, Property and Law," 4.

27. The widow's maintenance portion was supposed to come from purchased or service lands. In the absence of such lands, the 1649 Law Code and subsequent legislation allowed widows an allotment from patrimonial estates or from the father-in-law's service lands.

28. Kaiser, "Women, Property and Law," 13.

29. Eighteenth- and nineteenth-century inheritance laws applied to patrimonial or inherited property, not to acquired property, which a testator could bequeath freely but which became patrimonial once it was received in inheritance by a direct heir. Muscovite laws drew a similar distinction between patrimonial and purchased lands, allowing testators to bequeath the latter as they pleased. The eighteenth-century improvement in the status of women derived from their being guaranteed a share of the patrimony. Wagner, *Marriage, Property and Law*, 228–33.

30. Marrese, "Woman's Kingdom." Female landowners also enjoyed indirect voting rights in elections to *zemstvo* assemblies (from 1864) and the national Duma (from 1906). See Dorothy Atkinson, "Society and the Sexes in the Russian Past," in *Women in Russia*, ed. Dorothy Atkinson, Alexander Dallin, and Gail Warshofsky Lapidus (Stanford, 1977), 32.

31. Although collateral male kin could not displace heiresses who lacked brothers, if a man had so many daughters that his sons would not receive one-fourteenth of his estate, then the legal requirement that daughters receive one-fourteenth did not apply. Adultery also could be grounds for awarding to a husband lands that legally belonged to his wife. Needless to say, an adulterous husband did not face such sanctions. Marrese, "Woman's Kingdom," chaps. 1–2.

32. On these points, see ibid.; Wagner, *Marriage, Property and Law*, 232–371.

33. Although the same laws applied to urban social categories and potentially also to peasants who owned private lands, to date research has been completed only on noble estate owners.

34. Historians have as yet insufficient data to determine whether there was a real increase in female economic agency during the eighteenth century, or whether an apparent increase resulted from legal changes and the extent of enforcement, accidents of record keeping, chronological and regional variations, or the relative importance of patrimonial and service or acquired lands. For some of the conflicting possibilities, see Kaiser, "Women, Property and Law"; Kivelson, "Partible Inheritance"; Marrese, "Woman's Kingdom."

35. Stephen P. Frank, *Crime, Cultural Conflict, and Justice in Rural Russia, 1856–1914* (forthcoming); Marrese, "Woman's Kingdom," chap. 4.

36. Farrow, "Single Inheritance."

37. Preliminary research based on wills and dowries, covering the period from 1500 to 1725, indicates that land dispositions were broadly consistent with existing legal prescriptions. Kaiser, "Women's Property."

38. Kivelson, "Partible Inheritance."

39. A law of 1679 forbade a husband to sell his wife's hereditary estate, and from 1763 until 1825, land sales from spouse to spouse also were prohibited. Marrese, "Woman's Kingdom," chap. 1.

40. The question of gender difference in economic behavior is in need of serious research. One study of sixteenth- and seventeenth-century wills reveals some notewor-

thy distinctions, though on the whole male and female testatments seem remarkably consistent. Kaiser, "Women's Property."

41. On these issues, see W. Bruce Lincoln, *In the Vanguard of Reform: Russia's Enlightened Bureaucrats 1825–1861* (DeKalb, Ill., 1982), 148–62; Lina Bernstein, "Women on the Verge of a New Language: Russian Salon Hostesses in the First Half of the Nineteenth Century," in *Russia—Women—Culture*, ed. Helena Goscilo and Beth Holmgren (Bloomington, Ind., 1996), 209–24; Gitta Hammarberg, "Flirting with Words: Domestic Albums, 1770–1840," in Goscilo and Holmgren, *Russia—Women—Culture*, 297–320.

42. Traditionally, educated women enjoyed few alternatives to marriage: they could become governesses or teachers in schools for noblewomen, or they could enter nunneries. Priscilla Roosevelt, *Life on the Russian Country Estate: A Social and Cultural History* (New Haven, 1995), 180–83.

43. On the cult of domesticity, see Wortman, *Scenarios of Power* 1: 247–378.

44. Linda Edmondson, *Feminism in Russia, 1900–17* (Stanford, 1984); idem, ed., *Women and Society in Russia and the Soviet Union* (New York, 1992); Barbara Alpern Engel, *Mothers and Daughters of the Intelligentsia in Nineteenth-Century Russia* (New York, 1983); Christine Johanson, *Women's Struggle for Higher Education in Russia, 1855–1900* (Kingston, Ont., 1987); Richard Stites, *The Women's Liberation Movement in Russia: Feminism, Nihilism, and Bolshevism, 1860–1930* (Princeton, 1990).

45. The one important exception was the plantation economy of southwest Ukraine in the late imperial period. Robert Edelman, *Proletarian Peasants: The Revolution of 1905 in Russia's Southwest* (Ithaca, N.Y., 1987).

46. Princess Dashkova provides countless examples of these activities. Dashkova, *Memoirs*.

47. Lincoln, *Vanguard of Reform,* 148–62; Lindenmeyr, *Poverty,* 109–29.

48. The radical worker S. I. Kanatchikov describes the importance of such gatherings to his political education and radicalization. Reginald E. Zelnik, ed. and trans., *A Radical Worker in Tsarist Russia: The Autobiography of Semën Ivanovich Kanatchikov* (Stanford, 1971).

49. Daniel Gordon, "Philosophy, Sociology, and Gender in the Enlightenment Conception of Public Opinion," *French Historical Studies* 17 (1992): 899–902.

50. According to Jürgen Habermas, the independent public sphere or public opinion evolved from the private familial sphere. Jürgen Habermas, *The Structural Transformation of the Public Sphere: An Inquiry into a Category of Bourgeois Society,* trans. Thomas Burger with Frederick Lawrence (Cambridge, Mass., 1989). On these categories, see also Gordon, "Philosophy." On the contribution of "the rising state" to the development of a civil society in France, see Bell, "'Public Sphere.'" On civil society in Russia, see chap. 3.

51. The Smolny Institute was established in 1764; Pirogov's statement is dated 1856. On the purposes of women's education, see Engel, *Mothers and Daughters,* 3–61.

52. Quoted in Adele Lindenmeyr, "Public Life, Private Virtues: Women in Russian Charity," *Signs: Journal of Women in Culture and Society* 18 (1993): 572–73.

53. Sarah Maza, "Women, the Bourgeoisie, and the Public Sphere: Response to Daniel Gordon and David Bell," *French Historical Studies* 17 (1992): 945–49.

54. Dorothee Wierling, "The History of Everyday Life and Gender Relations: On Historical and Historiographical Relationships," in *The History of Everyday Life:*

Reconstructing Experiences and Ways of Life, ed. Alf Lüdtke, trans. William Templer (Princeton, 1995), 149–68; Joan W. Scott, "Gender: A Useful Category of Historical Analysis," *AHR* 91 (1986): 1053–75.

55. Brenda Meehan, *Holy Women of Russia: The Lives of Five Orthodox Women Offer Spiritual Guidance for Today* (San Francisco, 1993), 60.

56. For detailed analyses that differ somewhat from my conclusions, see Laurie Bernstein, *Sonia's Daughters: Prostitutes and Their Regulation in Imperial Russia* (Berkeley, 1995); Laura Engelstein, *The Keys to Happiness: Sex and the Search for Modernity in Fin-de-Siècle Russia* (Ithaca, N.Y., 1992); Meehan, *Holy Women;* Christine Ruane, "Divergent Discourses: The Image of the Russian Woman Schoolteacher in Post-Reform Russia," *Russian History* 20 (1993): 109–23; and Wagner, *Marriage, Property and Law.*

57. A work that highlights this interdependence is Worobec, *Peasant Russia.*

58. The relationship of the inner to the outer is a question of significant debate among psychologists. See L. S. Vygotsky, *Mind in Society: The Development of Higher Psychological Processes* (Cambridge, Mass., 1978); Jeanette A. Lawrence and Jaan Valsiner, "Conceptual Roots of Internalization: From Transmission to Transformation," *Human Development* 36 (1993): 150–67; James V. Wertsch, "Commentary," *Human Development* 36 (1993): 168–71; Barbara Rogoff, "Children's Guided Participation and Participatory Appropriation in Sociocultural Activity," in *Development in Context: Acting and Thinking in Specific Environments,* ed. Robert H. Wozniak and Kurt W. Fischer (Hillsdale, N.J., 1993), 121–53. I am grateful to Catherine Raeff for sharing the last three items.

59. For example, the rural cantonal courts were not integrated into the general judicial system until 1912 (see chap. 4); the Stolypin agrarian reforms, which in most respects sought to eliminate legal distinctions between peasants and other social groups, preserved prohibitions on the sale of allotment land to nonpeasants. See David A. J. Macey, *Government and Peasant in Russia, 1861–1906: The Prehistory of the Stolypin Reforms* (DeKalb, Ill., 1987), 241–42; Gregory L. Freeze, "The *Soslovie* (Estate) Paradigm in Russian Social History," *AHR* 91 (1986): 11–36; Christoph Schmidt, "Über die Bezeichnung der Stände *(sostojanie-soslovie)* in Russland seit dem 18. Jahrhundert," *JGO* 38 (1990): 199–211; idem, *Ständerecht und Standeswechsel in Russland, 1851–1897* (Wiesbaden, 1994); L. E. Shepelev, *Otmenennye istorei chiny, zvaniia i tituly v Rossiiskoi imperii* (Leningrad, 1977); P. A. Zaionchkovskii, *Pravitel'stvennyi apparat samoderzhavnoi Rossii v XIX v.* (Moscow, 1978).

60. "Monsieur Diderot, I have heard with the greatest pleasure that which your brilliant spirit has inspired in you, but with all your great principles, which I understand very well, one would make beautiful books and bad works. You forget in all your plans of reform the difference between our two positions; you, you only work on paper, which bears everything; it is all smooth, supple, and opposes no obstacles, neither to your imagination nor to your pen; while I, poor empress, I work on human skin, which is quite otherwise irritable and ticklish." Quoted in Larry Wolff, *Inventing Eastern Europe: The Map of Civilization on the Mind of the Enlightenment* (Stanford, 1994), 230.

CHAPTER 2: "RULING" CLASSES AND SERVICE ELITES

1. Quoted in Jacob Walkin, *The Rise of Democracy in Pre-Revolutionary Russia: Political and Social Institutions under the Last Three Czars* (New York, 1962), 76.

2. Brenda Meehan-Waters, *Autocracy and Aristocracy: The Russian Service Elite of 1730* (New Brunswick, N.J., 1982), 1–3.

3. Ibid., 8–22. On the continuing importance of the landed aristocracy in the ruling elite, see Dominic Lieven, *Russia's Rulers under the Old Regime* (New Haven, 1989), chap. 2.

4. *SZ* (1832), t. 9, razdel 1, glava 1, otdelenie 1, st. 13–15.

5. John P. LeDonne, *Absolutism and Ruling Class: The Formation of the Russian Political Order, 1700–1825* (New York, 1991), viii.

6. On alienation, see Marc Raeff, *Origins of the Russian Intelligentsia: The Eighteenth-Century Nobility* (New York, 1966); Michael Confino, "Histoire et psychologie: À propos de la noblesse russe au XVIIIe siècle," *Annales: Économies—Sociétés—Civilisation* 22 (1967): 1163–205. On the close connection to the land, see Michael Confino, *Domaines et seigneurs en Russie vers la fin du XVIIIe siècle* (Paris, 1963); idem, *Systèmes agraires et progrès agricole: L'assolement triennal en Russie aux XVIIIe–XIXe siècles* (Paris and La Haye, 1969); Kivelson, "Partible Inheritance"; Marrese, "Woman's Kingdom."

7. Meehan-Waters, *Autocracy and Aristocracy,* 47–48.

8. Ibid., 16–39.

9. Paul Dukes, *Catherine the Great and the Russian Nobility* (London, 1967), 26.

10. Ibid., 159–60.

11. Paul Dukes, *The Making of Russian Absolutism, 1613–1801* (New York, 1982), 116. See also idem, *Catherine and Nobility;* Robert E. Jones, *The Emancipation of the Russian Nobility, 1762–1785* (Princeton, 1973).

12. Dukes, *Catherine and Nobility,* 9–15, 141; L. F. Pisar'kova, "Ot Petra do Nikolaia I: Politika pravitel'stva v oblasti formirovaniia biurokratii," *Sosloviia i gosudarstvennaia vlast' v Rossii: XV–seredina XIX vv. Mezhdunarodnaia konferentsiia—Chteniia pamiati akad. L. V. Cherepnina,* 2 vols. (Moscow, 1994), 2: 23–25.

13. Jones, *Emancipation of Nobility,* chaps. 6–7; Dukes, *Catherine and Nobility,* 106. On the right of serfs to complain against their masters, see chap. 4.

14. Jones, *Emancipation of Nobility,* 267–72.

15. Ibid., 20–21, 74–77, 276–84. See also Dukes, *Catherine and Nobility,* 226–28.

16. Marc Raeff, "The Domestic Policies of Peter III and His Overthrow," reprinted in idem, *Political Ideas and Institutions in Imperial Russia* (Boulder, 1994), 188–212; Jones, *Emancipation of Nobility,* v–vii, 3–38, 44–46, 88–94, 154–69, 234–99; Dukes, *Catherine and Nobility,* 38–46, 226–27, 248–51.

17. W. Bruce Lincoln, *The Great Reforms: Autocracy, Bureaucracy, and the Politics of Change in Imperial Russia* (DeKalb, Ill., 1990); idem, *Vanguard of Reform.*

18. Leopold H. Haimson, ed., *The Politics of Rural Russia, 1905–1914* (Bloomington, Ind., 1979), especially idem, "Conclusion: Observations on the Politics of the Russian Countryside (1905–1914)," 261–300.

19. Terence Emmons, *The Russian Landed Gentry and the Peasant Emancipation of 1861* (London, 1968); Daniel Field, *The End of Serfdom: Nobility and Bureaucracy in Russia, 1855–1861* (Cambridge, Mass., 1976).

20. The experience of P. D. Boborykin suggests the ease of the transition from noble landowner to urban intellectual, though his also was a path fraught with financial pitfalls. See P. D. Boborykin, *Vospominaniia v dvukh tomakh,* 2 vols. (Moscow, 1965).

21. Seymour Becker, *Nobility and Privilege in Late Imperial Russia* (DeKalb, Ill., 1985), chap. 3; Haimson, *Politics of Rural Russia;* Lieven, *Russia's Rulers.*

22. Cherniavsky, *Tsar and People;* Daniel Field, *Rebels in the Name of the Tsar* (Boston, 1976); Elise Kimerling Wirtschafter, "The Ideal of Paternalism in the Prereform Army," in *Imperial Russia, 1700–1917: State, Society, Opposition: Essays in Honor of Marc Raeff,* ed. Ezra Mendelsohn and Marshall Shatz (DeKalb, Ill., 1988), 95–114.

23. See the discussion of peasants in chap. 4. On the inadequacy of rural economic crisis as an explanation for noble and peasant disaffection, see Peter Gatrell, *The Tsarist Economy, 1850–1917* (London, 1986); S. Becker, *Nobility and Privilege;* Steven L. Hoch, "On Good Numbers and Bad: Malthus, Population Trends and Peasant Standard of Living in Late Imperial Russia," *SR* 53 (1994): 42–75.

24. Recent scholarship does much to redress the imbalance. See Roosevelt, *Country Estate;* Marrese, "Woman's Kingdom"; Robin Bisha, "The Promise of Patriarchy: Marriage in Eighteenth-Century Russia" (Ph.D. diss., Indiana University, 1994).

25. On this issue, there is a tendency to oversimplify the interpretation presented in Raeff, *Origins of Intelligentsia.* Raeff does not describe an absolute lack of identification with the family patrimony, although he does argue that the income and serfs attached to noble estates were more important than the land itself (see p. 46). On the whole, however, his notion of noble rootlessness refers to the absence of an identity that was rooted in a given territorial locality, as distinct from a given familial estate. For a comparative perspective, see Dominic Lieven, *The Aristocracy in Europe, 1815–1914* (New York, 1992).

26. In 1863, exemption from the capitation was extended to lesser townspeople *(meshchane).* S. Becker, *Nobility and Privilege,* 25–26.

27. Secretarial rights refer to service rank. Pisar'kova, "Ot Petra do Nikolaia I," in *Sosloviia* 2:24–25.

28. Elise Kimerling Wirtschafter, *Structures of Society: Imperial Russia's "People of Various Ranks"* (DeKalb, Ill., 1994), 26–31, 78–85. See also the discussion of peasants in chap. 4.

29. Haimson, *Politics of Rural Russia;* Roberta Thompson Manning, *The Crisis of the Old Order in Russia: Gentry and Government* (Princeton, 1982).

30. Meehan-Waters, *Autocracy and Aristocracy,* 153.

31. Ibid., 92–96, 149–66. On the insecurity of property, see Lee A. Farrow, "Property, Security and the Security of Property in Eighteenth-Century Russia," paper prepared for delivery at the AAASS conference, Boston, November 17, 1996.

32. Dukes, *Russian Absolutism,* 168–69, 177, 182; Dashkova, *Memoirs;* Marc Raeff, *Michael Speransky: Statesman of Imperial Russia, 1772–1839* (The Hague, 1957), 170–203; Wirtschafter, *Serf to Soldier,* chap. 5.

33. M. A. Rakhmatullin, *Krest'ianskoe dvizhenie v velikorusskikh guberniiakh v 1825–1857 godakh* (Moscow, 1990), 179–86; Boris N. Mironov, "Local Self-Government in Russia in the First Half of the Nineteenth Century: Provincial Government and Estate Self-Government," *JGO* 42 (1994): 193–94.

34. Dukes, *Russian Absolutism,* 184; Meehan-Waters, *Autocracy and Aristocracy,* 166.

35. Jones, *Emancipation of Nobility,* 295. This view is restated in Becker, *Nobility and Privilege,* 19–20.

36. V. R. Leikina-Svirskaia, *Intelligentsiia v Rossii vo vtoroi polovine XIX veka* (Moscow, 1971); S. M. Troitskii, *Russkii absoliutizm i dvorianstvo v XVIII v.: Formirovanie biurokratii* (Moscow, 1974); Zaionchkovskii, *Pravitel'stvennyi apparat;* S. Becker, *Nobility and Privilege,* 25–26, 117–24.

37. RGVIA, f. 801 (Auditoriatskii departament voennogo ministerstva), op. 60, d. 29, ll. 6ob.–8. Polish *szlachta* who failed to document their ancestry became "single householders" with the right to regain noble status through military service on the same basis as their Russian counterparts. *Otchet ministerstva iustitsii za 1845* (St. Petersburg, 1846), li. See also Thomas Esper, "The Odnodvortsy and the Russian Nobility," *SEER* 45 (1967): 124–34.

38. Wirtschafter, *Serf to Soldier*, 33–34, 44–49.

39. Thus in 1782 two factory owners in Nizhnii Novgorod requested exclusion from the poll tax registers and enrollment in the noble lists on a hereditary basis. V. I. Snezhnevskii, "Opis' zhurnalam nizhegorodskogo namestnicheskogo pravleniia (za 1781–1783 gg.)," *DNGUAK: Sbornik statei, soobshchenii, opisei, del i dokumentov,* t. 3 (Nizhnii Novgorod, 1898), 156.

40. Dukes, *Catherine and Nobility*, 84, 145–46.

41. For the specifics, see Wirtschafter, *Structures of Society*, chaps. 2–4.

42. Troitskii, *Russkii absoliutizm*, 180–82, 204–12.

43. Ibid., 180–81.

44. Douglas Smith, "Freemasonry and the Public in Eighteenth-Century Russia," *Eighteenth-Century Studies* 29 (1995): 25–44.

45. Sergei Aksakov, *A Russian Gentleman,* trans. J. D. Duff (New York, 1982).

46. Field, *End of Serfdom*, 131.

47. Following reforms in 1831–1832, only nobles who owned more than one hundred serfs qualified for direct participation in the corporate assemblies. Emmons, *Landed Gentry,* 3–14.

48. Ibid., 4–5. For a similar depiction of noble stratification and lifestyles in the eighteenth century, see Confino, *Systèmes agraires,* chap. 7.

49. *Aleksandr Nikolaevich Engelgardt's Letters from the Country, 1872–1887,* trans. and ed. Cathy A. Frierson (New York, 1993), 176.

50. S. Becker, *Nobility and Privilege,* 36–39.

51. Manning, *Crisis of Old Order,* xiii; Haimson, *Politics of Rural Russia,* vii-viii; idem, "Introduction: The Russian Landed Nobility and the System of the Third of June," in ibid., 1–29; S. Becker, *Nobility and Privilege,* 138.

52. Manning, *Crisis of Old Order;* Gary M. Hamburg, *Politics of the Russian Nobility, 1881–1905* (New Brunswick, N.J., 1984). For a critique, see S. Becker, *Nobility and Privilege.*

53. On the economic successes of some landowners, see Edelman, *Proletarian Peasants;* S. Becker, *Nobility and Privilege,* chaps. 2–4; Gatrell, *Tsarist Economy,* chap. 4.

54. S. Becker, *Nobility and Privilege,* xiv.

55. Some poor nobles also remained on the land as agricultural laborers. Ibid., 12–14, 113–24.

56. On the economic viability of nobles, see S. Becker, *Nobility and Privilege,* chap. 2. On the nobility's continuing political influence, see ibid., chaps. 7–8; Haimson, *Politics of Rural Russia.*

57. S. Becker, *Nobility and Privilege,* 168–69. For a regional perspective, see Robert Edelman, *Gentry Politics on the Eve of the Russian Revolution: The Nationalist Party, 1907–1917* (New Brunswick, N.J., 1980).

58. Meehan-Waters, *Autocracy and Aristocracy,* 118–30; Farrow, "Single Inheritance."

59. Meehan-Waters, *Autocracy and Aristocracy,* 131.

60. On trading nobles, see "Vedomost' o narodonaselenii Rossii za 1851 god po

9 narodnoi perepisi," *ZMVD* (November 1853), otdelenie 3, 61–76; Victor Kamendrowsky and David M. Griffiths, "The Fate of the Trading Nobility Controversy in Russia: A Chapter in the Relationship between Catherine II and the Russian Nobility," *JGO* 26 (1978): 198–221.

61. S. V. Rozhdestvenskii, *Istoricheskii obzor deiatel'nosti ministerstva narodnogo prosveshcheniia, 1802–1902* (St. Petersburg, 1902), 196–98. For similar observations made by contemporaries in the eighteenth and nineteenth centuries, see Confino, *Systèmes agraires,* 256–57; Anatole Leroy-Beaulieu, *The Empire of the Tsars and the Russians,* ed. and trans. Zenaide A. Ragozin, 3 vols. (New York, 1893–1896) 1: 309–10.

62. Iurii Lotman believes that the literary elite of the late eighteenth and early nineteenth centuries viewed life as a game of chance, which was structured, ordered, and hierarchical but also highly random, fundamentally insecure and unstable, and filled with unexpected and unpredictable outcomes. In her stimulating study of the idea of nationalism, Liah Greenfeld also sees insecurity and status anxiety as essential characteristics of the eighteenth-century Russian nobility. The social and institutional phenomena emphasized in this discussion are consistent with these cultural interpretations. Iu. M. Lotman, "Tema kart i kartochnoi igry v russkoi literature nachala XIX veka," *Trudy po znakovym sistemam* 7 (1978): 120–42; idem, *Besedy o russkoi kul'ture: Byt i traditsii russkogo dvorianstva (XVIII–nachalo XIX veka)* (St. Petersburg, 1994), 136–63; Liah Greenfeld, *Nationalism: Five Roads to Modernity* (Cambridge, Mass., 1992), 204–22. I am grateful to Douglas Smith for the reference to the article by Lotman.

63. Michael Confino, "Servage russe, esclavage américain (note critique)," *Annales: Économies—Sociétés—Civilisation* 45 (1990): 1119–41; Raeff, *Origins of Intelligentsia.*

64. Raeff, *Origins of Intelligentsia;* see also Marc Raeff, "The Russian Autocracy and Its Officials," reprinted in *PIIIR,* 76–87; Daniel T. Orlovsky, *The Limits of Reform: The Ministry of Internal Affairs in Imperial Russia, 1802–1881* (Cambridge, Mass., 1981); Lincoln, *Vanguard of Reform;* idem, *Great Reforms;* Richard G. Robbins, Jr., *The Tsar's Viceroys: Russian Provincial Governors in the Last Years of the Empire* (Ithaca, N.Y., 1987); Lieven, *Russia's Rulers.*

65. These processes are well studied in a variety of contexts. See the bibliography for some of the more important references.

66. On the absence of constituted bodies and the administrative difficulties resulting therefrom, see Raeff, *Police State.*

67. I include "legislative" authority here because at all levels of imperial government there was no clear distinction between the legislative process and administrative decision making.

68. Lieven, *Russia's Rulers,* chaps. 1–2.

69. Ibid., 47–48, 156–67; Marc Raeff, "The Bureaucratic Phenomena of Imperial Russia, 1700–1905," *AHR* 84 (1979): 402.

70. Raeff, "Autocracy and Officials," in *PIIIR,* 76–87.

71. Ibid., 78.

72. On the State Council, see Lieven, *Russia's Rulers.* On the specialist ministries of agriculture, communications, trade and industry, and finance, see Daniel T. Orlovsky, "Professionalism in the Ministerial Bureaucracy on the Eve of the February Revolution of 1917," in *Russia's Missing Middle Class: The Professions in Russian History,* ed. Harley D. Balzer (Armonk, N.Y., 1996), 267–92.

73. Raeff, "Bureaucratic Phenomena." On cliques at court, see Ransel, *Politics*

of Catherinian Russia. On ministerial politics, see, among others, Orlovsky, *Limits of Reform;* idem, "Professionalism in Bureaucracy" in *RMMC;* and William C. Fuller, Jr., *Civil-Military Conflict in Imperial Russia, 1881–1914* (Princeton, 1985).

74. Raeff, "Bureaucratic Phenomena," 410–11.

75. On inadequate linkages in the military, see Bruce W. Menning, *Bayonets before Bullets: The Imperial Russian Army, 1861–1914* (Bloomington, Ind., 1992).

76. It is also important to distinguish imperial corruption from the Muscovite practice of local administration *(kormlenie),* which permitted provincial officials to maintain themselves by "feeding" off the territory and people under their authority. The practice remained legal until 1775 but continued at least until the end of the century. G. P. Enin, "Drevnerusskoe kormlenie v voevodskoi praktike XVII–XVIII vv.," in *Sosloviia i gosudarstvennaia vlast'* 1: 75–83.

77. Hans J. Torke, "Continuity and Change in the Relations between Bureaucracy and Society in Russia, 1613–1861," *Canadian Slavic Studies* 5 (1971): 472. On the necessity of bribe taking to supplement low pay and administrative staff, see Robbins, *Tsar's Viceroys,* 184–86.

78. These conditions are documented in Wirtschafter, *Serf to Soldier,* especially chap. 4.

79. Ibid., 116–18.

80. Richard G. Robbins, Jr., "The Limits of Professionalization: Russian Governors at the Beginning of the Twentieth Century," in *RMMC,* 251–66.

81. Robbins, *Tsar's Viceroys,* 12–64, 81–127, 146–79, 198–99, 243–45.

82. Ibid., 89.

83. Dietrich Geyer, "'Gesellschaft' als staatliche Veranstaltung. Sozialgeschichtliche Aspekte des russischen Behördenstaats im 18. Jahrhundert," in *Wirtschaft und Gesellschaft im vorrevolutionären Russland,* ed. Dietrich Geyer (Cologne, 1975), 20–52; Raeff, "Bureaucratic Phenomena," 399–411.

84. As an important exception, noblewomen did not face derogation, regardless of whom they married.

85. On implementing the capitation, see E. V. Anisimov, *Podatnaia reforma Petra I: Vvedenie podushnoi podati v Rossii, 1719–1728 gg.* (Leningrad, 1982).

86. Troitskii, *Russkii absoliutizm,* 243–52; Zaionchkovskii, *Pravitel'stvennyi apparat,* 28–37, 53; Shepelev, *Otmenennye istoriei chiny,* 67–69; Harold A. McFarlin, "Recruitment Norms for the Russian Civil Service in 1833: The Chancery Clerkship," *Societas—A Review of Social History* 3 (1973): 61–73; idem, "The Extension of the Imperial Russian Civil Service to the Lowest Office Workers: The Creation of the Chancery Clerkship, 1827–1833," *Russian History* 1 (1974): 1–17; Pisar'kova, "Ot Petra do Nikolaia I," in *Sosloviia* 2:22–26; M. F. Rumiantseva, "Rossiiskoe chinovnichestvo vtoroi poloviny XVIII v.: Formirovanie sosloviia," in *Sosloviia* 2:59–70.

87. Wirtschafter, *Serf to Soldier,* chap. 2.

88. On conscription, soldiers' families, and retired soldiers, see ibid., chaps. 1–2; Kimerling [Wirtschafter], "Soldiers' Children"; Wirtschafter, "Social Misfits"; Henry Hirschbiel, "The District Captains of the Ministry of State Properties in the Reign of Nicholas I: A Case Study of Russian Officialdom, 1838–1856" (Ph.D. diss., New York University, 1978); V. A. Aleksandrov, *Sel'skaia obshchina v Rossii (XVII–nachalo XIX v.)* (Moscow, 1976); L. S. Prokof'eva, *Krest'ianskaia obshchina v Rossii vo vtoroi polovine XVIII–pervoi polovine XIX veka* (Leningrad, 1981); Farnsworth, "Soldatka"; John L. H. Keep, "Catherine's Veterans," *SEER* 59 (1981): 385–96.

89. Wirtschafter, *Structures of Society,* chap. 3; Fedor Enskii, *Otstavnye soldaty* (St. Petersburg, 1873), 105–11.

90. John Bushnell, *Mutiny amid Repression: Russian Soldiers in the Revolution of 1905–1906* (Bloomington, Ind., 1985); idem, "Peasants in Uniform: The Tsarist Army as a Peasant Society," *Journal of Social History* 13 (1980): 565–76.

91. Bushnell, *Mutiny amid Repression.*

92. On this issue, see Fuller, *Civil-Military Conflict.*

93. On the postreform regimental economy, see John Bushnell, "The Tsarist Officer Corps, 1881–1914: Customs, Duties, Inefficiency," *AHR* 86 (1981): 753–80.

94. Wirtschafter, *Serf to Soldier,* chaps. 4–6.

95. Lieven, *Russia's Rulers;* Lincoln, *Vanguard of Reform;* McFarlin, "Recruitment Norms"; idem, "Extension of Civil Service"; Walter M. Pintner, "The Social Characteristics of the Early Nineteenth-Century Russian Bureaucracy," *SR* 29 (1970): 429–43; idem, "The Russian Higher Civil Service on the Eve of the 'Great Reforms'," *Journal of Social History* 8 (1975): 55–68; idem, "The Evolution of Civil Officialdom, 1755–1855," in *Russian Officialdom: The Bureaucratization of Russian Society from the Seventeenth to the Twentieth Century,* ed. Walter M. Pintner and Don Karl Rowney (Chapel Hill, N.C., 1980), 190–226; idem, "Civil Officialdom and the Nobility in the 1850s," in *RO:BRS,* 227–49.

96. LeDonne, *Absolutism and Ruling Class,* 14, 56–58; RGADA, f. 248 (Senat i ego uchrezhdeniia), kn. 3301, ll. 484–89.

97. Troitskii, *Russkii absoliutizm,* 180–81, 208–9, 240–42.

98. Pintner, "Social Characteristics," 430–37; idem, "Higher Civil Service," 56–57, 64; idem, "Civil Officialdom and Nobility," in *RO:BRS,* 238.

99. Pintner, "Evolution of Civil Officialdom," in *RO:BRS,* 201–5.

100. These data are discussed in greater detail in Wirtschafter, *Structures of Society,* chap. 3.

101. *PSZ* (I) 10, no. 7226.

102. Wirtschafter, "Social Misfits," 234–35.

103. *ZMVD* (June 1831): 113–32, (July 1832): 29–47, (February 1842): 115–34, (September 1859): 69–111.

104. I. S. Belliustin, *Description of the Clergy in Rural Russia: The Memoir of a Nineteenth-Century Parish Priest,* trans. Gregory L. Freeze (Ithaca, N.Y., 1985), 126.

105. Gregory L. Freeze, "Introduction," in *CRR,* 15–18. See also Gregory L. Freeze, "Handmaiden of the State? The Church in Imperial Russia Reconsidered," *Journal of Ecclesiastical History* 36 (1985): 82–102.

106. On church finances, see Igor Smolitsch, *Geschichte der russischen Kirche, 1700–1917,* 2 vols. (Leiden and Wiesbaden, 1964 and 1990) 1: 185, 482–84.

107. Gregory L. Freeze, *Church, Religion and Society in Modern Russia, 1740–1940* (forthcoming).

108. Ibid.; Gregory L. Freeze, "The Rechristianization of Russia: The Church and Popular Religion, 1750–1850," *Studia Slavica Finlandensia* 7 (Helsinki, 1990): 101–36.

109. Freeze, *Church, Religion and Society;* idem, "Rechristianization of Russia," 107–8. For vibrant descriptions of the intermingling of local beliefs, agricultural cycles, the Orthodox religious calendar, and the worship of Christian saints in popular holidays and celebrations, see M. M. Gromyko, *Trudovye traditsii russkikh krest'ian Sibiri (XVIII–pervaia polovina XIX v.)* (Novosibirsk, 1975), 83–156; and Alison Hilton, *Russian Folk Art* (Bloomington, Ind., 1995), chap. 10. On the need to view pop-

ular religious beliefs as genuine forms of Orthodoxy rather than remnants of paganism, see Christine D. Worobec, "New Sources on Popular Religion in Imperial Russia," unpublished paper (Kent State University, 1995).

110. Gregory L. Freeze, *The Parish Clergy in Nineteenth-Century Russia: Crisis, Reform, Counter-Reform* (Princeton, 1983), 146–55.

111. N. D. Zol'nikova, *Soslovnye problemy vo vzaimootnosheniiakh tserkvi i gosudarstva v Sibiri (XVIII v.)* (Novosibirsk, 1981), 24–98.

112. Gregory L. Freeze, *The Russian Levites: Parish Clergy in the Eighteenth Century* (Cambridge, Mass., 1977), 34–41; idem, *Parish Clergy*, 161–71; idem, "Caste and Emancipation: The Changing Status of Clerical Families in the Great Reforms," in *The Family in Imperial Russia: New Lines of Historical Research*, ed. David L. Ransel (Urbana, Ill., 1978), 129–33.

113. Freeze, "Caste and Emancipation," in *FIR*, 129.

114. The surfeit did not extend to some outlying areas, such as the Irkutsk, Perm, Kishinev, and Olonets dioceses, which still experienced severe shortages of seminary graduates. Freeze, *Russian Levites*, chap. 4; idem, *Parish Clergy*, chaps. 2–4; idem, "Introduction," in *CRR*, 19–21; idem, "Handmaiden of State?" 96–99; idem, "Caste and Emancipation," in *FIR*, 128.

115. Freeze, "Introduction," in *CRR*, 51–57; idem, "Caste and Emancipation," in *FIR*, 124–50; idem, *Parish Clergy*, 308–19, 383–97. See also Iu. Osval't, "Dukhovenstvo i reforma prikhodskoi zhizni, 1861–1865," *Voprosy istorii* 11 (1993): 140–49.

116. Gregory L. Freeze, "The Orthodox Church and Serfdom in Prereform Russia," *SR* 48 (1989): 361–87; idem, "Bringing Order to the Russian Family: Marriage and Divorce in Imperial Russia, 1760–1860," *JMH* 62 (1990): 709–46; idem, "Handmaiden of State?" 93–95.

117. Gregory L. Freeze, "The Disintegration of Traditional Communities: The Parish in Eighteenth-Century Russia," *JMH* 48 (1976): 32–43.

118. N. D. Zol'nikova, "Dukhovenstvo Tobol'skoi eparkhii i prikhodskie obshchiny 2-oi poloviny XVIII v. v usloviiakh sotsial'nogo konflikta: Problema mentaliteta i povedeniia," in *Sosloviia* 1: 94–103. For discussion of the parish's possible importance as a source of social bonds, see Wirtschafter, *Structures of Society*, 53–64, 145–50.

119. Freeze, *Russian Levites*, 172–83; idem, "Handmaiden of State?" 98–99; idem, "A Case of Stunted Anticlericalism: Clergy and Society in Imperial Russia," *European Studies Review* 13 (1983): 181; idem, "Disintegration of Communities," 42–43.

120. Freeze, "Rechristianization of Russia," 102–18; idem, "Stunted Anticlericalism," 181–82; idem, "Disintegration of Communities," 43–45; idem, "Handmaiden of State?" 93–95; Zol'nikova, "Dukhovenstvo Tobol'skoi eparkhii," in *Sosloviia* 1:94–103.

121. Freeze, "Disintegration of Communities," 44–50; idem, "Church, State and Society in Catherinean Russia: The Synodal Instruction to the Legislative Commission," in *". . . aus der anmuthigen Gelehrsamkeit" : Tübinger Studien zum 18. Jahrhundert*, ed. Eberhard Müller (Tübingen, 1988), 164–65.

122. Freeze, "Disintegration of Communities," 50.

123. Ibid., 43–44; Freeze, "Stunted Anticlericalism," 179; idem, "Introduction," in *CRR*, 19–20, 26; idem, *Russian Levites*, chap. 5; idem, *Parish Clergy*, chap. 2.

124. Freeze, *Parish Clergy*, 65–101, 306–19; idem, "Church, State and Society," 165; idem, "Stunted Anticlericalism," 180–81, 186–88; idem, "Introduction," in *CRR*, 54.

125. Freeze, "Handmaiden of State?" 99; idem, "Disintegration of Communities," 43; idem, "Introduction," in *CRR*, 60–61. There also is significant evidence of co-operation between parishioners and priests during the Pugachev rebellion, when peasants and clergymen joined together to defend local churches against the rebel onslaught. In some villages parishioners also saved the lives of priests who refused to recognize Pugachev's followers. Zol'nikova, "Dukhovenstvo Tobol'skoi eparkhii," in *Sosloviia* 1:94–103.

126. Freeze, *Russian Levites,* chap. 7; idem, *Parish Clergy,* 164–87; idem, "Caste and Emancipation," in *FIR*, 137–50; idem, "Disintegration of Communities," 45–46; idem, "Introduction," in *CRR*, 22–23.

127. Freeze, *Parish Clergy,* 155–64; idem, "Introduction," in *CRR*, 21–35; idem, "Handmaiden of State?" 95–97.

128. *CRR;* Zol'nikova, *Soslovnye problemy,* 4–5; Freeze, "Introduction," in *CRR*, 21, 33–35; idem, "Stunted Anticlericalism," 185–86; idem, "Handmaiden of State?" 96–98.

129. Freeze, "Handmaiden of State?" 99–100; idem, "Introduction," in *CRR*, 40–52, 56–57, 60–61.

130. Freeze, *Church, Religion and Society;* idem, "Handmaiden of State?" 100–102; idem, "Introduction," in *CRR*, 58–61; idem, *Parish Clergy*, 194–247, 389–97, 449–74; idem, "Die Laisierung des Archimandriten Feodor (Bucharev) und ihre kirchenpolitischen Hintergründe: Theologie und Politik im Russland der Mitte des 19. Jahrhunderts," in *Kirche im Osten: Studien zur osteuropäischen Kirchengeschichte und Kirchenkunde,* ed. Peter Hauptmann (Göttingen, 1985) 28: 26–52; Smolitsch, *Geschichte der russischen Kirche* 1: 152–60; Osval't, "Dukhovenstvo i reforma."

131. G. L. Friz [Freeze], "Tserkov', religiia i politicheskaia kul'tura na zakate staroi Rossii," *Istoriia SSSR* 2 (1991): 107–19; Freeze, "Subversive Piety: Religion and the Political Crisis in Late Imperial Russia," *JMH* 68 (1996): 308–50.

132. Freeze, "Subversive Piety," 313–14, 349–50; idem, "Introduction," in *CRR*, 58–62.

133. Freeze, "Subversive Piety," 309–11; Friz [Freeze], "Tserkov', religiia," 107–8.

134. Freeze, *Church, Religion and Society.*

135. Ibid.

136. Ibid.

137. Ibid.

138. Zol'nikova, "Dukhovenstvo Tobol'skoi eparkhii," in *Sosloviia* 1: 94–103.

CHAPTER 3: MIDDLE GROUPS

1. The discussion of *raznochintsy* draws heavily from my *Structures of Society.*

2. N. N. Repin, "Uchastie 'raznochintsev' vo vneshnei torgovle Rossii XVIII veka," in *Torgovlia i predprinimatel'stvo v feodal'noi Rossii XVIII veka* (Moscow, 1994), 252.

3. On the *iasak* tax or tribute, see John P. LeDonne, *Ruling Russia: Politics and Administration in the Age of Absolutism, 1762–1796* (Princeton, 1984), 281, 289; Marc Raeff, *Siberia and the Reforms of 1822* (Seattle, 1956), 91–96.

4. I. T. Pososhkov, *The Book of Poverty and Wealth,* ed. and trans. A. P. Vlasto and L. R. Lewitter (London, 1987).

5. Wirtschafter, *Structures of Society,* 53–63.

6. Freeze, "*Soslovie* Paradigm"; Manfred Hildermeier, *Bürgertum und Stadt in Russland, 1760–1860: Rechtliche Lage und soziale Struktur* (Cologne, 1986); Dietrich Geyer, "Zwischen Bildungsbürgertum und Intelligencija: Staatsdienst und akademische Professionalisierung im vorrevolutionären Russland," in *Bildungssystem und Professionalisierung in internationalen Vergleichen*, vol. 1 of *Bildungsbürgertum im 19. Jahrhundert*, ed. Werner Conze and Jürgen Kocka (Stuttgart, 1985) 207–30.

7. This view is challenged in James T. Flynn, "Tuition and Social Class in Russian Universities: S. S. Uvarov and 'Reaction' in the Russia of Nicholas I," *SR* 35 (1976): 232–48.

8. *Sbornik rasporiazhenii po ministerstvu narodnogo prosveshcheniia*, 2 vols. (St. Petersburg, 1866), 1: 6.IX.1813 and 14.IX.1813, 223; *Sbornik postanovlenii po ministerstvu narodnogo prosveshcheniia*, 2 vols. (St. Petersburg, 1875–1876) 2: 19.VIII.1827, no. 1308, 71-73; 9.V.1837, no. 10,217; 29.XII.1846.

9. *Sbornik postanovlenii* 2: 19.VIII.1827, no. 1308, 71–73; 9.V.1837, no. 10,217; *Sbornik rasporiazhenii* 2: 10.X.1844, 768–70; 30.VI.1845, 825–26; 31.XII.1845, 882. See also L. A. Bulgakova, "Soslovnaia politika v sfere obrazovaniia (XVIII–pervaia polovina XIX veka)," in *Sosloviia* 1: 39–51.

10. Rozhdestvenskii, *Istoricheskii obzor*, 196–98.

11. On exclusion from the capitation, see *Zhurnal departamenta narodnogo prosveshcheniia*, ch. 3 (1821): 234–35; *Sbornik postanovlenii* 2: 765, 870–71.

12. Before undergoing a formal change of status in the form of a specialized calling, graduates of state schools who came from social categories liable for the capitation had to obtain releases from their communities of origin. During the reign of Alexander I, at least two townsmen from Nizhnii Novgorod successfully sought releases to become teachers. The community granted the first in 1808, only after the governor intervened, and the second in 1821, after receiving a guarantee that the former townsman would continue to pay taxes until the next census. V. I. Snezhnevskii, "Opis' del i dokumentov nizhegorodskogo gorodovogo magistrata za 1787–1861 gg.," *DNGUAK: Sbornik statei, soobshchenii, opisei, del i dokumentov*, t. 2, vypusk 15 (Nizhnii Novgorod, 1895), 86, 97.

13. V. I. Snezhnevskii, "Opis' delam nizhegorodskogo uezdnogo suda, 1846–1868," *DNGUAK*, t. 1, vypusk 11 (Nizhnii Novgorod, 1891), 559–60.

14. On private pharmacies and medical practices see TsGIAgM, f. 54 (Moskovskoe gubernskoe pravlenie), op. 1, d. 1820 (1799 g.); *Zhurnal departamenta narodnogo prosveshcheniia*, ch. 3 (1821): 69–94; *Sbornik rasporiazhenii* 1: 23.X.1811, 200; John T. Alexander, *Bubonic Plague in Early Modern Russia: Public Health and Urban Disaster* (Baltimore, 1980), 95.

15. M. D. Kurmacheva, *Krepostnaia intelligentsiia Rossii: Vtoraia polovina XVIII–nachalo XIX veka* (Moscow, 1983).

16. The sources consulted here do not provide complete information about the children of Kulibin, but the family was upwardly mobile. According to published letters, one son entered the Academy of Arts in 1801 on a state stipend, a second son served as a secretary in the Mining Administration in 1831, and a son-in-law held a comfortable civil service position at the Nerchinsk factory. A second daughter, widowed by 1833, was the mistress of a populated estate and apparently a noblewoman. *ES* (32) 16, pt. 2: 955–56; "Materialy k biografii Ivana Petrovicha Kulibina," *DNGUAK: Sbornik statei, soobshchenii, opisei, del i dokumentov*, t. 2, vypusk 15 (Nizhnii Novgorod, 1895), 67–119.

17. Walter M. Pintner, *Russian Economic Policy under Nicholas I* (Ithaca, N.Y., 1967), 151–52.

18. The early development of railroads tells a similar story. In the late eighteenth century, there were at least two short lines operating at a mine and a factory; a third appeared in the early nineteenth century and in 1833 two serfs at a factory in the Urals belonging to the Demidov family actually built a locomotive. None of these achievements received broader application. Ibid., 131–51. On Russia's abundance of expertise but crying lack of capital for development, see A. I. Del'vig, *Polveka russkoi zhizni: Vospominaniia A. I. Del' viga, 1820–1870,* 2 vols. (Moscow and Leningrad, 1930) 2: 87–88.

19. Instruction from Norskaia sloboda (Moscow government) to the Legislative Commission in 1767. Printed in *SIRIO* 93: 299–300.

20. In 1792 the Dmitrov merchant I. A. Tolchenov sold his four-person serf family to Count A. G. Orlov because an impending financial disaster forced him to liquidate assets, not because state officials were enforcing the laws forbidding non-nobles to own serfs. David L. Ransel, "An Eighteenth-Century Russian Merchant Family in Prosperity and Decline (unpublished manuscript, 1996).

21. Wirtschafter, *Serf to Soldier,* 19–20; Victoria E. Bonnell, *Roots of Rebellion: Workers' Politics and Organizations in St. Petersburg and Moscow, 1900–1914* (Berkeley, 1983), 20–71; idem, ed., *The Russian Worker: Life and Labor under the Tsarist Regime* (Berkeley, 1983).

22. Wirtschafter, *Structures of Society,* 83–84.

23. N. N. Shipov, "Istoriia moei zhizni i moikh stranstvii: Rasskaz byvshego krepostnogo krest'ianina Nikolaia Shipova, 1802–1862 gg.," in *V. N. Karpov, Vospominaniia—N. N. Shipov, Istoriia moei zhizni,* reprint (Moscow and Leningrad, 1933). On peasant traders, see Repin, "Uchastie 'raznochintsev'," in *Torgovlia.*

24. August von Haxthausen, *Studies on the Interior of Russia,* ed. S. Frederick Starr, trans. Eleanore L. M. Schmidt (Chicago, 1972), 23.

25. N. P. Durov, "Fedor Vasil'evich Karzhavin," *RS* 12 (1875): 272–97.

26. Haxthausen, *Interior of Russia,* 27–29.

27. Samuel H. Baron, "Entrepreneurs and Entrepreneurship in Sixteenth/Seventeenth-Century Russia," in *Entrepreneurship in Imperial Russia and the Soviet Union,* ed. Gregory Guroff and Fred V. Carstensen (Princeton, 1983), 52; Wallace Daniel, "Entrepreneurship and the Russian Textile Industry: From Peter the Great to Catherine the Great," *RR* 54 (1995): 1–25.

28. For the contradictory results of recent research, see, among others, A. V. Tiustin, "Kupecheskie dinastii Penzy," *Zemstvo: Arkhiv provintsial'noi istorii Rossii* 3 (1995): 164–93; E. I. Sazonova, "Rostovskie kuptsy Serebrennikovy," *Soobshcheniia Rostovskogo Muzeia,* vypusk 6 (Rostov, 1994), 68–77; E. A. Zueva, "Basniny: Sibirskaia kupecheskaia dinastiia. Preemstvennost' pokolenii," in *Sotsial'no-politicheskie problemy istorii Sibiri XVII–XX vv.: Bakhrushinskie chteniia 1994 g.* (Novosibirsk, 1994), 21–27; idem, "Vedomosti ucheta kupecheskikh kapitalov kak istoricheskii istochnik (na materialakh g. Irkutska kontsa XVIII–pervoi chetverti XIX v.)," *Massovye istochniki po istorii Sibiri: Bakhrushinskie chteniia 1989 g.* (Novosibirsk, 1989), 98–108; idem, "Razmery i strukturno-pokolennyi sostav sem'i Tobol'skogo kupechestva po dannym tret'ei revizii," in *Materialy XXVI vsesoiuznoi nauchnoi studencheskoi konferentsii* (Novosibirsk, 1988), 24–28; Ransel, "Russian Merchant Family"; A. I. Aksenov, *Genealogiia moskovskogo kupechestva XVIII v.: Iz istorii formirovaniia russkoi burzhuazii* (Moscow, 1988); idem, *Ocherki genealogii uezdnogo kupechestva XVIII v.* (Moscow, 1993).

29. B. N. Mironov, "Sotsial'naia mobil'nost' Rossiiskogo kupechestva v XVIII–nachale XIX veka (opyt izucheniia)," in *Problemy istoricheskoi demografii SSSR*, ed. R. N. Pullat (Tallinn, 1977), 207–17; idem, *Russkii gorod v 1740–1860-e gody: Demograficheskoe, sotsial'noe i ekonomicheskoe razvitie* (Leningrad, 1990), 151–69; idem, "Bureaucratic or Self-Government: The Early Nineteenth Century Russian City," *SR* 52 (1993): 241; Aksenov, *Genealogiia moskovskogo kupechestva*, 61–62, 84–92; Ransel, "Russian Merchant Family."

30. Thomas C. Owen, "Entrepreneurship and the Structure of Enterprise in Russia, 1800–1880," in *EIRSU*, 63.

31. Other accounts confirm the absence of continuity in the composition of the merchant category from the late eighteenth to the mid-nineteenth century. On third-guild Siberian merchants, see E. A. Zueva, "Russkaia kupecheskaia semi'a v Sibiri kontsa XVIII–pervoi poloviny XIX v.," avtoreferat (Novosibirsk, 1992). See also V. P. Boiko, "Proiskhozhdenie i sostav tomskogo kupechestva v kontse XVIII–nachale XIX veka," in *Rossiiskoe kupechestvo ot srednikh vekov k novomu vremeni* (Moscow, 1993), 92–93; A. I. Aksenov, "Kupecheskii rod i semeinye sud'by," in *Rossiiskoe kupechestvo, 102–4*; Hildermeier, *Bürgertum und Stadt.*

32. S. M. Troitskii, "Dvorianskie proekty sozdaniia 'tret'ego china'," in *Obshchestvo i gosudarstvo feodal'noi Rossii* (Moscow, 1975), 226–36; David M. Griffiths, "Eighteenth-Century Perceptions of Backwardness: Projects for the Creation of a Third Estate in Catherinean Russia," *CASS* 13 (1979): 452–72; Wallace Daniel, "Grigorii Teplov and the Conception of Order: The Commission on Commerce and the Role of the Merchants in Russia," *CASS* 16 (1982): 410–31; Hugh D. Hudson, Jr., "Urban Estate Engineering in Eighteenth-Century Russia: Catherine the Great and the Elusive *Meshchanstvo*," *CASS* 18 (1984): 393–410; Hildermeier, *Bürgertum und Stadt*, pt. 1, chap. 2; *Catherine the Great's Instruction (Nakaz) to the Legislative Commission, 1767*, ed. and trans. Paul Dukes (Newtonville, Mass., 1977); *PSZ* (I) 18, no. 12949.

33. *Catherine II's Charters of 1785 to the Nobility and the Towns*, ed. and trans. David M. Griffiths and George E. Munro (Bakersfield, Calif., 1990); *PSZ* (I) 22, no. 16188; *SZ* (1832), t. 9, kn. 1, razdel 3, glava 1, otdelenie 1, st. 240–45. For comparable definitions, see V. Androssov, *Statisticheskaia zapiska o Moskve* (Moscow, 1832); L. O. Ploshinskii, *Gorodskoe ili srednee sostoianie russkogo naroda* (St. Petersburg, 1852); L. I. Nasonkina, "V. P. Androssov i ego issledovanie o Moskve kak istoricheskii istochnik," *Russkii gorod (issledovaniia i materialy)*, vypusk 8 (Moscow, 1986), 177–205.

34. *Ministerstvo finansov, 1802–1902*, ch. 1 (St. Petersburg, 1902), 72–96; Hildermeier, *Bürgertum und Stadt*, 124–58, 183–217.

35. The title "honored citizen" brought exemption from conscription, the capitation, and corporal punishment. Groups eligible to obtain this title included children of personal nobles and church employees, first-guild merchants, low-ranking civil servants, and recognized artists and scholars. Shepelev, *Otmenennye istoriei chiny*, 99–100; Hildermeier, *Bürgertum und Stadt*, 218–33. On ennoblement, see chap. 2.

36. A. Sergeev, "Gr. A. Kh. Benkendorf o Rossii v 1827–1830 gg.," *Krasnyi arkhiv* 6.37 (1929): 146, 168; 1.38 (1930): 109, 133, 138.

37. Among the unprivileged multitudes, Karpov included townspeople (*meshchane*), artisans, state peasants, serfs who paid monetary dues (*obrok*) or who had been contracted out to work for merchants, shop assistants (*prikazchiki*), laborers, and domestic servants. V. N. Karpov, "Vospominaniia," in *V. N. Karpov, 164–67*.

38. For more detailed discussion of these issues, see chap. 4. See also A. A.

Kizevetter, *Posadskaia obshchina v Rossii XVIII st.* (Moscow, 1903); P. G. Ryndziun-skii, *Gorodskoe grazhdanstvo doreformennoi Rossii* (Moscow, 1958); idem, *Utverzh-denie kapitalizma v Rossii 1850–1880 gg.* (Moscow, 1978); S. I. Smetanin, "Razlozhe-nie soslovii i formirovanie klassovoi struktury gorodskogo naseleniia Rossii v 1800–1861 gg.," *IZ* 102 (1978): 153–82.

39. L. N. Pushkarev, "Povesti o kuptsakh kak istochnik po izucheniiu soslovnogo mentaliteta russkogo kupechestva kontsa XVII–nachala XVIII vv.," in *Sosloviia* 2: 42–47.

40. Jeffrey Brooks, *When Russian Learned to Read: Literacy and Popular Liter-ature, 1861–1917* (Princeton, 1985); *Mentalitet i kul'tura predprinimatelei Rossii XVII–XIX vv.: Sbornik statei* (Moscow, 1996).

41. For the debate on the dating of Russia's accelerated industrial growth, see Peter Gatrell, "The Meaning of the Great Reforms in Russian Economic History," in *Russia's Great Reforms, 1855–1881,* ed. Ben Eklof, John Bushnell, and Larissa Za-kharova (Bloomington, Ind., 1994), 84–101.

42. These basic points are covered in William Blackwell, ed., *Russian Eco-nomic Development from Peter the Great to Stalin* (New York, 1974); Ian Blanchard, *Russia's "Age of Silver": Precious-Metal Production and Economic Growth in the Eighteenth Century* (New York, 1989); Olga Crisp, *Studies in the Russian Economy before 1914* (London, 1976); Gatrell, *Tsarist Economy;* Alexander Gerschenkron, "Problems and Patterns of Russian Economic Development," in *The Transformation of Russian Society: Aspects of Social Change since 1861,* ed. Cyril Black (Cam-bridge, Mass., 1960), 42–72; Arcadius Kahan, *The Plow, the Hammer and the Knout: An Economic History of Eighteenth-Century Russia* (Chicago, 1985); Thomas C. Owen, *The Corporation under Russian Law, 1800–1917: A Study in Tsarist Eco-nomic Policy* (Cambridge, 1991); Pintner, *Russian Economic Policy;* Peter Liashchenko, *History of the National Economy of Russia* (New York, 1949); Gilbert Rozman, *Urban Networks in Russia, 1750–1800, and Premodern Periodization* (Princeton, 1976); Mikhail I. Tugan-Baranovsky, *The Russian Factory in the Nine-teenth Century,* trans. Arthur Levin and Claora S. Levin (Homewood, Ill., 1970); and the literature cited herein.

43. William L. Blackwell, *The Beginnings of Russian Industrialization 1800–1860* (Princeton, 1968); idem, *The Industrialization of Russia: An Historical Perspective* (Arlington Heights, Ill., 1970), and the literature cited herein; Theodore H. Von Laue, *Sergei Witte and the Industrialization of Russia* (New York, 1969); Boris V. Anan'ich, "The Economic Policy of the Tsarist Government and Enterprise in Russia from the End of the Nineteenth through the Beginning of the Twentieth Century," in *EIRSU,* 125–39.

44. The project won official approval in 1891. Blackwell, *Industrialization of Russia,* 33–35; Von Laue, *Sergei Witte,* 78–92.

45. Fred V. Carstensen, "Foreign Participation in Russian Economic Life: Notes on British Enterprise, 1869–1914," in *EIRSU,* 140–42.

46. Ibid., 142.

47. Rozman, *Urban Networks,* 12–15, 69–75, 113–29, 253, 267–71, 276–83, and esp. chap. 1.

48. Mironov, *Russkii gorod.*

49. Ibid., 36–41, 64–68, 74, 87–90, 101–8, 116–25, 151–55, 205–21, 227–34.

50. For a comprehensive summary of the revisionist views of economic histori-ans, most of whom examine the period after 1850, see Gatrell, *Tsarist Economy.*

51. Anne Lincoln Fitzpatrick, *The Great Russian Fair: Nizhnii Novgorod, 1840–90* (New York, 1990), 11–12.

52. Both the textile and sugar industries adopted modern technology in the preemancipation period. In the cotton industry, this resulted from the British government's 1842 decision to lift the ban on exporting textile machinery. Crisp, *Russian Economy,* 12–16; Fitzpatrick, *Great Russian Fair,* 56.

53. Fitzpatrick, *Great Russian Fair,* 5–13, 32–98, 111, 131–33, 202–7.

54. For a classic statement of the view that serfdom retarded economic and particularly industrial development, see Gerschenkron, "Problems and Patterns," 42–72.

55. Carstensen, "Foreign Participation," in *EIRSU,* 140–41.

56. Ibid., 157.

57. Ibid., 141–46, 156.

58. Ibid., 157–58.

59. Shipov, "Istoriia moei zhizni," in *V. N. Karpov;* Owen, "Entrepreneurship and Enterprise," in *EIRSU,* 73–76. This was equally true of the sixteenth and seventeenth centuries. See Baron, "Entrepreneurs and Entrepreneurship," in *EIRSU,* 38–47.

60. The thesis of patrimonialism is presented in Richard Pipes, *Russia under the Old Regime* (New York, 1974).

61. These conditions are described in numerous sources. See, among others, Shipov, "Istoriia moei zhizni," in *V. N. Karpov;* Baron, "Entrepreneurs and Entrepreneurship," in *EIRSU,* 35–41, 52–55; Owen, "Entrepreneurship and Enterprise," in *EIRSU,* 60–71; idem, *Corporation under Russian Law;* Daniel, "Russian Textile Industry"; Fitzpatrick, *Great Russian Fair,* 7–12, 44, 70–85, 96–103, 113–14, 206–7.

62. Baron, "Entrepreneurs and Entrepreneurship," in *EIRSU,* 46.

63. Ibid., 47–50.

64. Wirtschafter, *Structures of Society;* Alfred J. Rieber, *Merchants and Entrepreneurs in Imperial Russia* (Chapel Hill, N.C., 1982), 9–12, 41–52.

65. William Blackwell, "The Russian Entrepreneur in the Tsarist Period: An Overview," in *EIRSU,* 16.

66. On the evolution of business practices, see Owen, *Corporation under Russian Law;* Fitzpatrick, *Great Russian Fair,* 92–103, 145–46; Gatrell, "Meaning of Great Reforms," in *RGR,* 84–101.

67. Gatrell, *Tsarist Economy,* 231–33.

68. Heather Hogan, *Forging Revolution: Metalworkers, Managers, and the State in St. Petersburg, 1890–1914* (Bloomington, Ind., 1993), 10–12.

69. See chap. 4. Some of the most recent examples include S. Frederick Starr, "Local Initiative in Russia before the Zemstvo," in *The Zemstvo in Russia: An Experiment in Local Self-Government,* ed. Terence Emmons and Wayne S. Vucinich (New York, 1982), 5–30; Daniel R. Brower, *The Russian City between Tradition and Modernity, 1850–1900* (Berkeley, 1990); Mironov, "Bureaucratic or Self-Government"; John Bushnell, "Did Serf Owners Control Serf Marriage? Orlov Serfs and Their Neighbors, 1773–1861," *SR* 52 (1993): 419–45.

70. On defining institutionalization, see Gregory L. Freeze, "The Meaning of Institutionalization in Modern Russian History," unpublished paper presented to the Iowa Symposium on Imperial Russia (November 1991).

71. During the second quarter of the nineteenth century, autonomous, self-supporting literary and journalistic figures engaged in an informal, unofficial dialogue with government officials. Professional groups also participated in officially recognized, formal organizations, but not before the 1860s.

72. N. V. Kozlova, "Kuptsy v strukture gosudarstvennogo upravleniia Rossii XVIII v.," in *Sosloviia* 1: 179–88; A. V. Semenova, "Kupecheskoe soslovie i gosudarstvennaia vlast' v Rossii. XVI–seredina XIX veka," in *Sosloviia* 2: 98–106; V. A. Nardova, *Gorodskoe samoupravlenie v Rossii v 60-kh-nachale 90-kh godov XIX v.: Pravitel'stvennaia politika* (Leningrad, 1984); idem, *Samoderzhavie i gorodskie dumy v Rossii v kontse XIX–nachale XX veka* (St. Petersburg, 1994); Lester T. Hutton, "The Reform of City Government in Russia, 1860–1870" (Ph.D. diss., University of Illinois at Urbana-Champaign, 1972).

73. Thomas C. Owen, *Capitalism and Politics in Russia: A Social History of the Moscow Merchants, 1855–1905* (New York, 1981), 37–70; Fitzpatrick, *Great Russian Fair,* 142–69; Jo Ann Ruckman, *The Moscow Business Elite: A Social and Cultural Portrait of Two Generations, 1840–1905* (DeKalb, Ill., 1984), 109–15, 138–43.

74. On the co-optation of middle groups before 1905, see Charles E. Timberlake, "The Middle Classes in Late Tsarist Russia," in *Social Orders and Social Classes in Europe since 1500: Studies in Social Stratification,* ed. M. L. Bush (New York, 1992), 86–113.

75. Baron, "Entrepreneurs and Entrepreneurship," in *EIRSU,* 51.

76. Fitzpatrick, *Great Russian Fair,* 98, 144–46.

77. Ibid., 150–69, 208–9.

78. This theme is developed with particular attention to formal social definitions in Wirtschafter, *Structures of Society.* On popular evasion and the manipulation of laws, see also Wirtschafter, *Serf to Soldier;* David Moon, *Russian Peasants and Tsarist Legislation on the Eve of Reform: Interaction between Peasants and Officialdom, 1825–1855* (London, 1992).

79. Ruckman, *Moscow Business Elite,* ix–xi, 1–3, 19, 73–80. On the stability of Moscow's textile elite, see also Robert E. Johnson, *Peasant and Proletarian: The Working Class of Moscow in the Late Nineteenth Century* (New Brunswick, N.J., 1979), 22–23.

80. Ruckman, *Moscow Business Elite,* 155–66.

81. On the cultural, educational, and philanthropic activities of merchants in provincial towns, see E. B. Dolgov, "Rol' kupechestva v formirovanii zastroiki uezdnykh gorodov Srednego Povolzh'ia (na materialakh g. Chistopolia)," in *Rossiiskoe kupechestvo,* 77–78; I. Iu. Paramonova, "Iz istorii tul'skogo kupechestva XVIII–XIX vekov," in *Rossiiskoe kupechestvo,* 79–80; L. P. Roshchevskaia, "Blagotvoritel'naia deiatel'nost' tiumenskogo kupechestva," in *Rossiiskoe kupechestvo,* 93–96; O. E. Glagoleva, "Predprinimatel'stvo i kul'tura v provintsii v kontse XVIII–pervoi polovine XIX veka (po materialam Tul'skoi gubernii)," in *Rossiiskoe kupechestvo,* 144–46; E. A. Zueva, "Dosug i razvlecheniia Sibirskogo kupechestva vo vtoroi polovine XVIII–nachale XIX v.," *Materialy XXIV vsesoiuznoi nauchnoi studencheskoi konferentsii* (Novosibirsk, 1986), 43–47; idem, "Basniny"; Ransel, "Russian Merchant Family."

82. The St. Petersburg Mercantile Society, established in 1784, served as a merchant arena for the exchange of information about business conditions and as a site for friendly sociability. P. A. Buryshkin, *Moskva kupecheskaia: Memuary,* reprint (Moscow, 1991); Smith, "Freemasonry and Public," 30; Glagoleva, "Predprinimatel'stvo i kul'tura," in *Rossiiskoe kupechestvo* 144–46; Ransel, "Russian Merchant Family."

83. Ruckman, *Moscow Business Elite,* 7–8, 16–20; Rieber, *Merchants and Entrepreneurs,* 165–91; Semenova, "Kupecheskoe soslovie," in *Sosloviia* 2: 102–5; Dolgov, "Rol' kupechestva," in *Rossiiskoe kupechestvo,* 77–78; Paramonova, "Iz istorii

tul'skogo kupechestva," in *Rossiiskoe kupechsetvo,* 79–80; Roshchevskaia, "Blagotvoritel'naia deiatel'nost' tiumenskogo kupechestva" in *Rossiiskoe kupechestvo,* 93–96; L. N. Pushkarev, "Kuptsy—chitateli i khraniteli drevnerusskoi povesti," in *Rossiiskoe kupechestvo,* 129–30; M. P. Mokhnacheva, "'Uchenye' zhurnaly i knigoizdatel'skoe predprinimatel'stvo v Rossii," in *Rossiiskoe kupechestvo,* 130–34; A. A. Preobrazhenskii, "'Pamiatnaia kniga' moskovskogo kuptsa serediny XIX veka," in *Rossiiskoe kupechestvo,* 140–43; Glagoleva, "Predprinimatel'stvo i kul'tura," in *Rossiiskoe kupechestvo,* 144–46; Zueva, "Dosug i razvlecheniia."

84. Zueva, "Basniny," 24–25.

85. Owen, *Capitalism and Politics,* 32–53, 64–65; Ruckman, *Moscow Business Elite,* 135–36, 185–87.

86. Jürgen Habermas, "Work and Weltanschauung: The Heidegger Controversy from a German Perspective," in idem, *The New Conservatism: Cultural Criticism and the Historians' Debate,* ed. and trans. Shierry Weber Nicholsen (Cambridge, Mass., 1989), 140–72.

87. There is an acute need for comprehensive study of the inner workings of city government, particularly before the Great Reform era. Historians lack detailed knowledge of administrative mechanisms and decision making. Even less is known about the nature of such institutions as the "society of townspeople" *(meshchanskoe obshchesvo)* and the "society of merchants" *(kupecheskoe obshchestvo).* These institutions—which performed important social and community functions in the areas of welfare, tax collection, and the distribution of service obligations—may have paralleled the peasant commune. If this was indeed the case, it would help to explain the ease with which individuals moved between urban and rural society and into and out of particular communities.

88. Nardova, *Gorodskoe samoupravlenie,* 162–68; Owen, *Capitalism and Politics,* 76–89; Ruckman, *Moscow Business Elite,* 136–37.

89. These policies included official consultation with representatives of trade and industry, protective tariffs (which by increasing the cost of raw materials and semi-manufactured goods did not always promote industrial growth), the abolition in 1884 of the foreign transit trade from the Black Sea across Transcaucasia, the development of "domestic" Central Asian sources of cotton, and the construction of a railroad system. Owen, *Capitalism and Politics,* 113–20.

90. For this characterization of the palace coups, see Lincoln, *Vanguard of Reform,* 104.

91. Owen, *Capitalism and Politics,* 120–42.

92. For discussion of the working classes, see chap. 4.

93. Robbins, *Famine in Russia.*

94. Ruckman, *Moscow Business Elite,* 189–93; Owen, *Capitalism and Politics,* 163–79.

95. Ruckman, *Moscow Business Elite,* 194–207; Owen, *Capitalism and Politics,* 163–79.

96. Ruckman, *Moscow Business Elite,* 194–207; Owen, *Capitalism and Politics,* 180–94.

97. Ruth Amende Roosa, "Russian Industrialists during World War I: The Interaction of Economics and Politics," in *EIRSU,* 159–87.

98. Ibid.

99. Ruth Amende Roosa, "Russian Industrialists and 'State Socialism,' 1906–1917," *Soviet Studies* 23 (1972): 395–417; idem, "Workers Insurance Legislation and the Role of the Industrialists in the Period of the Third State Duma," *RR* 34

(1975): 410–52; A. Ia. Avrekh, *Stolypin i tret'ia duma* (Moscow, 1968); V. Ia. Laverychev, *Tsarizm i rabochii vopros v Rossii, 1861–1917 gg.* (Moscow, 1972).

100. Ruckman, *Moscow Business Elite,* 180–87, 196–209.

101. Ibid., 18–19, 27–28, 33–34, 41–48; Zueva, "Dosug i razvlecheniia," 43–47.

102. Ruckman, *Moscow Business Elite,* 67–69.

103. Ibid., 87–108; Joseph Bradley, *Muzhik and Muscovite: Urbanization in Late Imperial Russia* (Berkeley, 1985), 249–91. On the Russian "culture of almsgiving" and the particular generosity of merchants, see Lindenmeyr, *Poverty,* 7–25.

104. S. I. Shchukin, quoted in Ruckman, *Moscow Business Elite,* 145.

105. Amitai Etzioni, ed., *The Semi-Professions and Their Organization: Teachers, Nurses, and Social Workers* (New York, 1969); William J. Goode, "The Theoretical Limits of Professionalization," in Etzioni, *Semi-Professions,* 266–313.

106. Geyer, "Zwischen Bildungsbürgertum," in *BPIV,* 207–30; James C. McClelland, *Autocrats and Academics: Education, Culture, and Society in Tsarist Russia* (Chicago, 1979); Nancy Mandelker Frieden, *Russian Physicians in an Era of Reform and Revolution, 1856–1905* (Princeton, 1981).

107. Goode, "Theoretical Limits," in Etzioni, *Semi-Professions,* 291–94; Etzioni, "Preface," in ibid., xiii.

108. Alexander, *Bubonic Plague;* idem, "Medical Professionals and Public Health," *CASS* 12 (1978): 116–35; idem, "Medical Developments in Petrine Russia," *CASS* 8 (1974): 198–221; M. M. Shtrange, *Demokraticheskaia intelligentsiia Rossii v XVIII veke* (Moscow, 1965); Kurmacheva, *Krepostnaia intelligentsiia;* Alan Kimball, "Russian Civil Society and Political Crisis in the Era of the Great Reforms," unpublished manuscript (Eugene, Ore., 1989).

109. Miranda Beaven, "Aleksandr Smirdin and Publishing in St. Petersburg, 1830–1840," *Canadian Slavonic Papers* 27 (1985): 15–30; Boborykin, *Vospominaniia;* Brooks, *When Russia Learned;* Karpov, "Vospominaniia," in *V. N. Karpov;* Gary Marker, *Publishing, Printing, and the Origins of Intellectual Life in Russia, 1700–1800* (Princeton, 1985); Louise McReynolds, *The News under Russia's Old Regime: The Development of a Mass-Circulation Press* (Princeton, 1991); Anthony Netting, "Russian Liberalism: The Years of Promise, 1842–1855" (Ph.D. diss., Columbia University, 1967); Etta Louise Perkins, "Careers in Art: An Exploration in the Social History of Post-Petrine Russia" (Ph.D. diss., Indiana University, 1980); idem, "Mobility in the Art Profession in Tsarist Russia," *JGO* 39 (1991): 225–33; idem, "Nicholas I and the Academy of Fine Arts," *Russian History* 18 (1991): 51–63; Nurit Schliefman, "A Russian Daily Newspaper and Its New Readership: *Severnaia Pchela* 1825–1840," *CMRS* 28 (1987): 127–44; S. Frederick Starr, "Russian Art and Society, 1800–1850," in *Art and Culture in Nineteenth-Century Russia,* ed. Theofanis George Stavrou (Bloomington, Ind., 1983), 87–112.

110. Frieden, *Russian Physicians.*

111. On the frustration of medical experts in the eighteenth century, see Alexander, *Bubonic Plague,* 45–50. Alexander does not distinguish trained individuals with professional expertise from professionals in the modern organizational and social sense.

112. The notion of "status-inconsistency" is used by Liah Greenfeld to describe the gap between the achievements and aspirations of the *Bildungsbürgertum* in the eighteenth-century German states and their actual position in society. As in Russia, for very different reasons, this gap was a source of discontent among the educated elites. Greenfeld, *Nationalism,* 293–310.

113. Edith W. Clowes, Samuel D. Kassow, and James L. West, eds, *Between Tsar and People: Educated Society and the Quest for Public Identity in Late Imperial Russia* (Princeton, 1991); *RMMC;* Frieden, *Russian Physicians;* John F. Hutchinson, *Politics and Public Health in Revolutionary Russia, 1890–1918* (Baltimore, 1990); idem, "Society, Corporation or Union? Russian Physicians and the Struggle for Professional Unity (1890–1913)," *JGO* 30 (1982): 37–53; McClelland, *Autocrats and Academics;* Scott J. Seregny, *Russian Teachers and Peasant Revolution: The Politics of Education in 1905* (Bloomington, Ind., 1989); Gerald D. Surh, "A Matter of Life or Death: Politics, Profession, and Public Health in St. Petersburg before 1914," *Russian History* 20 (1993): 125–46. Important exceptions include Ben Eklof, *Russian Peasant Schools: Officialdom, Village Culture, and Popular Pedagogy, 1861–1914* (Berkeley, 1986); *ZR;* William E. Pomeranz, "Justice from Underground: The History of the Underground *Advokatura,*" *RR* 52 (1993): 321–40; Alfred J. Rieber, "The Rise of Engineers in Russia," *CMRS* 31 (1990): 539–68; Ruane, "Divergent Discourses," 109–23.

114. An important exception to this general characterization is the early twentieth-century career of G. E. Rein, who articulated a "conservative" model of medical professionalization designed to place expert knowledge at the disposal of the state. John F. Hutchinson, "Politics and Medical Professionalization after 1905," in *RMMC,* 89–116.

115. Geyer, "Zwischen Bildungsbürgertum," in *BPIV.*

116. Many historians make this point. See Pipes, *Russia under Old Regime;* Otto Müller, *Intelligencija: Untersuchungen zur Geschichte eines politischen Schlagwortes* (Frankfurt, 1971).

117. For a recent effort to address this issue, which stresses the impact of governmental repression, see Scott J. Seregny, "Teachers and Rural Cooperatives: The Politics of Education and Professional Identities in Russia, 1908–17," *RR* 55 (1996): 567–90.

118. Clowes, Kassow, and West, *Between Tsar and People.*

119. These characteristic features include "(1) a deep concern for problems and issues of public interest—social, economic, cultural, and political; (2) a sense of guilt and personal responsibility for the state and the solution of these problems and issues; (3) a propensity to view political and social questions as moral ones; (4) a sense of obligation to seek ultimate logical conclusions—in thought as well as in life—at whatever cost; (5) the conviction that things are not as they should be, and that something should be done." Michael Confino, "On Intellectuals and Intellectual Traditions in Eighteenth- and Nineteenth-Century Russia," *Daedalus* 101 (1972): 117–18.

120. The characteristic traits of this subculture were "(1) a dissociation of some educated Russians from the institutional structure and prevailing values of Russian society (church, state, and class structure); (2) a commitment to new values (ideologies) outside of traditional beliefs on the part of these Russians." Daniel R. Brower, "The Problem of the Russian Intelligentsia," *SR* 26 (1967): 638–39, 646.

121. Müller, *Intelligencija.*

122. Ibid., 105–21.

123. For a summary of the spectrum of meanings that evolved by the late nineteenth century, see ibid., 376–79.

124. Ibid., 195–207, 220–29, 246–51.

125. Wortman, *Scenarios of Power,* vol. 1; Roosevelt, *Country Estate,* chap. 5;

Irina Paperno, *Chernyshevsky and the Age of Realism: A Study in the Semiotics of Behavior* (Stanford, 1988); *The Semiotics of Russian Cultural History: Essays by Iurii M. Lotman, Lidiia Ia. Ginsburg, and Boris A. Uspenskii,* ed. Alexander D. Nakhimovsky and Alice Stone Nakhimovsky (Ithaca, N.Y., 1985).

126. Seregny, *Russian Teachers,* 7–8, 23, 57–58, 89, 96, 112–45, 169, 201–8; Hutchinson, "Society, Corporation or Union?" 42–52.

127. Seregny, *Russian Teachers,* 169.

128. This total comes from 1908 data, which include approximately 22,000 civil and military physicians; 10,500 pharmacists and apothecaries; 4,341 student apothecaries; 24,150 medical orderlies *(fel'dshery);* 12,290 midwives; 2,531 dentists *(zubnye vrachi);* and 2,946 dental practitioners *(dantisty).* Hutchinson, "Society, Corporation or Union?" 39–40, 45.

129. For the impact of geography on Russian political culture, see Edward L. Keenan, "Muscovite Political Folkways," *RR* 45 (1986): 115–81; Marc Raeff, "The People, the Intelligentsia and Russian Political Culture," *Political Studies* 41 (1993): 93–106; Pipes, *Russia under Old Regime,* chap. 1.

130. Seregny, *Russian Teachers,* 34–35; Eklof, *Peasant Schools,* 215–20, 231–37.

131. Clowes, Kassow, and West, *Between Tsar and People;* Frieden, *Russian Physicians;* idem, "The Politics of Zemstvo Medicine," in *ZR,* 315–42; Hutchinson, "Society, Corporation or Union?"; idem, *Politics and Public Health.* This was not a universal pattern even in St. Petersburg. See Surh, "Life or Death."

132. On elite efforts to reform popular culture in the early modern period, see Peter Burke, *Popular Culture in Early Modern Europe* (New York, 1978).

133. Pomeranz, "Justice from Underground," 321–40.

134. Ibid., 327–28.

135. Ibid., 329–40.

136. In 1920, 61 percent of fourteen-year-olds in the countryside of European Russia were literate. Jeffrey Brooks, "The Zemstvo and the Education of the People," in *ZR,* 243–78. On stability and continuity in the achievements of rural education, see also Eklof, *Peasant Schools.*

137. Teachers in these schools were exempted from the certification requirements prescribed in the 1874 School Statute. Brooks, "Zemstvo and Education," in *ZR,* 252–53; Eklof, *Peasant Schools,* chaps. 3–4.

138. On these roles, which sometimes led to involvement in popular rebellion, see Seregny, *Russian Teachers;* Freeze, "Church and Serfdom"; Wirtschafter, "Social Misfits"; idem, *Structures of Society.* On the discursive strategies adopted by women teachers to counteract their image as outsiders, see Ruane, "Divergent Discourses."

139. P. Burke, *Popular Culture,* 257.

140. Samuel C. Ramer, "The Zemstvo and Public Health," in *ZR,* 280–95; Samuel C. Ramer, "The Transformation of the Russian Feldsher," in *IR:SSO,* 136–60.

141. Ramer, "Zemstvo and Health," in *ZR,* 295–99; Worobec, "Popular Religion."

142. Brooks, *When Russia Learned;* McReynolds, *News under Old Regime;* Engelstein, *Keys to Happiness.*

143. Jürgen Kocka, "Middle Classes and Civil Society in Nineteenth-Century Europe: The German Case in Comparative Perspective" (paper presented at the Univer-

sity of California, Los Angeles, March 16, 1995); idem, "The Middle Classes in Europe," *JMH* 67 (1995): 783–806; Mack Walker, *German Home Towns: Community, State, and General Estate, 1648–1871* (Ithaca, N.Y., 1971).

144. Raeff, *Police State.*

145. Isabel de Madariaga, *Russia in the Age of Catherine the Great* (New Haven, 1981); Lincoln, *Vanguard of Reform;* Clowes, Kassow, and West, *Between Tsar and People;* Lindenmeyr, *Poverty,* chaps. 5, 6, 9.

CHAPTER 4: LABORING PEOPLE

1. On the relationship between labor and intellectual progress, see Peter Lavrov, *Historical Letters,* ed. and trans. James P. Scanlan (Berkeley, 1967).

2. For a plea to consider a functional definition of peasant culture and custom, see M. M. Gromyko, "Kul'tura russkogo krest'ianstva XVIII–XIX vekov kak predmet istoricheskogo issledovaniia," *Istoriia SSSR* 3 (1987): 39–60.

3. On the divergent results of micro- and macrolevel data, see Gregory L. Freeze, "New Scholarship on the Russian Peasantry," *European History Quarterly* 22 (1992): 605–17.

4. Schmidt, *Ständerecht und Standeswechsel,* 87–89, 190–91.

5. Ibid., 87.

6. Henry Rosovsky, "The Serf Entrepreneur in Russia," *Explorations in Entrepreneurial History* 4 (1954): 207–33; Kurmacheva, *Krepostnaia intelligentsiia.*

7. Ben Eklof, "Ways of Seeing: Recent Anglo-American Studies of the Russian Peasant (1861–1914)," *JGO* 36 (1988): 57–79.

8. See, for example, Zueva, "Russkaia kupecheskaia sem'ia."

9. According to Soviet historians, protoindustrial villages were those in which more than half the adult male population earned its living from manufacturing rather than from farming. It is important to distinguish protoindustrial manufacturing from handicraft production for household use or local trade, though capitalist relationships could characterize either. In a recent discussion of the concept of protoindustrialization and its critics, Sheilagh C. Ogilvie and Markus Cerman define the phenomenon as "the expansion of domestic industries producing goods for non-local markets." The less technical definition of Soviet historians seems appropriate for this discussion, given the still quite limited extent of relevant research for imperial Russia. Isser Woloch also adopts a relatively loose definition when he describes as protoindustrial "mixed agricultural and textile districts" containing significant "concentrations of capital and labor," that also were "free of guild restrictions." Woloch's chronological framework is 1715–1789, and as examples of protoindustrial areas, he identifies East Anglia in England, West Riding in Yorkshire, French Normandy, Flanders, Westphalia, Saxony, Silesia, and Moravia. See Sheilagh C. Ogilvie and Markus Cerman, eds., *European Proto-Industrialization* (New York, 1996), 1; Isser Woloch, *Eighteenth-Century Europe: Tradition and Progress, 1715–1789* (New York, 1982), 140–41. On various Soviet criteria of classification, see Ia. E. Vodarskii, *Promyshlennye seleniia tsentral'noi Rossii* (Moscow, 1972), 5–52.

10. Robert Redfield, *The Little Community and Peasant Society and Culture* (Chicago, 1960), 1–182.

11. The components of peasant culture include economic experience and knowledge of nature, customary law and the partial use of governmental legislation, relationships in the familial and the communal contexts, responses to empirewide political

events, historical and ethical conceptions, norms of behavior, social utopian ideals, peasant literature, folklore, music, applied decorative arts, and holidays. Gromyko, "Kul'tura russkogo krest'ianstva," 39–41, 59–60.

12. Keenan, "Muscovite Political Folkways," 125–26.

13. Ibid., 119–28; Dorothy Atkinson, "Egalitarianism and the Commune," in *Land Commune and Peasant Community in Russia: Communal Forms in Imperial and Early Soviet Society,* ed. Roger Bartlett (London, 1990), 7–19.

14. Steven L. Hoch, "The Serf Economy and the Social Order in Russia," in *Serfdom and Slavery: Studies in Legal Bondage,* ed. M. L. Bush (New York, 1996), 312–14.

15. The discussion of family and commune relies upon Aleksandrov, *Obychnoe pravo;* idem, *Sel'skaia obshchina;* Bartlett, *Land Commune;* Bohac, "Peasant Inheritance Strategies"; Peter Czap, Jr., "The Perennial Multiple Family Household, Mishino, Russia, 1782–1858," *Journal of Family History* 7 (1982): 5–26; Barbara Alpern Engel, *Between the Fields and the City: Women, Work, and Family in Russia, 1861–1914* (New York, 1994); idem, "Russian Peasant Views of City Life, 1861–1914," *SR* 52 (1993): 446–59; Gromyko, *Trudovye traditsii;* idem, *Traditsionnye normy povedeniia i formy obshcheniia russkikh krest'ian XIX v.* (Moscow, 1986); Hoch, *Serfdom and Control;* Esther Kingston-Mann and Timothy Mixter, eds., *Peasant Economy, Culture, and Politics of European Russia, 1800–1921* (Princeton, 1991); Edgar Melton, "Household Economies and Communal Conflicts on a Russian Serf Estate, 1800–1817," *Journal of Social History* 26 (1993): 559–85; Boris N. Mironov, "The Russian Peasant Commune after the Reforms of the 1860s," *SR* 44 (1985): 438–67; Prokof'eva, *Krest'ianskaia obshchina;* Minenko, *Russkaia krest'ianskaia sem'ia;* Olga Semyonova Tian-Shanskaia, *Village Life in Late Tsarist Russia,* ed. David L. Ransel (Bloomington, Ind., 1993); Worobec, *Peasant Russia.*

16. Evidence from eighteenth- and early-nineteenth-century Siberia shows that women whose husbands were absent or ill and who exercised guardianship over underage children sometimes voted in village assemblies. Gromyko, *Trudovye traditsii,* 316–21.

17. On divorce, see Freeze, "Bringing Order"; Wagner, *Marriage, Property and Law.*

18. Edgar Melton, "Enlightened Seigniorialism and Its Dilemmas in Serf Russia, 1750–1830," *JMH* 62 (1990): 675–708. On cooperative work, see Gromyko, *Trudovye traditsii,* 77–83.

19. Both before and after emancipation, the boundaries of villages, communes, parishes, estates, and administrative domains were not necessarily coterminous. A single commune could contain multiple villages, and a single village could be divided among different communes. For aesthetic purposes, I use the terms "village" and "commune" interchangeably to mean the unit of peasant self-government that was responsible for deciding the economic, administrative, and judicial affairs of the collective community. On the commune's considerable local authority and internal autonomy, see Bushnell, "Did Serf Owners?"; Mironov, "Local Self-Government." On familism and the autonomy of household heads, see Hoch, "Serf Economy," in Bush, *Serfdom.*

20. The official statistics seem to equate "communal" with "repartitional." In this they apply a legal definition of "repartitional" that does not indicate whether communes actually divided land in the economic sense. Consequently, these data tell us

only how many communes had the right to redistribute land. A further ambiguity arises in the sources because peasants who held their land in hereditary tenure also generally belonged to communes that did not possess the right to redivide land. I am grateful to Steve Hoch for helping me to sort out these problems, though I remain responsible for any errors of interpretation. The data and geographical delineations are reproduced in Dorothy Atkinson, *The End of the Russian Land Commune, 1905–1930* (Stanford, 1983), 383–84. See also Judith Pallot, "The Development of Peasant Land Holding from Emancipation to the Revolution," in *Studies in Russian Historical Geography,* ed. James H. Bater and R. A. French, 2 vols. (London, 1983), 1: 85–87.

21. Technically all land in Siberia was state property. A. S. Zuev, "Sibirskoe kazachestvo v soslovnoi politike Rossiiskogo pravitel'stva (XVIII–pervaia polovina XIX vv.)," in *Sosloviia* 1: 103–113; John Channon, "Regional Variation in the Commune: The Case of Siberia," in *LCPC,* 66–85.

22. Gromyko, *Trudovye traditsii,* 302–19.

23. Czap, "Multiple Family Household."

24. Moshe Lewin, "The *Obshchina* and the Village," in *LCPC,* 36–44.

25. Ibid.; Judith Pallot, "The Northern Commune: Archangel Province in the Late Nineteenth Century," in *LCPC,* 45–65; Channon, "Regional Variation," in *LCPC.*

26. These connections and relationships are explored in Gromyko, *Trudovye traditsii;* Pallot, "Northern Commune," in *LCPC,* 45–64; and idem, "Peasant Land Holding," in *SRHG.*

27. Melton, "Household Economies," 560–62. For similar conditions among monastery peasants, see L. N. Vdovina, "Krest'ianskoe ponimanie prava na zemliu v pervoi polovine XVIII v. (po materialam chelobitnykh monastyrskikh krest'ian)," in *Mentalitet i agrarnoe razvitie Rossii (XIX–XX vv.)* (Moscow, 1996), 124–34.

28. Hoch, *Serfdom and Control;* Melton, "Household Economies," 562–63.

29. Melton, "Enlightened Seigniorialism," 703–7; idem, "Household Economies," 559–85.

30. Hoch, *Serfdom and Control,* 151–60.

31. Jeffrey Burds, "The Social Control of Peasant Labor in Russia: The Response of Village Communities to Labor Migration in the Central Industrial Region, 1861–1905," in *PECP,* 62–63; Cathy A. Frierson, "Peasant Family Divisions and the Commune," in *LCPC,* 303–20; Engel, *Between Fields and City;* idem, "Russian Peasant Views." For a discussion of property divisions and the nineteenth-century tendency to form nuclear families that also draws attention to the interplay between economic interests, marriage patterns, and individual aspirations, see E. A. Zueva, "Kupecheskaia sem'ia i sobstvennost': Semeinye razdely i nasledovanie v srede kuptsov-sibiriakov v poslednei chetverti XVIII–pervoi polovine XIX veka," in *Rossiiskoe kupechestvo,* 104–7; idem, "Russkaia kupecheskaia sem'ia."

32. In the words of the officially recorded peasant proverb, "One son is not a son, two sons are half a son, three sons are a son." "Rekrut," *Chtenie dlia soldat* 6 (1856): 99.

33. Early-nineteenth-century legislation prescribed that large households be first in line to provide recruits. Communal officials, by contrast, often looked to smaller, economically weak families as their first source of potential recruits. Wirtschafter, *Serf to Soldier,* 20–24; Melton, "Enlightened Seigniorialism," 696–702; Elvira M. Wilbur, "Peasant Poverty in Theory and Practice: A View from Russia's 'Impoverished Center' at the End of the Nineteenth Century," in *PECP,* 119–23.

34. The presence of smaller families does not necessarily imply a change in patterns of fertility; it simply means that extended, multigenerational families may have been less essential for economic survival.

35. Burds, "Control of Peasant Labor," in *PECP,* 59–60; Engel, *Between Fields and City;* idem, "Russian Peasant Views."

36. Freeze, "Russian Peasantry."

37. Carol S. Leonard, "Landlords and the *Mir:* Transaction Costs and Economic Development in Pre-Emancipation Russia (Iaroslav Guberniia)," in *LCPC,* 121–42.

38. For brief and comprehensive descriptions of these economic regions, see *PECP,* xvi–xviii; Judith Pallot, "Agrarian Modernization on Peasant Farms in the Era of Capitalism," in *SRHG* 2: 423–31.

39. Edgar Melton, "Proto-Industrialization, Serf Agriculture, and Agrarian Social Structure: Two Estates in Nineteenth-Century Russia," *Past and Present* 115 (1987): 69–106; Hoch, *Serfdom and Control,* 15–64, 91–94; Boris N. Mironov, "Vliianie revoliutsii tsen v Rossii XVIII veka na ee ekonomicheskoe i sotsial'no-politicheskoe razvitie," *Istoriia SSSR* 1 (1991): 86–101; Confino, *Systèmes agraires.*

40. Hoch, *Serfdom and Control,* 9.

41. Melton, "Proto-Industrialization," 94–96.

42. Ibid., 104–5.

43. Melton, "Household Economies," 563–68.

44. Ogilvie and Cerman define the "putting out" system as one in which "rural producers no longer had independent access to the market, either for buying raw materials or for selling their product." Ogilvie and Cerman, *European Proto-Industrialization,* 4. On Russian protoindustrialization, see Melton, "Proto-Industrialization," 73–79; Gatrell, "Meaning of Great Reforms," in *RGR,* 95–96; Rosovsky, "Serf Entrepreneur," 207–33; Vodarskii, *Promyshlennye seleniia.*

45. Gatrell, "Meaning of Great Reforms," in *RGR,* 95–96; Roosevelt, *Country Estate,* esp. chap. 9; Hilton, *Russian Folk Art,* chaps. 2–4, 16.

46. In a study of Moscow province in the period 1880–1900, Judith Pallot distinguishes "traditional peasant craft industries that served local markets, used local raw materials and household labor, and were part of the 'natural economy' of the peasants" from peasant manufactures that reached national and international markets. She then identifies three types of peasant manufactures: (1) those "in which households used family labor to manufacture items for which they produced or bought raw materials themselves"; (2) those "in which the peasant worked under contract to a merchant who did the marketing and supplied raw materials"; and (3) "industrial work in which labor was contracted by factories or their 'putters-out' to complete a single stage of a production process at home, an arrangement that contemporaries referred to as the domestic system of large-scale production." Judith Pallot, "Women's Domestic Industries in Moscow Province, 1880–1900," in Clements, Engel, and Worobec, *Russia's Women,* 163–64.

47. Gatrell, "Meaning of Great Reforms," in *RGR,* 95; Melton, "Proto-Industrialization," 80–81.

48. Melton, "Proto-Industrialization," 80–89; Vodarskii, *Promyshlennye seleniia,* 192–93, 240; Hilton, *Russian Folk Art,* 266.

49. Only through extensive statistical studies of microcontexts can historians begin to sort out the complex economic results of the reform, including the enormous local variations. As a model, see S. G. Kashchenko, *Reforma 19 fevralia 1861 goda v Sankt-Peterburgskoi gubernii* (Leningrad, 1990); A. Ia. Degtiarev, S. G. Kashchenko,

and D. I. Raskin, *Novgorodskaia derevnia v reforme 1861 goda: Opyt izucheniia s is-pol'zovaniem EVM* (Leningrad, 1989).

50. The law required conversion to quitrent for all peasants in 1862, but local arrangements varied widely and de facto labor services continued to exist. State peasants began to redeem their lands only in January 1887. Gatrell, "Meaning of Great Reforms," in *RGR*, 92; Hoch, "Good Numbers and Bad," 44.

51. Most peasants entered the redemption phase before 1881. Gatrell, "Meaning of Great Reforms," in *RGR*, 92.

52. In the 1880s over one-third of peasant households rented land. In separate emancipation statutes, proprietary serfs in the nine western provinces of European Russia and Poland, as well as state and crown peasants throughout the empire, received more land and paid significantly less to redeem it. Geroid Tanquary Robinson, *Rural Russia under the Old Regime* (Berkeley, 1960), 84–93; Daniel Field, "The Year of Jubilee," in *RGR*, 40–57; Gatrell, "Meaning of Great Reforms," in *RGR*, 92–93; Pallot, "Peasant Land Holding," in *SRHG* 1: 87.

53. In 1905–1906, peasants from Vladimir province (a non-black earth area where villagers actually lost land) defined "cut-offs" as the difference "between the legal maximum and their actual allotments." Andrew Verner, "Discursive Strategies in the 1905 Revolution: Peasant Petitions from Vladimir Province," *RR* 54 (1995): 82–83.

54. N. I. Anan'ich, "K istorii otmeny podushnoi podati v Rossii," *IZ* 94 (1974): 183–212; Linda Bowman, "Russia's First Income Taxes: The Effects of Modernized Taxes on Commerce and Industry, 1885–1914," *SR* 52 (1993): 256–82.

55. The government reduced the annual redemption assessments in 1883 because the amount of the payments exceeded receipts from agriculture. Gatrell, "Meaning of Great Reforms," in *RGR*, 93–97. On peasant land purchases and the successes of the Peasant Land Bank, see Atkinson, *End of Commune*, 56–100.

56. Ibid., 99.

57. Judith Pallot and Denis J. B. Shaw, *Landscape and Settlement in Romanov Russia, 1613–1917* (London, 1986), 114–16. ˙

58. In 1858, annual household incomes ranged from 50 to 1,000 rubles in the protoindustrial village of Mstera (Vladimir province). By contrast, on the agricultural estate of Rastorg (Kursk province), there were no households with incomes exceeding 500 rubles in the prereform period. Esther Kingston-Mann, "Peasant Communes and Economic Innovation: A Preliminary Inquiry," in *PECP*, 30–36; Melton, "Proto-Industrialization," 90, 96.

59. Cultivation of potatoes began to penetrate parts of Siberia as early as the 1760s. Gromyko, *Trudovye traditsii,* 57–58. On innovations in New Russia (Tauride, Kherson, and Ekaterinoslav provinces) at the end of the nineteenth century, see Leonard G. Friesen, "Bukkers, Plows and Lobogreikas: Peasant Acquisition of Agricultural Implements in Russia before 1900," *RR* 53 (1994): 399–418.

60. Robert Bideleux, "Agricultural Advance under the Russian Village Commune System," in *LCPC*, 200–207; Kingston-Mann, "Peasant Communes," in *PECP*, 36–42; Pallot and Shaw, *Landscape and Settlement,* 116–17.

61. Judith Pallot, "*Khutora* and *Otruba* in Stolypin's Program of Farm Individualization," *SR* 42 (1984): 242–56; idem, "Peasant Land Holding," in *SRHG* 1: 84–85, 92–107; Pallot and Shaw, *Landscape and Settlement,* chap. 7; Macey, *Government and Peasant;* Atkinson, *End of Commune,* 56–100; Francis William Wcislo, *Reforming Rural Russia: State, Local Society, and National Politics, 1855–1914* (Princeton, 1990), chaps. 6–7.

62. Pallot, "Agrarian Modernization," in *SRHG* 2: 423–49.

63. Ibid., 437–41. For a positive appraisal of flax cultivation, see *Aleksandr Nikolaevich Engelgardt's Letters,* 222–23.

64. Kingston-Mann, "Peasant Communes," in *PECP,* 38–51; Pallot, "Agrarian Modernization," in *SRHG* 2: 438–45.

65. This discussion of off-farm labor relates only to its impact on communal village life. The relationship of migration to industrialization, urban development, and the formation of a working class is treated later in this chapter.

66. Burds, "Control of Peasant Labor," in *PECP,* 62–63, 68–70, 99–100; Engel, *Between Fields and City,* 62.

67. Engel, *Between Fields and City,* 34–37, 49–50; idem, "Russian Peasant Views," 446–49; Burds, "Control of Peasant Labor," in *PECP,* 62–70, 94–97. Siberian peasants were consumers of tea already in the 1840s. See Gromyko, *Trudovye traditsii,* 273–74.

68. Peter Gatrell, "Introduction: Olga Crisp's Contribution to the Economic History of Russia," in *Economy and Society in Russia and the Soviet Union, 1860–1930. Essays for Olga Crisp,* ed. Linda Edmondson and Peter Waldron (New York, 1992), 4.

69. Engel, *Between Fields and City,* 50–52, 75–77.

70. Some peasant women shriekers *(klikushi)*—women who were believed to be bewitched by evildoers and possessed by devils—had migrant husbands who were forced to return to the village when their wives became incapacitated. Christine D. Worobec, *"Klikushestvo:* Devil Possession among Russian Peasant Women, 1861–1926," unpublished paper (Kent State University, 1994).

71. Engel, *Between Fields and City,* 34–35; idem, "Russian Peasant Views," 455–58; Burds, "Control of Peasant Labor," in *PECP,* 55, 99–100.

72. Engel, *Between Fields and City,* 103.

73. Edelman, *Proletarian Peasants.*

74. Works devoted to these issues include Bater and French, *Studies in Russian Historical Geography;* Crisp, *Russian Economy before 1914;* Edmondson and Waldron, *Economy and Society;* Gatrell, *Tsarist Economy;* Pallot and Shaw, *Landscape and Settlement.*

75. The discussion of economic stagnation and the peasants' standard of living is based primarily on Paul R. Gregory, "Grain Marketings and Peasant Consumption, Russia, 1885–1913," *Explorations in Economic History* 17 (1980): 135–64; idem, "Rents, Land Prices and Economic Theory: The Russian Agrarian Crisis," in *E&S,* 6–23; G. M. Hamburg, "The Crisis in Russian Agriculture: A Comment," *SR* 37 (1978): 481–86; Hoch, "Good Numbers and Bad"; Heinz-Dietrich Löwe, *Die Lage der Bauern in Russland, 1880–1905: Wirtschaftliche und soziale Veränderungen in der ländlichen Gesellschaft des Zarenreiches* (St. Katharinen, 1987); Roger Munting, "Economic Change and the Russian Gentry, 1861–1914," in *E&S,* 24–43; Pallot and Shaw, *Landscape and Settlement;* John Thomas Sanders, "'Once More into the Breach, Dear Friends': A Closer Look at Indirect Tax Receipts and the Condition of the Russian Peasantry, 1881–1899," *SR* 43 (1984): 657–66; James Y. Simms, Jr., "The Crisis in Russian Agriculture at the End of the Nineteenth Century: A Different View," 36 *SR* (1977): 377–98; idem, "On Missing the Point: A Rejoinder," *SR* 37 (1978): 487–90; idem, "Reply," *SR* 43 (1984): 667–71; idem, "More Grist for the Mill: A Further Look at the Crisis in Russian Agriculture at the End of the Nineteenth Century," *SR* 50 (1991): 999–1009; Stephen G. Wheatcroft, "Crises and the Condition of the Peasantry

in Late Imperial Russia," in *PECP,* 128–72; idem, "The 1891–92 Famine in Russia: Towards a More Detailed Analysis of Its Scale and Demographic Significance," in *E&S,* 44–64; Elvira M. Wilbur, "Was Russian Peasant Agriculture Really That Impoverished? New Evidence from a Case Study from the 'Impoverished Center' at the End of the Nineteenth Century," *Journal of Economic History* 43 (1983): 137–44; idem, "Peasant Poverty," in *PECP,* 101–27.

76. Gregory, "Rents, Land Prices," in *E&S,* 19–20.

77. In the early 1820s, Minister of Finance E. F. Kankrin similarly interpreted shortfalls in tax revenues as a crisis of urban trade. RGIA, f. 1167 (Komitet 6 dekabria 1826 goda), op. 16, dd. 102, 224; Hoch, "Good Numbers and Bad," 42–48; Manning, *Crisis of Old Order,* 220; Wheatcroft, "Condition of Peasantry," in *PECP,* 136–42. Demographic studies currently underway offer a possible solution to this conundrum.

78. Wheatcroft, "Condition of Peasantry," in *PECP,* 128–66; idem, "The 1891–92 Famine," in *E&S;* Gregory, "Grain Marketings," 146–53; Munting, "Economic Change and Gentry," in *E&S.*

79. Wheatcroft, "Condition of Peasantry," in *PECP,* 128–29, 147–66.

80. Gregory, "Grain Marketings," 146; Wheatcroft, "Condition of Peasantry," in *PECP,* 130–31.

81. E. P. Thompson, *Customs in Common: Studies in Traditional Popular Culture* (New York, 1993), 301–2.

82. Traditionally, monastery peasants were closest to proprietary serfs, but early in the reign of Peter the Great, the government began to regulate church property, and in 1762–1764 all ecclesiastical lands were secularized under the College of Economy. Monastic peasants thus became a category of state peasants called "economic peasants." Unless otherwise specified, "state peasant" refers to state *(gosudarstvennye, kazennye),* economic *(ekonomicheskie),* and appanage or crown *(dvortsovye;* after 1797, *udel'nye)* peasants. Before emancipation these categories of peasants came under separate administrative domains but shared similar—though not identical—legal statuses compared to serfs. For a general introduction to these and other subcategories of state peasants, see Jerome Blum, *Lord and Peasant in Russia from the Ninth to the Nineteenth Century* (Princeton, 1971); N. M. Druzhinin, *Gosudarstvennye krest'iane i reforma P. D. Kiseleva,* 2 vols. (Moscow, 1946 and 1958).

83. State peasants also were forbidden to enter bureaucratic service on the basis of social origin but were admitted if they possessed technical or educational credentials that carried rights of appointment to governmental posts. Zaionchkovskii, *Pravitel'stvennyi apparat,* 24–26. On the legal rights of state peasants, see Druzhinin, *Gosudarstvennye krest'iane* 1: 78–83.

84. David Griffiths, "Of Estates, Charters and Constitutions," in Griffiths and Munro, *Catherine II's Charters,* xvii–lxix; "Appendix A," in *Catherine II's Charters,* 63–105.

85. Steven L. Hoch and Wilson R. Augustine, "The Tax Censuses and the Decline of the Serf Population in Imperial Russia," *SR* 38 (1979): 403–25; Hoch, *Serfdom and Control,* 1.

86. Melton, "Enlightened Seigniorialism," 683–84; V. O. Kliuchevskii, "Proiskhozhdenie krepostnogo prava v Rossii," in *Sochineniia v deviati tomakh,* vol. 8 (Moscow, 1990), 120–93.

87. Isabel de Madariaga, "Catherine II and the Serfs: A Reconsideration of Some Problems," *SEER* 52, no. 126 (1974): 47–54. On the seventeenth century, see *Krest'ianskie chelobitnye XVII v.* (Moscow, 1994).

88. As early as 1719, Peter the Great instructed military governors to intervene to prevent the physical abuse of peasants. In 1838, 140 estates were under guardianship due to the mistreatment of serfs; in 1858, this number had increased to 193 estates containing 28,508 peasants. Isabel de Madariaga, *Catherine the Great: A Short History* (New Haven, 1990), 27–30; Peter Kolchin, *Unfree Labor: American Slavery and Russian Serfdom* (Cambridge, Mass., 1987), 142–48; M. F. Prokhorov, "O pravosoznanii pomeshchich'ikh krest'ian Rossii v tret'ei chetverti XVIII veka," in *Sosloviia* 2: 31–42.

89. It is unclear whether landlords ever had the power to send peasants to hard labor in Siberia; a law of 1765 allowed the Admiralty College to receive serfs and employ them in hard labor but made no mention of Siberia, where convicts served their terms of punishment. A law of 1809 interpreted the 1775 Statute on Local Administration as having eliminated hard labor except for criminals sentenced by a court.

90. According to the 1811 law, the provincial reform of 1775 had established these provisions.

91. Madariaga, "Catherine II and Serfs," 38–47.

92. Ibid., 51. On the difficulties encountered by peasants who tried to submit petitions to state institutions, see Prokhorov, "O pravosoznanii pomeshchich'ikh krest'ian," in *Sosloviia* 2: 38–40.

93. On Tsar Paul's ideal of a regulated and regularized serfdom, see Mikhail M. Safonov, "Imperatorskaia vlast', gosudarstvennyi apparat i dvorianstvo v kontse XVIII v.," *CMRS* 34 (1993): 149–58.

94. A. B. Kamenskii, "Soslovnaia politika Ekateriny II," *Voprosy istorii* 3 (1995): 41–42.

95. Robinson, *Rural Russia,* 42–43, 63.

96. It is important to note that conditions varied within these broad categories of peasants. This point recently was made in a study of villages attached to silver foundries in western Siberia, where peasants, essentially owned by the ruler, endured a regime described as worse than that imposed on some private serfs. A. N. Zheravina, "Soslovnyi status i sotsial'naia sushchnost' pripisnykh krest'ian Sibiri v seredine XVIII–seredine XIX vv. (po dannym zakonodatel'stva)," in *Sosloviia* 1: 83–93.

97. D. I. Raskin, "Ispol'zovanie zakonodatel'nykh aktov v krest'ianskikh chelobitnykh serediny XVIII veka (materialy k izucheniiu obshchestvennogo soznaniia russkogo krest'ianstva)," *Istoriia SSSR* 4 (1979): 179–92; A. V. Kamkin, "Pravosoznanie gosudarstvennykh krest'ian vtoroi poloviny XVIII veka (na materialakh Evropeiskogo Severa)," *Istoriia SSSR* 2 (1987): 163–73; Prokhorov, "O pravosoznanii pomeshchich'ikh krest'ian," in *Sosloviia* 2; Melton, "Enlightened Seigniorialism," 708; Vdovina, "Krest'ianskoe ponimanie," in *Mentalitet i agrarnoe.*

98. It was possible to appeal the decisions of lower courts to higher instances, reaching all the way to the Senate. Madariaga, *Catherine the Great,* 66–79; Druzhinin, *Gosudarstvennye krest'iane* 1: 52–56, 575–88; Janet M. Hartley, "Catherine's Conscience Court—An English Equity Court?" in *Russia and the West in the Eighteenth Century,* ed. A. G. Cross (Newtonville, Mass., 1983), 306–18.

99. Wirtschafter, *Structures of Society,* 26–34, 78–85.

100. Wirtschafter, "Social Misfits"; idem, *Structures of Society,* 65–70, 84–85.

101. V. N. Trapeznikov, "O liudiakh, iskavshikh vol'nosti iz vladeniia gospod svoikh," *Trudy Permskoi uchenoi arkhivnoi kommissii,* vypusk 4 (Perm, 1901), 142–52.

102. Hoch and Augustine, "Tax Censuses," 419–20.

103. See chap. 2.

104. Moon, *Peasants and Legislation,* 180.

105. Vdovina, "Krest'ianskoe ponimanie," in *Mentalitet i agrarnoe.*

106. From 1889, appointed land captains selected peasant judges from a list of candidates put forth by the cantonal assembly and also were empowered to overrule the decisions of cantonal courts. Jane Burbank, "A Question of Dignity: Peasant Legal Culture in Late Imperial Russia," *Continuity and Change* 10 (1995): 391–404; Peter Czap, Jr., "Peasant Class Courts and Peasant Customary Justice in Russia, 1851–1912," *Journal of Social History* 1 (1967): 148–78; Cathy Frierson, "Crime and Punishment in the Russian Village: Rural Concepts of Criminality at the End of the Nineteenth Century," *SR* 46 (1987): 55–69; idem, "Rural Justice in Public Opinion: The Volost' Court Debate, 1861–1912," *SEER* 64 (1986): 526–45; Stephen P. Frank, "Popular Justice, Community, and Culture among the Russian Peasantry, 1870–1900," reprinted in *The World of the Russian Peasant: Post-Emancipation Culture and Society,* ed. Ben Eklof and Stephen P. Frank (Boston, 1990), 133–53; Alexander K. Afanas'ev, "Jurors and Jury Trials in Imperial Russia, 1866–1885," in *RGR,* 214–30; Joan Neuberger, "Popular Legal Cultures: The St. Petersburg *Mirovoi Sud,*" in *RGR,* 231–46; *Aleksandr Nikolaevich Engelgardt's Letters;* S. A. Golunskii and D. S. Karev, *Istoriia suda i ugolovnogo protsessa* (Moscow, 1938). I am grateful to Stephen Frank for helping me to sort out the very confusing and little understood judicial structure, although I of course remain responsible for any errors in the description of the courts presented here.

107. N. V. Kozlova, *Pobegi krest'ian v Rossii v pervoi treti XVIII veka (iz istorii sotsial'no-ekonomicheskoi zhizni strany)* (Moscow, 1983), 35–36; Wirtschafter, *Structures of Society,* 82. For further discussion, see Christoph Schmidt, *Sozialkontrolle in Moskau: Justiz, Kriminalität und Leibeigenschaft, 1649–1785* (Stuttgart, 1996), 267–91.

108. Wirtschafter, *Serf to Soldier,* 4–9, 24–25.

109. Melton, "Enlightened Seigniorialism," 702–4.

110. Rodney Bohac, "Everyday Forms of Resistance: Serf Opposition to Gentry Exactions, 1800–1861," in *PECP,* 236–60.

111. Madariaga, *Catherine the Great,* 57–64; Marc Raeff, "Pugachev's Rebellion," in *PIIIR,* 234–67; John T. Alexander, *Autocratic Politics in a National Crisis: The Imperial Russian Government and Pugachev's Revolt, 1773–1775* (Bloomington, Ind., 1969).

112. Madariaga, *Catherine the Great,* 50–52.

113. Field, *Rebels in Name of Tsar;* Gregory L. Freeze, "A Social Mission for Russian Orthodoxy: The Kazan Requiem of 1861 for the Peasants in Bezdna," in *IR:SSO,* 115–35; Thomas M. Barrett, "Good News Comes to a Russian Village: The Peasant Articles of Kharkov and the Emancipation of the Serfs," *Peasant Studies* 17 (1989): 23–42.

114. Verner, "Discursive Strategies," 79–85; Atkinson, *End of Commune,* 49–51.

115. As employed here, the concept of "moral economy" refers to the principles and practices of tsarist political culture manifested in interactions between official or seignorial authority and popular ideas of justice. Although E. P. Thompson associates "the moral economy of provision" with "paternalist authority," his subject of study is the eighteenth-century English food "riot," an event that, so far as is presently known, was a rarity in imperial Russia. Thompson's "norm of reciprocity" and "right to subsistence" did play a role in concrete instances of Russian popular protest, but the issue

requires further research. Interestingly, the February revolution of 1917 may have begun with just such a "riot," initiated by women in Petrograd searching for bread in a time of dearth. See E. P. Thompson, *Customs in Common,* 185–258, 259–351; James C. Scott, *The Moral Economy of the Peasant: Rebellion and Subsistence in Southeast Asia* (New Haven, 1976).

116. See, for example, Matthew Schneer, "The Markovo Republic: A Peasant Community during Russia's First Revolution, 1905–1906," *SR* 53 (1994): 104–19.

117. On desacralization, see Roger Chartier, *The Cultural Origins of the French Revolution,* trans. Lydia G. Cochrane (Durham, N.C., 1991).

118. Verner, "Discursive Strategies," 79–90; David A. J. Macey, "The Peasant Commune and the Stolypin Reforms: Peasant Attitudes, 1906–1914," in *LCPC,* 220–21; Frank, *Crime, Cultural Conflict.*

119. Wheatcroft, "Condition of Peasantry," in *PECP,* 166–67; Abraham Ascher, *The Revolution of 1905: Russia in Disarray* (Stanford, 1988), 161–67.

120. Maureen Perrie, "The Russian Peasant Movement of 1905–7: Its Social Composition and Revolutionary Significance," reprinted in Eklof and Frank, *World of Peasant,* 208.

121. Verner, "Discursive Strategies," 68–77.

122. Peasants did not believe that landholdings between different villages and communes should be "equalized" by repartition; throughout the period of revolution and civil war, their solidarities and social bonds corresponded to the immediate farming community, the source of physical survival. Pallot and Shaw, *Landscape and Settlement,* chap. 7; Orlando Figes, "Peasant Farmers and the Minority Groups of Rural Society: Peasant Egalitarianism and Village Social Relations during the Russian Revolution (1917–1921)," in *PECP,* 378–401; idem, "The Russian Peasant Community in the Agrarian Revolution, 1917–18," in *LCPC,* 237–53; Macey, "Commune and Reforms," in *LCPC.* For a discussion of problems with the official data concerning implementation of the Stolypin land reforms and for a slightly lower estimate of the number of peasants who withdrew from the commune and consolidated (about 10%), or who withdrew but did not consolidate (another 15%), from 1906 until the period of war and revolution, see Pallot, "Peasant Land Holding," in *SRHG* 1: 84–85, 102–6.

123. Atkinson, *End of Commune,* 108–13.

124. This process in eighteenth-century England "added more than one hundred new capital offences to the statute book." Thompson, *Customs in Common,* 48–49.

125. On the relationship of peasants, unofficial "experts," and trained professionals, see chap. 3. On literary images of peasants, see Cathy A. Frierson, *Peasant Icons: Representations of Rural People in Late Nineteenth-Century Russia* (New York, 1993). On the appropriation of folk art by professional artists, collectors, exhibitors, and the Soviet state, see Hilton, *Russian Folk Art,* chaps. 14–18.

126. Wirtschafter, "Social Misfits," 226.

127. For another account that stresses the intensification of state intrusions in the postemancipation period, see Hoch, "Serf Economy," in Bush, *Serfdom.*

128. Eklof, *Peasant Schools;* Hilton, *Russian Folk Art,* chap. 8; Brooks, *When Russia Learned;* Anthony Netting, "Images and Ideas in Russian Peasant Art," *SR* 35 (1976): 48–68; A. V. Kamkin, "Iz istorii krest'ianskikh i prikhodskikh bibliotek russkogo severa XVIII v.," in *Kniga v Rossii: Iz istorii dukhovnogo prosveshcheniia. Sbornik nauchnykh trudov* (St. Petersburg, 1993), 112–20.

129. The term *kuptsy* (merchants) should not be confused with the categories of guild merchants also recognized in Petrine legislation, who bought certificates granting

specific economic and commercial privileges. The urban instructions to Catherine II's Legislative Commission (1767), for example, identified all town participants as *kuptsy*. Only with the Catherinean reforms of 1775 and 1785 was a clear terminological and sociolegal distinction established between merchants *(kuptsy)* and lesser townspeople *(meshchane)*.

130. Manfred Hildermeier, "Was war das Meščanstvo? Zur rechtlichen und sozialen Verfassung des unteren städtischen Standes in Russland," *FOG* 36 (1985): 53.

131. Ploshinskii, *Gorodskoe ili srednee sostoianie,* 107–52; Richard Hellie, "The Stratification of Muscovite Society: The Townsmen," *Russian History* 5 (1978): 119–75; Kizevetter, *Posadskaia obshchina,* iii–v, 1–3; Pallot and Shaw, *Landscape and Settlement,* 241–48.

132. Anisimov, *Podatnaia reforma,* 190–95. On this issue, see also M. Ia. Volkov, *Goroda verkhnego povolzh'ia i severo-zapada Rossii: Pervaia chetvert' XVIII v.* (Moscow, 1994).

133. Kizevetter, *Posadskaia obshchina;* Anisimov, *Podatnaia reforma; PSZ* (I) 22, no. 16187 (16188); A. V. Elpat'evskii, "Zakonodatel'nye istochniki po istorii dokumentirovaniia soslovnoi prinadlezhnosti v tsarskoi Rossii (XVIII–nachalo XX v.)," in *Istochnikovedenie otechestvennoi istorii* (Moscow, 1984), 45–51; P. G. Ryndziunskii, "Soslovno-podatnaia reforma 1775 g. i gorodskoe naselenie," in *Obshchestvo i gosudarstvo,* 86–95.

134. Wirtschafter, *Structures of Society,* 39–47, 85–89.

135. Ibid., 89. On trading peasants, see Daniel Morrison, "'Trading Peasants' and Urbanization in Eighteenth Century Russia: The Central Industrial Region" (Ph.D. diss., Columbia University, 1981); Repin, "Uchastie 'raznochintsev'," in *Torgovlia.*

136. Heredity had never been the sole basis for these rights of townspeople in any case. After the reforms, peasants, whose allotment lands could not be sold to non-peasants, remained the majority exception.

137. Hildermeier, *Bürgertum und Stadt,* 307–22; Anan'ich, "K istorii otmeny," 184–86; N. Evreinov, *Istoriia telesnykh nakazanii v Rossii,* reprint (Khar'kov, 1994), 126–33.

138. Examples of cultural and political usages include E. A. Shtakenshneider, *Dnevniki i zapiski (1854–1886)* (Moscow, 1934; reprint, Newtonville, Mass., 1980), 269–70; G. V. Plekhanov, "Ideologiia meshchanina nashego vremeni," in *Sochineniia,* 24 vols. (Moscow, 1923–1927), 14: 259–344; Mark Krinitskii, "Krizis domashnikh idealov sovremennago meshchanstva," *Riazanskaia zhizn',* no. 18, 21.XII.1911, 1–2. I am grateful to Stephen Frank for sharing this last article.

139. Hildermeier, *Bürgertum und Stadt,* 35–48.

140. Wirtschafter, *Structures of Society,* 53–64, 85–92, 109–12; Brower, *Russian City.*

141. Mironov, *Russkii gorod;* Schmidt, *Ständerecht und Standeswechsel;* Bradley, *Muzhik and Muscovite.*

142. In 1769, the official urban population constituted 3.1 percent of the country's registered inhabitants; almost a century later, in 1861, 10 percent of the empire's subjects lived in towns, and by 1914, the figure reached 15.3 percent in European Russia. Pallot and Shaw, *Landscape and Settlement,* 248–59.

143. Mironov, *Russkii gorod,* 3–41, 64–68, 74, 87–90, 105–6, 116–25, 151–55; Hildermeier, *Bürgertum und Stadt,* 234–45; Ryndziunskii, *Gorodskoe grazhdanstvo,* chaps. 1–3; James H. Bater, "Modernization and the Municipality: Moscow and St. Petersburg on the Eve of the Great War," in *SRHG* 2: 306–7.

144. Mironov, "Bureaucratic or Self-Government," 249.

145. Hildermeier, "Was war Meščanstvo?," 35–36.

146. Ia. Abramov, "Zabytoe soslovie," *Nabliudatel'* 4, no. 1 (1885): 288.

147. Bater, "Modernization and Municipality," in *SRHG* 2: 309.

148. N. B. Golikova, *Ocherki po istorii gorodov Rossii kontsa XVII–nachala XVIII v.* (Moscow, 1982), chap. 4; M. G. Rabinovich, *Ocherki etnografii russkogo feodal'nogo goroda: Gorozhane, ikh obshchestvennyi i domashnii byt* (Moscow, 1978), 31–66, 104–12; A. I. Kopanev, *Naselenie Peterburga v pervoi polovine XIX veka* (Leningrad, 1957), 24–100; Kizevetter, *Posadskaia obshchina,* 46–168; Smetanin, "Razlozhenie soslovii"; M. Ia. Volkov, "Goroda Tverskoi provintsii v pervoi chetverti XVIII v.," in *Istoricheskaia geografiia Rossii XII–nachalo XX v.: Sbornik statei k 70-letiiu professora L. G. Beskrovnogo* (Moscow, 1975), 143–63; idem, "Formirovanie gorodskoi burzhuazii v Rossii XVII–XVIII vv.," in *Goroda feodal'noi Rossii: Sbornik statei pamiati N. V. Ustiugova* (Moscow, 1966), 199–203; A. A. Kondrashenkov, "Zapadnosibirskii posad v kontse XVIII v.," in *Goroda feodal'noi Rossii,* 506–10.

149. P. G. Ryndziunskii, "Melkaia promyshlennost' (remeslo i melkotovarnoe proizvodstvo)," in *Ocherki ekonomicheskoi istorii Rossii pervoi poloviny XIX veka,* ed. M. K. Rozhkova (Moscow, 1959), 64–99.

150. Hildermeier, "Was war Meščanstvo?", 47.

151. Pallot and Shaw, *Landscape and Settlement,* 253–56; B. N. Mironov, "Russkii gorod vo vtoroi polovine XVIII–pervoi polovine XIX veka: Tipologicheskii analiz," *Istoriia SSSR* 5 (1988): 150–68.

152. Hilton, *Russian Folk Art,* 25.

153. Ryndziunskii, *Gorodskoe grazhdanstvo,* 40–51, 179–82, 504–53; M. M. Gromyko, "Razvitie Tiumeni kak remeslenno-torgovogo tsentra v XVIII v.," in *Goroda feodal'noi Rossii,* 408–9; Abramov, "Zabytoe soslovie," 273–74.

154. Hildermeier, "Was war Meščanstvo?" 40–41, 51–52.

155. Abramov, "Zabytoe soslovie," 274.

156. Even the most basic population data for cities are contradictory. Alternative figures list Odessa's population at 499,500 and 630,000 in 1914. Pallot and Shaw, *Landscape and Settlement,* 257–62; Michael F. Hamm, ed., *The City in Late Imperial Russia* (Bloomington, Ind., 1986), 3, 127; Patricia Herlihy, *Odessa: A History, 1794–1914* (Cambridge, Mass., 1986), 234.

157. Literary depictions of despair and poverty in a lower-class urban milieu at the time of the Great Reforms include S. Makashin, "Nasledstvennaia bednost'": Rasskaz," in M. A. Voronov and S. A. Makashin, *Rasskazy o starom Saratove,* (Saratov, 1937), 157–89; N. G. Pomialovskii, *Brat i sestra* in *Sochineniia v dvukh tomakh,* 2 vols. (Moscow-Leningrad, 1965) 2: 191–258. Works that stress the blurred boundaries between factory and nonfactory workers include Joan Neuberger, *Hooliganism: Crime, Culture, and Power in St. Petersburg, 1900–1914* (Berkeley, 1993); Bradley, *Muzhik and Muscovite;* Bonnell, *Russian Worker;* idem, *Roots of Rebellion.* See also E. P. Thompson, *The Making of the English Working Class* (New York, 1963); Jürgen Kocka, *Weder Stand noch Klasse: Unterschichten um 1800* (Bonn, 1990).

158. Brower, *Russian City,* chap. 2; Abramov, "Zabytoe soslovie," 269–71; Sergei T——v, "Ranenburgskie meshchane," *Riazanskaia zhizn',* no. 146, 24.VI.1912, 3. I am grateful to Stephen Frank for sharing this last article.

159. On municipalization and city services, see Bater, "Modernization and Municipality," in *SRHG* 2; Michael F. Hamm, *Kiev: A Portrait, 1800–1917* (Princeton, 1993), 18–54.

160. James H. Bater, *St. Petersburg: Industrialization and Change* (Montreal, 1976); idem, "The Industrialization of Moscow and St. Petersburg," in *SRHG* 2: 279–303; idem, "Modernization and Municipality," in *SRHG* 2; Hamm, *Kiev;* idem, *City in Late Imperial Russia;* idem, *The City in Russian History* (Lexington, Ky., 1976); Robert W. Thurston, *Liberal City, Conservative State: Moscow and Russia's Urban Crisis, 1906–1914* (New York, 1987).

161. Pallot and Shaw, *Landscape and Settlement,* 253–54; Bater, "Industrialization of Moscow," in *SRHG* 2.

162. On community and sociability, see A. F. Nekrylova, *Russkie narodnye gorodskie prazdniki, uveseleniia i zrelishcha* (Leningrad, 1988); A. I. Kupriianov, *Russkii gorod v pervoi polovine XIX veka: Obshchestvennyi byt i kul'tura gorozhan zapadnoi Sibiri* (Moscow, 1995).

163. LeDonne, *Ruling Russia,* 50–52.

164. Wirtschafter, *Structures of Society,* 122.

165. As a result of secularization, begun in 1762, monastery peasants became a special category of state peasants, called "economic peasants," under the administration of the College of Economy.

166. Wirtschafter, *Structures of Society,* 122. Seventeenth- and early-eighteenth-century *bobyli* could be rural or urban. In places where their occupations and obligations to the monastery were equivalent to those of state *posadskie,* the church used the category in order to preserve its authority over traders and artisans, who were in danger of being absorbed into the tsar's official urban community. K. N. Serbina, "K voprosu o bobyliakh (bobyli Tikhvinskogo posada)," in *Akademiku B. D. Grekovu ko dniu semidesiatiletiia: Sbornik statei* (Moscow, 1952), 172–77.

167. Janet Hartley, "Town Government in Saint Petersburg Guberniya after the Charter to the Towns of 1785," *SEER* 62 (1984): 61–84. For similar conclusions, see also Kupriianov, *Russkii gorod,* 17–36.

168. Hartley, "Town Government," 65.

169. Nardova, *Gorodskoe samoupravlenie;* idem, *Samoderzhavie i gorodskie dumy.*

170. Abramov, "Zabytoe soslovie," 274–75.

171. Agricultural and urban historians of Russia have yet to study the elimination of commons in favor of private property, a transformation that began with emancipation, intensified with the Stolypin reforms, but still remained far from complete in 1917. For a general summary of the English situation, see Thompson, *Customs in Common,* 97–184. On the Sheremetevs, see Lieven, *Aristocracy in Europe,* 116.

172. By century's end, Okhta had been incorporated into St. Petersburg. Abramov, "Zabytoe soslovie," 278–81.

173. Ibid., 281–84.

174. Few could afford this alternative. Ibid., 285–87.

175. Ibid., 290–91.

176. Brower, *Russian City;* Neuberger, *Hooliganism;* Mark D. Steinberg, *Moral Communities: The Culture of Class Relations in the Russian Printing Industry, 1867–1907* (Berkeley, 1992). Brower, in particular, stresses the need to look at the neighborhood, market, tavern, church, public bath, and of course the family as the foundations of urban life. Brower, *Russian City,* 30, 130.

177. Here merchants should be distinguished from the late-nineteenth-century commercial-industrial elite, which has been studied by a number of scholars. See chap. 3.

178. Brower, *Russian City,* chap. 4; Clowes, Kassow, and West, *Between Tsar and People.*

179. John Rule, *Albion's People: English Society, 1714–1815* (New York, 1992).

180. Robert J. Brym and Evel Economakis, "Peasant or Proletarian? Militant Pskov Workers in St. Petersburg, 1913," *SR* 53 (1994): 138–39.

181. The focus adopted here most closely resembles that of works such as Tim McDaniel, *Autocracy, Capitalism, and Revolution in Russia* (Berkeley, 1988) and Laverychev, *Tsarizm i rabochii vopros.*

182. This analysis is likewise devoted to factory workers. A glimpse of nonfactory workers is available in Bonnell, *Russian Worker;* Bradley, *Muzhik and Muscovite.* For a full-scale study, see Angela Rustemeyer, *Dienstboten in Petersburg und Moskau, 1861–1917* (Stuttgart, 1996).

183. Pallot and Shaw, *Landscape and Settlement,* 221; Bater, *St. Petersburg,* 46, 91; Bonnell, *Roots of Rebellion,* 25–27. Bonnell employs a broad definition of the working class that "includes a multiplicity of groups in manufacturing, sales-clerical, construction, transportation, communication, and service occupations who belonged to the hired labor force and were engaged in manual or low-level white-collar jobs." In reality (because of the nature of the source base) her study is limited to workers who joined trade unions, a minority in almost all occupations and industrial sectors. Bonnell, *Roots of Rebellion,* 24–25, 233.

184. Bater, *St. Petersburg,* 9–12, 40–49.

185. The empire's total population at the close of the eighteenth century was 35.5 million. Pallot and Shaw, *Landscape and Settlement,* 196–97.

186. In 1852, the Russian empire possessed fewer than one thousand kilometers of railway line. Bater, *St. Petersburg,* 86.

187. Pallot and Shaw, *Landscape and Settlement,* 195–220.

188. Johnson, *Peasant and Proletarian,* 24–25.

189. W. L. Blackwell, "The Historical Geography of Industry in Russia during the Nineteenth Century," in *SRHG* 2: 415–16.

190. Bater, "Industrialization of Moscow," in *SRHG* 2: 282.

191. Pallot and Shaw, *Landscape and Settlement,* 270; Blackwell, "Geography of Industry," in *SRHG* 2: 387–420.

192. Bater, *St. Petersburg,* 173–201, 308–53, 408–10; idem, "Industrialization of Moscow," in *SRHG* 2: 279–83; idem, "Modernization and Municipality," in *SRHG* 2: 311–15; Blackwell, "Geography of Industry," in *SRHG* 2: 402–12; Bradley, *Muzhik and Muscovite;* Theodore H. Friedgut, *Iuzovka and Revolution,* vol. 1, *Life and Work in Russia's Donbass, 1869–1924;* vol. 2, *Politics and Revolution in Russia's Donbass, 1869–1924* (Princeton, 1989 and 1994), and 2: 207.

193. By late 1916, as a result of the shift to defense production, metalworking employed almost 28 percent of Moscow workers, and textiles only 24 percent. Diane P. Koenker, *Moscow Workers and the 1917 Revolution* (Princeton, 1981), 25–26.

194. Bater, *St. Petersburg,* 219–22, 389; idem, "Industrialization of Moscow," in *SRHG* 2: 283–89; Bonnell, *Roots of Rebellion,* 31–35; Johnson, *Peasant and Proletarian,* 21.

195. Bonnell, *Roots of Rebellion,* 5–6, 230–33.

196. In 1885, one in five workers under the jurisdiction of the factory inspectorate was female; by 1914, the proportion of women factory workers had increased to one in three. In textiles women made up well over half (59 percent) of the 1914 industrial workforce. Rose B. Glickman, *Russian Factory Women: Workplace and Society, 1880–1914* (Berkeley, 1984), 83–85.

197. Johnson, *Peasant and Proletarian*, 17–24.

198. Bonnell, *Roots of Rebellion*, 47–67; Zelnik, *Radical Worker;* Steinberg, *Moral Communities*, 82–84.

199. Bonnell, *Roots of Rebellion*, 28–67.

200. Charters Wynn, *Workers, Strikes, and Pogroms: The Donbass-Dnepr Bend in Late Imperial Russia, 1870–1905* (Princeton, 1992), 16–50; Friedgut, *Iuzovka and Revolution* 1: 71–128, 193–230, 329–34.

201. Ibid., 194–99.

202. Ibid., 71–100, 207–30.

203. On these groups, see Steinberg, *Moral Communities;* Hogan, *Forging Revolution.*

204. Johnson, *Peasant and Proletarian*, 21.

205. Bater, "Modernization and Municipality," in *SRHG* 2: 306–10.

206. Bater, *St. Petersburg*, 160–73; idem, "Modernization and Municipality," in *SRHG* 2: 306–10; Johnson, *Peasant and Proletarian*, 42–50.

207. Schmidt, *Ständerecht und Standeswechsel*, 122–24. These factors may help to explain the greater peasant interest in consumer societies and small credit associations after 1905. See Seregny, "Teachers and Cooperatives."

208. Zelnik, *Radical Worker*, 6–19.

209. Ibid., 7–13.

210. Friedgut, *Iuzovka and Revolution* 1: 113–14, 260; Johnson, *Peasant and Proletarian*, 68–79.

211. University students also formed fraternal societies based on province of origin. Johnson, *Peasant and Proletarian*, 50, 68–70.

212. Ibid., 79.

213. Friedgut, *Iuzovka and Revolution* 1: 230–73; Johnson, *Peasant and Proletarian*, 68–81.

214. Koenker, *Moscow Workers*, 156–57.

215. Johnson, *Peasant and Proletarian*, 87–92. For accounts that emphasize employer control and domination, see Steinberg, *Moral Communities*, 48–51; Friedgut, *Iuzovka and Revolution* 1: 132–36.

216. Soviets *(sovety)* were councils of workers' deputies created in 1905 and councils of workers' and/or soldiers' deputies created again in 1917, usually on the initiative of radical intellectuals.

217. Bonnell, *Roots of Rebellion*, 403.

218. Ibid., 381, 403.

219. Koenker, *Moscow Workers*, 73–74.

220. Bonnell, *Roots of Rebellion*, 204–9, 233. In a recent study of printers, Mark Steinberg argues that participation rates in mutual aid societies were low, noting that fewer than one-half of St. Petersburg printers and only one-seventh of Moscow printers had any experience of these funds in the early 1900s. Even so, his figures suggest levels of involvement that are significantly higher than the overall rates of participation in trade unions provided by Bonnell. Steinberg, *Moral Communities*, 92–93.

221. Johnson, *Peasant and Proletarian*, 74–79.

222. Labor mobilization is treated later in this chapter.

223. In his powerful and wrenching novel *Invisible Man*, Ralph Ellison shows how slippery notions of "mentality" and "consciousness" can be, and how easily individuals and groups can move between violent destruction and organized political action. Ralph Ellison, *Invisible Man* (New York, 1990). On the Russian situation, see Wynn, *Workers, Strikes, and Pogroms;* Neuberger, *Hooliganism.*

224. There are numerous descriptions of these conditions. See, for example, Johnson, *Peasant and Proletarian;* Friedgut, *Iuzovka and Revolution,* vol. 1; Bonnell, *Russian Worker;* Zelnik, *Law and Disorder;* idem, *Labor and Society in Tsarist Russia: The Factory Workers of St. Petersburg, 1855–1870* (Stanford, 1971). On possible improvements in living standards at the end of the nineteenth and beginning of the twentieth centuries, see Iu. I. Kir'ianov, *Zhiznennyi uroven' rabochikh Rossii (konets XIX–nachalo XX v.)* (Moscow, 1979).

225. Hogan, *Forging Revolution,* chaps. 7–9.

226. Friedgut, *Iuzovka and Revolution* 1: 176–83; Steinberg, *Moral Communities,* 38–39; Bonnell, *Roots of Rebellion,* 77–80; Zelnik, *Radical Worker,* 13.

227. Steinberg, *Moral Communities,* 33–60.

228. Zelnik, *Labor and Society,* 32–34; Bater, "Industrialization of Moscow," in *SRHG* 2: 281–82.

229. Zelnik, *Labor and Society,* 35–37; Friedgut, *Iuzovka and Revolution* 1: 137–40; Laverychev, *Tsarizm i rabochii vopros,* 30–31; Tugan-Baranovskii, *Russian Factory,* chap. 5.

230. The government instituted an eight-hour workday for children between the ages of twelve and fourteen and forbade all factory employment for children under age twelve and all night work for women and juveniles under age seventeen.

231. Zelnik, *Radical Worker,* 18–21.

232. The discussion of labor legislation in the 1880s and 1890s is based on Johnson, *Peasant and Proletarian,* 86; Frederick C. Giffen, "The Formative Years of the Russian Factory Inspectorate, 1882–1885," *SR* 25 (1966): 641–50; idem, "The 'First Russian Labor Code': The Law of June 3, 1886," *Russian History* 2 (1975): 83–102; Gaston V. Rimlinger, "Autocracy and the Factory Order in Early Russian Industrialization," *Journal of Economic History* 20 (1960): 67–92; idem, "The Management of Labor Protest in Tsarist Russia: 1870–1905," *International Review of Social History* 5, pt. 2 (1960): 226–48; Theodore H. Von Laue, "Factory Inspection under the 'Witte System': 1892–1903," *American Slavic and East European Review* 19 (1960): 347–62; Zelnik, *Radical Worker,* 18–21.

233. Unfortunately, there is no study of these workers' actions and their outcomes.

234. S. V. Zubatov, a tsarist police official employed by the ministry of internal affairs, initiated and directed the formation of the government-approved labor organizations in Moscow, Minsk, Vil'na (Vilnius), Odessa, and St. Petersburg. Although militant strikes led to Zubatov's dismissal in 1903, a comparable St. Petersburg organization arose in 1904 under the leadership of a local priest, Father G. A. Gapon.

235. The total number of participants in the demonstration is estimated at 50–100 thousand; in addition to those who were killed, another 299 were seriously wounded. Ascher, *Revolution of 1905,* 24–25, 75–92; McDaniel, *Autocracy, Capitalism, and Revolution,* 60–88; Bonnell, *Roots of Rebellion,* 70–103; Kyril Tidmarsh, "The Zubatov Idea," *American Slavic and East European Review* 19 (1960): 335–46.

236. McDaniel, *Autocracy, Capitalism, and Revolution,* 64.

237. Ibid., 73–82, 88.

238. P. E. Liubarov, "Tret'ia gosudarstvennaia duma i vopros o strakhovanii rabochikh kazennykh predpriiatii," *Vestnik moskovskogo universiteta* 2 (1967): 38; R. S. Rotenberg, "Bor'ba rabochego klassa Rossii za gosudarstvennoe sotsial'noe strakhovanie (1900–1914 gg.)," *Voprosy istorii* 11 (1958): 129; McDaniel, *Autocracy,*

Capitalism, and Revolution, 89–100; Bonnell, *Roots of Rebellion,* 94–97; Friedgut, *Iuzovka and Revolution* 1: 280–99.

239. Diane Koenker defines strikes "as work stoppages with common goals." Koenker, *Moscow Workers,* 295.

240. These points were suggested to me in reading Bonnell, *Roots of Rebellion,* 11–18, chaps. 3–4.

241. Johnson, *Peasant and Proletarian,* 124–52.

242. Diane P. Koenker and William G. Rosenberg, *Strikes and Revolution in Russia, 1917* (Princeton, 1989), 23–63; Iu. I. Kir'ianov, "Byli li antivoennye stachki v Rossii v 1914 godu?" *Voprosy istorii* 2 (1994): 43–52; Ascher, *Revolution of 1905,* 92–95; Bonnell, *Roots of Rebellion,* 352–54.

243. On the role of skill acquisition and exposure to the secular culture of educated elites in the formation of a revolutionary working-class consciousness, see Zelnik, *Radical Worker;* Steinberg, *Moral Communities;* idem, "Vanguard Workers and the Morality of Class," in *Making Workers Soviet: Power, Class, and Identity,* ed. Lewis H. Siegelbaum and Ronald Grigor Suny (Ithaca, N.Y., 1994), 66–84.

244. Zelnik, *Law and Disorder;* Johnson, *Peasant and Proletarian,* 159–60. Workers across Russia attended marriage celebrations in nearby villages and returned home for major religious holidays. On strikes and disturbances caused by management's efforts to prevent workers from observing religious holidays, see Friedgut, *Iuzovka and Revolution* 1: 312–24.

245. Zelnik, *Law and Disorder,* chaps. 4–5.

246. Ibid., chap. 4.

247. Jonathan E. Sanders, "The Union of Unions: Political, Economic, Civil, and Human Rights Organizations in the 1905 Revolution" (Ph.D. diss., Columbia University, 1985).

248. The same may be said of economic and educated elites. See Rieber, *Merchants and Entrepreneurs;* Clowes, Kassow, and West, *Between Tsar and People.*

249. Abstract thinking, as opposed to symbolic thinking, begins to develop in human beings by age twelve. According to Jean Piaget, children of eighteen months have the capacity for representation, which allows them "to use mental symbols and words to refer to absent objects." As a result of the development of symbolic thinking, the young child increasingly is freed "from the concrete here and now" and introduced "to the world of possibilities." In the adolescent, who thinks abstractly and theoretically, "the possible and the ideal captivate both mind and feeling. . . . In the stage of formal thought, the adolescent develops the ability to imagine the possibilities inherent in a situation," and before acting on a problem, he "analyzes it and attempts to develop hypotheses concerning what *might* occur." Herbert Ginsburg and Sylvia Opper, *Piaget's Theory of Intellectual Development: An Introduction* (Englewood Cliffs, N.J., 1969), 63–65, 205–6. I am grateful to Michele Winkler for the references to Piaget. See also Edmund Burke, *Reflections on the Revolution in France and on the Proceedings in Certain Societies in London Relative to That Event,* ed. Conor Cruise O'Brien (London, 1968); and Conor Cruise O'Brien, "A Vindication of Edmund Burke," *National Review,* December 17, 1990, 28–35.

250. *Prianiki* were spice cakes decorated with stamped designs. Hilton, *Russian Folk Art,* 45–46, 69–72.

251. Bonnell, *Roots of Rebellion,* 107–209, 239–45, 256–59.

252. Ralph Ellison's "invisible man" illustrates the lack of a clear distinction in

the mind and actions of one politically conscious individual. Ellison, *Invisible Man.*

253. Daniel R. Brower, "Labor Violence in Russia in the Late Nineteenth Century," *SR* 41 (1982): 417–31.

254. Laura Engelstein, *Moscow 1905: Working-Class Organization and Political Conflict* (Stanford, 1982), 79–94, 107–13, 142–49; Wynn, *Workers, Strikes, and Pogroms,* chaps. 4, 6, 7; Friedgut, *Iuzovka and Revolution* 2: 66–83, 107–11, 151–77, 247–48; Neuberger, *Hooliganism,* chap. 5; Robert Weinberg, *The Revolution of 1905 in Odessa: Blood on the Steps* (Bloomington, Ind., 1993).

255. The extent and meaning of worker violence in the revolutionary events of the late tsarist era clearly deserve further study.

256. Friedgut, *Iuzovka and Revolution* 2: 110–11, 470–71.

257. Reginald E. Zelnik, "On the Eve: Life Histories and Identities of Some Revolutionary Workers, 1870–1905," in Siegelbaum and Suny, *Making Workers Soviet,* 27–65.

258. Clowes, Kassow, and West, *Between Tsar and People;* Leopold H. Haimson, "Civil War and the Problem of Social Identities in Early Twentieth-Century Russia," in *Party, State, and Society in the Russian Civil War: Explorations in Social History,* ed. Diane P. Koenker, William G. Rosenberg, and Ronald Grigor Suny (Bloomington, Ind., 1989), 24–47.

259. Pierre Bourdieu draws an interesting distinction between "practical knowledge, based on the continuous decoding of the perceived" and knowledge that is "consciously noticed." Pierre Bourdieu, *Outline of a Theory of Practice,* trans. Richard Nice (New York, 1977), 10.

260. Koenker, *Moscow Workers,* 151–52, 362; Koenker and Rosenberg, *Strikes and Revolution,* 181, 326–29. On the defensive nature of worker radicalism, see also David Mandel, *The Petrograd Workers and the Fall of the Old Regime* (London, 1984).

261. Following the abdication of Nicholas II in Petrograd, a self-appointed committee of Duma deputies constituted itself as the Provisional Government. The composition of this government changed three times in 1917. Throughout the year, it competed for political and moral authority with local soviets of elected workers' and soldiers' deputies, dominated by the socialist parties. What limited power it possessed rested on the belief it would organize free elections to a Constituent Assembly whose task would be to write a constitution that would provide the basis for a new political order. The idea of soviet power meant that a socialist coalition would replace the Provisional Government, assuming temporary administrative authority and responsibility for the convocation of the Constituent Assembly. In September and October 1917, the Bolsheviks were the only socialist party advocating the immediate seizure of power by the soviets.

262. Allan K. Wildman, *The End of the Russian Imperial Army,* vol. 1, *The Old Army and the Soldiers' Revolt (March–April 1917);* vol. 2, *The Road to Soviet Power and Peace* (Princeton, 1980 and 1987).

263. Works that convey the confusion on the ground include Friedgut, *Iuzovka and Revolution,* vol. 2; Richard Pipes, *The Russian Revolution* (New York, 1990); Alexander Rabinowitch, *Prelude to Revolution: The Petrograd Bolsheviks and the July 1917 Uprising* (Bloomington, Ind., 1968); idem, *The Bolsheviks Come to Power: The Revolution of 1917 in Petrograd* (New York, 1976); John Reed, *Ten Days That Shook the World* (New York, 1960).

264. For a theoretical statement of the continuity between "popular" and "proletarian" cultures in early industrialization, see Wolfgang Kaschuba, "Popular Culture

and Workers' Culture as Symbolic Orders: Comments on the Debate about the History of Culture and Everyday Life," in Lüdtke, *History of Everyday Life,* 169–97.

265. Daniel R. Brower, "The Penny Press and Its Readers," in Frank and Steinberg, *Cultures in Flux,* 147–67.

CONCLUSION

1. On this issue, see Georges Duby, *The Three Orders: Feudal Society Imagined,* trans. Arthur Goldhammer (Chicago, 1980).

2. Griffiths, "Estates, Charters," in Griffiths and Munro, *Catherine II's Charters;* Kamenskii, "Soslovnaia politika Ekateriny II."

3. Pososhkov, *Poverty and Wealth.*

4. V. O. Kliuchevskii, *Istoriia soslovii v Rossii,* reprinted in *Sochineniia v deviati tomakh,* vol. 6 (Moscow, 1989).

5. This terminology is from Brunn, Hroch, and Kappeler, "Introduction," in Kappeler, *Formation of National Elites,* 1–10.

6. Gyan Pakrash, "Subaltern Studies as Postcolonial Criticism," *AHR* 99 (1994): 1475–90; Florencia E. Mallon, "The Promise and Dilemma of Subaltern Studies: Perspectives from Latin American History," *AHR* 99 (1994): 1491–515.

7. Wolff, *Inventing Eastern Europe.*

8. Wortman, *Scenarios of Power* 1: 5–7, 22–26, 42–61.

9. Quoted in L. T. Senchakova, *Prigovory i nakazy Rossiiskogo krest'ianstva 1905–1907 gg.,* vol. 1 (Moscow, 1994), 16.

10. Wayne Dowler, "The Politics of Language in Non-Russian Elementary Schools in the Eastern Empire," *RR* 54 (1995): 516.

11. Yuri Slezkine, "Naturalists versus Nations: Eighteenth-Century Russian Scholars Confront Ethnic Diversity," *Representations* 47 (1994): 183, 188.

12. Mark Bassin, "Inventing Siberia: Visions of the Russian East in the Early Nineteenth Century," *AHR* 96 (1991): 763–75.

13. Greenfeld, *Nationalism;* Hans Rogger, *National Consciousness in Eighteenth-Century Russia* (Cambridge, Mass., 1960).

14. Greenfeld, *Nationalism,* 255.

15. Redfield, *Little Community,* 113.

16. Wirtschafter, *Structures of Society,* 109.

17. Ibid., chaps. 2, 4–6.

18. Harley D. Balzer, "Introduction," in *RMMC,* 17–18.

19. Verner, "Discursive Strategies," 80–81.

20. Robert O. Crummey, "Old Belief as Popular Religion: New Approaches," *SR* 52 (1993): 710–11.

21. On the development of Old Belief within local structures of power and culture, see Georg Michels, "The Solovki Uprising: Religion and Revolt in Northern Russia," *RR* 51 (1992): 1–15.

22. From the time the capitation was introduced in the reign of Peter the Great until 1782, Old Believers were subjected to double taxation. See A. S. Riazhev, "Gosudarstvennaia politika po otnosheniiu k staroobriadtsam-pereselentsam iz Rechi Pospolitoi vo vtoroi polovine XVIII v.," in *Sosloviia* 2: 70–77.

23. Robert O. Crummey, *The Old Believers and the World of Antichrist: The Vyg Community and the Russian State, 1694–1855* (Madison, Wisc., 1970); Roy R. Robson, *Old Believers in Modern Russia* (DeKalb, Ill., 1995).

24. Roy R. Robson, "Liturgy and Community among Old Believers, 1905–1917," *SR* 52 (1993): 713–24; idem, *Old Believers*, 36–37, 43–46.

25. The best scholarly estimate is that of A. von Bushen, published in 1863, which concludes that Old Believers constituted about 10 percent of the empire's total population. Von Bushen's calculations did not include Orthodox dissenters who fell outside the identifiable boundaries of Old Belief.

26. Robson, *Old Believers*, 24–40.

27. Georg Michels, "Women and Religious Dissent in Late Muscovy" (unpublished paper presented at the UCLA "Winter" Workshop: Topics in Medieval Russian Culture, March 1, 1996).

28. On local religion and heterodoxy, see chap. 2.

29. See chap. 3.

30. Smith, "Freemasonry and Public," 29.

31. In 1846, the radical publicist V. G. Belinskii wrote of "*potrebnost' obshchestva* [a strong need for society]" and "*stremlenie k obshchestvu* [a striving toward society]" (Wirtschafter, *Structures of Society*, 143). See also, Müller, *Intelligencija;* Clowes, Kassow, and West, *Between Tsar and People;* Klaus Frölich, *The Emergence of Russian Constitutionalism, 1900–1904: The Relationship between Social Mobilization and Political Group Formation in Pre-Revolutionary Russia* (The Hague, 1981).

32. Peter Gay, *Weimar Culture: The Outsider as Insider* (New York, 1968).

33. On these points, see Freeze, "Church and Serfdom"; Zol'nikova, "Dukhovenstvo Tobol'skoi eparkhii," in *Sosloviia* 1: 94–103; Roosevelt, *Country Estate,* chap. 10; Bradley, *Muzhik and Muscovite,* 66–68; Zelnik, *Radical Worker,* 7–13, 24–36.

34. For recent treatments, see Keenan, "Muscovite Political Folkways"; Marker, *Publishing, Printing;* Marc Raeff, "Transfiguration and Modernization: The Paradoxes of Social Disciplining, Paedagogical Leadership, and the Enlightenment in Eighteenth-Century Russia," in *Alteuropa—Ancien Régime—Frühe Neuzeit,* ed. Hans Erich Bödeker and Ernst Hinrichs (Stuttgart–Bad Cannstatt, 1991), 99–115; idem, "People, Intelligentsia"; idem, *Police State;* Nicholas Riasanovsky, *A Parting of Ways: Government and the Educated Public in Russia, 1801–1855* (Oxford, 1976); Douglas Campbell Smith, "Working the Rough Stone: Freemasonry and Society in Eighteenth-Century Russia" (Ph.D. diss., University of California, Los Angeles, 1996).

35. Lotman, "Tema kart."

36. Worobec, "Popular Religion"; Roosevelt, *Country Estate,* chap. 10; Lindenmeyr, *Poverty,* chap. 1; Freeze, "Subversive Piety." Thus it is people steeped in rationalism and modern science who fear their inability to control the powerful forces known to be governed by natural law, whereas those who continue to follow local religious practices believe that they or someone in their midst can in fact control nature through rituals, incantations, witchcraft, and appeals to ancestral or divine spirits.

37. On this issue, see Eve Levin, "*Dvoeverie* and Popular Religion," in *Seeking God: The Recovery of Religious Identity in Orthodox Russia, Ukraine, and Georgia,* Stephen K. Batalden, (DeKalb, Ill., 1993), 31–52.

38. Greenfeld, *Nationalism,* 256.

39. Friz [Freeze], "Tserkov', religiia," 107–8.

40. Rogger, "Skobelev Phenomenon."

41. Julius Kirshner, "Introduction: The State Is 'Back In,'" *Journal of Modern History* 67, Supplement (1995): S6–S9.

42. In 1895 there were 340 learned societies in Russia, compared to only 25 in

1855, and "an official survey of 1899 counted more than 7,000 non-governmental organizations of a charitable and social service nature." The Moscow city directory of 1912 listed over 600 voluntary associations "covering a wide range of charitable, technical, literary, sporting, artistic, educational, cultural, and learned activities." Frölich, *Russian Constitutionalism,* 147–56; Walkin, *Democracy in Pre-Revolutionary Russia,* chap. 6; Joseph Bradley, "Voluntary Associations, Civic Culture, and *Obshchestvennost'* in Moscow," in Clowes, Kassow, and West, *Between Tsar and People,* 136–37.

43. On educated society's failure to forge large-scale organizational bonds, see Clowes, Kassow, and West, *Between Tsar and People;* Seregny, *Teachers and Revolution;* Lindenmeyr, *Poverty.*

44. Thomas Porter and William Gleason, "The *Zemstvo* and Public Initiative in Late Imperial Russia," *Russian History* 21 (1994): 419–37.

45. Menning, *Bayonets before Bullets,* 122, 236, 270.

46. Konstantin P. Pobedonostsev, *Reflections of a Russian Statesman* (Ann Arbor, Mich., 1965); Hans Rogger, *Jewish Policies and Right-Wing Politics in Imperial Russia* (Berkeley, 1986), 66–68.

47. Fröhlich, *Russian Constitutionalism,* 104.

48. Haimson, "Civil War and Identities," in Koenker, Rosenberg, and Suny, *Party, State, and Society.*

49. Schmidt, *Ständerecht und Standeswechsel;* Elpat'evskii, "Zakonodatel'nye istochniki."

50. Neuberger, *Hooliganism.* The psychology involved in the phenomenon of hooliganism also may be gleaned from Ellison, *Invisible Man.*

51. In a discussion of Louis Althusser's concept of ideology, Peter Schöttler notes that "individuals are always caught up in an *imaginary relation* to their real conditions of existence, and it is this imaginary relation which largely structures their behavior and thought." Peter Schöttler, "Mentalities, Ideologies, Discourses: On the 'Third Level' as a Theme in Social-Historical Research," in Lüdtke, *Everyday Life,* 82.

SELECTED BIBLIOGRAPHY

This selected bibliography is not intended to be fully representative of recent Russian-, English-, German-, and French-language scholarship, especially in the subfields of economic history, peasant studies, labor history, and the study of nationalities. It reflects only what has gone into the making of this book.

Abramov, Ia. "Zabytoe soslovie." *Nabliudatel'*, vol. 4, no. 1 (January 1885): 269–302.

Aksakov, S. T. *A Russian Gentleman*. Translated by J. D. Duff. Oxford: Oxford University Press, 1982.

Aksenov, A. I. *Genealogiia moskovskogo kupechestva XVIII v.: Iz istorii formirovaniia russkoi burzhuazii*. Moscow, 1988.

———. *Ocherki genealogii uezdnogo kupechestva XVIII v.* Moscow, 1993.

Aleksandr Nikolaevich Engelgardt's Letters from the Country, 1872–1887. Translated and edited by Cathy A. Frierson. New York: Oxford University Press, 1993.

Aleksandrov, V. A. *Obychnoe pravo krepostnoi derevni Rossii: XVIII–nachalo XIX v.* Moscow, 1984.

———. *Sel'skaia obshchina v Rossii (XVII–nachalo XIX v.).* Moscow, 1976.

Alexander, John T. *Autocratic Politics in a National Crisis: The Imperial Russian Government and Pugachev's Revolt, 1773–1775*. Bloomington: Indiana University Press, 1969.

———. *Bubonic Plague in Early Modern Russia: Russian Public Health and Urban Disaster*. Baltimore: Johns Hopkins University Press, 1980.

———. "Medical Developments in Petrine Russia." *Canadian-American Slavic Studies* 8 (1974): 198–221.

———. "Medical Professionals and Public Health in 'Doldrums' Russia (1725–1762)." *Canadian-American Slavic Studies* 12 (1978): 116–35.

Amburger, Erik. *Geschichte der Behördenorganisation Russlands von Peter dem Grossen bis 1917*. Leiden: Brill, 1966.

Anan'ich, N. I. "K istorii otmeny podushnoi podati v Rossii." *Istoricheskie zapiski* 94 (1974): 183–212.

Androssov, V. *Statisticheskaia zapiska o Moskve*. Moscow, 1832.

Anfimov, A. M. *Ekonomicheskoe polozhenie i klassovaia bor'ba krest'ian evropeiskoi Rossii, 1881–1904.* Moscow, 1984.

———. *Krupnoe pomeshchich'e khoziaistvo evropeiskoi Rossii.* Moscow, 1969.

Anfimov, A. M., and P. N. Zyrianov. "Nekotorye cherty evoliutsii russkoi krest'ianskoi obshchiny v poreformennyi period (1861–1914 gg.)." *Istoriia SSSR* 4 (1980): 26–41.

Anisimov, E. V. *Podatnaia reforma Petra I: Vvedenie podushnoi podati v Rossii v 1719–1728.* Leningrad, 1982.

Appleby, Joyce, Lynn Hunt, and Margaret Jacob. *Telling the Truth about History.* New York: Norton, 1994.

Arsen'ev, K. I. "Istoriko-statisticheskii ocherk narodnoi obrazovannosti v Rossii do kontsa XVIII veka." *Uchenye zapiski vtorogo otdeleniia imperatorskoi Akademii nauk,* kn. 1, otdelenie 2 (St. Petersburg, 1854): 1–32.

Ascher, Abraham. *The Revolution of 1905: Authority Restored.* Stanford: Stanford University Press, 1992.

———. *The Revolution of 1905: Russia in Disarray.* Stanford: Stanford University Press, 1988.

Atkinson, Dorothy. *The End of the Russian Land Commune, 1905–1930.* Stanford: Stanford University Press, 1983.

Atkinson, Dorothy, Alexander Dallin, and Gail Warshofsky Lapidus, eds. *Women in Russia.* Stanford: Stanford University Press, 1977.

Augustine, Wilson R. "Notes toward a Portrait of the Eighteenth-Century Russian Nobility." *Canadian Slavic Studies* 4 (1970): 373–425.

Avrekh, A. Ia. *Stolypin i tret'ia duma.* Moscow, 1968.

Avrich, Paul. *Russian Rebels, 1600–1800.* New York: Norton, 1972.

Balzer, Harley David. "Educating Engineers: Economic Politics and Technical Training in Tsarist Russia." Ph.D. diss., University of Pennsylvania, 1980.

———, ed. *Russia's Missing Middle Class: The Professions in Russian History.* Armonk, N.Y.: Sharpe, 1996.

Banac, Ivo, and Paul Bushkovitch, eds. *The Nobility in Russia and Eastern Europe.* New Haven: Yale Concilium on International and Area Studies, 1983.

Baron, Samuel H. "The Weber Thesis and the Failure of Capitalist Development in 'Early Modern' Russia." *Jahrbücher für Geschichte Osteuropas* 18 (1970): 320–36.

Barrett, Thomas M. "Good News Comes to a Russian Village: The Peasant Articles of Kharkov and the Emancipation of the Serfs." *Peasant Studies* 17 (1989): 23–42.

Bartlett, Roger. "J. J. Sievers and the Russian Peasantry under Catherine II." *Jahrbücher für Geschichte Osteuropas* 32 (1984): 16–33.

———, ed. *Land Commune and Peasant Community in Russia: Communal Forms in Imperial and Early Soviet Society.* London: Macmillan, 1990.

Bassin, Mark. "Inventing Siberia: Visions of the Russian East in the Early Nineteenth Century." *American Historical Review* 96 (1991): 763–94.

———. "Russia between Europe and Asia: The Ideological Construction of Geography." *Slavic Review* 50 (1991): 1–17.

———. "Turner, Solov'ev, and the 'Frontier Hypothesis': The Nationalist Significa-tion of Open Spaces." *Journal of Modern History* 65 (1993): 473–511.

Batalden, Stephen K., ed. *Seeking God: The Recovery of Religious Identity in Orthodox Russia, Ukraine, and Georgia.* DeKalb: Northern Illinois University Press, 1993.

Bater, James H. *St. Petersburg: Industrialization and Change*. Montreal: McGill-Queen's University Press, 1976.

Bater, James H., and R. A. French, eds. *Studies in Russian Historical Geography*. 2 vols. London: Academic Press, 1983.

Bauer, Henning, Andreas Kappeler, and Brigitte Roth, eds. *Die Nationalitäten des russischen Reiches in der Volkzählung von 1897*. 2 vols. Stuttgart: Steiner, 1991.

Bayer, Waltraud. *Die Moskauer Medici: Der russische Bürger als Mäzen 1850 bis 1917*. Vienna: Böhlau, 1996.

Beaven, Miranda. "Aleksandr Smirdin and Publishing in St. Petersburg, 1830–1840." *Canadian Slavonic Papers* 27 (1985): 15–30.

Becker, Christopher. "*Raznochintsy:* The Development of the Word and of the Concept." *Slavic Review* 18 (1959): 63–74.

Becker, Seymour. *Nobility and Privilege in Late Imperial Russia*. DeKalb: Northern Illinois University Press, 1985.

Belinskii, V. G. *Polnoe sobranie sochinenii*. 13 vols. Moscow, 1953–1959.

Bell, David A. "The 'Public Sphere,' the State, and the World of Law in Eighteenth-Century France." *French Historical Studies* 17 (1992): 913–34.

Belliustin, I. S. *Description of the Clergy in Rural Russia: The Memoir of a Nineteenth-Century Parish Priest*. Edited and translated by Gregory L. Freeze. Ithaca, N.Y.: Cornell University Press, 1985.

Bennett, Helju Aulik. "The Chin System and the Raznochintsy in the Government of Alexander III, 1881–1894." Ph.D. diss., University of California, Berkeley, 1971.

———. "Evolution of the Meanings of Chin: An Introduction to the Russian Institution of Rank Ordering and Niche Assignment from the Time of Peter the Great's Table of Ranks to the Russian Revolution." *California Slavic Studies* 10 (1977): 1–43.

Bernstein, Laurie. *Sonia's Daughters: Prostitutes and Their Regulation in Imperial Russia*. Berkeley: University of California Press, 1995.

Besançon, Alain. *Éducation et société en Russie dans le second tiers du XIXe siècle*. Paris and La Haye: Mouton, 1974.

Beyrau, Dietrich. *Militär und Gesellschaft im vorrevolutionären Russland*. Cologne: Böhlau, 1984.

Bisha, Robin. "The Promise of Patriarchy: Marriage in Eighteenth-Century Russia." Ph.D. diss., Indiana University, 1993.

Black, Cyril, ed. *The Transformation of Russian Society: Aspects of Social Change since 1861*. Cambridge, Mass.: Harvard University Press, 1960.

Blackwell, William L. *The Beginnings of Russian Industrialization, 1800–1860*. Princeton: Princeton University Press, 1968.

———. *The Industrialization of Russia: A Historical Perspective*. 2d ed. Arlington Heights, Ill.: Davidson, 1970.

———, ed. *Russian Economic Development from Peter the Great to Stalin*. New York: Franklin Watts, 1974.

Blanchard, Ian. *Russia's "Age of Silver": Precious-Metal Production and Economic Growth in the Eighteenth Century*. New York: Routledge, 1989.

Blum, Jerome. *Lord and Peasant in Russia from the Ninth to the Nineteenth Century*. Princeton: Princeton University Press, 1971.

Boborykin, P. D. *Vospominaniia v dvukh tomakh*. Edited by E. Vilenskaia and L. Roitberg. 2 vols. Moscow, 1965.

Bohac, Rodney D. "Peasant Inheritance Strategies in Russia." *Journal of Interdisciplinary History* 16 (1985): 23–42.

Bonnell, Victoria E. *Roots of Rebellion: Workers' Politics and Organization in St. Petersburg and Moscow, 1900–1914.* Berkeley: University of California Press, 1983.

———, ed. *The Russian Worker: Life and Labor under the Tsarist Regime.* Berkeley: University of California Press, 1983.

Bourdieu, Pierre. *Outline of a Theory of Practice.* Translated by Richard Nice. New York: Cambridge University Press, 1977.

Bowman, Linda. "Russia's First Income Taxes: The Effects of Modernized Taxes on Commerce and Industry, 1885–1914." *Slavic Review* 52 (1993): 256–82.

Bradley, Joseph. *Muzhik and Muscovite: Urbanization in Late Imperial Russia.* Berkeley: University of California Press, 1985.

Braudel, Fernand. *On History.* Translated by Sarah Matthews. Chicago: University of Chicago Press, 1980.

Brooks, Jeffrey. *When Russia Learned to Read: Literacy and Popular Literature, 1861–1917.* Princeton: Princeton University Press, 1985.

Brower, Daniel R. "Estate, Class, and Community: Urbanization and Revolution in Late Tsarist Russia." The Carl Beck Papers in Russian and East European Studies, no. 302. Pittsburgh: University of Pittsburgh Press, 1983.

———. "Labor Violence in Russia in the Late Nineteenth Century." *Slavic Review* 41 (1982): 417–31.

———. "The Problem of the Russian Intelligentsia." *Slavic Review* 26 (1967): 638–47.

———. *The Russian City between Tradition and Modernity, 1850–1900.* Berkeley: University of California Press, 1990.

———. *Training the Nihilists: Education and Radicalism in Tsarist Russia.* Ithaca, N.Y.: Cornell University Press, 1975.

Brown, Julie Vail. "The Professionalization of Russian Psychiatry: 1857–1911." Ph.D. diss., University of Pennsylvania, 1981.

Brubaker, Rogers. "Rethinking Nationhood: Nation as Institutionalized Form, Practical Category, Contingent Event." *Contention: Debates in Society, Culture, and Science* 4 (1994): 3–14.

Brunner, Otto, Werner Conze, and Reinhart Koselleck, eds. *Geschichtliche Grundbegriffe: Historisches Lexikon zur politisch-sozialen Sprache in Deutschland.* 7 vols. Stuttgart: Klett, 1972–1992.

Brym, Robert J., and Evel Ekonomakis. "Peasant or Proletarian? Militant Pskov Workers in St. Petersburg, 1913." *Slavic Review* 53 (1994): 120–39.

Buganov, V. I. "Rossiiskoe dvorianstvo." *Voprosy istorii* 1 (1994): 29–41.

Bulgakova, L. A. "Intelligentsiia v Rossii vo vtoroi chetverti XIX veka: Sostav, pravovoe i material'noe polozhenie." Kand. diss., Leningrad, 1983.

———. "Soslovnaia politika v oblasti obrazovaniia vo vtoroi chetverti XIX v." In *Voprosy politicheskoi istorii SSSR.* Moscow, 1974.

Burbank, Jane. "Discipline and Punishment in the Moscow Bar Association." *Russian Review* 54 (1995): 44–64.

———. "A Question of Dignity: Peasant Legal Culture in Late Imperial Russia." *Continuity and Change* 10 (1995): 391–404.

Burke, Edmund. *Reflections on the Revolution in France and on the Proceedings in Certain Societies in London Relative to That Event.* Edited with an introduction by Conor Cruise O'Brien. Reprint, London: Penguin, 1968.

Burke, Kenneth. *On Symbols and Society*. Edited by Joseph R. Gusfield. Chicago: University of Chicago Press, 1989.

Burke, Peter. *Popular Culture in Early Modern Europe*. Reprint, New York: Harper and Row, 1978.

Buryshkin, P. A. *Moskva kupecheskaia: Memuary*. Reprint, Moscow, 1991.

Bush, M. L., ed. *Serfdom and Slavery: Studies in Legal Bondage*. New York: Longman, 1996.

———. *Social Orders and Social Classes in Europe since 1500: Studies in Social Stratification*. New York: Longman, 1992.

Bushnell, John. "Did Serf Owners Control Serf Marriage? Orlov Serfs and Their Neighbors, 1773–1861." *Slavic Review* 52 (1993): 419–45.

———. *Mutiny amid Repression: Russian Soldiers in the Revolution of 1905–1906*. Bloomington: Indiana University Press, 1985.

———. "Peasant Economy and Peasant Revolution at the Turn of the Century. Neither Immiseration nor Autonomy." *Russian Review* 47 (1988): 75–88.

———. "Peasants in Uniform: The Tsarist Army as a Peasant Society." *Journal of Social History* 13 (1980): 565–76.

———. "The Tsarist Officer Corps, 1881–1914: Customs, Duties, Inefficiency." *American Historical Review* 86 (1981): 753–80.

Chartier, Roger. *The Cultural Origins of the French Revolution*. Translated by Lydia G. Cochrane. Durham, N.C.: Duke University Press, 1991.

Cherniavsky, Michael. *Tsar and People: Studies in Russian Myths*. New Haven: Yale University Press, 1961.

Clements, Barbara Evans, Barbara Alpern Engel, and Christine D. Worobec, eds. *Russia's Women: Accommodation, Resistance, Transformation*. Berkeley: University of California Press, 1991.

Clowes, Edith W., Samuel D. Kassow, and James L. West, eds. *Between Tsar and People: Educated Society and the Quest for Public Identity in Late Imperial Russia*. Princeton: Princeton University Press, 1991.

Confino, Michael. *Domaines et seigneurs en Russie vers la fin du XVIIIe siècle*. Paris: Institut d'Études Slaves de l'Université de Paris, 1963.

———. "Histoire et psychologie: À propos de la noblesse russe au XVIIIe siècle." *Annales: Économies-Sociétés-Civilisation* 22 (1967): 1163–205.

———. "On Intellectuals and Intellectual Traditions in Eighteenth- and Nineteenth-Century Russia." *Daedalus* 101 (1972): 117–49.

———. "Present Events and the Representation of the Past: Some Current Problems in Russian Historical Writing." *Cahiers du Monde russe et soviétique* 35 (1994): 839–68.

———. "Russian Customary Law and the Study of Peasant *Mentalités*." *Russian Review* 44 (1985): 35–43.

———. "Servage russe, esclavage américain (note critique)." *Annales: Économies-Sociétés-Civilisation* 45 (1990): 1119–41.

———. *Systèmes agraires et progrès agricole: L'assolement triennal en Russie aux XVIIIe–XIXe siècles*. Paris and La Haye: Mouton, 1969.

Conze, Werner, and Jürgen Kocka, eds. *Bildungsbürgertum im 19. Jahrhundert*. Vol. 1, *Bildungssystem und Professionalisierung in internationalen Vergleichen*. Stuttgart: Klett-Cotta, 1985.

Cracraft, James. *The Church Reforms of Peter the Great*. London: Macmillan, 1971.

Crisp, Olga. *Studies in the Russian Economy before 1914*. London: Macmillan, 1976.

Cross, A. G., ed. *Russia and the West in the Eighteenth Century.* Newtonville, Mass.: Oriental Research Partners, 1983.

Crummey, Robert O. "Old Belief as Popular Religion: New Approaches." *Slavic Review* 52 (1993): 700–712.

———. *The Old Believers and the World of Antichrist: The Vyg Community and the Russian State, 1694–1855.* Madison: University of Wisconsin Press, 1970.

Curtiss, John Shelton. *The Russian Army under Nicholas I, 1825–1855.* Durham, N.C.: Duke University Press, 1965.

Czap, Peter, Jr. "Peasant Class Courts and Peasant Customary Justice in Russia, 1861–1912." *Journal of Social History* 1 (1967): 148–78.

———. "The Perennial Multiple Family Household, Mishino, Russia, 1782–1858." *Journal of Family History* 7 (1982): 5–26.

Daniel, Wallace. "Entrepreneurship and the Russian Textile Industry: From Peter the Great to Catherine the Great." *Russian Review* 54 (1995): 1–25.

———. "Grigorii Teplov and the Conception of Order: The Commission on Commerce and the Role of the Merchants in Russia." *Canadian-American Slavic Studies* 16 (1982): 410–31.

———. "The Merchantry and the Problem of Social Order in the Russian State: Catherine II's Commission on Commerce." *Slavonic and East European Review* 55 (1977): 185–203.

———. "The Merchants' View of the Social Order in Russia as Revealed in the Town *Nakazy* from Moskovskaia Guberniia to Catherine's Legislative Commission." *Canadian-American Slavic Studies* 11 (1977): 503–22.

Darnton, Robert. *The Great Cat Massacre and Other Episodes in French Cultural History.* New York: Basic Books, 1984.

Dashkova, E. R. *The Memoirs of Princess Dashkova: Russia in the Time of Catherine the Great.* Translated and edited by Kyril Fitzlyon. Reprint, Durham, N.C.: Duke University Press, 1995.

Davydov, M. A. *Oppozitsiia ego velichestva: Dvorianstvo i reformy v nachale XIX veka.* Göttingen: Max Planck Institut für Geschichte, 1994.

Degtiarev, A. Ia., S. G. Kashchenko, and D. I. Raskin. *Novgorodskaia derevnia v reforme 1861 goda: Opyt izucheniia s ispol'zovaniem EVM.* Leningrad, 1989.

Del'vig, A. I. *Polveka russkoi zhizni: Vospominaniia A. I. Del'viga, 1820–1870.* 2 vols. Moscow and Leningrad, 1930.

Desiatiletie ministerstva narodnogo prosveshcheniia, 1833–1843. St. Petersburg, 1864.

Diakin, V. S. "Natsional'nyi vopros vo vnutrennei politike tsarizma (XIX v.)." *Voprosy istorii* 9 (1995): 130–42.

Dowler, Wayne. "The Politics of Language in Non-Russian Elementary Schools in the Eastern Empire, 1865–1914." *Russian Review* 54 (1995): 516–38.

Druzhinin, N. M. *Gosudarstvennye krest'iane i reforma P. D. Kiseleva.* 2 vols. Moscow, 1946 and 1958.

———. *Russkaia derevnia na perelome, 1861–1880 gg.* Moscow, 1978.

Duby, Georges. *The Three Orders: Feudal Society Imagined.* Translated by Arthur Goldhammer. Chicago: University of Chicago Press, 1980.

Duffy, Christopher. *Russia's Military Way to the West: Origins and Nature of Russian Military Power, 1700–1800.* London: Routledge and Kegan Paul, 1981.

Dukes, Paul. *Catherine the Great and the Russian Nobility.* London: Cambridge University Press, 1967.

———. *The Making of Russian Absolutism, 1613–1801.* New York: Longman, 1982.

————, ed. and trans. *Russia under Catherine the Great*. 2 vols. Newtonville, Mass.: Oriental Research Partners, 1977–1978.

Dulov, A. V. *Geograficheskaia sreda i istoriia Rossii konets XV–seredina XIX v.* Moscow, 1983.

Dunn, Stephen, and Ethel Dunn. *The Peasants of Central Russia*. New York: Waveland, 1988.

Durov, N. P. "Fedor Vasil'evich Karzhavin." *Russkaia starina* 12 (1875): 272–97.

Edelman, Robert. *Gentry Politics on the Eve of the Russian Revolution: The Nationalist Party, 1907–1917*. New Brunswick, N.J.: Rutgers University Press, 1980.

————. *Proletarian Peasants: The Revolution of 1905 in Russia's Southwest*. Ithaca, N.Y.: Cornell University Press, 1987.

Edmondson, Linda. *Feminism in Russia, 1900–1917*. Stanford: Stanford University Press, 1984.

————, ed. *Women and Society in Russia and the Soviet Union*. New York: Cambridge University Press, 1992.

Edmondson, Linda, and Peter Waldron, eds. *Economy and Society in Russia and the Soviet Union, 1860–1930: Essays for Olga Crisp*. New York: St. Martin's Press, 1992.

Eklof, Ben. "Russian Literacy Campaigns, 1861–1939." In *National Literacy Campaigns: Historical and Comparative Perspectives*. Edited by Robert F. Arnove and Harvey J. Graff. New York: Plenum Press, 1987.

————. *Russian Peasant Schools: Officialdom, Village Culture, and Popular Pedagogy, 1861–1914*. Berkeley: University of California Press, 1986.

————. "Ways of Seeing: Recent Anglo-American Studies of the Russian Peasant (1861–1914)." *Jahrbücher für Geschichte Osteuropas* 36 (1988): 57–79.

Eklof, Ben, and Stephen P. Frank, eds. *The World of the Russian Peasant: Post-Emancipation Culture and Society*. Boston: Unwin Hyman, 1990.

Eklof, Ben, John Bushnell, and Larissa Zakharova, eds. *Russia's Great Reforms, 1855–1881*. Bloomington: Indiana University Press, 1994.

Ellison, Ralph. *Invisible Man*. New York: Vintage, 1990.

Elpat'evskii, A. V. "Zakonodatel'nye istochniki po istorii dokumentirovaniia soslovnoi prinadlezhnosti v tsarskoi Rossii (XVIII–nachalo XX v.)." In *Istochnikovedenie otechestvennoi istorii*. Moscow, 1984.

Emmons, Terence. *The Formation of Political Parties and the First National Elections in Russia*. Cambridge, Mass.: Harvard University Press, 1983.

————. *The Russian Landed Gentry and the Peasant Emancipation of 1861*. London: Cambridge University Press, 1968.

Emmons, Terence, and Wayne S. Vucinich, eds. *The Zemstvo in Russia: An Experiment in Local Self-Government*. New York: Cambridge University Press, 1982.

Engel, Barbara Alpern. *Between the Fields and the City: Women, Work, and Family in Russia, 1861–1914*. New York: Cambridge University Press, 1994.

————. "Engendering Russia's History: Women in Post-Emancipation Russia and the Soviet Union." *Slavic Review* 51 (1992): 309–21.

————. *Mothers and Daughters: Women of the Intelligentsia in Nineteenth-Century Russia*. New York: Cambridge University Press, 1983.

————. "Russian Peasant Views of City Life, 1861–1914." *Slavic Review* 52 (1993): 446–59.

Engelstein, Laura. *The Keys to Happiness: Sex and the Search for Modernity in Fin-de-Siècle Russia*. Ithaca, N.Y.: Cornell University Press, 1992.

————. *Moscow 1905: Working-Class Organization and Political Conflict.* Stanford: Stanford University Press, 1982.

Enskii, Fedor. *Otstavnye soldaty.* St. Petersburg, 1873.

Esper, Thomas. "The Odnodvortsy and the Russian Nobility." *Slavonic and East European Review* 45 (1967): 124–34.

Etzioni, Amitai, ed. *The Semi-Professions: Teachers, Nurses, and Social Workers.* New York: Free Press, 1969.

Evreinov, N. *Istoriia telesnykh nakazanii v Rossii.* Reprint, Khar'kov, 1994.

Farnsworth, Beatrice. "The Soldatka: Folklore and Court Record." *Slavic Review* 49 (1990): 58–73.

Farnsworth, Beatrice, and Lynne Viola, eds. *Russian Peasant Women.* New York: Oxford University Press, 1992.

Farrow, Lee A. "Peter the Great's Law of Single Inheritance: State Imperatives and Noble Resistance." *Russian Review* 55 (1996): 430–47.

————. "Property, Security, and the Security of Property in Eighteenth-Century Russia." Paper prepared for delivery at the AAASS conference, Boston, November 17, 1996.

Fedorov, A. V. *Russkaia armiia v 50–70 gg. XIX veka.* Leningrad, 1959.

Fedorov, V. A. *Soldatskoe dvizhenie v gody dekabristov, 1816–1825 gg.* Moscow, 1963.

Fenster, Aristide. *Adel und Ökonomie im vorindustriellen Russland: Die unternehmirische Betätigung der Gutsbesitzer in der grossgewerblichen Wirtschaft im 17. und 18. Jahrhundert.* Wiesbaden: Kommission bei F. Steiner, 1983.

Field, Daniel. *The End of Serfdom: Nobility and Bureaucracy in Russia, 1855–61.* Cambridge, Mass.: Harvard University Press, 1976.

————. "Peasants and Propagandists in the Russian Movement to the People of 1874." *Journal of Modern History* 59 (1987): 415–38.

————. *Rebels in the Name of the Tsar.* Boston: Houghton Mifflin, 1976.

Filippov, N. G. "Nauchno-tekhnicheskie obshchestva dorevoliutsionnoi Rossii." *Voprosy istorii* 3 (1985): 31–45.

Fitzpatrick, Anne Lincoln. *The Great Fair: Nizhnii Novgorod, 1840–90.* New York: St. Martin's Press, 1990.

Fitzpatrick, Sheila. "Ascribing Class: The Construction of Social Identity in Soviet Russia." *Journal of Modern History* 65 (1993): 745–70.

Florinsky, Michael. *Russia: A History and an Interpretation.* 2 vols. New York: Macmillan, 1947 and 1953.

Flynn, James T. "Tuition and Social Class in the Russian Universities: S. S. Uvarov and 'Reaction' in the Russia of Nicholas I." *Slavic Review* 35 (1976): 232–48.

"Forum: The Public Sphere in the Eighteenth Century." *French Historical Studies* 17 (1992): 882–956.

Foucault, Michel. *The Archaeology of Knowledge and the Discourse on Language.* Translated by A. M. Sheridan Smith. New York: Pantheon, 1972.

————. *Madness and Civilization: A History of Insanity in the Age of Reason.* Translated by Richard Howard. New York: Vintage, 1988.

————. *The Order of Things: An Archaeology of the Human Sciences.* New York: Random House, 1970.

Frank, Stephen P. *Crime, Cultural Conflict, and Justice in Rural Russia, 1856–1914.* Forthcoming.

————. "'Simple Folk, Savage Customs?' Youth, Sociability, and the Dynamics of

Culture in Rural Russia, 1856–1914." *Journal of Social History* 25 (1992): 711–36.

Frank, Stephen P., and Mark D. Steinberg, eds. *Cultures in Flux: Lower-Class Values, Practices, and Resistance in Late Imperial Russia*. Princeton: Princeton University Press, 1994.

Freeze, Gregory L. "Bringing Order to the Russian Family: Marriage and Divorce in Imperial Russia, 1760–1860." *Journal of Modern History* 62 (1990): 709–46.

———. "A Case of Stunted Anti-Clericalism: Clergy and Society in Imperial Russia." *European Studies Review* 13 (1983): 177–200.

———. *Church, Religion and Society in Modern Russia, 1740–1940*. Forthcoming.

———. "Church, State and Society in Catherinean Russia: The Synodal Instruction to the Legislative Commission." In *"...aus der anmuthigen Gelehrsamkeit": Tübinger Studien zum 18. Jahrhundert*. Edited by Eberhard Müller. Tübingen: Attempto, 1988.

———. "The Disintegration of Traditional Communities: The Parish in Eighteenth-Century Russia." *Journal of Modern History* 48 (1976): 32–50.

———. *From Supplication to Revolution: A Documentary Social History of Imperial Russia*. New York: Oxford University Press, 1988.

———. "Handmaiden of the State? The Church in Imperial Russia Reconsidered." *Journal of Ecclesiastical History* 36 (1985): 82–102.

———. "Introduction." In I. S. Belliustin, *Description of the Clergy in Rural Russia: The Memoir of a Nineteenth-Century Parish Priest*, edited and translated by Gregory L. Freeze. Ithaca, N.Y.: Cornell University Press, 1985.

———. "Die Laisierung des Archimandriten Feodor (Bucharev) und ihre kirchenpolitischen Hintergründe: Theologie und Politik im Russland der Mitte des 19. Jahrhunderts." In *Kirche im Osten: Studien zur osteuropäischen Kirchengeschichte und Kirchenkunde*. Vol. 28. Edited by Peter Hauptmann. Göttingen: Vandenhoeck and Reprecht, 1985.

———. "The Meaning of Institutionalization in Modern Russian History." Unpublished paper presented to the Iowa Symposium on Imperial Russia, November 1991.

———. "New Scholarship on the Russian Peasantry." *European History Quarterly* 22 (1992): 605–17.

———. "The Orthodox Church and Serfdom in Prereform Russia." *Slavic Review* 48 (1989): 361–87.

———. *The Parish Clergy in Nineteenth-Century Russia: Crisis, Reform, Counter-Reform*. Princeton: Princeton University Press, 1983.

———. "The Rechristianization of Russia: The Church and Popular Religion, 1750–1850." *Studia Slavica Finlandensia* 7 (Helsinki, 1990): 101–36.

———. *The Russian Levites: Parish Clergy in the Eighteenth Century*. Cambridge, Mass.: Harvard University Press, 1977.

———. "The *Soslovie* (Estate) Paradigm in Russian Social History." *American Historical Review* 91 (1986): 11–36.

———. "Subversive Piety: Religion and the Political Crisis in Late Imperial Russia." *Journal of Modern History* 68 (1996): 308–50.

———. "Tserkov', religiia i politicheskaia kul'tura na zakate staroi Rossii." *Istoriia SSSR* 2 (1991): 107–19.

Frieden, Nancy Mandelker. *Russian Physicians in an Era of Reform and Revolution, 1856–1905*. Princeton: Princeton University Press, 1981.

Friedgut, Theodore H. *Iuzovka and Revolution*. Vol. 1, *Life and Work in Russia's Donbass, 1869–1924*. Vol. 2, *Politics and Revolution in Russia's Donbass, 1869–1924*. Princeton: Princeton University Press, 1989 and 1994.

Frierson, Cathy A. "Crime and Punishment in the Russian Village: Rural Concepts of Criminality at the End of the Nineteenth Century." *Slavic Review* 46 (1987): 55–69.

———. *Peasant Icons: Representations of Rural People in Late Nineteenth-Century Russia*. New York: Oxford University Press, 1993.

———. "Rural Justice in Public Opinion: The Volost' Court Debate, 1861–1912." *Slavonic and East European Review* 64 (1986): 526–45.

Friesen, Leonard G. "Bukkers, Plows and Lobogreikas: Peasant Acquisition of Agricultural Implements in Russia before 1900." *Russian Review* 53 (1994): 300–418.

Fröhlich, Klaus. *The Emergence of Russian Constitutionalism, 1900–1904: The Relationship between Social Mobilization and Political Group Formation in Pre-Revolutionary Russia*. The Hague: Nijhoff, 1981.

Fuller, William C., Jr. *Civil-Military Conflict in Imperial Russia, 1881–1914*. Princeton: Princeton University Press, 1985.

———. *Strategy and Power in Russia, 1600–1914*. New York: Free Press, 1992.

Garrard, J. G., ed. *The Eighteenth Century in Russia*. Oxford: Clarendon Press, 1973.

Gatrell, Peter. *The Tsarist Economy, 1850–1917*. London: Batsford, 1986.

Gaudin, Corinne. "Les *zemskie načal' niki* au village: Coutumes administratives et culture paysanne en Russie, 1889–1914." *Cahiers du Monde russe* 36 (1995): 249–72.

Gay, Peter. *Weimar Culture: The Outsider as Insider*. New York: Harper and Row, 1968.

Geraci, Robert Paul. "Window on the East: Ethnography, Orthodoxy, and Russian Nationality in Kazan, 1870–1914." Ph.D. diss., University of California, Berkeley, 1995.

Geyer, Dietrich. *Russian Imperialism: The Interaction of Domestic and Foreign Policy, 1860–1914*. Translated by Bruce Little. New Haven: Yale University Press, 1987.

———, ed. *Wirtschaft und Gesellschaft im vorrevolutionären Russland*. Cologne: Kiepenheuer and Witsch, 1975.

Giffen, Frederick C. "The 'First Russian Labor Code': The Law of June 3, 1886." *Russian History* 2 (1975): 83–102.

———. "The Formative Years of the Russian Factory Inspectorate, 1882–1885." *Slavic Review* 25 (1966): 641–50.

Ginsburg, Herbert, and Sylvia Opper. *Piaget's Theory of Intellectual Development: An Introduction*. Englewood Cliffs, N.J.: Prentice-Hall, 1969.

Ginzburg, Carlo. *Clues, Myths, and the Historical Method*. Translated by John and Anne C. Tedeschi. Baltimore: Johns Hopkins University Press, 1989.

Gleason, Abbott. *Young Russia: The Genesis of Russian Radicalism in the 1860s*. New York: Viking, 1980.

Gleason, Walter J. *Moral Idealists, Bureaucracy, and Catherine the Great*. New Brunswick, N.J.: Rutgers University Press, 1981.

Glickman, Rose B. "The Literary Raznochintsy in Mid-Nineteenth Century Russia." Ph.D. diss., University of Chicago, 1968.

———. *Russian Factory Women: Workplace and Society, 1880–1914*. Berkeley: University of California Press, 1984.

Goehrke, Carsten. "Zum Problem des Regionalismus in der russischen Geschichte. Vorüberlegungen für eine künftige Untersuchung." *Forschungen zur osteuropäischen Geschichte* 25 (1978): 75–107.

Goldberg, Carl Allan. "The Association of Industry and Trade, 1906–1917: The Successes and Failures of Russia's Organized Businessmen." Ph.D. diss., University of Michigan, 1974.

Golikova, N. B. *Ocherki po istorii gorodov Rossii kontsa XVII–nachala XVIII v.* Moscow, 1982.

Golunskii, S. A., and D. S. Karev. *Istoriia suda i ugolovnogo protsessa: Al' bom nagliadnykh posobii.* Moscow, 1938.

Gordon, Daniel. "Philosophy, Sociology, and Gender in the Enlightenment Conception of Public Opinion." *French Historical Studies* 17 (1992): 882–911.

Gorky, Maxim. "On the Russian Peasantry." *Journal of Peasant Studies* 4 (1976): 11–27.

Goroda feodal' noi Rossii: Sbornik statei pamiati I. V. Ustiugova. Moscow, 1966.

Goscilo, Helena, and Beth Holmgren, eds. *Russia—Women—Culture.* Bloomington: Indiana University Press, 1996.

Graf, Harvey J., ed. *Literacy and Social Development in the West: A Reader.* New York: Cambridge University Press, 1981.

Grantham, George, and Carol S. Leonard, eds. *Agrarian Organization in the Century of Industrialization: Europe, Russia, and North America.* Greenwich, Conn.: JAI Press, 1989.

Greenfeld, Liah. *Nationalism: Five Roads to Modernity.* Cambridge, Mass.: Harvard University Press, 1992.

Gregory, Paul R. "Grain Marketings and Peasant Consumption, Russia, 1885–1913." *Explorations in Economic History* 17 (1980): 135–64.

Grenzer, Andreas. *Adel und Landbesitz im ausgehenden Zarenreich: Der russische Landadel zwischen Selbstbehauptung und Anpassung nach Aufhebung der Leibeigenschaft.* Stuttgart: Steiner, 1995.

———. "Zur Sozialgeschichte des russischen Adels im Zarenreich." *Jahrbücher für Geschichte Osteuropas* 37 (1989): 250–63.

Griffiths, David M. "Eighteenth-Century Perceptions of Backwardness: Projects for the Creation of a Third Estate in Catherinean Russia." *Canadian-American Slavic Studies* 13 (1979): 452–72.

Griffiths, David M. and George E. Munro, eds. *Catherine II's Charters of 1785 to the Nobility and the Towns.* Bakersfield, Calif.: C. Schlacks, Jr., 1990.

Gromyko, M. M. "Kul'tura russkogo krest'ianstva XVIII–XIX vekov kak predmet istoricheskogo issledovaniia." *Istoriia SSSR* 3 (1987): 39–60.

———. *Traditsionnye normy povedeniia i formy obshcheniia russkikh krest'ian XIX v.* Moscow, 1986.

———. *Trudovye traditsii russkikh krest'ian Sibiri (XVIII–pervaia polovina XIX v.).* Novosibirsk, 1975.

Guroff, Gregory, and Fred V. Carstensen, eds. *Entrepreneurship in Imperial Russia and the Soviet Union.* Princeton: Princeton University Press, 1983.

Habermas, Jürgen. *The New Conservatism: Cultural Criticism and the Historians' Debate.* Edited and translated by Shierry Weber Nicholsen. Cambridge, Mass.: MIT Press, 1989.

———. *The Structural Transformation of the Public Sphere: An Inquiry into a Category of Bourgeois Society.* Translated by Thomas Burger with Frederick Lawrence. Cambridge, Mass.: MIT Press, 1989.

Haimson, Leopold H. "The Problem of Social Stability in Urban Russia, 1905–1917."
    Slavic Review 23 (1964): 619–42; 24 (1965): 1–22.
———. "Social Identities in Early Twentieth Century Russia." *Slavic Review* 47
    (1988): 1–21.
———, ed. *The Politics of Rural Russia, 1905–1914.* Bloomington: Indiana University
    Press, 1979.
Haimson, Leopold H., and Charles Tilly, eds. *Strikes, Wars and Revolutions in an In-
    ternational Perspective.* New York: Cambridge University Press, 1989.
Hamburg, Gary M. "The Crisis in Russian Agriculture: A Comment." *Slavic Review* 37
    (1978): 481–86.
———. *Politics of the Russian Nobility, 1881–1905.* New Brunswick, N.J.: Rutgers
    University Press, 1984.
Hamm, Michael F. *Kiev: A Portrait, 1800–1917.* Princeton: Princeton University Press,
    1993.
———, ed. *The City in Late Imperial Russia.* Bloomington: Indiana University Press,
    1986.
———, ed. *The City in Russian History.* Lexington: University Press of Kentucky,
    1976.
Hartley, Janet M. *Alexander I.* New York: Longman, 1994.
———. "The Boards of Social Welfare and the Financing of Catherine II's State
    Schools." *Slavonic and East European Review* 67 (1989): 211–27.
———. "Town Government in St. Petersburg Guberniya after the Charter to the Towns
    of 1785." *Slavonic and East European Review* 62 (1984): 61–84.
Haxthausen, August von. *Studies on the Interior of Russia.* Edited by S. Frederick
    Starr. Translated by Eleanore L. M. Schmidt. Chicago: University of Chicago
    Press, 1972.
Hellie, Richard. "The Stratification of Muscovite Society: The Townsmen." *Russian
    History* 5 (1978): 119–75.
Herlihy, Patricia. *Odessa: A History, 1794–1914.* Cambridge, Mass.: Harvard Ukrain-
    ian Research Institute, 1986.
Hildermeier, Manfred. *Bürgertum und Stadt in Russland, 1760–1860: Rechtliche Lage
    und soziale Struktur.* Cologne: Böhlau, 1986.
———. "Gesellschaftsbild und politische Artikulation der Kaufmannschaft im vor-
    und frühindustriellen Russland." *Forschungen zur osteuropäischen Geschichte*
    38 (1986): 392–418.
———. "Was war das Meščanstvo? Zur rechtlichen und sozialen Verfassung des un-
    terenstädtischen Standes in Russland." *Forschungen zur osteuropäischen
    Geschichte* 36 (1985): 15–53.
Hilton, Alison. *Russian Folk Art.* Bloomington: Indiana University Press, 1995.
Himmelfarb, Gertrude. *The New History and the Old: Critical Essays and Reap-
    praisals.* Cambridge, Mass.: Harvard University Press, 1987.
———. *On Looking into the Abyss: Untimely Thoughts on Culture and Society.* New
    York: Knopf, 1994.
Hirschbiel, Henry. "The District Captains of the Ministry of State Properties in the
    Reign of Nicholas I: A Case Study of Russian Officialdom, 1838–1856." Ph.D.
    diss., New York University, 1978.
Hittle, J. M. *The Service City: State and Townsmen in Russia, 1600–1800.* Cambridge,
    Mass.: Harvard University Press, 1979.
Hoch, Steven L. "The Banking Crisis, Peasant Reform, and Economic Development in

Russia, 1857–1861." *American Historical Review* 96 (1991): 795–820.

———. "On Good Numbers and Bad: Malthus, Population Trends and Peasant Standard of Living in Late Imperial Russia." *Slavic Review* 53 (1994): 42–75.

———. *Serfdom and Social Control in Russia: Petrovskoe, a Village in Tambov.* Chicago: University of Chicago Press, 1986.

Hoch, Steven L., and Wilson R. Augustine. "The Tax Censuses and the Decline of the Serf Population in Imperial Russia, 1833–1858." *Slavic Review* 38 (1979): 403–25.

Hogan, Heather. *Forging Revolution: Metalworkers, Managers, and the State in St. Petersburg, 1890–1914.* Bloomington: Indiana University Press, 1993.

Hosking, Geoffrey A. *The Russian Constitutional Experiment: Government and Duma, 1907–1914.* Cambridge: Cambridge University Press, 1973.

Hudson, Hugh D., Jr. "Urban Estate Engineering in Eighteenth-Century Russia: Catherine the Great and the Elusive 'Meshchanstvo.'" *Canadian-American Slavic Studies* 18 (1984): 393–410.

Hunt, Lynn. *Politics, Culture, and Class in the French Revolution.* Berkeley: University of California Press, 1984.

———, ed. *The New Cultural History.* Berkeley: University of California Press, 1989.

Hutchinson, John F. *Politics and Public Health in Revolutionary Russia, 1890–1918.* Baltimore: Johns Hopkins University Press, 1990.

———. "Society, Corporation or Union? Russian Physicians and the Struggle for Professional Unity (1890–1913)." *Jahrbücher für Geschichte Osteuropas* 30 (1982): 37–53.

Hutton, Lester T. "The Reform of City Government in Russia, 1860–1870." Ph.D. diss., University of Illinois at Urbana-Champaign, 1972.

Iatsunskii, V. K. *Sotsial'no-ekonomicheskaia istoriia Rossii XVIII–XIX vv.* Moscow, 1973.

Istoricheskaia geografiia Rossii XII–nachalo XX v.: Sbornik statei k 70-letiiu professora L. G. Beskrovnogo. Moscow, 1975.

Istoriia rabochego klassa Rossii, 1861–1900 gg. Edited by L. M. Ivanov and M. S. Volin. Moscow, 1972.

Istoriia rabochego klassa SSSR: Rabochii klass ot zarozhdeniia do nachala XX v. Moscow, 1983.

Istoriia rabochego klassa SSSR: Rabochii klass Rossii 1907–fevral' 1917 g. Moscow, 1982.

Jarausch, Konrad Hugo, ed. *The Transformation of Higher Learning, 1860–1930: Expansion, Diversification, Social Opening and Professionalization in England, Germany, Russia and the United States.* Chicago: University of Chicago Press, 1983.

Joffe, Muriel. "The Cotton Manufacturers in the Central Industrial Region, 1880s–1914: Merchants, Economics and Politics." Ph.D. diss., University of Pennsylvania, 1981.

Johanson, Christine. *Women's Struggle for Higher Education in Russia, 1855–1900.* Kingston, Ont.: McGill-Queen's University Press, 1987.

Johnson, Robert E. *Peasant and Proletarian: The Working Class of Moscow in the Late Nineteenth Century.* New Brunswick, N.J.: Rutgers University Press, 1979.

———. "Primitive Rebels? Reflections on Collective Violence in Imperial Russia." *Slavic Review* 41 (1982): 436–42.

Jones, Robert E. *The Emancipation of the Russian Nobility, 1762–1785.* Princeton: Princeton University Press, 1973.

————. *Provincial Development in Russia: Catherine II and Jakob Sievers.* New Brunswick, N.J.: Rutgers University Press, 1984.

Kabuzan, V. M. "Gosudarstvennye krest'iane Rossii v XVIII–50-kh godakh XIX veka: Chislennost', sostav i razmeshchenie." *Istoriia SSSR* 1 (1988): 68–83.

————. *Izmeneniia v razmeshchenii naseleniia Rossii v XVIII–pervoi polovine XIX v. (po materialam revizii).* Moscow, 1971.

————. *Narodonaselenie Rossii v XVIII–pervoi polovine XIX v. (po materialam revizii).* Moscow, 1963.

————. *Narody Rossii v pervoi polovine XIX v.: Chislennost' i etnicheskii sostav.* Moscow, 1992.

Kahan, Arcadius. *The Plow, the Hammer and the Knout: An Economic History of Eighteenth-Century Russia.* Chicago: University of Chicago Press, 1985.

————. *Russian Economic History: The Nineteenth Century.* Edited by Roger Weiss. Chicago: University of Chicago Press, 1989.

Kaiser, Daniel H. "Women, Property and the Law in Early Modern Russia." Unpublished paper. Grinnell, Iowa, 1988.

————. "Women's Property in Muscovite Families, 1500–1725." Unpublished paper. Grinnell, Iowa, 1988.

Kamendrowsky, Victor, and David M. Griffiths. "The Fate of the Trading Nobility Controversy in Russia: A Chapter in the Relationship between Catherine II and the Russian Nobility." *Jahrbücher für Geschichte Osteuropas* 26 (1978): 198–221.

Kamenskii, A. B. *"Pod seniiu Ekateriny...": Vtoraia polovina XVIII veka.* St. Petersburg, 1992.

————. "Rossiiskoe dvorianstvo v 1767 godu (k probleme konsolidatsii)." *Istoriia SSSR* 1 (1990): 58–77.

————. "Soslovnaia politika Ekateriny II." *Voprosy istorii* 3 (1995): 29–45.

Kamkin, A. V. "Pravosoznanie gosudarstvennykh krest'ian vtoroi poloviny XVIII veka (na materialakh Evropeiskogo Severa)." *Istoriia SSSR* 2 (1987): 163–73.

Kappeler, Andreas. "Historische Voraussetzungen des Nationalitätenproblems im russischen Vielvölkerreich." *Geschichte und Gesellschaft* 8 (1982): 159–83.

————. *Russland als Vielvölkerreich: Entstehung, Geschichte, Zerfall.* Munich: Beck, 1992.

————, ed. *The Formation of National Elites.* New York: New York University Press, 1992.

Kashchenko, S. G. *Reforma 19 fevralia 1861 goda v Sankt-Peterburgskoi gubernii.* Leningrad, 1990.

Kaspin, Albert. "Ostrovsky and the Raznochinets in His Plays." Ph.D. diss., University of California, Berkeley, 1957.

Keenan, Edward L. "Muscovite Political Folkways." *Russian Review* 45 (1986): 115–81.

Keep, John L. H. "Catherine's Veterans." *Slavonic and East European Review* 59 (1981): 385–96.

————. *Soldiers of the Tsar: Army and Society in Russia, 1462–1874.* New York: Oxford University Press, 1985.

Kenez, Peter. "A Profile of the Prerevolutionary Officer Corps." *California Slavic Studies* 7 (1973): 121–58.

Khasanova, S. I. "K voprosu ob izuchenii intelligentsii dorevoliutsionnoi Rossii." *Revoliutsionno-osvoboditel'noe dvizhenie v XIX–XX vv. v Povolzh'e i Priural'e.* Edited by G. N. Vul'fson. Kazan, 1974.

Khodarkovsky, Michael. "The Stepan Razin Uprising: Was It a 'Peasant War'?" *Jahrbücher für Geschichte Osteuropas* 42 (1994): 1–19.

Kimball, Alan. "Russian Civil Society and Political Crisis in the Era of the Great Reforms, 1859–1863." Unpublished manuscript. Eugene, Ore., 1989.

Kimerling [Wirtschafter], Elise. "Soldiers' Children, 1719–1856: A Study of Social Engineering in Imperial Russia." *Forschungen zur osteuropäischen Geschichte* 30 (1982): 61–136.

Kingston-Mann, Esther, and Timothy Mixter, eds. *Peasant Economy, Culture, and Politics of European Russia, 1800–1921*. Princeton: Princeton University Press, 1991.

Kir'ianov, Iu. I. "Byli li antivoennye stachki v Rossii v 1914 godu?" *Voprosy istorii* 2 (1994): 43–52.

———. *Zhiznennyi uroven' rabochikh Rossii: Konets XIX–nachalo XX v.* Moscow, 1979.

Kirshner, Julius. "Introduction: The State Is 'Back In.'" *Journal of Modern History* 67 (1995): S1–S10

Kivelson, Valerie A. "The Effects of Partible Inheritance: Gentry Families and the State in Muscovy." *Russian Review* 53 (1994): 197–212.

———. "Kinship Politics/Autocratic Politics: A Reconsideration of Eighteenth-Century Autocratic Culture." Unpublished manuscript. January 30, 1996.

Kizevetter, A. A. *Posadskaia obshchina v Rossii XVIII st.* Moscow, 1903.

Kleimola, Ann M., and Gail Lenhoff, eds. *Culture and Identity in Muscovy, 1359–1584/Moskovskaia Rus' (1359–1584): Kul'tura i istoricheskoe samosoznanie*. Moscow, 1996.

Klier, John D., and Shlomo Lambroza, eds. *Pogroms: Anti-Jewish Violence in Modern Russian History*. New York: Cambridge University Press, 1992.

Kliuchevskii, V. O. *Istoriia soslovii v Rossii*. Reprinted in *Sochineniia v deviati tomakh*. Vol. 6. Moscow, 1989.

———. "Proiskhozhdenie krepostnogo prava v Rossii." Reprinted in *Sochineniia v deviati tomakh*. Vol. 8. Moscow, 1990.

Knabe, Bernd. *Die Struktur des russischen Posadgemeindes und das Katalog der Beschwerden und Forderungen der Kaufmanschaft, 1762–1767. Forschungen zur osteuropäischen Geschichte* 22 (1975).

Kniga v Rossii: Iz istorii dukhovnogo prosveshcheniia: Sbornik nauchnykh trudov. St. Petersburg, 1993.

Kocka, Jürgen. "Middle Classes and Civil Society in Nineteenth-Century Europe: The German Case in Comparative Perspective." Paper presented at the University of California, Los Angeles, March 16, 1995.

———. "The Middle Classes in Europe." *Journal of Modern History* 67 (1995): 783–806.

———. *Weder Stand noch Klasse: Unterschichten um 1800*. Bonn: Dietz, 1990.

Koenker, Diane P. *Moscow Workers and the 1917 Revolution*. Princeton: Princeton University Press, 1981.

Koenker, Diane P., and William G. Rosenberg. *Strikes and Revolution in Russia, 1917*. Princeton: Princeton University Press, 1989.

Koenker, Diane P., William G. Rosenberg, and Ronald Grigor Suny, eds. *Party, State, and Society in the Russian Civil War: Explorations in Social History*. Bloomington: Indiana University Press, 1989.

Kolchin, Peter. *Unfree Labor: American Slavery and Russian Serfdom*. Cambridge, Mass.: Harvard University Press, 1987.

Kollmann, Nancy Shields. "Ritual and Social Drama at the Muscovite Court." *Slavic Review* 45 (1986): 486–502.

———. "The Seclusion of Elite Muscovite Women." *Russian History* 10 (1983): 170–87.

Kopanev, A. I. *Naselenie Peterburga v pervoi polovine XIX veka*. Leningrad, 1957.

Korelin, A. P. *Dvorianstvo v poreformennoi Rossii, 1861–1904 gg*. Moscow, 1979.

Koselleck, Reinhart. *Critique and Crisis: Enlightenment and the Pathogenesis of Modern Society*. New York: Berg, 1988

Kössler, Reinhart. *Arbeitskultur im Industrialisierungsprozess: Studien an englischen und sowjetrussischen Paradigmata*. Münster: Westfalisches Dampfboot, 1990.

Koval'chenko, I. D. *Russkoe krepostnoe krest'ianstvo v pervoi polovine XIX veka*. Moscow, 1967.

Kozlova, N. V. "Organizatsiia kommercheskogo obrazovaniia v Rossii v XVIII v." *Istoricheskie zapiski* 117 (1989): 288–314.

———. *Pobegi krest'ian v Rossii v pervoi treti XVIII veka (iz istorii sotsial'no-ekonomicheskoi zhizni strany)*. Moscow, 1983.

Krest'ianskie chelobitnye XVII v. Moscow, 1994.

Krinitskii, Mark. "Krizis domashnikh idealov sovremennago meshchanstva." *Riazanskaia zhizn', no. 18, 21.XII.1911*.

Kristeva, Julia. *Revolution in Poetic Language*. Translated by Margaret Waller. New York: Columbia University Press, 1984.

Kuchmova, L. I. "Sel'skaia pozemel'naia obshchina Evropeiskoi Rossii v 60–70-e gody XIX v." *Istoricheskie zapiski* 106 (1981): 323–47.

Kupriianov, A. I. *Russkii gorod v pervoi polovine XIX veka: Obshchestvennyi byt i kyl'tura gorozhan zapadnoi Sibiri*. Moscow, 1995.

Kurmacheva, M. D. *Krepostnaia intelligentsiia Rossii: Vtoraia polovina XVIII–nachalo XIX veka*. Moscow, 1983.

LaCapra, Dominick, and Steven L. Kaplan, eds. *Modern European Intellectual History: Reappraisals and New Perspectives*. Ithaca, N.Y.: Cornell University Press, 1982.

Laverychev, V. Ia. *Tsarizm i rabochii vopros v Rossii, 1861–1917 gg*. Moscow, 1972.

Lavrov, Peter. *Historical Letters*. Edited and translated by James P. Scanlan. Berkeley: University of California Press, 1967.

Lawrence, Jeanette A., and Jaan Valsiner. "Conceptual Roots of Internalization: From Transmission to Transformation." *Human Development* 36 (1993): 150–67.

LeDonne, John P. *Absolutism and Ruling Class: The Formation of the Russian Political Order, 1700–1825*. New York: Oxford University Press, 1991.

———. *Ruling Russia: Politics and Administration in the Age of Absolutism, 1762–1796*. Princeton: Princeton University Press, 1984.

Leikina-Svirskaia, V. R. *Intelligentsiia v Rossii vo vtoroi polovine XIX veka*. Moscow, 1971.

———. *Russkaia intelligentsiia v 1900–1917 godakh*. Moscow, 1981.

Lenhoff, Gail. *The Martyred Princes Boris and Gleb: A Socio-Cultural Study of the Cult and the Texts*. Columbus, Ohio: Slavica, 1989.

Lenski, Gerhard. "Societal Taxonomies: Mapping the Social Universe." *Annual Review of Sociology* 20 (1994): 1–26.

Leroy-Beaulieu, Anatole. *The Empire of the Tsars and the Russians*. Translated by Zenaide A. Ragozin. 3 vols. New York: Putnam's, 1893–1896.

Lewin, Moshe. "Customary Law and Russian Rural Society in the Post-Reform Era." *Russian Review* 44 (1985): 1–19.

Liashchenko, Peter I. *History of the National Economy of Russia to the 1917 Revolution*. Translated by L. M. Herman. New York: Macmillan, 1949.

Lieven, Dominic C. B. *The Aristocracy in Europe, 1815–1914*. New York: Columbia University Press, 1992.

———. *Russia's Rulers under the Old Regime*. New Haven: Yale University Press, 1989.

Lincoln, W. Bruce. *The Great Reforms: Autocracy, Bureaucracy, and the Politics of Change in Imperial Russia*. DeKalb: Northern Illinois University Press, 1990.

———. *In the Vanguard of Reform: Russia's Enlightened Bureaucrats, 1825–1861*. DeKalb: Northern Illinois University Press, 1982.

Lindenmeyr, Adele. *Poverty Is Not a Vice: Charity, Society, and the State in Imperial Russia*. Princeton: Princeton University Press, 1996.

———. "Public Life, Private Virtues: Women and Russian Charity, 1762–1914." *Signs: Journal of Women in Culture and Society* 18 (1993): 562–91.

Liubarov, P. E. "Tret'ia gosudarstvennaia duma i vopros o strakhovanii rabochikh kazennykh predpriiatii." *Vestnik moskovskogo universiteta* 2 (1967): 36–48.

Lotman, Iu. M. *Besedy o russkoi kul'ture: Byt i traditsii russkogo dvorianstva (XVIII–nachalo XIX veka)*. St. Petersburg, 1994.

———. "Tema kart i kartochnoi igry v russkoi literature nachala XIX veka." *Trudy po znakovym sistemam* 7 (1978): 120–42.

Löwe, Heinz-Dietrich. *Die Lage der Bauern in Russland, 1880–1905: Wirtschaftliche und soziale Veränderungen in der ländlichen Gesellschaft des Zarenreiches*. St. Katharinen, Germany: Scripta Mercaturae, 1987.

Lüdtke, Alf, ed. *The History of Everyday Life: Reconstructing Experiences and Ways of Life*. Translated by William Templer. Princeton: Princeton University Press, 1995.

Lyotard, Jean-François. *The Postmodern Condition: A Report on Knowledge*. Translated by Geoff Bennington and Brian Massumi. Minneapolis: University of Minnesota Press, 1984.

Macey, David A. J. *Government and Peasant in Russia, 1861–1906: The Prehistory of the Stolypin Reforms*. DeKalb: Northern Illinois University Press, 1987.

Madariaga, Isabel de. "Catherine II and the Serfs: A Reconsideration of Some Problems." *Slavonic and East European Review* 52 (1974): 34–62.

———. *Catherine the Great: A Short History*. New Haven: Yale University Press, 1990.

———. *Russia in the Age of Catherine the Great*. New Haven: Yale University Press, 1981.

Malia, Martin. *Alexander Herzen and the Birth of Russian Socialism*. Cambridge, Mass.: Harvard University Press, 1961.

Mallon, Florencia E. "The Promise and Dilemma of Subaltern Studies: Perspectives from Latin American History." *American Historical Review* 99 (1994): 1491–1515.

Manchester, Laurie. "Secular Ascetics: The Mentality of Orthodox Clergymen's Sons in Late Imperial Russia." Ph.D. diss., Columbia University, 1995.

Mandel, David. *The Petrograd Workers and the Fall of the Old Regime*. London: Macmillan, 1984.

Manning, Roberta Thompson. *The Crisis of the Old Order in Russia: Gentry and Government*. Princeton: Princeton University Press, 1982.

Marker, Gary. *Publishing, Printing, and the Origins of Intellectual Life in Russia,*

1700–1800. Princeton: Princeton University Press, 1985.

———. "Who Rules the Word? Public Education and the Fate of Universality in Russia, 1782–1803." *Russian History* 20 (1993): 15–34.

Marrese, Michelle Lamarche. "A Woman's Kingdom: Women and the Control of Property in Russia, 1700–1861." Ph.D. diss., Northwestern University, 1995.

Marsh, Rosalind, ed. *Women in Russia and Ukraine*. New York: Cambridge University Press, 1996.

Mayzel, Matitiahu. "The Formation of the Russian General Staff, 1880–1917: A Social Study." *Cahiers du Monde russe et soviétique* 16 (1975): 297–321.

Maza, Sarah. "Women, the Bourgeoisie, and the Public Sphere: Response to Daniel Gordon and David Bell." *French Historical Studies* 17 (1992): 935–50.

McCaffray, Susan P. *The Politics of Industrialization in Tsarist Russia: The Association of Southern Coal and Steel Producers, 1874–1914*. DeKalb: Northern Illinois University Press, 1996.

McClelland, James C. *Autocrats and Academics: Education, Culture, and Society in Tsarist Russia*. Chicago: University of Chicago Press, 1979.

McDaniel, Tim. *Autocracy, Capitalism, and Revolution in Russia*. Berkeley: University of California Press, 1988.

McFarlin, Harold. "The Extension of the Imperial Russian Civil Service to the Lowest Office: The Creation of the Chancery Clerkship, 1827–1833." *Russian History* 1 (1974): 1–17.

———. "Recruitment Norms for the Russian Civil Service in 1833: The Chancery Clerkship." *Societas: A Review of Social History* 3 (1973): 61–73.

McKean, Robert B. *St. Petersburg between the Revolutions: Workers and Revolutionaries, June 1907–February 1917*. New Haven: Yale University Press, 1990.

McNeal, Robert H. *Tsar and Cossack, 1855–1914*. New York: St. Martin's Press, 1985.

McReynolds, Louise. *The News under Russia's Old Regime: The Development of a Mass-Circulation Press*. Princeton: Princeton University Press, 1991.

Meehan, Brenda. *Holy Women of Russia: The Lives of Five Orthodox Women Offer Spiritual Guidance for Today*. San Francisco: Harper, 1993.

Meehan-Waters, Brenda. *Autocracy and Aristocracy: The Russian Service Elite of 1730*. New Brunswick, N.J.: Rutgers University Press, 1982.

———. "Catherine the Great and the Problem of Female Rule." *Russian Review* 34 (1975): 293–307.

Melton, Edgar. "Enlightened Seigniorialism and Its Dilemmas in Serf Russia, 1750–1830." *Journal of Modern History* 62 (1990): 675–708.

———. "Household Economies and Communal Conflicts on a Russian Serf Estate, 1800–1817." *Journal of Social History* 26 (1993): 559–85.

———. "Proto-Industrialization, Serf Agriculture, and Agrarian Social Structure: Two Estates in Nineteenth-Century Russia." *Past and Present* 115 (1987): 69–106.

Mendelsohn, Ezra, and Marshall S. Shatz, eds. *Imperial Russia, 1700–1917: State, Society, Opposition. Essays in Honor of Marc Raeff*. DeKalb: Northern Illinois University Press, 1988.

Menning, Bruce W. *Bayonets before Bullets: The Imperial Russian Army, 1861–1914*. Bloomington: Indiana University Press, 1992.

Mentalitet i agrarnoe razvitie Rossii (XIX–XX vv.). Moscow, 1996.

Mentalitet i kul'tura predprinimatelei Rossii XVII–XIX vv.: Sbornik statei. Moscow, 1996.

Merton, Robert K. *Social Theory and Social Structure*. New York: Free Press, 1968.

Michels, Georg. "The Solovki Uprising: Religion and Revolt in Northern Russia." *Russian Review* 51 (1992): 1–15.

———. "Women and Religious Dissent in Late Muscovy." Unpublished paper presented at the UCLA "Winter" Workshop: Topics in Medieval Russian Culture, March 1, 1996.

Minenko, N. A. *Kul'tura russkikh krest'ian zaural'ia XVIII–pervaia polovina XIX v.* Moscow, 1991.

———. *Russkaia krest'ianskaia sem'ia v zapadnoi Sibiri (XVIII–pervoi poloviny XIX v.).* Novosibirsk, 1979.

Ministerstvo finansov. *Ministerstvo finansov, 1802–1902.* St. Petersburg, 1902.

Ministerstvo narodnogo prosveshcheniia. *Sbornik materialov dlia istorii prosveshcheniia v Rossii.* 3 vols. St. Petersburg, 1893–1898.

———. *Sbornik postanovlenii po ministerstvu narodnogo prosveshcheniia.* 2 vols. St. Petersburg, 1875–1876.

———. *Sbornik rasporiazhenii po ministerstvu narodnogo prosveshcheniia.* 2 vols. St. Petersburg, 1866.

Mironov, B[oris]. N. "Bureaucratic or Self-Government: The Early Nineteenth Century Russian City." *Slavic Review* 52 (1993): 233–55.

———. "Local Self-Government in Russia in the First Half of the Nineteenth Century: Provincial Government and Estate Self-Government." *Jahrbücher für Geschichte Osteuropas* 42 (1994): 161–201.

———. "The Russian Peasant Commune after the Reforms of the 1860s." *Slavic Review* 44 (1985): 438–67.

———. "Russkii gorod vo vtoroi polovine XVIII–pervoi polovine XIX veka: Tipologicheskii analiz." *Istoriia SSSR* 5 (1988): 150–68.

———. *Russkii gorod v 1740–1860-e gody.* Leningrad, 1990.

———. "Vliianie revoliutsii tsen v Rossii XVIII veka na ee ekonomicheskoe i sotsial'no-politicheskoe razvitie." *Istoriia SSSR* 1 (1991): 86–101.

Monkkonen, Eric H. "The Dangers of Synthesis." *American Historical Review* 91 (1986): 1146–57.

Moon, David. "Reassessing Russian Serfdom." *European History Quarterly* 26 (1996): 483–526.

———. *Russian Peasants and Tsarist Legislation on the Eve of Reform: Interaction between Peasants and Officialdom, 1825–1855.* London: Macmillan, 1992.

Morrison, Daniel. "'Trading Peasants' and Urbanization in Eighteenth Century Russia: The Central Industrial Region." Ph.D. diss., Columbia University, 1981.

Muir, Edward, and Guido Ruggiero, eds. *Microhistory and the Lost Peoples of Europe.* Translated by Eren Branch. Baltimore: Johns Hopkins University Press, 1991.

Müller, Otto. *Intelligencija: Untersuchungen zur Geschichte eines politischen Schlagwortes.* Frankfurt: Athenaeum, 1971.

Murvar, Vatro. "Max Weber's Typology and Russia." *Sociological Quarterly* 8 (1967): 481–94.

Nahirny, Vladimir C. "The Russian Intelligentsia: From Men of Ideas to Men of Convictions." *Comparative Studies in Society and History* 4 (1962): 403–35.

———. *The Russian Intelligentsia: From Torment to Silence.* New Brunswick, N.J.: Transaction, 1983.

Nakhimovsky, Alexander D., and Alice Stone Nakhimovsky, eds. *The Semiotics of Russian Cultural History: Essays by Iurii M. Lotman, Lidiia Ia. Ginsburg, and Boris A. Uspenskii.* Ithaca, N.Y.: Cornell University Press, 1985.

Nardova, V. A. *Gorodskoe samoupravlenie v Rossii v 60-kh–nachale 90-kh godov: XIX v.: Pravitel'stvennaia politika.* Leningrad, 1984.

———. *Samoderzhavie i gorodskie dumy v Rossii v kontse XIX–nachale XX veka.* St. Petersburg, 1994.

Nechkina, M. V. *Dekabristy.* 2d ed. Moscow, 1982.

Nekrylova, A. F. *Russkie narodnye gorodskie prazdniki, uveseleniia i zrelishcha.* Leningrad, 1988.

Netting, Anthony. "Images and Ideas in Russian Peasant Art." *Slavic Review* 35 (1976): 48–68.

———. "Russian Liberalism: The Years of Promise, 1842–1855." Ph.D. diss., Columbia University, 1967.

Neuberger, Joan. *Hooliganism: Crime, Culture, and Power in St. Petersburg, 1900–1914.* Berkeley: University of California Press, 1993.

———. "Stories of the Street: Hooliganism and the St. Petersburg Popular Press." *Slavic Review* 48 (1989): 177–94.

Noblesse, état et société en Russie XVIe–début du XIXe siècle. Cahiers du Monde russe et soviétique, 34, nos. 1–2 (1993).

O'Brien, Conor Cruise. "A Vindication of Edmund Burke." *National Review,* December 17, 1990, 28–35.

O'Brien, Tim. *In the Lake of the Woods.* New York: Penguin, 1995.

Obshchestvo i gosudarstvo feodal'noi Rossii: Sbornik statei posviashchennyi 70-letiiu L. V. Cherepnina. Moscow, 1975.

Obzor deiatel'nosti ministerstva narodnogo prosveshcheniia i podvedomstvennykh emu uchrezhdenii v 1862, -63 i -64 godakh. St. Petersburg, 1865.

Ogilvie, Sheilagh C., and Markus Cerman, eds. *European Proto-Industrialization.* New York: Cambridge University Press, 1996.

Olábarri, Ignacio. "'New' New History: A *Longue Durée* Structure." *History and Theory* 34 (1995): 1–29.

"Opis' del Permskoi uchenoi arkhivnoi kommissii vyslannykh iz Senatskogo arkhiva." *Trudy Permskoi uchenoi arkhivnoi kommissii,* vypusk 3, otdel 2 (Perm, 1897): 54–61.

Opisanie del arkhiva ministerstva narodnogo prosveshcheniia. Vol. 1. Petrograd, 1917.

The Origins of the State in Italy, 1300–1600. Supplement to *Journal of Modern History* 67 (1995).

Orlovsky, Daniel T. *The Limits of Reform: The Ministry of Internal Affairs in Imperial Russia, 1802–1881.* Cambridge, Mass.: Harvard University Press, 1981.

———. "Recent Studies on the Russian Bureaucracy." *Russian Review* 35 (1976): 448–67.

Ostrovskii, A. N. *Polnoe sobranie sochinenii.* 16 vols. Moscow, 1949–1953.

Osval't, Iu. "Dukhovenstvo i reforma prikhodskoi zhizni, 1861–1865." *Voprosy istorii* 11 (1993): 140–49.

Otchet ministerstva iustitsii za 1845. St. Petersburg, 1846.

Owen, Thomas C. *Capitalism and Politics in Russia: A Social History of the Moscow Merchants, 1855–1905.* New York: Cambridge University Press, 1981.

———. *The Corporation under Russian Law, 1800–1917: A Study in Tsarist Economic Policy.* Cambridge: Cambridge University Press, 1991.

Pakrash, Gyan. "Subaltern Studies as Postcolonial Criticism." *American Historical Review* 99 (1994): 1475–90.

Pallot, Judith. "*Khutora* and *Otruba* in Stolypin's Program of Farm Individualization." *Slavic Review* 42 (1984): 242–56.

Pallot, Judith, and Denis J. B. Shaw. *Landscape and Settlement in Romanov Russia 1613–1917.* New York: Oxford University Press, 1990.

Paperno, Irina. *Chernyshevsky and the Age of Realism: A Study in the Semiotics of Behavior.* Stanford: Stanford University Press, 1988.

Pearson, Thomas S. *Russian Officialdom in Crisis: Autocracy and Local Self- Government, 1861–1900.* New York: Cambridge University Press, 1989.

Perkin, Harold. *The Origins of Modern English Society, 1780–1880.* London: Routledge and Kegan Paul, 1969.

Perkins, Etta Louise. "Careers in Art: An Exploration in the Social History of Post-Petrine Russia." Ph.D. diss., Indiana University, 1980.

———. "Mobility in the Art Profession in Tsarist Russia." *Jahrbücher für Geschichte Osteuropas* 39 (1991): 225–33.

———. "Nicholas I and the Academy of Fine Arts." *Russian History* 18 (1991): 51–63.

Perrie, Maureen. "Folklore as Evidence of Peasant *Mentalité:* Social Attitudes and Values in Russian Popular Culture." *Russian Review* 48 (1989): 119–43.

Peterburg i guberniia: Istoriko-etnograficheskie issledovaniia. Leningrad, 1989.

Pintner, Walter M. *Russian Economic Policy under Nicholas I.* Ithaca, N.Y.: Cornell University Press, 1967.

———. "The Russian Higher Civil Service on the Eve of the 'Great Reforms.'" *Journal of Social History* 8 (1975): 55–68.

———. "The Social Characteristics of the Early Nineteenth-Century Russian Bureaucracy." *Slavic Review* 29 (1970): 429–43.

Pintner, Walter McKenzie, and Don Karl Rowney, eds. *Russian Officialdom: The Bureaucratization of Russian Society from the Seventeenth to the Twentieth Century.* Chapel Hill: University of North Carolina Press, 1980.

Pipes, Richard. *The Russian Revolution.* New York: Vintage, 1990.

———. *Russia under the Old Regime.* New York: Scribner's, 1974.

———, ed. *The Russian Intelligentsia.* New York: Columbia University Press, 1961.

Pirumova, N. M. *Zemskaia intelligentsiia i ee rol' v obshchestvennoi bor'be.* Moscow, 1986.

———. *Zemskoe liberal'noe dvizhenie: Sotsial'nye korni i evoliutsiia do nachala XX veka.* Moscow, 1977.

Plekhanov, G. V. "Ideologiia meshchanina nashego vremeni." In *Sochineniia.* 24 vols. Vol. 14. Moscow, 1923.

Ploshinskii, L. O. *Gorodskoe ili srednee sostoianie russkogo naroda.* St. Petersburg, 1852.

Pobedonostsev, Konstantin P. *Reflections of a Russian Statesman.* Ann Arbor: University of Michigan Press, 1965.

Pocock, J. G. A. *Politics, Language, and Time: Essays on Political Thought and History.* Chicago: University of Chicago Press, 1989.

Pollard, Alan. "The Russian Intelligentsia: The Mind of Russia." *California Slavic Studies* 3 (1964): 1–32.

Pomeranz, William E. "Justice from Underground: The History of the Underground *Advokatura.*" *Russian Review* 52 (1993): 321–40.

Pomialovskii, N. G. *Sochineniia v dvukh tomakh.* 2 vols. Moscow-Leningrad, 1965.

Portal, Roger. "Aux origines d'une bourgeoisie industrielle en Russie." *Revue d'Histoire Moderne et Contemporaine* 7 (1961): 35–61.

———. "Du servage à la bourgeoisie: La Famille Konovalov." *Revue des études slaves* 38 (1961): 143–50.

————. "Manufactures et classes sociales en Russie au XVIIIe siècle." *Revue Historique* 201 (1949): 161–85; 202 (1949): 1–23.

Porter, Roy. *English Society in the Eighteenth Century.* London: Lane, 1982.

Porter, Thomas, and William Gleason. "The *Zemstvo* and Public Initiative in Late Imperial Russia." *Russian History* 21 (1994): 419–37.

Pososhkov, Ivan. *The Book of Poverty and Wealth.* Edited and translated by A. P. Vlasto and L. R. Lewitter. London: Athlone, 1987.

Prokof'eva, L. S. *Krest'ianskaia obshchina v Rossii vo vtoroi polovine XVIII– pervoi polovine XIX veka.* Leningrad, 1981.

Promyshlennost' i torgovlia v Rossii, XVII–XVIII vv. Moscow, 1983.

Pullat, R. N., ed. *Problemy istoricheskoi demografii SSSR.* Tallinn, 1977.

Pushkarev, L. N. *Dukhovnyi mir russkogo krest'ianina po poslovitsam XVII–XVIII vekov.* Moscow, 1994.

Pushkin, Michael. "The Professions and the Intelligentsia in Nineteenth-Century Russia." *University of Birmingham Historical Journal* 12 (1969–1970): 72–99.

————. "*Raznochintsy* in the University—Government Policy and Social Change in Nineteenth-Century Russia." *International Review of Social History* 26 (1981): 25–65.

Rabinovich, M. G. *Ocherki etnografii russkogo feodal'nogo goroda: Gorozhane, ikh obshchestvennyi i domashnii byt.* Moscow, 1978.

————. "Sotsial'noe proiskhozhdenie i imushchestvennoe polozhenie ofitserov reguliarnoi armii v kontse Severnoi voiny." In *Rossiia v period reform Petra I.* Edited by N. I. Pavlenko. Moscow, 1973.

Rabinowitch, Alexander. *The Bolsheviks Come to Power: The Revolution of 1917 in Petrograd.* New York: Norton, 1976.

————. *Prelude to Revolution: The Petrograd Bolsheviks and the July 1917 Uprising.* Bloomington: Indiana University Press, 1968.

Raeff, Marc. "The Bureaucratic Phenomena of Imperial Russia, 1700–1905." *American Historical Review* 84 (1979): 399–411.

————. *Michael Speransky: Statesman of Imperial Russia, 1772–1839.* The Hague: Nijhoff, 1957.

————. "La Noblesse et le discours politique sous le règne de Pierre le Grand." *Cahiers du Monde russe et soviétique* 34 (1993): 33–45.

————. *Origins of the Russian Intelligentsia: The Eighteenth-Century Nobility.* New York: Harcourt, Brace and World, 1966.

————. "The People, the Intelligentsia and Russian Political Culture." *Political Studies* 41 (1993): 93–106.

————. *Political Ideas and Institutions in Imperial Russia.* Boulder, Colo.: Westview Press, 1994.

————. *Politique et culture en Russie, 18e–20e siècles.* Paris: Écoles des Hautes Études en Sciences Sociales, 1996.

————. *Siberia and the Reforms of 1822.* Seattle: University of Washington Press, 1956.

————. "Transfiguration and Modernization: The Paradoxes of Social Disciplining, Paedagogical Leadership, and the Enlightenment in Eighteenth-Century Russia." In *Alteuropa—Ancien Régime—Frühe Neuzeit: Probleme und Methoden der Forschung.* Edited by Hans Erich Bödeker and Ernst Hinrichs. Stuttgart–Bad Cannstatt: Frommann-Holzboog, 1991.

————. *Understanding Imperial Russia: State and Society in the Old Regime.* Translated by Arthur Goldhammer. New York: Columbia University Press, 1984.

―――. *The Well-Ordered Police State: Social and Institutional Change through Law in the Germanies and Russia, 1600–1800.* New Haven: Yale University Press, 1983.

―――, ed. *Plans for Political Reform, 1730–1905.* Englewood Cliffs, N.J.: Prentice Hall, 1966.

Rakhmatullin, M. A. *Krest'ianskoe dvizhenie v velikorusskikh guberniiakh v 1825–1857 godakh.* Moscow, 1990.

Ransel, David L. "Character and Style of Patron-Client Relations in Russia." In *Klientelsysteme im Europa der Frühen Neuzeit.* Edited by Antoni Mączak. Munich: Oldenbourg, 1988.

―――. "An Eighteenth-Century Russian Merchant Family in Prosperity and Decline." Unpublished manuscript, 1996.

―――. *Mothers of Misery: Child Abandonment in Russia.* Princeton: Princeton University Press, 1988.

―――. *The Politics of Catherinian Russia: The Panin Party.* New Haven: Yale University Press, 1975.

―――, ed. *The Family in Imperial Russia: New Lines of Historical Research.* Urbana: University of Illinois Press, 1978.

Rashin, A. G. *Formirovanie rabochego klassa Rossii.* Moscow, 1958.

―――. *Naselenie Rossii za sto let (1811–1913): Statisticheskie ocherki.* Moscow, 1956.

Raskin, D. I. "Ispol'zovanie zakonodatel'nykh aktov v krest'ianskikh chelobitnykh serediny XVIII veka (materialy k izucheniiu obshchestvennogo soznaniia russkogo krest'ianstva)." *Istoriia SSSR* 4 (1979): 179–92.

Rawson, Don C. *Russian Rightists and the Revolution of 1905.* Cambridge: Cambridge University Press, 1995.

Redfield, Robert. *The Little Community and Peasant Society and Culture.* Chicago: University of Chicago Press, 1960.

Reed, John. *Ten Days That Shook the World.* New York: Vintage, 1960.

Reformy v Rossii XVI–XIX vv.: Sbornik nauchnykh trudov. Moscow, 1992.

Repin, I. *Dalekoe blizkoe.* Moscow, 1986.

Riasanovsky, Nicholas. *Nicholas I and Official Nationality in Russia, 1825–1855.* Berkeley: University of California Press, 1959.

―――. *A Parting of Ways: Government and the Educated Public in Russia, 1801–1855.* Oxford: Oxford University Press, 1976.

Rieber, Alfred J. *Merchants and Entrepreneurs in Imperial Russia.* Chapel Hill: University of North Carolina Press, 1982.

―――. "The Rise of Engineers in Russia." *Cahiers du Monde russe et soviétique* 31 (1990): 539–68.

Rimlinger, Gaston V. "Autocracy and the Factory Order in Early Russian Industrialization." *Journal of Economic History* 20 (1960): 67–92.

―――. "The Management of Labor Protest in Tsarist Russia: 1870–1905." *International Review of Social History* 5, pt. 2 (1960): 226–48.

Robbins, Richard G., Jr. *Famine in Russia, 1891–1892: The Imperial Government Responds to a Crisis.* New York: Columbia University Press, 1975.

―――. *The Tsar's Viceroys: Russian Provincial Governors in the Last Years of the Empire.* Ithaca, N.Y.: Cornell University Press, 1987.

Robinson, Geroid Tanquary. *Rural Russia under the Old Regime.* Berkeley: University of California Press, 1972.

Robson, Roy R. "Liturgy and Community among Old Believers, 1905–1917." *Slavic Review* 52 (1993): 713–24.

———. *Old Believers in Modern Russia*. DeKalb: Northern Illinois University Press, 1995.

Rogger, Hans. *Jewish Policies and Right-Wing Politics in Imperial Russia*. Berkeley: University of California Press, 1986.

———. *National Consciousness in Eighteenth-Century Russia*. Cambridge, Mass.: Harvard University Press, 1960.

———. "Nationalism and the State: A Russian Dilemma." *Comparative Studies in Society and History* 4 (1961–1962): 253–64.

———. *Russia in the Age of Modernisation and Revolution, 1881–1917*. New York: Longman, 1983.

———. "The Skobelev Phenomenon: The Hero and His Worship." *Oxford Slavonic Papers*. N.s. 9 (1976): 46–78.

Rogoff, Barbara. "Children's Guided Participation and Participatory Appropriation in Sociocultural Activity." In *Development in Context: Acting and Thinking in Specific Environments*. Edited by Robert H. Wozniak and Kurt W. Fischer. Hillsdale, N.J.: Erlbaum, 1993.

Roosa, Ruth Amende. "Russian Industrialists and 'State Socialism,' 1906–1917." *Soviet Studies* 23 (1972): 395–417.

———. "Workers Insurance Legislation and the Role of the Industrialists in the Period of the Third Duma." *Russian Review* 34 (1975): 410–52.

Roosevelt, Priscilla. *Life on the Russian Country Estate: A Social and Cultural History*. New Haven: Yale University Press, 1995.

Rosenberg, Hans. *Bureaucracy, Aristocracy, and Autocracy: The Prussian Experience 1660–1815*. Cambridge, Mass.: Harvard University Press, 1958.

Rosenberg, William G. "Representing Workers and the Liberal Narrative of Modernity." *Slavic Review* 55 (1996): 245–69.

Rosovsky, Henry. "The Serf Entrepreneur in Russia." *Explorations in Entrepreneurial History* 4 (1954): 207–33.

Rossiia: Entsiklopedicheskii slovar'. Reprint, Leningrad, 1991.

Rossiiskii proletariat: Oblik, bor'ba, gegemoniia. Edited by L. M. Ivanov. Moscow, 1970.

Rossiiskoe kupechestvo ot srednikh vekov k novomu vremeni. Nauchnaia konferentsiia. Moskva, 2–4 noiabria 1993 g. Tezisy dokladov. Moscow, 1993.

Rotenberg, R. S. "Bor'ba rabochego klassa Rossii za gosudarstvennoe sotsial'noe strakhovanie (1900–1914 gg.)." *Voprosy istorii* 11 (1958): 126–41.

Rozhdestvenskii, S. V. *Istoricheskii obzor deiatel'nosti ministerstva narodnogo prosveshcheniia, 1802–1902*. St. Petersburg, 1902.

Rozhkova, M. K., ed. *Ocherki ekonomicheskoi istorii Rossii pervoi poloviny XIX veka*. Moscow, 1959.

Rozman, Gilbert. *Urban Networks in Russia, 1750–1800, and Premodern Periodization*. Princeton: Princeton University Press, 1976.

Ruane, Christine. "Divergent Discourses: The Image of the Russian Woman Schoolteacher in Post-Reform Russia." *Russian History* 20 (1993): 109–23.

———. *Gender, Class, and the Professionalization of Russian City Teachers, 1860–1914*. Pittsburgh: University of Pittsburgh Press, 1994.

Rubinshtein, N. L. *Sel'skoe khoziaistvo Rossii vo vtoroi polovine XVIII v*. Moscow, 1957.

Ruckman, Jo Ann. *The Moscow Business Elite: A Social and Cultural Portrait of Two Generations, 1840–1905.* DeKalb: Northern Illinois University Press, 1984.

Ruffmann, Karl-Heinz. "Russischer Adel als Sondertypus der europäischen Adelswelt." *Jahrbücher für Geschichte Osteuropas* 9 (1961): 161–78.

Rule, John. *Albion's People: English Society, 1714–1815.* New York: Longman, 1992.

Russkii gorod (issledovaniia i materialy). Vypusk 1–9. Moscow, 1976–1990.

Rustemeyer, Angela. *Dienstboten in Petersburg und Moskau, 1861–1917.* Stuttgart: Steiner, 1996.

Ryndziunskii, P. G. *Gorodskoe grazhdanstvo doreformennoi Rossii.* Moscow, 1958.

———. *Utverzhdenie kapitalizma v Rossii, 1850–1880 gg.* Moscow, 1978.

Safonov, Mikhail M. "Imperatorskaia vlast', gosudarstvennyi apparat i dvorianstvo v kontse XVIII v." *Cahiers du Monde russe et soviétique* 34 (1993): 149–58.

Sanders, John Thomas. "'Once More into the Breach, Dear Friends'": A Closer Look at Indirect Tax Receipts and the Condition of the Russian Peasantry, 1881–1899." *Slavic Review* 43 (1984): 657–66.

Sanders, Jonathan E. "The Union of Unions: Political, Economic, Civil, and Human Rights Organizations in the 1905 Russian Revolution." Ph.D. diss., Columbia University, 1985.

Saunders, David. *Russia in the Age of Reaction and Reform, 1801–1881.* New York: Longman, 1992.

Sazonova, E. I. "Rostovskie kuptsy Serebrennikovy." In *Soobshcheniia Rostovskogo muzeia.* Vypusk 6. Rostov, 1994.

Sbornik imperatorskogo Rossiiskogo istoricheskogo obshchestva. 148 vols. St. Petersburg, 1867–1916.

Schliefman, Nurit. "A Russian Daily Newspaper and Its New Readership: *Severnaia Pchela,* 1825–1840." *Cahiers du Monde russe et soviétique* 28 (1987): 127–44.

Schmidt, Christoph. *Sozialkontrolle in Moskau: Justiz, Kriminalität und Leibeigenschaft, 1649–1785.* Stuttgart: Steiner, 1996.

———. *Ständerecht und Standeswechsel in Russland, 1851–1897.* Wiesbaden: Harrassowitz, 1994.

———. "Über die Bezeichnung der Stände (*sostojanie-soslovie*) in Russland seit dem 18. Jahrhundert." *Jahrbücher für Geschichte Osteuropas* 38 (1990): 199–211.

Schneer, Matthew. "The Markovo Republic: A Peasant Community during Russia's First Revolution, 1905–1906." *Slavic Review* 53 (1994): 104–19.

Scott, James C. *The Moral Economy of the Peasant: Rebellion and Subsistence in Southeast Asia.* New Haven: Yale University Press, 1976.

Scott, Joan W. "Gender: A Useful Category of Historical Analysis." *American Historical Review* 91 (1986): 1053–75.

Screen, J. E. O. *The Helsinki Yunker School, 1846–1879: A Case Study of Officer Training in the Russian Army.* Studia Historica 22. Helsinki: Painokaari, 1986.

Semenova, L. N. *Ocherki istorii byta i kul'turnoi zhizni Rossii: Pervaia polovina XVIII v.* Leningrad, 1982.

———. *Rabochie Peterburga v pervoi polovine XVIII veka.* Leningrad, 1974.

Semevskii, V. I. *Krest'iane v tsarstvovanie imperatritsy Ekateriny II.* St. Petersburg, 1903.

———. *Krest'ianskii vopros v Rossii v XVIII i pervoi polovine XIX veka.* St. Petersburg, 1888.

Senchakova, L. T. *Prigovory i nakazy Rossiiskogo krest'ianstva 1905–1907 gg.* 2 vols. Moscow, 1994.

Serbina, K. N. "K voprosu o bobyliakh (bobyli Tikhvinskogo posada)." In *Akademiku B. D. Grekovu ko dniu semidesiatiletiia: Sbornik statei*. Moscow, 1952.

Seregny, Scott J. *Russian Teachers and Peasant Revolution: The Politics of Education in 1905*. Bloomington: Indiana University Press, 1989.

———. "Teachers and Rural Cooperatives: The Politics of Education and Professional Identities in Russia, 1908–17." *Russian Review* 55 (1996): 567–90.

Sergeev, A. "Graf A. Kh. Benkendorf o Rossii v 1827–1830 gg." *Krasnyi arkhiv* 6.37 (1929): 138–74; 1.38 (1930): 109–47.

Seton-Watson, Hugh. *The Russian Empire, 1801–1917*. Oxford: Clarendon Press, 1967.

Sewell, William H. "État, Corps, Ordre: Some Notes on the Social Vocabulary of the French Old Regime." In *Sozialgeschichte Heute: Festschrift für Hans Rosenberg zum 70. Geburtstag*. Vol. 11. Edited by Hans-Ulrich Wehler. Göttingen: Vandenhoeck and Ruprecht, 1974.

Shanin, Teodor. *The Awkward Class: Political Sociology of Peasantry in a Developing Society: Russia, 1910–1925*. Oxford: Clarendon Press, 1972.

———. *The Roots of Otherness: Russia's Turn of the Century*. Vol. 1, *Russia as a 'Developing Society.'* Vol. 2, *Russia, 1905–07: Revolution as a Moment of Truth*. New Haven: Yale University Press, 1986.

Shepelev, L. E. *Otmenennye istoriei chiny, zvaniia i tituly v Rossiiskoi imperii*. Leningrad, 1977.

Shevzov, Vera. "Chapels and the Ecclesial World of Prerevolutionary Russian Peasants." *Slavic Review* 35 (1996): 585–613.

Shtakenshneider, E. A. *Dnevniki i zapiski (1854–1886)*. Moscow, 1934. Reprint, Newtonville, Mass.: Oriental Research Partners, 1980.

Shtrange, M. M. *Demokraticheskaia intelligentsiia Rossii v XVIII veke*. Moscow, 1965.

Shuster, U. A. *Peterburgskie rabochie v 1905–1907 gg*. Leningrad, 1976.

Sidorova, I. B. "Kto takie raznochintsy? (polemika v literature)." In *Voprosy otechestvennoi, zarubezhnoi istorii, literaturovedeniia i iazykoznaniia*. Ch. 1. Kazan, 1981.

———. "Otrazhenie nuzhd raznochintsev v gorodskikh nakazakh 1767 goda." In *Voprosy otechestvennoi, zarubezhnoi istorii, literaturovedeniia i iazykoznaniia*. Ch. 1. Kazan, 1981.

———. "Polozhenie raznochintsev v russkom obshchestve (XVIII–pervaia polovina XIX v.)." Kand. diss., Kazan, 1982.

Siegelbaum, Lewis, and Ronald Grigor Suny, eds. *Making Workers Soviet: Power, Class, and Identity*. Ithaca, N.Y.: Cornell University Press, 1994.

Simms, James Y., Jr. "The Crisis in Russian Agriculture at the End of the Nineteenth Century: A Different View." *Slavic Review* 36 (1977): 377–98.

———. "More Grist for the Mill: A Further Look at the Crisis in Russian Agriculture at the End of the Nineteenth Century." *Slavic Review* 50 (1991): 999–1009.

———. "On Missing the Point: A Rejoinder." *Slavic Review* 37 (1978): 487–90.

———. "Reply." *Slavic Review* 43 (1984): 667–71.

Sistema gosudarstvennogo feodalizma v Rossii: Sbornik statei. 2 vols. Moscow, 1993.

Sladkevich, I. G. "O soslovnykh proektakh Komiteta 6 dekabria 1826." In *Issledovaniia po otechestvennomu istochnikovedeniiu*. Moscow and Leningrad, 1964.

Slezkine, Yuri. "Naturalists versus Nations: Eighteenth-Century Russian Scholars Confront Ethnic Diversity." *Representations* 47 (1994): 170–95.

Smetanin, S. I. "Razlozhenie soslovii i formirovanie klassovoi struktury gorodskogo naseleniia Rossii v 1800–1861 gg." *Istoricheskie zapiski* 102 (1978): 153–82.

Smith, Douglas Campbell. "Freemasonry and the Public in Eighteenth-Century Russia." *Eighteenth-Century Studies* 29 (1995): 25–44.

———. "Working the Rough Stone: Freemasonry and Society in Eighteenth-Century Russia." Ph.D. diss., University of California, Los Angeles, 1996.

Smith, R. E. F., and David Christian. *Bread and Salt: A Social and Economic History of Food and Drink in Russia.* New York: Cambridge University Press, 1984.

Smolitsch, Igor. *Geschichte der russischen Kirche, 1700–1917.* 2 vols. Leiden: Brill, 1964; Wiesbaden: Harrassowitz, 1990.

Snezhnevskii, V. I. "K istorii pobegov krepostnykh v poslednei chetverti XVIII i v XIX stoletiiakh." *Nizhegorodskii sbornik* 10 (Nizhnii Novgorod, 1890): 517–95.

———. "Opis' zhurnalam nizhegorodskogo namestnicheskogo pravleniia (za 1781–1783 gg.)." *Deistviia nizhegorodskoi gubernskoi uchenoi arkhivnoi kommissii: Sbornik statei, soobshchenii, opisei, del i dokumentov,* t. 3 (Nizhnii Novgorod, 1898).

Solomon, Susan Gross, and John F. Hutchinson, eds. *Health and Society in Revolutionary Russia.* Bloomington: Indiana University Press, 1990.

Sosloviia i gosudarstvennaia vlast' v Rossii: XV–seredina XIX vv. Mezhdunarodnaia konferentsiia—Chteniia pamiati akad. L. V. Cherepnina. 2 vols. Moscow, 1994.

Starr, S. Frederick. *Decentralization and Self-Government in Russia, 1830–1870.* Princeton: Princeton University Press, 1972.

Stavrou, Theofanis George, ed. *Art and Culture in Nineteenth-Century Russia.* Bloomington: Indiana University Press, 1983.

Steffens, Thomas. *Die Arbeiter von Petersburg 1907 bis 1917: Soziale Lage, Organisation und spontaner Protest zwischen zwei Revolutionen.* Freiburg: Hochschulverlag, 1985.

Stein, Hans-Peter. "Der Offizier des russischen Heeres im Zeitabschnitt zwischen Reform und Revolution (1861–1905)." *Forschungen zur osteuropäischen Geschichte* 13 (1967): 346–507.

Steinberg, Mark D. *Moral Communities: The Culture of Class Relations in the Russian Printing Industry, 1867–1907.* Berkeley: University of California Press, 1992.

Stites, Richard. *The Women's Liberation Movement in Russia: Feminism, Nihilism, and Bolshevism, 1860–1930.* Princeton: Princeton University Press, 1990.

Suchkov, I. V. "Sotsial'nyi i dukhovnyi oblik uchitel'stva Rossii na rubezhe XIX–XX vekov." *Otechestvennaia istoriia* 1 (1995): 62–77.

Sunderland, Willard. "Peasants on the Move: State Peasant Resettlement in Imperial Russia, 1805–1830s." *Russian Review* 52 (1993): 472–85.

Suny, Ronald Grigor. "Revision and Retreat in the Historiography of 1917: Social History and Its Critics." *Russian Review* 53 (1994): 165–82.

Surh, Gerald D. "A Matter of Life or Death: Politics, Profession, and Public Health in St. Petersburg before 1914." *Russian History* 20 (1993): 125–46.

———. *1905 in St. Petersburg: Labor, Society, and Revolution.* Stanford: Stanford University Press, 1989.

T———v, Sergei. "Ranenburgskie meshchane." *Riazanskaia zhizn',* no. 146, 24.VI.1912.

Thelander, Dorothy R. "Mother Goose and Her Goslings: The France of Louis XIV as Seen through the Fairy Tale." *Journal of Modern History* 54 (1982): 467–96.

Thompson, E. P. *Customs in Common: Studies in Traditional Popular Culture.* New York: New Press, 1993.

―――. *The Making of the English Working Class.* New York: Vintage, 1963.

Thurston, Robert W. *Liberal City, Conservative State: Moscow and Russia's Urban Crisis, 1906–1914.* New York: Oxford University Press, 1987.

Thyrêt, Isolde. "Life in the Kremlin under the Tsars Mikhail Fedorovich and Aleksei Mikhailovich: New Perspectives on the Institution of the *Terem.*" Unpublished paper presented at the conference Private Life in Russia: Medieval Times to the Present, University of Michigan–Ann Arbor, October 4–6, 1996.

Tian-Shanskaia, Olga Semyonova. *Village Life in Late Tsarist Russia.* Edited by David L. Ransel. Translated by David L. Ransel with Michael Levine. Bloomington: Indiana University Press, 1993.

Tidmarsh, Kyril. "The Zubatov Idea." *American Slavic and East European Review* 19 (1960): 335–46.

Tilly, Charles. "A Bridge Halfway: Responding to Brubaker." *Contention: Debates in Society, Culture, and Science* 4 (1994): 15–19.

―――. "Did the Cake of Custom Break?" In *Consciousness and Class Experience in Nineteenth-Century Europe.* Edited by John M. Merriman. New York: Holmes and Meier, 1979.

Tishkin, G. A., ed. *Feminizm i Rossiiskaia kul'tura: Sbornik trudov.* St. Petersburg, 1995.

Tiustin, A. V. "Kupecheskie dinastii Penzy." *Zemstvo: Arkhiv provintsial'noi istorii Rossii* 3 (1995): 164–93.

Torgovlia i predprinimatel'stvo v feodal'noi Rossii. Moscow, 1994.

Torke, Hans Joachim. "Continuity and Change in the Relations between Bureaucracy and Society in Russia, 1613–1861." *Canadian Slavic Studies* 5 (1971): 457–76.

―――. "Das russische Beamtentum in der ersten Hälfte des 19. Jahrhunderts." *Forschungen zur osteuropäischen Geschichte* 13 (1967): 7–345.

Tovrov, Jessica. *The Russian Noble Family: Structure and Change.* Reprinted dissertation. New York: Garland, 1987.

Trapeznikov, V. N. "O liudiakh, iskavshikh vol'nosti iz vladeniia gospod svoikh." *Trudy Permskoi uchenoi arkhivnoi kommissii,* vypusk 4 (Perm, 1901): 142–52.

Troitskii, S. M. *Russkii absoliutizm i dvorianstvo v XVIII v.: Formirovanie biurokratii.* Moscow, 1974.

Tugan-Baranovskii, Mikhail I. *The Russian Factory in the Nineteenth Century.* Translated by Arthur Levin and Claora S. Levin. Homewood, Ill.: Irwin, 1970.

Turner, Victor. *Dramas, Fields, and Metaphors: Symbolic Action in Human Society.* Ithaca, N.Y.: Cornell University Press, 1974.

V. N. Karpov, Vospominaniia—N. N. Shipov, Istoriia moei zhizni. Moscow and Leningrad, 1933.

Valkenier, Elizabeth. *Russian Realist Art. The State and Society: The Peredvizhniki and Their Tradition.* New York: Columbia University Press, 1989.

Van Dyke, Carl. *Russian Imperial Military Doctrine and Education, 1832–1914.* Westport, Conn.: Greenwood Press, 1990.

"Vedomost' o narodonaselenii Rossii za 1851 god po 9 narodnoi perepisi." *Zhurnal ministerstva vnutrennikh del* (November 1853), otdelenie 3, 61–76.

Velychenko, Stephen. "Identities, Loyalties and Service in Imperial Russia: Who Administered the Borderlands?" *Russian Review* 54 (1995): 188–208.

Verner, Andrew. "Discursive Strategies in the 1905 Revolution: Peasant Petitions from Vladimir Province." *Russian Review* 54 (1995): 65–90.

Vladimirskii-Budanov, M. *Gosudarstvo i narodnoe obrazovanie v Rossii XVIII v.* Vol.

1. Iaroslavl, 1874. Reprint, Cambridge: Oriental Research Partners, 1972.

Vodarskii, Ia. E. *Naselenie Rossii v kontse XVII–nachale XVIII veka: Chislennost',
soslovno-klassovyi sostav, razmeshchenie.* Moscow, 1977.

———. *Promyshlennye seleniia tsentral'noi Rossii v period genezisa i razvitiia kapitalizma.* Moscow, 1972.

Volkov, M. Ia. *Goroda verkhnego povolzh'ia i severo-zapada Rossii. Pervaia chetvert'
XVIII v.* Moscow, 1994.

Volkov, S. V. *Russkii ofitserskii korpus.* Moscow, 1993.

Von Laue, Theodore H. "Factory Inspection under the 'Witte System': 1892–1903."
American Slavic and East European Review 19 (1960): 347–62.

———. *Sergei Witte and the Industrialization of Russia.* New York: Atheneum, 1969.

Voronov, M. A., and S. A. Makashin. *Rasskazy o starom Saratove.* Saratov, 1937.

Vucinich, Wayne S., ed. *The Peasant in Nineteenth-Century Russia.* Stanford: Stanford
University Press, 1968.

Vul'fson, G. N. "Poniatie 'raznochinets' v XVIII–pervoi polovine XIX veka." In
Ocherki istorii narodov Povolzh'ia i Priural'ia. Vypusk 1. Kazan, 1967.

Vygotsky, L. S. *Mind in Society: The Development of Higher Psychological Processes.*
Edited by Michael Cole, Vera John-Steiner, Sylvia Scribner, and Ellen Souber-
man. Cambridge, Mass.: Harvard University Press, 1978.

Wagner, William G. *Marriage, Property and Law in Late Imperial Russia.* New York:
Oxford University Press, 1994.

Walker, Mack. *German Home Towns: Community, State, and General Estate,
1648–1871.* Ithaca, N.Y.: Cornell University Press, 1971.

Walkin, Jacob. *The Rise of Democracy in Pre-Revolutionary Russia: Political and Social Institutions under the Last Three Tsars.* New York: Praeger, 1962.

Wallace, Donald Mackenzie. *Russia on the Eve of War and Revolution.* Edited by Cyril
E. Black. New York: Vintage, 1961.

Wcislo, Francis William. *Reforming Rural Russia: State, Local Society, and National
Politics, 1855–1914.* Princeton: Princeton University Press, 1991.

Weber, Eugen. *Peasants into Frenchmen: The Modernization of Rural France,
1870–1914.* Stanford: Stanford University Press, 1976.

Weber, Max. *From Max Weber: Essays in Sociology.* Edited and translated by H. H.
Gerth and C. Wright Mills. New York: Oxford University Press, 1946.

Weickhardt, George G. "Legal Rights of Women in Russia, 1100–1750." *Slavic Review* 55 (1996): 1–23.

Weinberg, Robert. *The Revolution of 1905 in Odessa: Blood on the Steps.* Bloomington: Indiana University Press, 1993.

Weissman, Neil B. *Reform in Tsarist Russia: The State Bureaucracy and Local Government, 1900–1914.* New Brunswick, N.J.: Rutgers University Press, 1981.

———. "Rural Crime in Tsarist Russia: The Question of Hooliganism, 1905–1914."
Slavic Review 37 (1978): 228–40.

Wertsch, James V. "Commentary." *Human Development* 36 (1993): 168–71.

Whelan, Heide W. *Alexander III and the State Council: Bureaucracy and Counter-
Reform in Late Imperial Russia.* New Brunswick, N.J.: Rutgers University
Press, 1982.

White, Hayden. *Metahistory: The Historical Imagination in Nineteenth-Century Europe.* Baltimore: Johns Hopkins University Press, 1973.

———. *Tropics of Discourse: Essays in Cultural Criticism.* Baltimore: Johns Hopkins
University Press, 1978.

Whittaker, Cynthia H. "The Reforming Tsar: The Redefinition of Autocratic Duty in Eighteenth-Century Russia." *Slavic Review* 51 (1992): 77–98.

Wilbur, Elvira M. "Was Russian Peasant Agriculture Really That Impoverished? New Evidence from a Case Study from the 'Impoverished Center' at the End of the Nineteenth Century." *Journal of Economic History* 43 (1983): 137–44.

Wildman, Allan K. *The End of the Russian Imperial Army*. Vol. 1, *The Old Army and the Soldiers' Revolt (March–April 1917)*. Vol. 2, *The Road to Soviet Power and Peace*. Princeton: Princeton University Press, 1980 and 1987.

Williams, Raymond. *Culture and Society: 1780–1950*. Reprint, New York: Columbia University Press, 1983.

Wirtschafter, Elise Kimerling. *From Serf to Russian Soldier*. Princeton: Princeton University Press, 1990.

———. "Social Misfits: Veterans and Soldiers' Families in Servile Russia." *Journal of Military History* 59 (1995): 215–35.

———. *Structures of Society: Imperial Russia's "People of Various Ranks."* DeKalb: Northern Illinois University Press, 1994.

Wolf, Eric R. *Europe and the People without History*. Berkeley: University of California Press, 1982.

Wolff, Larry. *Inventing Eastern Europe: The Map of Civilization on the Mind of the Enlightenment*. Stanford: Standford University Press, 1994.

Woloch, Isser. *Eighteenth-Century Europe: Tradition and Progress, 1715–1789*. New York: Norton, 1982.

———. *The New Regime: Transformations of the French Civic Order, 1789–1820s*. New York: Norton, 1994.

Worobec, Christine D. "*Klikushestvo:* Devil Possession among Russian Peasant Women, 1861–1926." Unpublished paper. Kent State University, 1994.

———. "New Sources on Popular Religion in Imperial Russia." Unpublished paper. Kent State University, 1995.

———. *Peasant Russia: Family and Community in the Post-Emancipation Period*. Princeton: Princeton University Press, 1991.

———. "Witchcraft Beliefs and Practices in Prerevolutionary Russian and Ukrainian Villages." *Russian Review* 54 (1995): 165–87.

Woronzoff-Dashkoff, A. "Disguise and Gender in Princess Dashkova's *Memoirs. Canadian Slavonic Papers* 32 (1991): 62–74.

Wortman, Richard S. *The Development of a Russian Legal Consciousness*. Chicago: University of Chicago Press, 1976.

———. *Scenarios of Power: Myth and Ceremony in Russian Monarchy*. Vol. 1, *From Peter the Great to the Death of Nicholas I*. Princeton: Princeton University Press, 1995.

Wynn, Charters. *Workers, Strikes, and Pogroms: The Donbass-Dnepr Bend in Late Imperial Russia, 1870–1905*. Princeton: Princeton University Press, 1992.

Yaney, George L. *The Systematization of Russian Government: Social Evolution in the Domestic Administration of Imperial Russia, 1711–1905*. Urbana: University of Illinois Press, 1973.

Zaionchkovskii, P. A. "Ofitserskii korpus russkoi armii pered pervoi mirovoi voinoi." *Voprosy istorii* 4 (1981): 21–29.

———. *Otmena krepostnogo prava v Rossii*. Moscow, 1960.

———. *Pravitel'stvennyi apparat samoderzhavnoi Rossii v XIX v.* Moscow, 1978.

———. *Rossiiskoe samoderzhavie v kontse XIX stoletiia*. Moscow, 1970.

————. *Samoderzhavie i russkaia armiia na rubezhe XIX–XX stoletii.* Moscow, 1973.

Zelnik, Reginald E. *Labor and Society in Tsarist Russia: The Factory Workers of St. Petersburg, 1855–1870.* Stanford: Stanford University Press, 1971.

————. *Law and Disorder on the Narova River: The Kreenholm Strike of 1872.* Berkeley: University of California Press, 1995.

————, ed. and trans. *A Radical Worker in Tsarist Russia: The Autobiography of Semën Ivanovich Kanatchikov.* Stanford: Stanford University Press, 1986.

Zhurnal departamenta narodnogo prosveshcheniia, ch. 3 (1821).

Zol'nikova, N. D. *Soslovnye problemy vo vzaimootnosheniiakh tserkvi i gosudarstva v Sibiri (XVIII v.).* Novosibirsk, 1981.

Zuev, A. S. *Russkoe kazachestvo Zabaikal'ia vo vtoroi chetverti XVIII–prevoi polovine XIX vv.* Novosibirsk, 1994.

Zueva, E. A. "Basniny: Sibirskaia kupecheskaia dinastiia. Preemstvennost' pokolenii." In *Sotsial'no-politicheskie problemy istorii Sibiri XVII–XX vv.: Bakhrushinskie chteniia 1994 g.* Novosibirsk, 1994.

————. "Dosug i razvlecheniia Sibirskogo kupechestva vo vtoroi polovine XVIII–nachale XIX v." In *Materialy XXIV vsesoiuznoi nauchnoi studencheskoi konferentsii.* Novosibirsk, 1986.

————. "Razmery i strukturno-pokolennyi sostav sem'i Tobol'skogo kupechestva po dannym tret'ei revizii." In *Materialy XXVI vsesoiuznoi nauchnoi studencheskoi konferentsii.* Novosibirsk, 1988.

————. "Russkaia kupecheskaia sem'ia v Sibiri kontsa XVIII–pervoi poloviny XIX v." Avtoreferat. Novosibirsk, 1992.

————. "Vedomosti ucheta kupecheskikh kapitalov kak istoricheskii istochnik (na materialakh g. Irkutska kontsa XVIII–pervoi chetverti XIX v.)" In *Massovye istochniki po istorii Sibiri: Bakhrushinskie chteniia 1989 g.* Novosibirsk, 1989.

INDEX